End<

[Beth Ward] pours out her heart in *'Dying in Indian Country'* as she chronicles the life of just one family caught in the tragic web of history. Having worked with native people in Canada and having three native children in our family, I know that what she writes is all too true and commonplace. I commend her book to you, the reader, and pray that somehow through the telling of this story, you might be moved to help to do something about this terrible scandal which shames both our nations.

'Dying in Indian Country' is a compassionate and honest portrayal of one couple's journey through hardship and pain, triumph and sorrow. [Beth Ward] has her feet in both worlds, native and non native and because of it has insights which many cannot have. The whole issue she addresses in the book, the caring for native children has become so politicized that it hardly seems that much that the bureaucracy does is in the best interest of the child. [Beth's] strong faith in God comes through loudly and clearly as the one constant sustaining factor in it all. She has dedicated her life to make the lot of native children better. That is what this book is all about and I highly recommend it to you!

Reed Elley, former Member of the Parliament, Vancouver Island, British Columbia, and former Chief Critic for Indian Affairs and Northern Development, Official Opposition, Canada. Baptist Pastor, father of four native and metis children

Those of us who have lived our lives among American Indians within the reservation system have seen firsthand the disastrous consequences of socialism and paternalism perpetrated on Indian Tribes by the federal government. A very readable book, DYING IN INDIAN COUNTY is [Beth Ward]'s brutally honest description of her family's life and experience on Indian Reservations; including direct personal experience with the Indian Child Welfare Act and

Tribal Government jurisdiction over her husband and children, even though they have no vote in that Government. The reader who is not hopelessly entrenched in "political correctness" and the "politics of guilt and pity" will find this book a tremendous resource and compelling argument for drastic change in Federal Indian Policy, away from paternalism to freedom and dignity for the individual Indian citizen.

Montana Representative Rick Jore
House District 73

I am a third generation reservation resident. People sometimes ask me why I am concerned about Indian reservations. This book provides the clearest explanation available to date. Reading it will give you the best feel for what it's like to live on a modern American Indian reservation that you are likely to find short of living there. At times, as you read her book, you will feel confused, discouraged, hopeless, depressed, and angry. Welcome to the *rez*. Many people have their aspirations destroyed here. Too many have their lives and health damaged. More than a few lives end prematurely here.

What is exciting about this book is that it doesn't end there. [Beth] and her family find hope emerging from despair. They are finding solutions both for their own lives and help for those around them. This is a story about an amazing life journey. Read it and weep. Read it and rejoice.

Darrel Smith. Writer, Rancher
South Dakota

Dying in Indian Country

A Family Journey from Self-Destruction to Opposing Tribal Sovereignty

BETH WARD

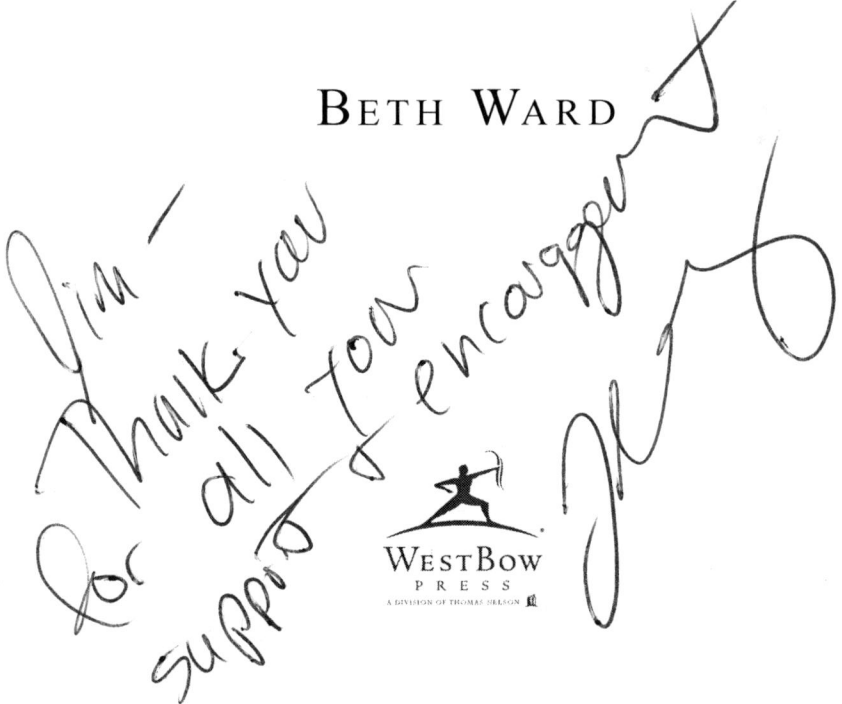

WestBow
PRESS
A DIVISION OF THOMAS NELSON

Copyright © 2000, 2012 by Beth Ward.

All rights reserved. No part of this book may be used or reproduced by any means, graphic, electronic, or mechanical, including photocopying, recording, taping or by any information storage retrieval system without the written permission of the publisher except in the case of brief quotations embodied in critical articles and reviews.

This is a completely true story. Many names have been changed to protect the privacy of children and loved ones. The point of this book is not to hurt people, but to reveal what is happening in the hope that something will change and lives will be saved

WestBow Press books may be ordered through booksellers or by contacting:

WestBow Press
A Division of Thomas Nelson
1663 Liberty Drive
Bloomington, IN 47403
www.westbowpress.com
1-(866) 928-1240

Because of the dynamic nature of the Internet, any web addresses or links contained in this book may have changed since publication and may no longer be valid. The views expressed in this work are solely those of the author and do not necessarily reflect the views of the publisher, and the publisher hereby disclaims any responsibility for them.

Poetry by Phonacelle Shapel by permission.
Cover Image by Mitch Krueger

ISBN: 978-1-4497-3792-4 (hc)
ISBN: 978-1-4497-3793-1 (sc)
ISBN: 978-1-4497-3794-8 (e)

Library of Congress Control Number: 2012900970

Printed in the United States of America

WestBow Press rev. date: 06/27/2012

Contents

A family, after years of poverty, alcoholism and violence, has come to understand that tribal government and federal Indian policy are part of the problem

Foreword xi
Preface xiii
Chapter one: May, 1980 1
Chapter two: Dying in the Suburbs 5
Chapter three: March 1980: Rolling Thunder 21
Chapter four: Living in Indian Country 31
Chapter five: The Noble Red Man 55
Chapter six: This isn't fun anymore 73
Chapter seven: Play it again, Sam 89
Chapter eight: Crying in Indian Country 103
Chapter nine: Dying in Indian Country 119
Chapter ten: Gi-ga-wa-ba-min me-na-wa 139
Chapter eleven: Dying in the Heart 155
Chapter twelve: Freed: Living in the protected place 179
Chapter thirteen: Are we ever really protected? 197
Chapter fourteen: March 1991; The Eye of the Storm 213
Chapter fifteen: The work begins 227
Chapter sixteen: One Day at a Time 243
Chapter seventeen: The Mission is Clear 263
Chapter eighteen: Joy 285
Chapter nineteen: Misty 299
Chapter twenty: The First People. 315
Chapter twenty-one: Human Rights for all? 331
Chapter twenty-two: September, 1999 349
Chapter twenty-three: October, 1999 359

Epilogue June 14, 2004 363

Appendix 372
   Appendix: 1 - Sweet Bye-and-Bye
   Appendix: 2 - Surrender
   Appendix: 3 - The Rub Tree; By Don Burgess
   Appendix: 4 - Roland, Christmas Newsletter, 2003

Appendix: 5 - Sampling of Emails re: Roland, May/June 2004
Appendix: 6 - Sample of Letters re: Roland's DVD, 2006
Appendix: 7 - Re: Montana Human Rights Network
Appendix: 8 - Family, 2000-2011
Appendix: 9 - A Daily Prayer
Appendix: 10 - Roland
Appendix: 11 - Scott Kayla Morrison
Appendix: 12 - Bill Lawrence
Appendix: 13 - Salvation Assured
Appendix: 14 - Facts and Statistics
Appendix: 15 - Senator Conrad
Appendix: 16 - Senator Max Baucus
Appendix: 17 - The Montana Delegation circa 1990's
Appendix: 18 - Federal Funding for Tribal Governments based on Census
Appendix: 19 - Important Points Concerning ICWA
Appendix: 20 - For More Information
Appendix: 21 - Pictures

In order to reduce confusion, not all family members are mentioned. This is not meant to slight anyone. All of Roland's relatives have been very important to us.

Gi-ga-wa-ba-min me-na-wa

"See you later"

In loving honor of our Parents and Grandparents and in memory of Lila Hunter, Buck Ward, Charlie Hunter, Julia Whitebird, Shanda Ward, Wanda Ward, Misty, little Leon Peters, Elaine's children, and many more, including the bruised little girl whose name I never knew.

I haven't used your real names in this book, but God knows who you are.

Roland loved all his Brothers, Sisters, Uncles, Aunts, Cousins, Nieces, Nephews, Children, Grandchildren, and Great-grandchild with all his heart, and wanted nothing more than to see everyone saved - healthy and happy.

Dedicated to our Children and Grandchildren; Grace be unto you, and peace, from God the Father, and from the Lord Jesus Christ.

May this story help keep you from making the same mistakes we did in our early years.
In Honor as well of *Elisabeth, Werner, Eugen, Hildegard, Ernst, Margarete, Max and Martha.*
I never knew you – but didn't want your names to disappear forever without any mention.
I DO care what happened to you.

THE JAGGED EDGE

the rusted dregs
of dreams, silent
as specters, drift
like latent thoughts
filling the cornices
of my mind

a crescendo of wind
rushes through the
storm tossed gables,
a narcotic searing
the shrouds of empty
ghosts who have fed
upon my fear

and, i am left standing
on the jagged edge of
space while stars shine
with sparks struck from
a philosopher's stone

© By PHONACELLE SHAPEL

In order to reduce confusion, not all family members are mentioned. This is not meant to slight anyone. All of Roland's relatives have been very important to us.

FAMILY TREES

WALTER HUNTER AND KATHY WARD FAMILY
THEIR CHILDREN & STEPCHILDREN:

Charlie, Mike, Buck, David, Glenn, Lila and...

Elaine: had James, who married Gloria
had Dale, who married Tammy and had Wally.

Yvonne: had Wanda and Roger, Julia, Sonya, and Marci Whitebird and had Matthew: who married Shanda
with Reggie; she had Bradley

Roland (him) married Shirley. Together they had:
> Cheri: who with Gene Peters, had Carrie, Leon, and Angela
> Misty: who with Wesley Redwood had Ross, Brooke, Caleb, Dewey, and Kelly
> Junior
> > Joy: who with Jordon had Ashley and Jordon Jr.

Dorothy: had Troy, Mickey and Paul

Annie: had Savannah and Shaine
with Arnold, she had Candis

OTHER RELATIVES:

> Cousins: Nova and Norine
> > Dan Hunter; best drinking buddy and dated Darlene Peters, Gene's mother

Elmer Dovetail; married Marcia, had Kirk, Celeste, and Lyndi.
Celeste married Kirk
Other Nephews and Niece: Verlin, Jerry, Pam
    Shirley's siblings: Alvin and Laurie

MY FAMILY:

MY SIBLINGS:
    Eric, Craig, Annie, Bobby, Stephanie, Tonya; who married Dusty
    Beth (me): married Roland and had Andrew, Haley, Heidi, Timothy, and Rosie

OTHER RELATIVES:
    Aunt: Sister Mary
    Cousin: Marion

Foreword

"Family" occurs in this work of approximately 175 pages just about 175 times. No word is more important. Close behind are "faith" and "freedom." Around those three terms the author constructs an alliterative homage to living in Indian Country. Yet, the work is entitled, "Dying in Indian Country." The paradox is that the vitality captured in this story emerges from beneath crucibles of suffering and denial. Yes, living in Indian Country has much to do with learning how to die, for suffocating laws and policies in Indian Country vie against unparalleled resilience in sapping the will to live. In some that resilience prevails to write stories of revival and accomplishment, while in others resilience fails and is overcome to write epitaphs of sorrow and regret.

Family, faith, and freedom are the terms that lay out the challenge of life in Indian Country. Here we cannot miss a plea for that freedom which would give families the chance to build faith as a defense against cultural deprivations and depravities. What an eloquent voice it is that directs our hearing and our gaze upon the incredible odds that conspire against independent ethical choices and individual accomplishments under the guise of supportive Federal, paternalistic policies and practices. If the policy were one of deliberate abandonment and repression it could not work more effectively than the supposedly helpful policies of "self-determination" now in place.

Of course, the key that unravels the mystery of sadness told here is the official policy of fossilizing the Indian as America's "other." A nation that does not accept the Indian as "one of us," is a nation that wages perpetual warfare upon the Indian's very humanity.

How ironic it is, then, that peoples who from their origins defined themselves only as "people" should now have become, not people but "native American." And how cruel is it to make this damning point by exploiting the most vulnerable of these people, the children? By defining them as others we refuse them the very milk of human kindness, sometimes that of their very own non-Indian mothers. Most of the names of tribes in North America simply meant "the people." Neither territorial nor cultural exceptionalism was expressed in these self-chosen names. The sensibility conveyed was an appreciation of humanity itself. And even Christopher Columbus, in referring to the inhabitants as "los Indios" ("the people of the Indies") demonstrated great respect for their self-understanding even while being confused about his geography. Now, though, we hide behind laws that refuse to receive "the people" simply as people, as human beings. Instead we seek to make cultural artifacts of them, to be treated as means rather than ends in themselves. Here is a story that loudly shouts, "We count!" "We are people, too!" Listen to it!

W. B. Allen
Emeritus Dean and Professor
Michigan State University
Formerly, Chair, U. S. Commission on Civil Rights

Preface

To Our Family:

About twenty five years ago, "Wanda" was admitted to a treatment center. While visiting her there, I told her why I hadn't been coming around so much anymore. I told her I couldn't keep watching the bad things going on. I couldn't keep watching everyone hurting and dying. At the time, Wanda said she understood.

Wanda passed away seven years ago of a drug overdose. Her mother passed on from a drug overdose a couple years later as well. I hope others now understand, because the reason I wrote this book is the same as I told Wanda. I know it isn't considered right to tell all the stories and to talk to people about things that happened in the family. At the same time, I also know that unless someone speaks up, nothing will ever change and family will keep on dying.

Roland and I tried to figure out what was causing all the pain and decided it had to do with the whole "victim / entitlement" mentality that's pushed in Indian Country. Many children are raised to feel angry at society and unsafe with their own family and friends. Many adults lack responsibility and accountability. Lost is the traditional sense of community, taking care of each other, and creative problem solving.

Roland and I believed the current reservation system is hurting people much more than it is helping. Roland tried to change things by going to Washington DC and speaking to Congressmen. Some were open and listened to him. Others wouldn't give him the time of day. It was interesting to notice that those who received the largest tribal government campaign contributions were least likely to listen to someone like Roland. Those ones would only listen to tribal leaders and no one else.

And through all the years we were doing this, many Caucasians kept telling us to leave everything alone and "don't rock the boat." People who have no idea what's going on would say that Indian people are happy and that we are "racist" for trying to change things. Meanwhile, people back home kept dying.

So telling the story is the only thing that Roland and I could do. I began this book in 1997, so it has been 15 years in the making. I am sorry if there is anything in it that will cause pain. We need to tell the story so that others will know, and maybe some pressure will build on Congress to change things. We don't want everyone's grandkids to have to go through what everybody else has gone through, and I know that deep down, you have the same hope.

Roland and I did this because we love you.

STEP THAT FALTERED

Somewhere I saw suffering.
Dear God, that it had been
just somewhere.

Once I saw it on the street
walking by and walking by,
and Dear God,
I saw it just walking by.

I met it on the face
of a child,
and I heard it
in a voice.

That it had been but one.
One walking by
One child
One voice

Had it not been
the muted cry
of so many.
So many muted cries…

I might have slept
the nights all through
I could have smiled,
said, "not mine to grieve."

Had it been but one,
I could have passed,
could have laughed.

Step that faltered.
Laugh that died.
   © By **PHONACELLE SHAPEL**

Chapter one: May, 1980

It had just turned daylight when we pulled the yellow Chevy station wagon into the small town of Cass Lake. The morning was dawning warm and sunny. Roland was driving. I had been sleeping in the front seat next to him, and his nephew Matthew and Matthew's girlfriend were sleeping in the back seat. Roland drove through the treeless streets of the tribal tract housing and pulled into the dirt driveway of a yellow house. It was early, but the sun was already beating down. It was going to be a hot day.

Roland honked his horn. Out of a rundown shed from back behind the house, a heavy woman with long black hair emerged unsteadily and stood in its doorway. Roland called her over to the car. Coughing, Annie unsteadily crossed the grass and came up next to the driver's side. The smell of alcohol wafted through the window.

They greeted each other and Roland asked where the wake was being held.

"Up to Bug school," she said, and then bent her head to throw up on the ground.

Roland averted his eyes and patiently waited.

Lifting her head, Annie and Roland spoke briefly again before he said good-bye and pulled the car back out of the driveway.

The wake was in a small building at Bug-a-ne-ge-shig school in a shady, wooded area known as "Mission." I felt very uncomfortable as we pulled up. It was easy to ride in a car going somewhere, but now we were here. I was now far away from home and knew no one but Roland. Numbly, I climbed out of the car. I had never been around many Indian people before. How should I act?

As we entered the dark building I stayed close to Roland. A quick glance around the room showed me I was the only white person there. Many people milled about talking to each other in the main room. Feeling out of place, I avoided looking at anyone and said nothing. Roland moved through the crowd to the kitchen. Hands sweating, I stiffly followed. The women in the kitchen were busy preparing food for the feed that would follow the service. Roland greeted his sister and introduced me.

"Elaine, this is Beth."

Elaine looked up from her work and said hello. She and Roland spoke for a moment, Roland motioned to me, and I tensely shadowed him back into the main room.

He led me through the crowd toward a miniature casket placed alone by the wall. I actually felt some relief as I trailed him. Standing at the casket would be easier than standing apart in the crowd. Roland took a moment at the casket and then stepped aside for me to see. Looking down I saw a precious sleeping child, a small, dark haired girl in a pretty little dress, no more than two years old. Lying peacefully, if you ignored her bruised and battered face.

Roland had told me earlier that his niece had died from a fall from the couch onto a cement floor, but as I looked down at the bruises on both sides of her face, I wondered if that were true.

Turning from the casket, Roland moved toward a tall, slim young man. James, he told me, was his nephew and the father of the little girl. For a short time they whispered together. Roland then turned to me, "Wait here while I go outside to talk to James alone." But afraid to stay inside surrounded by strangers, I followed them out and sat on the stoop, nervously watching and waiting as Roland and James walked down the dirt driveway and then out onto the dusty road. My eyes followed Roland as long as he was still visible through the trees. As he disappeared, two men emerged from inside and stood a short distance away as they shared a cigarette. How does one sit, what does one look at, what does one do with their hands when one is isolated, alone and out of place? It seemed an eternity before Roland returned, although I knew it was just a short time.

The tiny cemetery was in a heavily forested area near a lake. We followed other cars down a long, narrow, muddy road to get there. Circling through the cemetery, there was nowhere to park. The small area was packed with cars and people. We drove back down the road a ways until we found a spot and then walked back up to the crowd.

At the edge of the crowd, we stood some distance from the ceremony. The graveside service was brief. As it ended and the first shovel of dirt was thrown into the small hole, the baby's mother, Gloria, let out a loud wail and hung on to James, sobbing.

Roland nudged and we began walking back to the car. As I stepped over yesterday's puddles, I glanced back at the slowly dispersing crowd.

What happened to that baby girl? I wondered, why won't Roland tell me what happened?

Beth Ward

THE PLACE

When I was young
I had a lonesome place

It was there I went
To hide my face

Lest the tears that fell
Should live to tell
Of a child's woe

Years have passed
And now I know

That grown-ups have
No place to go

© By **PHONACELLE SHAPEL**

Chapter two: Dying in the Suburbs

I've heard it said that poverty breeds social misbehavior. That was hardly the cause in my case. In fact, it is notable how despite the obvious contrast of race, class, and money in our early lives, Roland and I grew up with surprisingly similar behavior and attitudes.

As I relate this story, I am not trying to bring blame on one person or a group of people. I am simply relating events as they happened and, right or wrong, my reactions to them. Nor am I pretending to be innocent of all wrongdoing. I am telling the truth of how I came to Indian Country and what I saw there, in the hope that at least some of the dying -- physical, emotional and spiritual, in the Native American community and in my own -- may be recognized and prevented.

I grew up in an upper-middle class suburb of a large metropolitan area during the 1960s. Our home, a two story, five-bedroom house with two-car garage, was comfortable. We had the only swimming pool in the all-white neighborhood, but other than that, we lived more simply than Dad's income could have allowed us to. Dad was, for the most part, frugal.

At home in the evenings, we kids sat behind my dad and played as he worked at the desk in his basement study. It never occurred to me to ask what he was working on.

Dad, a computer programmer for Honeywell in the days when computers were in their infancy, was always busy. I was a blond little girl with gray-green eyes, the third child of seven. As a five-year-old, I sat nearby on the edge of the carpet with my three-year-old sister Christine. Placing my paper on the cement floor, I drew a picture of a strong, bearded, rustic dad carrying his little girl on his shoulders.

This was in clear contrast with my real father, the son of wealthy and aristocratic German immigrants. A small, bespectacled man with receding hairline, he was seldom seen in public wearing anything but his black business suit. But that wasn't the paramount contrast. The physical difference I drew was just what I assumed to be the reason Dad couldn't -- wouldn't -- carry me. Although he enjoyed having us climb onto the bed with him so he could read to us in the evening, he was a man who seemed to avoid any other kind of physical contact.

Dad took us out on Saturday afternoons; Mom wanted time to herself and insisted he do this. While we played at the beach, he read books. And while he enjoyed taking us to museums, symphonies, and horseback riding, his interest during these trips seemed to be the event itself rather than the little people with him. Dad valued intelligence, German literature, mathematics and his personal space above most other things. When he did pay attention, it was frequently born of intolerance; only because we'd interrupted, done something wrong, or had gotten in his way.

"Who spilled jelly on the counter? Who spilled jelly on the counter?" he demanded to know.

All fingers pointed in my direction and I was rewarded with a slap. Not exactly the kind of touch I was craving. Even at a young age I knew something was missing.

My older brothers, Craig and Erik, seven and eight at the time, were also critical of Dad's inattention. But just like my dad, they were both very intelligent and indifferent. And while Dad was able to subtly give the message I was inferior in aptitude, my brothers were more up front about it. An emotional child, I felt stupid and worthless. This feeling was deep in my spirit, going down into my core. It's funny, but despite its weight and depth I had had no real knowledge of it, just as I was unaware of being overly sensitive, although to my family my sensitivity was a matter of fact. To me, this was just the way life was and the heartache I carried was a normal part of being.

Although we children, excluding two-year-old Bobby, reciprocated my father's inattention and began to harbor bitterness, I didn't always blame Dad for his faults. I knew, as did my siblings, that he simply wasn't capable of giving what we needed. In part this knowledge came from my mother's many comments about his inability and her reluctance to relinquish child-rearing decisions to him, but it also came from observation. While Mom was away at a League of Women Voters meeting one evening, Bobby slipped in the tub and cracked his head. Erik and Craig urged Dad to take care of him, but Dad had no idea what to do and so did nothing. His decision was to leave little Bobby in the tub until Mom came home so as not to get blood on the floor.

Dad withdrew even at family gatherings and at political parties. Mom was the social parent, the one bringing us. While everyone in the room mingled, talked, ate and laughed, Dad found the nearest bookshelf and hid himself in the corner reading. I was aware our relatives and friends admired him for his intelligence, but I was also aware he was different from other parents. People noticed the difference and, although our political friends were always kind to us, I sensed they made exceptions for our family.

I told myself that our whole family is different...people make fun of us. I then expanded it to 'we aren't like them, so we aren't as good.' So now, not only did I feel inferior to my own family, but also I came to believe our family was inferior to others.

Mom, the oldest daughter of Scottish-Irish Catholic laborers, was a loving woman, but had hopes and dreams never realized. Although she was a song leader at our Church, volunteered as director of a community assistance program, enjoyed going to the Governor's Inaugural Ball and sat in his office giving him advice, she didn't seem happy. She had five children to care for at that time and a husband who, although a dedicated provider, was emotionally distant.

Mom usually didn't get up with us in the morning. We got ourselves ready for school, dressing in our Catholic uniforms and walking to the bus. I think she meant well and did her best, but simply had too much going on inside herself to see what was happening inside some of her children.

One thing I enjoyed most was when she was busy on the phone, because then I could lay my head in her lap and she would run her fingers gently through my hair.

As a teenager I looked elsewhere for affection. Harv, a man in his thirties, lived two doors down. Alan lived between Harv and us. Both men took time to talk to me. During summers I spent hours watching them while they worked on car engines or tended their yards. Harv was a surrogate dad. I even started calling him "Dad" and began spending time just hanging around with him while he was working in his garage, even while he and his friends were drinking.

I never drank with them. They were adults; I was only fourteen. But Harv seemed to like having me around. He took care of me, doing little things like give me aspirin when I had a headache. I couldn't remember my real dad taking that kind of time for me.

Alan knew I was in trouble emotionally and tried to talk to me about things in a roundabout way. He was especially concerned about the time I spent at Harv's. I had no idea why. I just enjoyed the attention they both were giving me.

Mom finally asked Dad to move out in the early 70's. He moved to an apartment about seven blocks away. My two youngest sisters, Stephanie and Tonya, were about five and two at the time. All seven of the children remained with Mom.

One afternoon much later, I was at Dad's apartment helping him fold his clean sheets. He placed one end in my hands and taking the other end, he proceeded to show me how the maids folded the sheets in his nursery when he was a child.

"You had a nursery?" I asked while we worked.

"Well, one wing of the house was set aside for the children. This is where we lived. I had a very good mother though. She came to the nursery every day to have lunch with us."

Smiling and obviously pleased with the memory of the limited attention he'd gotten from his mother, he turned to put the folded sheet away. He said nothing more.

Mom never gave us chores and never really asked me to help her with anything. The fact that this woman was attempting to care for our large household without help from her teenagers was obvious to anyone who would enter the house. The rooms were in constant clutter.

Sitting on the roof of our garage one late summer afternoon, I could smell dinner cooking. It would be just a little while before she called us in. I lay back with my hands behind my head and soaked up the warmth of the roof. All through my teenage years I was still doing what I wanted with my day and expecting Mom to clean up after me, do my laundry and make dinner. Occasionally, when I was alone in the house I would take it upon myself to clean the living room or mop the kitchen floor, but this would happen only rarely and only when I felt like.

In junior high I left the Catholic school and started at the public one. There, I was withdrawn and afraid. It wasn't just the Catholic friends I had left behind; I was in a school district separate from our family friends as well. Going to Democratic fund-raisers, literature drops, and rallies, I had grown up with the children of the political crowd. Over the years, I felt safe with them and was more boisterous and talkative. But because our family resided in a different school district, my political friends knew nothing about my uncomfortable school life. Lord knows I never wanted them to find out – I thought I was as despised there. Wanting to fit in somehow, I began to hang with other misfits, some of whom used marijuana and alcohol. A school friend introduced me to hitchhiking and some nights we'd do nothing but hitchhike up and down Central Avenue, meeting people and getting high. Other times we'd go to the homes of her friends to smoke. Never really doing anything or saying anything, we'd stay a little while, then go. She introduced me to a lifestyle I had never seen before, but I was willing to accept it because it was easier than fitting in with people who were better than me.

But the more I smoked and drank with them, the worse I felt - truly, totally worthless. Thinking I was hated at the public school, I transferred to a Catholic one my sophomore year. However, my ability to deal with people, let alone myself, hadn't changed. I had a warped sense of friendship. Walking into the girls' bathroom – nicknamed 'The Can' - where all the drinking and drug activity was happening, I believed that merely being present there, sitting on the counter listening to the banter, was enough to make me a part of the crowd.

I had a talent for shoplifting. While shopping at a department store, I admired a cross pendant. I'd wanted one for quite some time. Glancing around, I pocketed it. It didn't dawn to me how little sense it made to steal a symbol of Jesus.

I didn't shoplift often, but I was good enough at it that friends would occasionally pay me to pick something up for them. It was easy. During one shopping spree, I had a casual conversation with the security man while holding stolen merchandise in my purse.

A member of the city Human Resources Committee, having a heart for young people, gathered us teenage Democrats and a handful of Republican kids together and asked if we would like to be on the Youth Project Committee (YPC) he was forming. We were all enthusiastic. We were going to be political appointees!

The official goal of the committee was to "promote the consideration and participation of youths in the affairs of the city," so we surveyed teenagers to find out what they really wanted and needed. We accomplished the survey to a limited extent, but nothing was ever done with the results and the YPC drifted off into non-existence. Nevertheless, my baptism into political rhetoric had been fun.

Because of Mom's activism and political connections, she was appointed as a Police Commissioner. Soon after her appointment, friends and I met at a park to smoke pot. One of the girls and I laughed. Her mom was on the Police Commission as well. Together, our moms constituted two-thirds of the commission. Wouldn't it be funny to get caught together?

We thought so, but Mom would have been devastated. She took her responsibility seriously. She even began riding in the squad cars once a week or so to get familiar with the men and their problems. She came home full of exciting stories. Her favorite cop to ride with was Mitch. I'd heard his name before from some kids. He was the 'cool' cop.

That same summer Mom began inviting Mitch and his foster boys over to swim in our outdoor pool. Having him over was fun enough, but after each swim Mitch would captivate us for the rest of the evening with exciting stories of true crime. He was hilarious.

Our whole family, excluding Dad, always looked forward to those nights.

But true crime got personal. My friend and I began dating Mitch's foster boys.

A few weeks later my friend said she hadn't been able to get hold of her guy. Someone suggested she call the jail.

"If you can't find your boyfriend, check the jail," the person had advised, as if it were a universal truth. Sure enough, there he was. He'd stolen Mitch's gun and tried robbing a convenience store.

As I drew closer to 16, even Harv started giving me pot.

"I don't really like this stuff," he said. "I'm buying it for you."

We smoked late at night with a friend of his that first time and ended up racing around the houses, laughing and hiding. During the next few weeks, I partied more with Harv and his friends.

A month or so after my 16th birthday, I stopped visiting Harv. During that month he 'played' with me in a new way - three times. At first I thought it was fun. After all…he wasn't doing "that." It was only 'kind of' that. But after each "event" he wouldn't speak to me for over a week. I'd go over to his place, as usual …but he would totally ignore me. I got the message. It wasn't fun anymore.

…I was so drunk. My mind was swimming. I was sick. I could see my friend sitting on her bedroom floor with her back against the door. Her boyfriend and others were banging on the door trying to get in. They wanted to throw me in the shower, but she wasn't letting them. I don't remember anything else. The next morning, she told me they'd run out of Coca-Cola so I first started mixing rum with just a little water, then began drinking it straight...

Mom came across the street to the house where I was baby-sitting. I think she was crying. She wanted to know what it was that I wanted and what she could do to make things better. I couldn't tell her. I didn't really know what my problem was.

My math teacher was also the school counselor. After talking with me a short while he suggested a treatment interview. I didn't believe I was an alcoholic, but the idea of going away someplace was inviting. When I agreed, he became excited. "You're the first person I've ever sent to treatment!" he said.

I skipped school the rest of the day and walked over to Mitch's house, telling myself I needed to talk to him about this treatment thing, but really just wanting to be around him.

He gave me a hug. "Get in there and I'll come visit you." I went back to school feeling light as air. Mitch cared.

The next day at the Treatment Center, I told the interviewer I wasn't going to say a word with my mom in the room. When they couldn't push me to cooperate, he brought her to another room to wait. Upon returning, the interviewer asked me if I realized how much I was hurting her.

"She's crying in the other room you know."

I didn't respond. I didn't care.

Treatment itself wasn't guaranteed. The two-week detox was meant to be an evaluation period. The counselors in detox were to decide whether or not treatment was necessary. To my mind, I hadn't been drinking all that long, only two years or so and not daily or anything. Lots of people do much more than I ever had. But I wanted to "pass" the test and be allowed to go to treatment. I didn't want to go home. In order to get to go to treatment, I needed to make the most of what drinking I'd done. Even expand a little if I had to.

Even in this setting I knew I didn't measure up. Even here I was afraid I'd fail.

When I saw him walk past that afternoon, I jumped up. Mitch! He really came! The staff showed us a small room where we could talk in private.

"Look," Mitch said, "we failed with most of the foster kids we've had. Stay in treatment and be one of our successes. I'll be back to visit again."

The counselors believed what I told them about my drinking and decided I needed treatment. I'd passed the test. My family came in for a meeting. It was my job to tell them what I'd been doing in the last two years and what the plans were for the next two-month period. The meeting was short. As I was taught during group, I hugged both

Dying in Indian Country

of my parents before they left. My dad was stiff as a board when he bent over to receive my hug. I left the room feeling confused and not sure what had happened. Why did I feel so empty?

A counselor explained to me that I felt empty because nothing at all had happened in the room. What he had seen was a complete lack of reaction from my parents and siblings.

In treatment we were taught the twelve steps of Alcoholics Anonymous. We were expected to complete the first five steps while still in the treatment Center. The other steps would come later. I never really took the steps to heart or followed them. More important to me while I was there was that people seemed to pay attention and like me.

In the evening before everyone went to bed, we got together in the TV room and hugged each other. This was fantastic! Like an insatiable sponge, I wanted this part of the evening to go on and on.

….I waited by the window for over an hour one evening, scanning every car that slowed down to turn into the parking lot. I watched the elevator every time it opened. Finally I went to the pay phone and called Mitch's house. He answered. My voice cracked.
"I thought you were coming tonight."
"Oh, man, I was helping the kids with their math homework. I can't come tonight."
"Oh. Okay."
I hung up quickly so he wouldn't hear me crying.

I was to be discharged to my cousin Marion's house until a bed opened at the halfway house. Why the Counselors seriously thought this would be better than going home, I don't know. Marion, 17, had just given up her baby for adoption. Her mother thought I'd be some kind of replacement, I guess. That was fine with me; I had no desire to go home while waiting for an opening at the halfway house.

My dad sent $100 a month for me to live on. That didn't leave much after paying my share of the rent. On the urging of friends, I applied for food stamps. I was nervous as I waited in the welfare office, but answering the financial workers questions and getting the assistance wasn't difficult. My "aftercare" group applauded when I told them I was getting $70 a month in stamps.

I didn't see much of my family. I stayed in the city and spent my time with Marion, my aftercare group, and Marion's friends from Narcotics Anonymous. We wasted the summer sleeping late, listening to the Moody Blues and Helen Reddy on LP, and splashing in gutter puddles when it rained. Marion's new boyfriend played the guitar and kept us all laughing.

Treatment may have brought me sobriety, but my character wasn't any different. Housework was never a habit of mine before; there was no reason to start now. Marion, frustrated one morning that I hadn't been doing my dishes, wrapped the whole sink load into my bed blankets.

Further, I didn't even consider getting a job. No reason to work unless I absolutely had to. I had Dad's $100 and the state's food stamps. The most I could muster the energy to do was go to a downtown temporary agency and make $18 a day. Marion and I only did that twice. I would have gone again, but she didn't want to. Just as well, I didn't really want to, either. I didn't like the eight hour shifts, standing most of the time, packing materials at a warehouse and incessantly watching the clock for break time.

Of course, there was no reason to report that small income to the food stamp office.

No, work wasn't primary on my mind. Our apartment was just two blocks from the lake and it was summer time. When I wasn't visiting friends or going to parties with the N.A. group, I could be found there.

For Marion's birthday gift in September, 1977, I went to the corner drug store and stole a candle.

Soon after, a bed finally opened for me at the adolescent halfway house in an affluent suburb. I knew one of the staff members from treatment. He was just another man in a long line that I hoped would care enough to be my dad. He was, in fact, part of the reason I'd chosen this particular halfway house. But why did he make fun of me the first few weeks I was there? What did I do wrong during the group where he had everyone laughing so hard at me? Of course, I was no match for the kids who already lived there. I couldn't measure up to them. He was right. I tried my best to fit in, but I suppose knowing I was unlovable only reinforced the outcome that I was unloved.

Mom was sick all fall. The doctor said she was depressed because we hadn't heard from Craig in months. One of my brothers thought she was depressed because of the way her political friends were treating her. She was a Pro-lifer among Democrats and they had stopped inviting her to the get-togethers.

"She can't compromise about abortion, so she doesn't want to be part of either party anymore," he said.

I wasn't sure if I should believe that or not, but I was homesick and wanted to be back with my family. Never having fit in or understood what was going on at the halfway house, I left and went home in time for Thanksgiving. When I got out of the car in the driveway, fourteen-year-old Bobby came out to hug me. I was surprised and touched. Unfortunately I still couldn't let Mom hug me. There was still an angry wall between us. I didn't know why or want it to be that way; it just was.

She had been losing weight all year, but for some reason her stomach had stayed big. She looked pregnant. Something was really wrong. In mid-December, Mom had exploratory surgery and just before Christmas, I was told she had ovarian cancer. Apparently, my younger brothers and sisters had been told earlier. My family had thought I wouldn't be able to handle the information.

Mom came home in time for Christmas. I cleaned and fixed up her bedroom as best I could. Grandma and Grandpa came back from

Yuma to be with us. We hadn't had Christmas with them in all my memory.

One evening I sat next to Mom as she lay on her bed. Although the doctor had tapped her stomach earlier in order to drain the accumulating fluid, it had returned. Her stomach was bloated again. Our conversation turned to Dad.

"Your dad and I have been in and out of counseling for years. I don't know if he'll ever get better," she said. "Your dad's father, who had Jewish heritage, left Nazi Germany in the 1930s. Two years later, your dad, along with your grandma and uncle, followed to America. You have to remember he came to America at the age of twelve, an age when most children are already having a difficult time. When he arrived, he spoke only German and America was just entering a period of hating Germans. On top of that, he came from a very rich and aristocratic family. Your grandpa was very domineering. Even when your dad was right, he was wrong in his father's eyes. I remember playing monopoly with his father once. I started to win, so he got mad and tossed the whole board off the table."

Later, my Aunt Charlotte told me more, "From the time your father and his brother (Charlotte's husband) were newborns until they moved to America, they were raised by a nanny named 'Baba'. For twelve years, she had been your dad's nurturer; she was there for him when he was sick and there for him when he was frightened. And apparently Baba had no other family. These two boys were her whole life. But Hitler would allow no money to be taken out of Germany, so your grandpa left Baba in Germany because he was afraid he couldn't afford to feed her. Can you imagine how this must have felt to the boys? Sometimes, when you think of these things, you can see how and why your father turned all his emotions inside."

Mom returned to the hospital in January. One night, on impulse, I called one of her friends and asked if we could present Mom with some kind of award for all the work she'd done for the city. The friend was enthusiastic. Within a couple of days, a plaque was made commemorating the work she had done for various organizations. Each group also wrote a letter to go with the plaque. We presented it to her in her hospital room.

"I only wish I could be there for the party," she said, smiling weakly.

While my sister and I were visiting Mom a few days later, the nurse and doctor took me aside and explained that Mom had only a week or so to live. Because Dad still lived in his apartment, the hospital staff was concerned about us kids. I calmly assured them that extended family was around and we'd be fine, then returned to Mom's room to visit a little more.

When I got home an hour later, I walked into the dining room to tell my brothers and sisters what the nurse had said. My family was seated around the table playing cards. I stood near the entry to the room and began, "The Nurse said..." but as I hit the word, "Mom...," my knees suddenly buckled and I fell against the wall and onto the floor. Sobbing, I couldn't finish what I was trying to say. My sister finished for me. After a few minutes, I got up and went to Mom's room, where I had been sleeping the last few nights. My whole body felt weak. This couldn't be. She couldn't be dying.

Sometime later I left the room. The rest of the house was quiet. I had no idea what anyone else was up to, I just knew I had to go back to the hospital. In control of myself again, I called a neighbor.

"Will you take me back to the hospital?"

The neighbor came right over. I don't even remember who it was. I didn't speak much to my driver. Once at the hospital, I went straight to Mom's bed. Unable to look at her, I said, "Mom, I love you and I'm sorry for all the times I've hurt you."

"I love you and I'm sorry for how I've hurt you, too."

I stood for a moment not knowing how to respond. How has she hurt me? I couldn't think of anything. But I didn't say that out loud. I thought if I asked her, it would ruin what she was trying to say. Instead, I did the second thing I'd come to do. Moving to the head of her bed, I sat down and began running my fingers softly through her hair.

I wanted to be with her as much as possible, but aunts told us our job was to be at school. What good was it to be at school? Did anyone really think I was concentrating on algebra equations?

During the school's required three-day senior retreat, Mom died. I hadn't wanted to go on the retreat. I knew she'd die while I was gone, but everyone told me to go. Mom's sister was with her that night. She said Mom woke up and turned toward her with the most peaceful look on her face. She then turned and went back to sleep. She died about ten minutes later.

I came home to a house in chaos a couple hours before the wake. My siblings, angry with each other and barking orders, were rushing to get dressed and ready. I quietly realized it was good I'd stayed on retreat.

I sat next to my dad during the funeral. At one point, I saw a single tear roll down his cheek.

The funeral procession was impressive. We kids watched out of the back of the limo, amazed at the long line of cars winding its way to the cemetery. As the limo made turns or went up and down hills, we were able to get an idea of the procession's length by the number of cars with headlights on turning to follow us.

The day after the funeral, Bobby and I sat on the living room floor and hugged each other.

The seven of us kids, Erik, 20-years-old, on down to Tonya, only nine, tried to live on our own for a few weeks. Craig and I fought constantly. In grief much of the time, the very few good moments were overwhelmed by bad.

One night, I watched all the cars that turned to come up our street. For over an hour, I waited and watched. My eyes followed as each car came near, then drove past. I finally called Mitch's house. His wife answered.

"I thought he was coming tonight."

"Oh, he forgot," she said.

"Thank you," I said, and hung up quickly so she wouldn't hear me cry.

Dying in Indian Country

Not understanding why God took Mom and not really believing in him anyway, I gave up on the Lord. A neighbor, concerned that I needed something to keep my mind off Mom, got a job for me volunteering at a local day care. Working with the preschoolers, I noticed how clear their eyes were. Not blood shot. They hadn't seen enough yet, I decided; they haven't felt the pain.

With the consent of most siblings, Dad moved back into the house. It only made sense. He was the one paying for it.

When summer arrived, Marion and I both began working for a temporary home health agency. After a few weeks of working, the two of us impulsively hitchhiked to Grand Teton National Park. While there, we met a family from our home state that was kind enough to bring us all the way back, depositing us on our respective doorsteps. Dave and Louise Nelson and I began a friendship that week. Constantly giving, they took me to their wood carving class, gave me a job at their photo studio, and even got me a job with a commercial artist friend of theirs.

But even their remarkable patience could be stretched only so far. It was a beautiful spring day when Marion picked me up for lunch from the artist's studio. The sun was warm, the air fresh, and I had no desire to return to work. Marion and I instead went to the zoo. It didn't dawn on me how embarrassed the Nelson's would be, having referred me as a good worker.

When I showed up for work at the Nelson's the next day, Louise was upset.

I protested, "But everyone thought it was great when 'Harold and Maude' did things like that."

"Harold and Maude is a movie."

I was fired.

Having gotten experience working in the Daycare, I went on to jobs taking care of the handicapped and mentally retarded and then to my job at Bridgeway Treatment Center, where I cared for elderly alcoholics.

BARGAIN

I would bargain with the devil,
sell my soul and call it well…

I would with demons traffic
on dark and cloudless nights

Ruthless I would seal the
title to my soul…

You would be the prize
and I would call it well

© By PHONACELLE SHAPEL

Chapter three:
March 1980: Rolling Thunder

I hurried down the long hallway of the treatment center toward a patient's room. As I quickly walked, two men ambled up the hall toward me. One was a staff member, the other a new patient on crutches. The new patient was a Native American with classic features. He eyed me closely as he walked by, making me feel extremely uncomfortable. I didn't like being stared at.

That Indian better stay away from me, I thought as he passed.

Bridgeway Treatment Center, on the seventh floor of Prospect Park Nursing Home, was an alcohol detox and treatment center specializing in geriatric nursing care. Because of Bridgeway's ability to provide specialized nursing along with alcoholism treatment, the program occasionally accepted younger people with physical needs other alcohol centers couldn't cope with.

I learned that the Indian man had been hit by a car after leaving a bar six weeks earlier. Late to meet a girlfriend at another bar, he was struck by a fast moving Buick while crossing the street and sustained a fractured leg. He had spent the last month and a half in traction at Hennepin County Medical Center. He was at Bridgeway because of the medications and physical therapy he still needed for his recovery.

Bridgeway was focused around the 12-step Alcoholics Anonymous program. As a Nursing Treatment Assistant, I worked with patients on a daily basis with both their physical and alcohol treatment. Doing the first step with people was always one of my favorite duties. Reviewing their past in an attempt to bring out the problems related to alcohol and their powerlessness over it, I heard their stories and got a chance to know them personally.

Although many caregivers involved with emotionally vulnerable patients are able to remain objective and detached, it's not uncommon for a nurse to occasionally develop a close relationship with a patient. Unfortunately, I had a tendency to get attached to patients. Doing step work with patients only fed that tendency.

I became attached to a seventy-year-old woman when she broke down and cried over the murder of her three-year-old daughter at the hands of her husband fifty years earlier. I fell in love with an eighty-year-old Florida transplant when she swore at me for trying to explain that those were elm trees outside her window, not palm trees.

But having grown up without a good relationship with my father, my biggest danger was that I had an overwhelming need to be protected and wanted. In February of 1980, Bruce Gates was the resident I was most fond of. A war veteran, he was fifty-ish with white hair and a fatherly appearance. I wasn't assigned to Bruce's first step, but I'd met him in group session and found him to be smart, warm-hearted and funny. Although I didn't go out of my way to find time to speak to him, I enjoyed his teasing when we were around each other. We developed a warm friendship. Once, at his request, I picked him up on my day off to go check out a new kind of street scooter he was interested in buying. He said the 'mo-ped' was the only transportation he could afford right then.

"Sometimes you have good credit, sometimes you have bad credit. Right now I have no credit."

About this same time, Bruce began developing a friendship with the new patient, Roland, the Indian man. Whenever I ran into Bruce in the halls, Roland was with him. Together they would tease me good-naturedly.

Roland also began hanging around the nurse's desk more.
He was kind of a nice person after all, I decided.

I wasn't assigned to help Roland with his first step either, but he wasn't comfortable with the person who was and asked me to help instead. There was nothing in his first step that struck me emotionally. In fact, my initial impression was that Roland was skimming the surface, not totally forthright in his story. But through the open door of this first step work, Roland began to tell me details of his life.

He was 100 percent Chippewa from the Leech Lake Reservation. Roland's generation was the last of primarily full bloods on that Reservation and until he was five-years-old, he spoke only Ojibwe. As a baby he lived near a lake with his family in a small house without plumbing. When his mother remarried after his father died, he stayed with his grandpa, Way-zhow-ush-quah-je-wabe, in the woods near Walker. The rest of his five or so siblings stayed with his mother and stepfather, Walter, who were drinking heavily. I say five children or so because the number varied. Both adults entered the marriage with five children each, but some of the older ones were already married and others moved in and out. Five more children came after Roland.

The drinking wasn't the reason Roland went to stay with his grandfather. Grandpa drank too, although not as often as his daughter. Grandpa needed Roland to help him around and be a companion. But the relationship was reciprocal; Roland cherished the help and companionship his grandpa gave him. Spending much of their time alone together, they grew very close.

Roland spoke fondly of his early childhood.
"We used to camp by the lake in large groups," he said, describing traditional events such as powwows and ricing. "Gathering wild rice every year was our time to be together and see friends and family. We looked forward to it, just like Christmas to you guys, because people you hadn't seen for a long time would get together while camping by the lake and had fun. Other times in the woods was when we gathered maple or went trapping and fishing."

Roland stayed with his grandfather until he was five and it was time to begin school. When the time came to leave, Roland hated to go. He adored his grandfather. But his parents still spent time with his grandfather at the gatherings in the woods. There, Roland continued to learn from both his parents and Grandpa the traditional way of life and food gathering.

However, Roland's mother and stepfather were also Christians now. As Christians, they were determined to raise their children to be sober and love the Lord. "They had all of us kids sit at the table after dinner for Bible study," Roland remembered.

Nevertheless, after his Grandpa's death six years later, Roland began drinking. His parents, who had no problem with spanking him when he was younger, now backed away.

"You make your choices. Just don't come crying to us when you get in trouble," Roland quoted his mother saying.

Roland took to running away from home and getting into trouble with the law. Finally, he was sent to a foster home and then to a boy's reformatory. After graduation from the reformatory he attended Haskell Institute, an Indian college in Kansas to study architecture. He enjoyed the work; creative design appealed to him.

Roland told me that he had worked as an architect for a couple of years before he got into trouble for dating the Sheriff's daughter once too often. He said that as he was wrestling with jailers while being thrown into a cell, he grabbed the doorjamb with his left hand to keep from being pushed in and they slammed the heavy door right on it. The next morning, according to Roland, the doctor worked to save most of his hand. Although the doctor was successful and he lost only half his thumb, he said he was unable to use that hand for a long time and so was unable to continue as an architect. I never questioned it.

Roland was in and out of jobs for the next few years. His life alternated between trying to pull himself together in alcohol treatment and being drunk. His life fluctuated from honest workman to social outcast and back again. Bridgeway wasn't his first time in treatment; it was his fourth, and he now had a wife and four kids. He hadn't lived with his wife for the last six months, though, and said he didn't see much chance of returning to his marriage. According to Roland, she was always critical of him and mean with the kids.

"Anyway, my wife won't like me sober," he said.

Most days, I began my shift in the afternoon and inevitably found Roland and Bruce leaning against the wall in the hallway. Roland, swinging his cane in his hand, was always nicely groomed. His clothes, including his jeans, were always pressed, and the cuffs of his sleeves carefully and perfectly rolled under twice. The two of them talked quietly to each other as they watched people pass. They always had a big smile and hello when I approached.

When I had the opportunity to take a group of residents for a walk, Roland joined me. It was spring, and another aide and I guided the group along the parkway toward the University. The river sparkled below us. Roland and I, while at the same time speaking and laughing with the group and enjoying the sunshine, walked together and talked.

In the late evening, Roland and Bruce were the only ones still in the smoking room watching TV long after the older residents had retired. With the shift almost over and the work all done, I took the time to sit down and unwind.

Roland went home to visit his wife and kids on Easter. I missed him that day at work, but he had children and it was good for him to be with them.
When Roland returned, he said he hadn't had a good time.
"My wife and her relatives were drinking," he told me. "I felt out of place."
He said he'd ended up just taking a walk around the block with the kids and then returning to Bridgeway. "My baby girl is only a year old. I want her to know who I am. I just go back anymore to see the kids."

He knew my interest in culture and after a time gave me a copy of the book "Rolling Thunder." It was a great book for a teenager prone to romantic notions. It was the story of a witty and lovable medicine man who lived as he wanted to, not as others expected him to. As I understood it, Rolling Thunder was wiser in the world than even our best scientists because he could do things that no one else could do. He understood the deep reality of the hidden spirit world, something I figured materialistic and destructive white people had no understanding of. I wanted to understand that world and be part of it. I also wanted to live my life free of the burdens and expectations of the white world and having to work 40 hours a week for 40 years.

But on top of all that, Rolling Thunder was a kind man who loved his wife and took care of his family. He was a good father. Are all Indians like that?

Maybe Roland is like Rolling Thunder, I thought. He was warm, attentive, and always glad to see me. On top of that, he'd given me that book. There had to be more that he could show me.

While working in various resident rooms fulfilling my obligations for the day, my mind was aware of where Roland was and what he was supposed to be doing all the time. I knew the sound of his cowboy boots approaching down the tile hallway. When standing at the nursing desk, my hands would begin to sweat when I heard the sound of his footsteps.

I began to work double shifts in order to spend more time with him. I also began to take him out on passes to Narcotics Anonymous meetings or for long drives. We once drove over two hours on the freeway. We hadn't done it by plan, but simply drove with no real thought of where we were going and then talked for over an hour before we realized how far we had gone. Roland even remarked that he was enjoying the conversation so much that he had forgotten to have a cigarette during that time.

"I've never done that before," he said.

One evening Roland and I sat on his bed while he showed me an Ojibwe language book. As we paged through it, he explained to me different words and tried to teach me to pronounce them.

I had already been thinking about the inevitability of this friendship being short-lived (he was married after all), so I asked him what the word for *"good-bye"* was.

"There is no word that means 'good-bye'," he answered, "There is only a word for 'see-you-later.' In our culture, we never say good-bye, because we know we will see each other again in the next life. 'Gi-ga-wa-ba-min me-na-wa'. That means 'see you later'."

"Gi-ga-wa-ba-min me-na-wa," I repeated.

"No," he said, "you're stressing it wrong. And don't bring your voice down at the end; bring it up. In your language you always end your words down. Ours is different."

He had me repeat it about twenty times before he was satisfied. I made myself memorize it then. I didn't tell Roland, but I figured that someday I would have to use it.

A week later I was standing at the nurses' desk when the elevator doors opened and a woman from laundry approached carrying several pressed shirts on hangers.

"Will you make sure Roland Ward gets these?" she asked.

"Sure," I answered.

The woman laid the shirts on the counter in front of me and got back on the elevator. I was surprised that Roland was getting such special treatment. The laundry department didn't normally press shirts and deliver them personally to patients. But I quickly put the question out of mind. I was happy to go to Roland's room and hang the shirts in the closet for him. My desire to spend time with Roland had become an obsession. I had been assigned to perform certain cares on various patients, but instead spent my evening talking to Roland in a small hallway. He sat on the chair used to weigh wheelchair patients, and I sat on the floor at his feet. I hadn't intended to avoid my work, I just couldn't seem to tear myself away and go do it. Late in the evening, a workmate confronted me about helping to get a quadriplegic patient into bed. Although I tried to come up with an excuse, I couldn't manage a good one. My nursing supervisor also questioned why the diabetic urine sticks hadn't been done. The staff at Bridgeway tended to be laid back and easy going, but I knew I was pushing their patience.

The Nursing Director called me to her office one afternoon. She wanted to talk to me about my relationship with Roland.

"Have you taken everything into consideration?" she asked, "Roland is fifteen years older than you, comes from a different culture, and has a family." I was sure that I had thought of everything, but being young and naïve, had no real clue what I was talking about.

An amazingly kind, patient and trusting woman, she gave me the benefit of the doubt and handed me a list she'd written. "You and Roland look these questions over and talk about them. Be sure that you are comfortable with each question and its answer before you go any further in this relationship."

The list asked questions that really needed to be considered, such as how our families would react and how we would handle spirituality. Knowing that my mother had passed on a year earlier, the Director asked how I thought she might have reacted. I recognized the wisdom of the questions and appreciated how she was handling this. But the reality was that I had already made up my mind. I counseled myself that my liberal family wouldn't mind the relationship a bit.

There's nothing wrong with this, I told myself, ignoring the question about my mother.

A few days later Roland was called to the phone at the nurses' desk. After speaking for a few minutes, he hung up and got permission to call long distance to his sister in Cass Lake. I sat at the desk while he talked. When he was done, he told me the small daughter of his nephew had died and the family wanted him to be at the funeral that weekend.

His counselor gave him permission to leave treatment for the funeral on Friday. Now Roland had to find a way to get to the reservation.

"It's my weekend off. I can take you," I offered.

The night we were to leave, there was a powwow at the American Indian Center. We decided to go there first and meet Roland's nephew, Matthew, afterwards. He also needed a ride to the funeral. I was excited about going to the powwow. I'd never been to one before. But as we approached the building and I saw all kinds of Indians hanging around outside of it; I felt nervous. Then we walked into the building and I saw no other white person among the hundreds of Indians.

I'd never been alone before, without any other whites, and had no idea it would be scary. I'd grown up with preconceived images of Indians. Images are safe and easy as long as they are never challenged. But these people were real and some were glancing at me with noticeable hostility. I stayed close to Roland.

Roland moved through the crowd, stopping to greet and talk with various people. My discomfort increased with the fact no one spoke to me. Although Roland introduced me, few of his friends would even look at me, let alone say anything.

We eventually made it to the bleachers and sat toward the top. This was better. There was no need to talk to anyone now and sitting next to Roland I felt safe. The costumes and dances were interesting for the first couple songs. Many of the younger people were wearing bright colors and danced swiftly with leaps and swirls. Other ones wore earth tones and danced with rhythmic, equal measure of the feet.

But after a time I began to get bored. There didn't seem to be much variation in the music and the dances made no sense to me. It helped a little when Roland told me what kind of dance it was and how it was to be performed correctly. The brightly colored dancers were called Fancy Dancers. The others were Traditional Dancers. But my favorite was the hoop dancer, a young man who swirled skillfully with several huge rings.

When the dancing stopped and elders went out to retrieve a fallen feather, Roland explained to me that not just anyone could reach over and pick up a feather from the ground.

"The feather is a sacred object," he said, "It needs to be prayed over before anyone can pick it up."

We met his nephew Matthew and Matthew's girlfriend in front of the center sometime after midnight. From there we got on Hwy 10 and headed north to Cass Lake. Roland drove the yellow Chevy wagon most of the way.

Beth Ward

ICARUS

the stars burn
and roar with the
coldness of clarity,
a wine that fills
greenglass caves

a sweet drop of
red memory on her
tongue, she stands
beneath the obelisk,
wings folded, she
hoards her warmth

and waits in solitude
for Icarus while a
feather falls at her
feet

© By PHONACELLE SHAPEL

Chapter four:
Living in Indian Country

When I returned to work a few days later, my supervisor took me aside to confront me on the quality of my work. My obsession with Roland was getting in the way of my assignments and she was concerned. Was I sure that I had taken all possibilities into consideration? Did I know what I was getting into? Together we decided I should take a leave of absence for the remainder of the time that Roland was in treatment.

Roland's counselor also called me to his office and began counseling me to stay away from Roland for awhile.

"If it is real love," he said, "a month apart will only prove it." When it was clear I wasn't listening to his gentle approach, he became blunter, "Roland is a loser. Don't get involved with him."

Too late. I took my leave, but a short time later, Roland decided to abandon the treatment program anyway. While being superficially disappointed that he left, I was truthfully delighted.

Roland moved in with Edwin, a friend of his, in a studio apartment downtown. However, most of the time he stayed with me in the four-bedroom house I shared with friends in the suburbs. We went on walks, saw movies, and ate at our favorite restaurant. Why I wasn't fired, I don't know.

Before meeting Roland, I had attended the DFL Caucuses and had gotten myself elected as an alternate to the Minnesota Democratic Convention. I attended the first day of the two-day June event at a

Minneapolis Convention Center. The second day, instead of keeping my commitment, I spent the day with Roland.

One morning as I was getting ready for work, Roland told me that his wife was employed in the laundry room of the nursing home housing Bridgeway.

Alarmed, I asked, "Was that your wife that brought your pressed shirts up to the floor?"

"Yes," he answered.

"You mean that I've met her and didn't even know it?"

"I guess so."

"Roland, she wouldn't have been pressing your shirts for you if she didn't still love you!"

"Oh," he answered, "she only did that so she could check you out."

"You mean your wife knew who I was?"

"Well, of course she did."

"Roland, if she still has feelings for you, maybe you should be back with her and the kids."

"Well, if you don't want me here, I'll just get going," he answered.

He grabbed his jacket and strode to the front door.

"Wait a minute," I said, "that's not what I meant, let's talk about it."

"No," he said, "that's the way you feel."

He was out the door and walking down the road before I even knew what happened. The guilt stayed with me all day while I worked. Not the guilt I had felt initially about being a home-wrecker, but the guilt of having Roland misunderstand and be hurt by what I was trying to say. After work, I went to look for him over at Edwin's. Roland was there. It had taken him most of the hot day to walk the 20 miles back into Minneapolis.

To my relief though, he was ready to forgive and returned with me to the house. I was blind to the manipulation. All I knew was I wanted him.

That summer we drove up north to Cass Lake. Main Street, just a few blocks long, looked shriveled and lifeless. Although there were some tired businesses such as a grocery, liquor store, laundromat, mercantile, bars, and a Dairy Queen, most of the street appeared worn out and empty. The Five and Dime, its window display of trinkets dusty and sun bleached, had a "for sale" sign in the door. Roland was sorry to see the elderly couple retire. Apparently they weren't asking much for the store. On later visits, the store was closed, but remained unsold, the same musty wares sitting in the window.

Roland's dad, Walter Hunter, lived in a yellow three-bedroom house on the tribal tract, a section of land built up with many of these identical homes. This tract was across the highway from the main part of this small resort town. Roland's relatives, laughing during the telling, related how white tourists drive slowly through the tract with their windows rolled up and their doors locked, looking at tribal members and their homes as if visiting a zoo. Roland's relatives laughed, then cursed the tourists.

Walter had been a Christian for almost thirty years now, but still practiced many of the old traditions he was raised with. In his eighties with white hair and weathered hands, he kept constantly busy. While many of the homes around him were barren and dirt packed, growing more old cars and dogs then trees or grass, his lawn was clean and well kept. A source of pride was his cucumber patch in the backyard. One of his favorite stories, which he would tell over and over, was how he had caught two boys stealing from his patch a couple years earlier. Walter laughed and laughed as he retold about how one boy stood and vehemently denied the theft, all the while cucumbers were peeking out of his pockets.

The house itself was a simple box design used by the Bureau of Indian Affairs on many reservations across the country at that time. The front door, toward the center, brought you into the living room. The linoleum-covered floor extended into the dining area and the kitchen was behind a wall to the side. The wall brought you down a hallway to the bedrooms. The number of bedrooms differed from house to house. The furniture was simple and the thin walls were adorned with pictures of grandchildren and Native American mementos.

I was the last one out of bed on my first morning there. I could hear people talking and laughing in the other room. They had ignored me when we'd come in the night before. I stayed in bed as long as possible out of fear of everyone.

Living with Walter was his youngest daughter, Annie, her two daughters, Savannah and Candis, and Roland's nephew Matthew. Finally their voices quieted down and I decided to get up. I got dressed and joined Roland and Walter in the kitchen. To my delight, there was a big bowl of unglazed doughnuts on the table.

"Can I have one?" I asked Roland.

"Sure."

Great. I grabbed one and took a big bite.

"Ugh! What's wrong with these doughnuts?"

Roland laughed. "Those aren't doughnuts. That's fry bread. That's the best kind of bread there is!"

Well, Roland may think so, but after that kind of disappointment, it took me a long time to warm up to the things.

Annie was outside on the dirt driveway, leaning on a car, talking to two social workers about her girls. Savannah and Candis were about seven and four. Candis, in her pajamas, kept peeking out the front door. Every time she did, her mom would holler at her to get back into the house and get dressed. Figuring this didn't impress the social workers much; I finally took Candis into the back room, found some clothes for her and brushed her hair.

As Roland left for the woods with his dad the next morning, he kissed me good-bye. Annie leaned over after he left and said, "He really must love you. I've never seen him kiss anyone in front of people before. Not even his wife."

I was sitting with Roland's sisters around the kitchen table. It was beginning to feel comfortable. Now most of them looked at me and smiled and laughed as we talked. The atmosphere was relaxing. They didn't seem to care how I looked or what I wore. I didn't feel any pressure to perform.

Matthew's older sister Wanda kind of slid into her grandpa's house that day. When she moved, she glided across a room. Intelligent and quick-witted, Wanda radiated confidence. A beautiful girl with shoulder length black hair, heart shaped face and sunglasses; she wore her jeans tight. She quickly took me under her wing and invited me to go play pool with her down at the bowling alley. I went with her and watched as she teased and flirted with the men. Wanda was full of life and held people's attention. After the bowling alley, we sat in the grass at the park talking about Roland while we ate snacks.

"Is Roland a good worker?" I asked.

After hesitating a moment, she answered, "When he works." I took that to be a positive answer.

Later I was told, "It's hard to get jobs around here. White people won't hire Indians, and a person can only get a job with the tribal government if they've got connections, like family on the council."

That evening, after hearing I'd been walking around the tract with Wanda, Roland warned me not to walk around the tract by myself.

"There's a rapist that lives in that house over there," Roland said, pursing his lips and pointing with them, a custom used rather than point with fingers.

"Everyone knows it?"

"Well, that's just the way he is. People just stay away from him."

The whole tract bore that feeling of "live and let be." Days were never structured; things got done when people did them. Most of people's time seemed to be spent visiting, not because there was anything special to say nor because they hadn't seen each other just the other day, but just for something to do. Roland would just up and decide to get in the car to go visit someone or someone would up and decide to come visit him. Roland didn't even need to arrive at a house in order to visit. He'd stop the car in the middle of the road if he saw someone he knew walking. The pedestrian would lean in the window, while at the same time not looking at Roland or me, but looking off to the side as if concentrating on someone or something off in the distance and after the initial *"Whach you up to?"* and *"aw, nothin. Same ol' stuff,"* no one would have a thing to say. Roland would sit staring straight ahead and the walker would stand outside the car staring at something else and after what to me seemed like an eternity, one of them would finally break the silence with, "Hey! Gotta go. See ya round, man!"

Once arriving at someone's home, we were always offered food. "Pull up a plate!" they'd say, "you'd better eat something."

I always felt shy about eating. I was raised not to interfere with other family's meal times. In my mind, it was rude to drop in and expect to eat at other people's homes. But in Roland's world, it was considered rude not to offer a visitor food. No matter if there was very little to offer, they gladly stretched it.

Dinner table conversation wasn't like the silent greetings from car windows. Joking and teasing each other was the norm. Laughter was frequent.

It was interesting when people came over to see Walter though. He was an elder, and although some people came only to ask him for money or a pound of wild rice, others came to make sure he was okay or to ask advice. The older people, although they all knew English, spoke only Ojibwe to Walter. These were the only times I heard the language spoken in lengthy conversation. The younger people, however, didn't seem to know much Ojibwe, so their conversations were always in English.

As the visitors sat and talked, their eyes wandered everywhere but at the person they were speaking to. This, I found out later, was traditional respect. I would experience this again and again as I met more people in Roland's family. The first time or two after meeting them they would ignore me. But after that, they warmed up and began to both look at me more and speak to me - most of them anyway. Some men Roland's age *have yet* to ever address me or make eye contact. As time passed, I learned this was done out of respect for Roland. In his culture, for a man to look at a woman in the eye is flirting, and to look someone of the same sex in the eye is a threat, the same as accusing them of something.

Most mornings Roland and his family had a bowl of oatmeal and poured some grease on it for flavoring. I decided one morning that it must taste something like the salted bacon grease my dad spread on his pumpernickel bread, so I made myself a bowl and sat down to eat it. Ugh! All I tasted was a mouth full of thick grease!

"Well, you're only supposed to use a little bit, not pour it on like milk!" Roland said laughing, "Next time have a little oatmeal with your grease!"

There was no next time, and I never did try the beverage in the teapot that they kept on the back of the stove either. The dark liquid with green leaves floating in it; the one they called "swamp tea."

Well, I couldn't be much of a food critic though; I was never much of a cook. In getting dinner done, Annie and I had an agreement. She would do the cooking and I would do the dishes. But one afternoon I decided to try to make a cake from scratch. I couldn't find white sugar, but I found some maple sugar on a shelf under the counter. Maple sugar was plentiful; Walter tapped trees every spring. So, I followed the recipe and used maple sugar instead. Big mistake. Maple sugar is not refined. When I served it, the cake was way overly sweet and you could feel the gritty granules of sugar in your mouth. No one would eat it - well, except Walter (bless his heart). He finished his whole piece of cake without saying a word, staring at the ceiling as he chewed and swallowed each bite.

Even hanging clothes on a line was new to me. I was actually afraid that women would look out their windows and see I was doing it wrong. So as I went about the chore, I tried very hard to hang each piece perfectly and just the way Roland had told me.

Following a day or so of sore throat, the cold came on quick and miserable. The kind of cold that keeps you from breathing and is full of dry, endless coughing.

I didn't want anyone to see me this way, let alone be near me. I looked and felt terrible.

"Here," Walter offered, "try some snake root. Put it in your mouth and chew it."

In his hand he held a gnarly looking root about 2 inches in length. He broke off a tiny bit and handed it to me. Putting it in my mouth, I almost spat it right out again. He laughed, "Just chew it. It'll help you."

Whether or not it worked, I don't know. Colds come and colds go. It was hard for me to tell if it was the medicine that did it.

After awhile a person gets used to cockroaches. After awhile, you don't always take the time to look for a weapon with which to smack the fast moving abominations. Sometimes, in an effort to just get them before they run off and generate one hundred more of themselves, you quick smack 'em with your hand.

"Our sister Dorothy brought those with her from California. We never had them before that," Annie said, motioning. "We've sprayed a lot of times, but just can't get rid of them."

The worst part of getting up at night for a glass of water was turning on the lights. Cockroaches swarmed the walls and counters. Sometimes you'd try to smack those too, but it was really a waste of time and you'd be up all night if you were serious. As much as possible, I used cups that had been drying in the dish rack, suspended an inch or so above the counter.

One morning I watched Annie pack things for Savannah and Candis to take with them to the foster home, including a few jars of blueberries she had canned. Apparently, Annie had crossed the line with the social workers, a line no one was telling me about. The girls weren't going far; they were going just to the other side of town. Roland and I drove Annie and the girls over. Little emotion was expressed. It seemed almost normal routine and the exchange between mother and foster parents was over in a matter of minutes.

One afternoon, Roland drove down a dirt road and stopped at a clearing near the lake. We got out and stood in the tall grass near a tree, enjoying the warmth. The breeze from the lake was fresh and the air smelled of pine. The sun sparkled on the water.

"I'll always take care of you," Roland told me.

"Really?" My heart soaked it in, "Do you really mean that?'

"Of course. I wouldn't have said it if I didn't mean it."

When we returned from Leech Lake in August, I resigned from Bridgeway. I wanted to be free to go with Roland at the end of the month for ricing season. Without a job, I spent my days doing nothing but be with him. One afternoon we hopped on a bus to go see Bruce. We hadn't seen him at all that summer. Arriving at his apartment house, we saw a panel of buzzers for the different apartments, the names of the occupants above each buzzer. We looked up Bruce's apartment number, but his name wasn't on it. No one answered the buzzer. Roland and I went home confused. That evening Roland called Bruce's son.

"Sorry," his son said, "Dad was killed last month. He was all tanked up on his mo-ped, and took a turn into a car. He was killed instantly"

The next day, Roland and I drove out to the veteran cemetery near the airport and found his grave, a simple white cross in a long row of white crosses. Maybe if we'd stayed in touch, he wouldn't have started drinking again. We felt guilty for not ever having visited him. As we stood at his grave, we knew he would always remain a very special and important person in our hearts.

The wild ricing season was the end of August and early September. Elders would go to the edge of the lake and inspect the crop, deciding the proper time to begin the harvest. The harvest had rules. No one can begin ricing until the season officially opens and canoes have to be within certain specifications. The point is to try to preserve the fields for another year.

Roland loved to pole for his dad. Standing at the end of the canoe with a 15 to 20 foot hand-hewn pole, he pushed the canoe through the rice stalks. Walter, sitting in the middle of the canoe, was the 'knocker'. In each hand he held hand-hewn sticks about 32 inches long. The knocker would take one stick and reach out to the rushes, pulling them toward him over the canoe while with the other hand knocking the rice off of the rush and into the boat. Both knocking and poling are hard-learned skills; people who are good at it are in demand.

Not wanting to stay on the tract by myself, I went along every day and waited on the bank of the lake. I took a good book and sometimes took walks through the woods. Walter called me "Roland's shadow."

One morning just after arriving at the lake, I saw Roland throw a Coke can into the brush. I went to get it. Looking over the tall weeds, I saw all kinds of pop and beer cans strewn about.

"Roland! How come everyone is throwing their trash here! You're Indians; you're supposed to respect the environment!"

"Don't worry about it," he said, obviously irritated with me. "The Boy Scouts will pick it up."

They usually riced until dark or until their boat was so full that they could take no more in. When they got back to the house I rubbed Walter's back and listened to him talk about when he was a young man playing the amateur baseball circuit or when he was in the service and stationed in Germany. ("Sprechen due deutch?" he'd ask, "nein," I'd answer.)

Walter offered to teach me to dance. Everyone thought he was joking. But up he stood and over he came. I wasn't a very good student, but I had a good time.

Step by step, Roland and his dad showed me the process of harvesting and preparing wild rice in the traditional way. Few did it that way anymore. If they kept their rice, most people brought it to a place for bulk processing. But many didn't even hang on to it. A lot of the younger people would sell their rice directly off the lake to brokers waiting on the shore and at certain stores. Some ricers would get their bags wet, causing it to weigh more and get a better price. Others would put rocks in the middle of their bags. Some saved their money until the end of the season, but many took their cash immediately and spent the night drinking. But Walter and Roland saved their rice. They preferred to keep it, process it the old way, and use it through the following year.

When Walter felt he had enough rice to get started, he went to the backyard and placed a load of cedar wood in a small pit. After lighting the fire, he put a metal sheet over it. The sheet was bent up around the sides in order to keep the rice from falling off as he took a pole and pushed the rice back and forth on the sheet. This prevented the rice from burning while it was being parched.

Next came the 'jigging'. The parched rice was placed in a concrete pot that was put into a hole in the ground. Wanda then stepped into the hole onto the grain. Her hands on the ground to steady herself, she quickly moved her feet up and down to grind the hulls off of the rice. This could take about two hours. When Wanda got tired, someone else took over. I was glad they never asked me. It didn't look easy.

When the rice looked ready, Walter took it out of the hole to fan it. He put the rice a few scoops at a time into a wide, fairly flat, birch bark bowl, then, while standing with his back to the wind, bounced the bowl to shake the hulls out of the rice. Finally, the rice was brought to the kitchen table, where we all went through it, cleaning out any left over hulls. This was the final product, ready to store for meals all winter.

"Would you like to try some Indian popcorn?" Walter asked me.

Taking some of the rice, he popped it on the stove just like corn. Imagine making popcorn with rice!

Parching the old way was also the best way to finish the rice. When preparing it for a meal, rice parched the old way didn't have to be boiled. All I had to do was pour the hot water from the boiled potatoes (a staple at each meal) over the rice, cover it, and let it set for about 15 minutes and it was ready for the table.

In Roland's mind, real wild rice is the only rice worth eating. But for me, it was bland and tasteless. I had to doctor it up with butter and salt at first in order to get used to it.

I learned a lot about cooking that month, though. It had never occurred to me that baked beans or macaroni and cheese could be made from scratch. Annie also tried to show me how to cut up a fish. This was not something I wanted to learn, so I weaseled out of it as quick as possible.

In my simpleness, I had always thought I knew how to cook. Well, I knew how to make hot-dogs anyway. It was a blessing for them all that I didn't cook much while I was there.

Back in the Twin Cities that fall, Roland enrolled in the Human Services Program at the Minneapolis Community College that fall and we got an apartment together. Every weekend after he got out of school, Roland went after his four kids - Cheri, 13; Misty, 10; Junior, 8; and Joy, who was almost two years old now and just beginning potty training.

Cheri, Junior and Joy were dark like their father. Misty was fairer, more like her mother. Cheri, Misty and Junior, although slightly plump, were all small for their age, sharing their parents' short height but not their slight frames. Baby Joy alone seemed to have some height potential. In the beginning all four were quiet and bashful. At times, they would timidly bring me a fistful of dandelions or a colored picture, but for the most part, they seemed to stand back, watching to see who I was and how long I'd be around.

I didn't mind the kids and felt I had no right to come between them and their father. I figured it was my duty to accept and care for them every weekend. I wasn't going to be the kind of woman who would try to keep a man from his children.

When the Saturday paper came, I went through the family entertainment section to see if there were any free or low cost events we could go to. We always found something to do on Saturdays, whether it was going to the zoo, a film at the library, a picnic, or walk in a park. Some evenings Roland would show his older girls and me how to do beadwork. He put together a little loom for me. I finished a wristband for him which he wore for a long time.

One weekend Roland went to Leech Lake with his brother. Cheri came alone to spend the weekend with me. Quiet, with thick wavy black hair and a beautiful smile, she was an adorable girl. I was both glad and flattered she had wanted to be with me. I didn't have much money, but wanted to do something fun with the weekend. I thought maybe I would show her some things she might not have seen before, so together we visited the historic Swan Turnblad House on Park and 26th. She seemed to like it. I know I loved it.

During the week, Roland and I took walks and ate out when we could afford it. Roland went to school and visited the blood bank twice a week to sell his plasma. They paid him nine dollars a pint. When he agreed to have a tetanus shot, they gave him a dollar more per pint.

I half-heartedly looked for a job. Mostly I waited for him to come home.

One weekend, at a powwow up north, Roland and I camped under the trees with Roland's sister Elaine and her family. Elaine's eight-year-old daughter danced the jingle dance and won first place. Her dress was adorned with what looked like bells, but were actually rolled snuff can lids.

"How are chewing tobacco lids traditional?" I asked Roland as we sat at a picnic table under a tree, "Indians didn't always have chewing tobacco. What did they use before they had chewing tobacco?"

"I don't know. They used whatever they could find."

"Maybe it's a relatively new traditional dance."

"Maybe."

"Roland, how come you don't teach your girls to dance?" I asked.

"They were never interested."

"Well, how come you yourself don't dance?"

"I don't know. I used to."

"Did you dance fancy or traditional?"

"Traditional."

Seeing Matthew and Elaine's kids walking with a group of teenagers on the road toward us, Roland laughed, "Looks like they're out snagging."

I crinkled my nose. "Snagging?"

"Yeah, well, picking up girls."

"Snagged? Sounds like something you do with snot."

Roland laughed, "You gotta get used to our slang."

I was getting used to it. I was taking it all in.

I met the Whitebird girls - Sonya, Marci, and Julia - that fall. Yvonne Whitebird, who was Roland's sister and Matthew and Wanda's mother, called and asked him to come after her and her young girls. She and her boyfriend Reggie were fighting and she needed a place to stay. We drove up to a housing project called Mississippi Courts on the north side of town between the freeway and the river.

The housing was the worst I'd ever seen. Garbage stood outside the homes and littered the dirt drive, doors with torn screens hung askew and windows were broken. Inside, cockroaches swarmed the dirty walls. Yvonne came out to the car with a bag of clothes. Her three girls, looking about six through ten years old, trailed her. While she loaded the girls and bag into the car, Yvonne turned to Reggie and made some final cracks at him. Standing on the cement stoop, Reggie didn't reply to her. In an almost whiny voice explaining it wasn't his fault, he directed his remarks toward Roland.

Once home, I showed them the guest bedroom. Giving Yvonne the twin bed with its crisp white comforter, I laid blankets for the girls on the floor. I had put a lot of time into fixing up that bedroom, so I hoped she would like it and be comfortable. But the next morning, I saw she hadn't slept under the covers at all. To my disappointment and puzzlement, she'd lain on top of the bedclothes and pulled the extra blanket over her.

But a much bigger frustration was the fact that during her overnight stay she didn't once look at or speak to me. Yvonne directed her comments and eyes toward Roland alone. I still didn't really understand the "no talk – no look" thing, so I felt slighted and assumed she didn't like me.

Yvonne spent the night with us, then returned home to Reggie. She left the girls with us another couple of days. While all three girls were quiet, the oldest, Julia, was particularly reserved. She didn't communicate with me at all and to her sisters only in hushed tone as though not to disturb me. But in her eyes, if you took time to pay attention (something she tried not to let you do) you could see a deep sadness.

Tall, slim, and delicately featured, Julia, along with her sisters, (and I learned later their older brother Roger) were some of the few full-blooded Cass Lake members of their generation. But Julia's siblings, though not heavy, were not quite as slim, not quite as delicate as she. And Julia's siblings, though not rowdy, were also not quite as subdued, not quite as melancholy.

Over the next couple months I met more and more of Roland's relatives. Between Roland's mother and stepfather there had been 15 children. Now middle aged, those children each had several of their own. There seemed to be no end to the relatives, including Roland's own uncles, aunts, cousins and second cousins yet to meet.

On a late night trip to the Leech Lake Reservation that winter, Roland and I ran out of gas on a stretch between Walker and Cass Lake. It was too cold to walk anywhere so Roland decided we'd just cover in blankets and spend the night there. He didn't treat the incident with any frustration. To him, it was just a minor inconvenience. Feeling his comfort, I felt safe because he felt safe.

In the morning we were picked up by a passer-by. When we arrived to Walter's home, Roland's sister Dorothy and her three sons, Troy, Mickey and Paul were sitting at the kitchen table. She had just returned from California and was getting a divorce from her husband, an Air Force sergeant.

Roland introduced us and the conversation turned to James and Gloria, the parents of the little girl in the casket several months earlier. James had been sent to prison for her beating death. However, Roland's family had their own thoughts about what really happened.

"You know," said one, "they had a fight the night that baby died. But he took off and it was her that was with those kids. When he came back, she took off and that's when he found that baby on the couch."

"He loved that Gloria too much," said another.

"Still does. She's running all over on him while he's sitting in jail."

Dorothy's boys sat quietly listening to the conversation. Mickey, named after a brother of Roland's who had died in an alcohol-related car wreck, was about eight-years-old. He and his brothers were half black, half Indian. A slim, mischievous kid, he also had a quiet and thoughtful side to him. He loved his uncle, Roland and when Roland was in town, Mickey was content to quietly tag along. Although they had a house on the other side of the tract, Mickey insisted on making himself a cot at the foot of our bed that night. When it was time for us to leave the next day, he seemed sad. I don't know why. I couldn't think of anything special that we'd done.

On our trip home Roland stopped to briefly visit a friend at an alcohol treatment facility.

"This building used to be a place for TB patients," Roland told me, "My dad had to stay here for months when I was little. He was quarantined."

Dan Hunter, the man we were visiting, was Roland's cousin and best friend growing up. They had their first drunk together when

Roland was eleven. Dan's nose was enlarged from his alcohol abuse but he was still a very handsome man.

He also had a sense of humor and good-naturedly ribbed the both of us while they played pool for about an hour.

Every weekend, Roland's four children came over. In the beginning it didn't bother me. I made it my job to find fun things for us to do. But as time went on I began to feel more and more used. Whether or not they came over was always a decision between Roland and his ex-wife, Shirley. They never considered it any of my business although I was the one who ended up doing most of the childcare. In addition, we usually couldn't afford the food. It was frustrating to come into the kitchen and find the kids had eaten the whole loaf of bread for a snack when we had no money to buy more. When I got upset, the kids ran to their dad and complained I was being mean. Roland then got angry with me. It was best just to keep those feelings to myself.

One day the phone rang and Junior answered it.

"Who is this? Who is this?" he asked, laughing in apparent response to the voice he was hearing. "Oh, Mom! You were teasing me!"

With all the negative things I'd been told, I was a little surprised by this exchange. It hadn't occurred to me that she may have a sense of humor and joke with the children.

Roland's sister Lila was beautiful and full of life. Her laugh was contagious.

She married a hard working man, and they had two beautiful children. But for some reason, Lila wasn't happy. She left her husband for a man who beat her. Roland couldn't understand it and never did accept that boyfriend or any that came after. No one could understand. Lila was smart and fun to be with. Why would she give up her family and security in order to live life on the streets?

Homeless and broke, Lila kept drinking. You would catch sight of her at times walking unsteadily down Franklin Avenue. Then you might not see her for weeks. Every now and then she would go to detox and sober up, taking methadone to help her. The doctors told her that her liver was bad. She knew that if she continued drinking, she would die. Sometimes when she was sober she would go see her children. While she was there her daughter would do her best to take care of her, even cooking hot meals for her. But Lila couldn't - wouldn't stay for more than a few days. Something was driving her and even she didn't seem to know what. She just went with it.

Roland's brothers, Charlie and Buck, were also on the street. Charlie's nickname was 'The Champ'. When he was younger, he was the best boxer in the prison. Tall and very slim with beautiful features, he must have been very good looking as a young man - but he never married. He was very quiet, one of those men that would never look at or speak to me. But he seemed quiet with everyone. When Roland stopped to talk to him, Charlie never said much. He always seemed nervous. I frequently saw him walking alone down Franklin Avenue, a brown paper bag in his hand. Sometimes he was with Buck.

The Ward family is of the Bear Clan and Buck's big and stocky frame, the stockiest of all the Ward boys, fit the image. He had a wife and children in Cass Lake but I never met them and he didn't seem to spend much time with them. During the summer he roamed Franklin Avenue or hung out up north. In the winter, he usually had himself admitted into a treatment center. It was a good way to stay warm and get three square meals a day.

Buck seemed to have a struggle with the world. In part, it could have been from having damaged his ear years earlier. As a result of that damage he had trouble with his balance. People assumed he was drunk even when he wasn't drinking. There were other problems, too. He, like Charlie, spent a lot of time on the street.

Buck loved Roland. He called Roland by his middle name and every now and then when we ran into him on the street, Buck would slip Roland some money. He was the one that always remembered Roland's birthday with a card or a twenty-dollar bill. But they rarely saw each other.

In April, Roland's divorce was final. Shirley told him he didn't have to show up for court, but he did anyway and sat in the back of the room and watched. When the judge asked why she wanted a divorce, she answered, "Because he doesn't want to be married anymore."

I knew what her words were saying; she didn't want the divorce. But I brushed my feelings of guilt aside. The divorce was done now and that's all that mattered.

But immediately afterwards Roland and I began arguing and he told me to move out. I left, but rather than move back to the suburbs, I stayed with a friend on the south side so I'd still be near Roland. I tried going out with someone else, but I didn't like it. I came back to see Roland whenever he'd let me. And he took advantage of it. I took his laundry to my dad's house and did it for him, I gave him money; I did anything he asked just for the opportunity of being able to spend more time with him. One afternoon when I came to see him, he held up a check that had come in the mail for me and asked if he and his youngest brother, Glenn, could use it.

"What for?" I asked.

"My niece, Wanda, has been in a car accident. She's in intensive care and may not live."

I agreed on the condition I could go with them.

That evening, Roland, Glenn and I drove up north. Wanda had been a passenger in the car driven by her boyfriend. Both were drinking, and the car had run into a truck at an intersection. We sat with Yvonne in the lobby of intensive care and took turns visiting the broken girl. Her face was a wreck and tubes trailed in and out of her. We were allowed only a few minutes at a time to speak to her.

Two weeks later, Wanda was transferred to a special clinic where she was put on a rotating bed. Wanda would never glide across a room again. Her spinal cord had been severely twisted. She would be a paraplegic for life.

When we returned home, I stayed with Roland. Eventually we moved into a cheaper apartment in the basement of our building. The apartment wasn't much to look at and, with only one exit, was probably illegal. Coming in a door on the side of the building, there were about six steps down into the apartment. The apartment felt perpetually moist and carried a musty smell. This provided for coolness during the hot summer months, but not much other benefit. The indoor/outdoor carpeting in the living room area had to be swept daily to rid it of the white paint chips flaking off the stone walls. Mildew climbed up the shower stall installed in the kitchen area. There wasn't an actual bathroom. A toilet room had also been installed in the kitchen. Washing up had to be done in the kitchen sink, where I also gave Joy her baths.

There was one bedroom, and another area we used for a bedroom but really housed the building's furnace. The one bedroom, for some reason, had been left with a huge, six-foot mirror with an ornately carved hardwood frame leaning against its rocky wall. Probably too heavy for the landlord to move, the mirror was the only redeemable thing in the whole apartment. It gave our bedroom, at least, some ambiance. Our extra 'bedroom', with its cement floor, second hand furniture, flaking stone walls, oil smell, and spider webs, was harder to work with.

Despite its small size and dingy atmosphere, we had visitors. Along with the weekend visits of the children, there was a steady trickle of Roland's siblings, nephews, nieces and cousins. Roland's dad also dropped by whenever in town visiting the oncology doctor at Veteran's Hospital.

"That doctor," he chuckled, "wanted to know what Indian medicine I was using. I told him he wouldn't know it anyhow."

One afternoon, we gave him our bed to nap in. Waking up, he spotted his reflection in the mirror and thought it was another man laying on a bed staring at him. He only realized it was a reflection after he tried speaking to it. This became another story he laughingly repeated over and over.

Other visits weren't quite as enjoyable. A friend of Roland's came to dinner with his ten-year-old son. During the meal he joked meanly about his seven-year-old daughter and his wife.

"That stupid kid ain't even mine. Hey, remember when she was falling asleep at the dinner table, her head hanging forward, and I pushed her face into her bowl? Wasn't that funny?"

The father and son laughed together.

Roland's niece came down with her two-year-old girl and boyfriend. The little girl needed some tests done at the University Hospital. She was suspected of having an irregular heart common in Fetal Alcohol Syndrome babies.

That night, after visiting other relatives, the small family came back to our subterranean apartment. Roland and I had gone to bed much earlier. The niece and her boyfriend, drunk, went straight to the extra bedroom and passed out.

Later, through the wall, I listened as the baby cried and cried.

"Aren't they going to wake up and take care of her?" I asked Roland. Roland climbed out of bed and stumbled into the other room, where I could hear him holler, "Hey...hey! Get up! Get up and take care of that baby! Get up and take care of that baby!"

His niece groaned and rolled over.

"Get up and take care of that kid!"

Roland returned to our room and a few minutes later, the crying subsided.

Later, we heard that a baby boy she had given birth to was taken from her right away. They said the placenta was green from drug and alcohol abuse.

I don't know if that was true, it was just what we'd heard. We never did see the baby.

Shirley's younger brother Alvin was rapping on our bedroom window one morning. It was just around dawn.

"Whaddya want?" Roland hollered groggily.

"I gotta talk to you 'bout somethin'."

Roland got up, pulled on his robe and went to open the door. Still tired, Roland came back into the bedroom and laid back down. Alvin followed. Kneeling near Roland, he pulled something from his pocket.

"I found this checkbook on Franklin Ave.," Alvin started, "What do you think?"

"It's not worth the trouble, Alvin. Forget it. You'll just end up in jail again.""Come on, it couldn't have been reported yet.""Forget it, Alvin,"

Alvin tried for a few more minutes, then left.

"He's doing it for that new girlfriend," Roland criticized, "He's always doing that. Falling in love and then letting some girl get him put back in jail."

Two weeks later, Roland's ex-wife was on the phone and angry. Cheri wasn't home yet that evening and it was late. After confirming

Dying in Indian Country

she wasn't at our house, Shirley wanted Roland to come over and help look for her. We got in the car and drove over. Their yellow HUD house was a couple of miles away in a nicer, quiet neighborhood. We arrived and went directly into the house.

We found Shirley screaming at Cheri in the dining room, giving her what Roland called an "ear beating." But then, swinging her fists wildly, Shirley lunged at Cheri, slugging and smacking her to the floor and knocking over a chair in the process. The next thing I knew, Shirley was on top of the thirteen-year-old girl beating her with her fists. Cheri lay curled in a tight ball trying to protect her face with her hands. I stood in shock, never having seen anything like this before. Roland moved quickly, shouting at Shirley to stop. Shirley turned and began hollering at Roland and smacking him. He held her off and moved toward the phone, but Shirley jumped in the way.

"You ain't calling no cops!" she shrieked.

"Come on Beth," he said, grabbing my arm and pulling me out the door.

When we got to the car, I asked, "Are you just going to leave her?"

Roland answered, "There's nothing I could do in there! I can't touch Shirley! She was just daring me to hit her so she could call the cops and put me in jail. We'll call the cops from a phone booth."

He called the police from a nearby store, then went back to the house. We were coming up the sidewalk when Shirley opened the door and started shouting again.

"So what do you expect me to do? Let her run all over? Next thing you know she'll be pregnant by a black guy!" Shirley hollered.

Roland yelled back, "You could try talking to her instead of beating her!"

"Talk! That's all you ever want to do. You never discipline these kids! You leave it up to me to do all the disciplining! You always have!"

At that moment two policemen arrived and joined us on the sidewalk. "What's going on?"

"She's beating on my girl!" Roland said.

"I wasn't beating her!" Shirley shouted. "I was disciplining her! She's been running around half the night!"

"You were beating her!" I yelled.

The policeman glanced at me, then asked to see Cheri. Cheri came to the door, already in her nightgown, her face red and streaked with tears. The policeman briefly shined his flashlight on Cheri and then shut it off.

"Well," he said, "I can't see any marks or bruises. Why don't you all just cool off and talk about it in the morning."

With that, the police left, Shirley closed the door, and we went home frustrated.

The following Sunday morning, after having the kids since Friday, one of the older girls announced that she had left something at home and needed it. Roland asked me to run the girls back to their house to get it.

"Sure," I said.

I drove up in front of the house and the older girls hopped out. Little Joy, two and a half and dressed in a cute red sweater, waited in the back seat. After what seemed an eternity, I was relieved to see the house door open. But it wasn't the girls coming; it was Shirley marching across the lawn toward me. Behind Shirley, her brother Alvin and sister Laurie stood in the doorway watching. Opening the passenger door, she quickly slid into the seat, turned and slapped me hard in the face.

"Don't you ever stick your nose into my business again!" she threatened.

Holding back tears so she wouldn't see me cry; I stared straight ahead and said nothing. Shirley then turned to Joy, who was standing on the back seat grinning at her mom, and quickly smiled.

"How are you little girl?" Shirley cooed, tickling Joy's face while Joy laughed in delight. Then Shirley slid out of the car and walked briskly back into the house.

A few minutes later, Misty ran out and grabbed Joy from the back seat.

"We can't go back with youse," she said quickly. Carrying Joy, she hurried back to the house.

As soon as I pulled away from their house, I let loose and cried all the way home. My heart and stomach were sick. What happened? Fighting was something junior high kids did, not adults! We're both grown women! How could she be so childish? But whatever happened, I hoped Roland would take care of it. He'll go over to Shirley and tell her off, I thought, He won't let her get away with this.

Still in tears, I went into the basement apartment. Roland asked where the girls were.

"Shirley slapped me and took the girls."

"Well, what are you crying for? Did you smack her back?" "No." "Why not? You don't just let someone smack you!" Roland said, disgusted, "Was her sister there?"

"Yes. She was watching from the steps with Alvin."

"Well, they probably put her up to it," he said coldly, then angrily added, "next time anyone slaps you, you smack 'em right back!"

With that, he gathered the girls' clothes and took Junior back home. Roland didn't tell Shirley off and was angry with me for a few days after the incident. I knew he was embarrassed by my weakness. Because he was so disgusted with me, I was disgusted with myself.

"Shirley ain't nothing," Roland's niece, Pam, advised later. "She told me she was going to come over and kick my a-- once, but I told her just come on. She never did. You stick up to her and she won't do nothin."

Separately, Cheri was also egging me on. "Joy was sleeping on the couch and a feather from the pillow tickled her face and she started crying. Mom got a board and spanked her just for crying cause of that feather! Just kick my mom's a--! SOMEONE'S gotta do it!"

Well, I wasn't going to haul off and pick a fight with Shirley the way Cheri wanted, but silently, I decided I would never let Shirley hit me again. I would be ready the next time. And I would respond quickly. I girded my heart and my mind for a future confrontation. For months whenever we drove up in front of her house to get the kids I was afraid, but I kept the fear quiet. I never let Roland know how scared I was. Over and over in my mind, I rehearsed what would happen if she were to come out and try to assault me again.

In fact, for years after my fear left, the preparedness would be on my mind every time we were near Shirley or her house.

Beth Ward

TODAY I DISAPPEARED MYSELF.

I took myself inside of me
and there's nothing left of me.

Today I disappeared myself.

© **By PHONACELLE SHAPEL**

Chapter five:
The Noble Red Man

After about two years, Roland began using marijuana again. I joined him. He always knew where to go to get it. Sometimes he got it from Shirley. Most of the time he went to the tribal housing project. I usually waited in the car, watching him as he disappeared between the white buildings for fifteen minutes or so while he went into one apartment or another. I never followed him into the projects, but occasionally I went with him into the house of one of his other dealers and stood just inside the door while Roland, laughing and talking, did business with his friends.

One place, the home of a young man and wife, was always dark inside. Children were sitting on the couch, amid blankets and clothing, sucking their thumbs and watching TV. The guy would be bagging the weed on a kitchen table cluttered with beer cans and ashtrays. When he was finished, he'd weigh the bag on the small scale. We wouldn't stay long and I never remembered their names.

The weed wasn't important to me at first. I joined Roland just for something to do. I was working jobs that lasted a month or two at a time. (Well, I either walked away from the jobs or was fired.) Sometimes Roland worked too, along with visiting the blood bank twice a week. He was also still trying to go to school. But primarily he and his family taught me how to use the welfare system. We made use of food stamps, General Assistance, fuel assistance, and picked up free cheese and butter once a month when the government offered it. In addition we picked up free food and clothing at various churches. With each program, we told the staff whatever we had to in order to get what we wanted.

"If you want to get anything, you have to lie about it," Roland's family told me.

I was willing to use other people's resources rather than my own whenever possible, but when I did have a job, it bothered me that only my money was used to buy groceries. It irritated me that Roland saved his plasma money for marijuana. But as time went on, I changed my mind and wanted him to use his blood money for that purpose, as well. I began to like getting high with him. I also knew I was getting extremely lazy. The marijuana made Roland lazy, too. He dropped out of school. I didn't like that we were getting that way. It felt ugly, and only fed the loathing I already had for myself. Off and on, I quit smoking with him.

Our relationship was also getting stormier and stormier. Roland was quick to temper and I felt as though I was walking on eggs all the time. He wasn't physical with me, but he could get very hostile, giving me the silent treatment for up to a week if I made him angry. I never felt that I had any freedom to say "no" to him or his family.

Many of our arguments had to do with his two older girls. I was missing things and suspected the girls had taken them. At one point, I found my mother's engagement ring, which had been stored safely in my jewelry box, hidden in the dirt of a houseplant. But Roland wouldn't admit there was a problem, preferring to blame me for the missing items.

The weekends with the kids began to take a toll. For the most part they just refused to listen to me. After I scolded little Joy for jumping on the bed, she ran to her dad screaming and crying,

"Beth beat me up!"

Later, in the car, this same innocent child with big brown eyes leaned over to me and whispered, "my Ma's going to kick your ass...."

When Misty was given a prescription lotion to apply before bed, I told her to bathe first, then use it.

She immediately went to her dad, "Do I have to take a bath? Beth said I had to!"

"Nah, you don't have to take no bath!"

And despite asking the girls to clean their area before leaving on Sunday evening, I inevitably spent that evening picking up toys from all around the apartment, sweeping up the kind of dirt four children always leave behind, and straightening the spare room.

We fought and Roland kicked me out.

I spent the night at my cousin Marion's and thought about suicide. Not knowing where to go after I left Marion's the next day, I went to Hennepin County Medical Center's Crisis Unit. I wasn't serious about killing myself; I just didn't know what else to do. I could have gone back to stay with my dad or with my brother Erik in his south side apartment, but I didn't want my family to know we were fighting again. I didn't want to hear what they would have to say.

The crisis center sent me to stay for a couple of days at an adult "crisis home," which ironically turned out to be the home of one of my former detox counselors. It was a quiet, nicely kept home. I was to sleep upstairs in the remodeled attic, sharing a room with a kind, older woman who had left an abusive husband. I was allowed to stay there two days with a requirement that I leave during the day hours to set up an alternate plan. However, the worst blizzard in years hit and everyone was socked into their homes. Mail delivery was stopped, offices shut down, and even the city buses were forced to quit running. With no bus service available, I wasn't required to leave. To my delight, this also meant not being required to make decisions about my life. I spent the time reading.

After a couple days things opened up again. I took the bus tokens given me and went back into town.

The arrangement the crisis workers had made was that I was to move into a brownstone on Park Avenue. The county was going to pay my rent. They gave me a voucher to give to the manager and I rode the bus over to see it. As I approached the building, people, black, Indian and white, were hanging out on the steps smoking cigarettes. They stared at me as I entered the building. Inside, the common rooms were shabby and in need of paint. Men with nicotine stained fingers and disheveled clothing looked up from the TV.

I found the office and handed them the voucher.

"I'll show you around," the manager said.

In the cafeteria, people turned to stare at me. I was introduced to the cook.

"Let me know if anyone causes you any trouble," he said.

The manager then led me up some stairs and through some halls to my room. The room, with a cot and dresser, was small. He issued me a pink blanket and then showed me where the bathroom was. We passed a black guy in the hall who slowed and looked me up and down as we went by.

"This is the bathroom. We don't have a shower, just this tub. The door locks with this swinging latch."

The bathroom was dingy, the door loose even when latched. I didn't say anything to the manager. He could have his voucher, but I wasn't going to spend one night there. After the manager left, I took the pink blanket and went to Erik's to ask if I could stay with him.

One afternoon a few days later, staring at the snow packed ground as I walked, I saw Roland's coat out of the corner of my eye. Looking up quickly, I was sure it was Roland standing against the wall. But on closer look, no, it was a man who looked just like him. Funny they'd chosen coats so similar. Farther down Franklin, I ran into Roland's sister and brother, Lila and Glenn. I stopped and spent the afternoon with them while they and their friends drank. Lila liked my scarf, so we traded.

That evening, I went to see if Roland was home. He was, and he was mad I'd traded scarves with Lila.

"Get rid of that thing. Don't you know you can get lice from that?"

But I think he was more mad that I'd spent time with Glenn. Roland let me come home again.

A few days later we walked home from the store balancing ourselves on the high snow packed mounds that still covered what had been sidewalks. An elderly white woman bundled in a long black coat tottered toward us, trying to maintain her own balance.

"Git out of my way," Roland growled.

"Would you have said that if she had been an Indian elder?" I asked him, shocked at his treatment of the woman. Roland looked at me, surprised by my reaction, but didn't respond.

Wanda, now a paraplegic from her car accident, had been transferred to a Rehab program that would help her learn how to live with her wheelchair. Roland and I spent two or three nights a week for a few months visiting her and playing scrabble. Many times Glenn would join us.

As Wanda's strength improved, she was allowed out on passes. The first time we took her out Roland rolled her to the car and swung the front door open.

"No," Wanda said, "I'm not ready for the front seat."

It was more difficult to handle a transfer into the back seat, but we managed.

We ran into Wanda's stepdad. He was a medicine man, and although I stood right next to Roland, he was one that would never look at or speak to me.

"When Wanda gets a little better, I'll have her lay on a blanket and I'll pray over her," he told Roland.

After he was gone, I asked Roland, "Do you really think he can fix her back?"

"Sure he can, if he sobers up."

Eventually the Rehab staff allowed Wanda to spend a weekend with us. It was my job to give her medication, including a shot of blood thinner. I'd never given a shot before but over the phone, a nurse talked me through it. After preparing the syringe, I grasped some flesh on Wanda's abdomen and stuck the needle in. There, that wasn't so hard after all.

A nurse pulled Roland and me aside on our arrival to the Rehab one afternoon and asked to speak to us.

"Wanda says she'll be moving in with you after discharge."

Roland and I looked at each other in surprise.

"She's never discussed that with us," Roland said, "We live in a basement apartment. We'd have to carry her up and down a set of narrow steps each time."

"Well," the nurse said as she shuffled papers, "I've been pushing her to find a place. Maybe she was just trying to get me off her back."

A month later Wanda was discharged to her mother Yvonne's house.

When I turned twenty-one, I received an inheritance of about $2,000. We decided to blow it on travel. I paid some bills, two months rent, and gave Roland the rest to hang on to. It made me feel "taken care of" to have Roland in charge of handling the money. In the back of my mind, I felt that if he knows I trust and will give to him, he will love and not leave me.

We first stopped at Shirley' house so Roland could say good-bye to the kids. As he was getting back into the car, he told me Shirley had asked him for some of the money.

"I told her it wasn't mine to give," he said.

I wished I knew if he was telling me the truth.

Traveling west, we stopped at Glacier Park in Montana, visited my brother Craig in Oregon and my Aunt Charlotte in California. Roland decided we should try to make it to Arkansas and visit his cousin, Elmer Dovetail. We had a pretty good time but were running out of money when we got to Arizona. By the time we reached Amarillo, Texas, we were flat broke and spent the night in a Salvation Army parking lot.

The next morning after washing up in the "Sally," Roland announced, "We'll hawk my boom box and try to make it to my cousin's."

But the boom box brought only $30. From the mall of another town down the road, Roland called Elmer and asked him to wire money. I had no idea who these people were and didn't believe they'd help us, but in no time at all, Elmer wired Roland enough money to help us make it all the way to Arkansas.

Stopping for gas at a full-service station in the small town of Alma, Arkansas, Roland asked me if I would run into the nearby restaurant and get some donuts for the road. I crossed the parking lot and entered the restaurant. The dining area was quiet and uninteresting. A couple of people sat at a table talking, but other than that, it was empty. I went to the glass counter to look for donuts. To my disappointment, there were no pastries. All that was in the glass case was a dismal display of audio cassettes and some 8-tracks. They all had the same picture on them - an uninteresting man and a woman standing close together. The woman was dressed in a long, blue gown. A Gospel singing couple, whose names I forgot moments after I read them.

No food in the display. This was a restaurant, right?

A man approached, looking at me expectantly, and said, "Do you know Jesus?"

My whole body tensed. I don't remember what exactly I said; something along the lines of, "Do you have any donuts? I'd like some donuts..."

Two more people joined the man. They, too, had an expectant look on their faces. "Would you like to know Jesus?" they asked. My heart began to race. I didn't want donuts anymore. They were telling me something, but because they were surrounding me, all I was thinking about was how to get out of there.

"Get down on your knees and we'll pray for you right now," they told me.

This was a restaurant, right? I wanted out. Now.

I refused to kneel and they finally gave in and sold me two cinnamon rolls. They didn't have any donuts. Even as I was at the register paying, they were still preaching.

Very scared, I hurried back across the parking lot to our station wagon as fast as I could. Reaching the car, I quickly climbed in. Closing the door, I turned to Roland and said, "You will not believe what just happened..." But he wasn't listening. Some guy had his head in his window, telling Roland about Jesus.

A car honked behind us. Someone wanted gas. Good. Now maybe the man would go and we could leave...

But no. The man pulled his head out just long enough to wave at the other car to wait its turn. He was busy, his wave seemed to say, and he stuck his head back into our window. Roland was polite and the one way conversation seemed endless, but eventually, our car was released. What a relief.

The rest of our trip to Elmer's took only a couple more hours. Along the way, we let off tension by joking about the unbelievable event, and I ranted about Southern preachers with their phony rhetoric and flipped-back, poufy hair.

Hot and tired, we finally arrived at Elmer's. He greeted us at the door...with flipped-back, poufy hair. Oh, yes, and did Roland tell me he was an evangelical preacher? Of course not.

Fortunately, despite the slick hair-do, he wasn't anything like Tony Alamo or his followers in Alma, Arkansas.

Elmer, the son of Walter's brother, was wonderful. He and Sharon had three children, Kirk, 19, Celeste, 18, and Lyndi, 10.

Celeste was already married with a four-year-old girl. This wasn't according to the Dovetail's hopes and plans, but when it happened, they dealt with the situation as best any parent could and the young family was doing well.

Elmer insisted we attend church with them. I managed to suffer through that along with his daily evangelizing, but despite the Jesus stuff, they were warm, loving people. Elmer was a practical joker, always enjoying a good laugh and getting everyone else to laugh with him. Elmer got Roland a job painting with him on a crew, and we spent four weeks there, saving enough money to make it back to Minnesota.

Elmer and Sharon made it up to Cass Lake for ricing that fall. Elmer drove around the tract with his canoe tied right side up on top of his tiny car. He didn't mind the people laughing at him. In fact, he enjoyed the attention.

Standing by the car in Walter's driveway, we introduced Elmer to Roland's children. But the kids were shy and said little. Cheri seemed to eye him with suspicion. Coincidentally, I was eyeing her and Misty with suspicion. After staying a night at Elmer's niece's house, they came back with several pieces of nice jewelry. "Alice's mom gave us this jewelry," they claimed. Roland appeared to believe them.

We stayed at Walter's house for a short time that ricing season then moved to Dorothy's house. One afternoon, Roland, his nephew, Dale, and others were sitting in the kitchen smoking weed. Mickey, about 10-years-old, walked into the room and asked for a drag. Roland handed it to him.

"Roland!" I said, "You shouldn't do that!"

"Oh," growled Roland. "Dorothy doesn't care!"

"It doesn't matter if she cares or not. You should be smart enough not to do it!"

They stopped giving it to Mickey, at least when I was around.

I made the mistake of taking my sister Tonya up to the reservation for ricing that year. She was about twelve-years-old. I thought I was showing her another side of life and that it would be good for her. But I was wrong. I don't know what about it I had expected would be good. People weren't friendly to her and there's nothing glamorous about poverty. After a few days, I walked her and little Joy uptown to catch the bus.

I was supposed to ride with her back to the cities, so I don't know why I brought Joy with me on the walk. Once there, I had to bring her back to the tract. Tonya waited for me at the bus stop. The truth was I didn't want to go and was purposefully dragging my feet.

A half-hour later at Dorothy's house, Tonya burst through the door and went straight to a bedroom. I followed. Tonya sat in tears on the dirty mattress that served as a bed.

"I made the bus wait for you. I told the driver you were coming right back," she sobbed. "It was so embarrassing, making them wait for you and you didn't come."

I sat and said nothing. I knew I should feel something. My sister was crying because I had hurt her terribly. What really disturbed me was that I knew I was guilty, but felt nothing. Instead of feeling compassion for my sister and shame for what I had done, I felt heaviness in my stomach from the realization that something was really wrong with me – I was no longer the human I once was.

The next day, I took the bus back with her, then returned up to Roland on my own. My desire to stay up there wasn't because I was having fun. I stayed because Roland was shunning me and I was afraid of losing him.

Everything was subtle. Roland never said outright that I couldn't say "no" to him or his family. It was just that every time I tried, I paid some consequences. In addition, if I had a problem with someone in his family, he always believed them before he would believe me. So I was getting the silent treatment a lot that summer.

Two weeks earlier, Dorothy had told him I was flirting with her boyfriend. So for two weeks Roland and his sister were hostile to me and I had no idea why. When Roland finally told me, I was stunned. All I had done was talk to the guy. He was telling me about having been an extra in Hollywood Indian movies. It was interesting! But in Roland's world, women can't simply talk to other men.

I heard rumors that Savannah had been beaten and molested by Annie's boyfriend out near Mission. It was a rumor said in passing; it was just part of a conversation. I'm not even sure who said it.

Late one night during that ricing season some relatives drove up to Dorothy's house. Roland and Dorothy went outside to talk to them. I stayed inside knowing it was none of my business. From the window I could hear Savannah screaming and crying, *"I want my mom! I want my mom!"*

Annie was gone again, drinking, and no one wanted the responsibility of keeping the girls. Poor Savannah, she knew that no one really wanted her and Candis, so she screamed for her mom to let her aunts and uncles know that she didn't want them either. I'm not sure who finally took the girls or where they went, but they didn't stay at Dorothy's.

Ricing was almost over.

"My dad said this will be the last time we rice together," Roland told me ruefully. Walter had a feeling and just "knew" this was the last time. His dad wouldn't come out and say something like that unless it was true.

At home, Roland's daughter Cheri had stopped coming on the weekends. She spent time with her friends instead. I was sorry she didn't want to see us but also secretly relieved and even more relieved when Misty also quit coming. The fewer kids to take care of, the easier the weekends were. Besides, we never really went anywhere anymore, except to visit my family, and Roland didn't go with us. It was easier the fewer children I had.

We were hearing from Junior and Joy that Cheri and Misty were running around. The little ones also said that their mother was paying the older girls to steal cigarettes from their corner store.

Sitting on the warm sidewalk with Junior and Joy one morning, I wondered why I was hanging around. Why couldn't I just walk away?

Suddenly, Joy looked up at me, smiled, and asked a question. Junior laughed at her question, and I hugged them both.

Maybe God wants me to stay here for them.

A man came to our door with a bike. Did Roland want to buy it? For some reason, I didn't think of my own small thievery as a real crime, nor was buying food stamps at half price, which I was more than happy to do for people who would rather have drinking money then a good meal. But fencing bikes, in my mind, was a real crime.

"Roland," I begged, "we can't buy stolen bikes."

Roland turned the man down and told him not to bring stolen stuff around anymore.

That spring we broke up again. During that time I heard about a program coordinating volunteer reading assistants with schools that needed them. Great, I thought, it will give me something to do.

They gave me a choice of schools to work at. I chose Cheri's Junior High and Misty and Junior's elementary school. I would remain connected to them somehow. With no training of any kind, only an instruction to help the teachers as directed, I reported to the junior high first and was assigned two students. I heard a lot about this school from Cheri; students carried guns and teachers were scared of them. I had only to be there part of a day to see it was true. The elderly, frail looking math teacher made no attempt to discipline her class. I reported to the office at Misty's school next.

"You'll be with the fourth grade," I was told.

Reporting to the classroom, I was assigned one student. Junior. Imagine, out of all the students in the school, I was placed with Roland's son. Junior greeted me happily. We went to a table in the hallway and he sat on my lap as we went over his worksheets together. When Roland heard of the arrangement later, he didn't seem happy, but he said nothing about it. I returned to living with him not long after.

Later that October, Yvonne was in the hospital in labor with Bradley and needed someone to go to her house to take care of Wanda. I didn't mind helping and the county would pay me, so I offered to go. There would be no phone for me to keep in contact with Roland, but he told me he'd come up and visit in a couple of days.

The first night went all right. The next day, I helped Wanda into my station wagon and we went for a drive. We ran into her cousins down on the Avenue. Climbing into the car, they asked if we'd drop them off at a bar down the road. One thing led to another, and we stopped at a couple of bars. I usually never drank at all, let alone with Roland's relatives. I am still not sure why I did this time.

Maybe because it was Indian summer and the weather was great. Maybe because I felt it was my job to take Wanda where she wanted to go and who was I to tell her what she could or could not do? Or... maybe it was because it was exciting for me to be away from Roland just having fun. So I had a couple of drinks with them.

"I always wanted to be like Roland," Verlin, one of the cousins, proclaimed to me over his beer, "Ever since I was a little kid watching him and Dan Hunter drinking with my ma in our kitchen, I always wanted to be like him."

Outside of the second bar, while transferring Wanda from the car to the wheelchair, I misjudged and dropped the chair backward with Wanda in it, catching it just before it hit the pavement. I decided that I shouldn't drive and asked Verlin to. I didn't drink anymore that evening.

Eventually we found ourselves back at Wanda's. Somewhere along the line, a couple of girls none of us really knew had joined our group. As everyone sat in the living room laughing and drinking, the new girls, one skinny with straggly, sandy-colored hair and the other heavier and more Indian looking, tried to snag on Roland's nephews.

As their partying progressed into the night, I became bored and uncomfortable and went in to the bedroom to read. But that didn't help.

Restless, I returned to the main room and sat down. I don't remember saying anything; I don't think I even had time to. I wasn't seated but a moment when suddenly, the skinny girl with straggly hair jumped up and came at me. In her right fist was a knife. It happened so fast I had no time to think beyond, "Oh my God, what do I do?"

She was just a couple of feet from me, ready to lunge, when Roland, Pam, and Pam's boyfriend came in the kitchen door. Roland took one look at what was happening and he and Pam's boyfriend chased the girl out the living room door.

Everyone else in the room stayed where they were, guffawing to each other about what just happened. Still in shock, I neither heard nor cared what they were saying. After what seemed just a moment, Roland came back in.

"The girl must have been stoned, because both of us together couldn't get her down," said Roland, "we hit her over the head with a 2x4 and she was still standing."

They didn't know where she went. She'd run off somewhere behind the houses.

I left with Roland then. As we stood with Pam and her boyfriend outside by our car, Roland asked me what had happened. I started to tell him, but to my embarrassment, began to cry. My whole body, tense as a rock until that moment, was now crumbling. What might have happened had Roland not come in when he did?

But I knew it wasn't okay to cry, especially with Pam watching, so I stopped.

In November, Cheri, having run away from her mom, showed up on our doorstep. I was glad she came to us, but once that happened, the other kids weren't allowed to see or talk to their dad anymore.

"Blame Cheri," their mom told them. And they did.

I wish I could say Cheri and I got along well together, but we didn't. She wouldn't help with chores, she didn't care about school, and my jewelry and make-up disappeared. During school hours one day, Cheri brought a group of friends down into our apartment.

"What are you doing out of school?" I asked her, "Get on back."

Another time she came home late at night with a couple friends, one of which needed help coming down our stairs. The girls all went straight to the bedroom and stayed there. When Roland told Cheri the next morning that she better not be out drinking like that again, she got mad and denied it.

"Well what did your friend need to be carried for?" Roland demanded.

"She was sick," Cheri lied.

I found out later that Cheri was also lying about me to her mother. But anytime I would try to bring up any of these issues, Roland would become angry and somehow show it was all my fault.

"She didn't steal your things. You gave her those earrings," he asserted, with Cheri standing defiantly beside him.

"No I didn't. I know I'd never give those away. I liked them!"

"Yes, you did. I saw you."

I was sure I hadn't.

At least I'd thought I hadn't.

Maybe I did, and just don't remember.

That spring I knew I was pregnant almost as soon as it happened. Roland was thrilled. Working as a night janitor at a downtown hotel, he began bringing sweet rolls home for me in the mornings. We sat together on the landing in the doorway of our apartment, enjoying the morning sun.

But I knew I now had to quit smoking marijuana and get a skill. There was no way I was going to raise my child on welfare and food stamps. My child was not going to live the depressed life I saw so many Rez kids living. On TV, I saw an ad for a school for Medical Assisting. It was only a nine-month course. I took a bus over, applied and was accepted.

In April we purchased a Buick. He paid for it, but it was in my name because Roland didn't have a driver's license due to his bad record.

The sunny mornings didn't last long. Cheri and I fought again and Roland threatened to kick me out.

Finally fed up with them both, I walked out.

This time I was through, I told myself, and I moved back to Dad's.

During the summer I went on long, daily walks with Tonya, but other than that, I hung around the house missing Roland and not wanting to miss any call. I slept in the basement bedroom and ached for him constantly. When I was given money from my school, I called Roland and gave him half of it. I was lost without him, despite the fact he had begun drinking again.

I was so bent on getting back with Roland that I bought airline tickets to Las Vegas with my credit card and talked Dad into lending us money for the trip, using the Buick as collateral. He reluctantly agreed.

A week before we were to leave, Roland called. "Someone stole the Buick. I got up this morning and it was gone."

I went to his house to call the police. The police located the car later that day in a wrecking yard. They had towed it from where it had gone off the road and through a guardrail. It was totaled.

Roland had some cuts on his arm and his glasses were missing, but told me he had fallen off of the curb while drinking the night before. After over four years of sobriety, he was drinking again.

"You were drunk and crashed it, didn't you?"

Roland denied it. But at the wrecking yard I found his glasses on the dash of the car under the broken windshield. Despite my suspicions, I told Roland that I believed him.

Cheri, angry at her dad for both drinking and seeing me again, moved back with her mother.

Although our collateral was gone, I took my dad's money and time off from school and we went on the trip to Las Vegas anyway. I wasn't really interested in gambling. I had only suggested Las Vegas because I knew it would interest Roland. The manipulation (his or mine?) had worked; we were a couple again. The first half of the week was fun. We played games, walked the brightly-lit streets and saw a show. On an evening about half way through the trip, Roland slid a wrench into his boot and went off by himself to what he said was the Indian side of town. I stayed at the motel and studied my homework. He wasn't gone as long as I thought he'd be.

"Some people thought I was a nark, so I didn't hang around," he said. Instead, he took some money and went downstairs to gamble. When he came back up, he was drunk.

While getting our breakfast at a buffet the next morning, Roland claimed he'd lost our last $100 dollars in a taxicab. I was four months pregnant, and we were broke. Our room was paid for, but the plane ticket couldn't be used until the reserved day. In the meantime, we'd have to find a way to eat. My dad refused to accept anymore collect calls. I didn't understand why.

Late one night, after a couple days of not eating, Roland returned to our room with a plate full of chicken. An employee had set it aside in a back room for his own dinner, and when the man had gone to grab a drink, Roland slipped in and took the plate. Chicken had never tasted so good.

And the plane ride back couldn't come soon enough. But we were now back together again.

A week or so later Roland woke up shaking. The weather was hot, but that wasn't the reason he was sweating. He needed a drink. After calling around, he found people were drinking over at his ex-brother-in-law's. We got in the car to drive the mile or so to his house. As we passed the park, a tire on our car suddenly blew.

"Here," he said, "go over to that store and call AAA. I'll meet you over at Reggie's."

And he left.

So five months pregnant, I waited in the heat for AAA to come fix the tire. But I said nothing when I finally arrived at the brother-in-laws. I just smiled and laughed with the rest of them.

"The reason you can't leave me is because I have medicine in my bag that keeps you with me. Wanda's dad gave it to me a month ago," Roland told me. But he wouldn't tell me just what a medicine bag was or what was in it. All he would tell me was that it was personal, and that he shouldn't have said as much as he did.

"I shouldn't have even told you I was carrying it."

It was hard for me to decide whether or not he was making that up, but I chose to believe him. I wanted to believe there was a real reason, not my fault, for continuing with this relationship.

How comforting it was now to have an excuse. My behavior was now beyond my control.

Beth Ward

with nets they call love
they've captured me

they say I'm free
free to be
their
image of me

but the need they feel
binds
chains of steel

© By **PHONACELLE SHAPEL**

Chapter six:
This isn't fun anymore

Roland went up for the ricing season and I stayed in his apartment. But Walter had been right the year before. Roland and he didn't rice together. Roland drank the whole time.

I briefly followed him up. There, I met Tammy, the fifteen-year-old girlfriend of Dale. Tammy had just given premature birth a month earlier. The tiny baby boy, named Wally (after his great grandpa), used a miniature bottle about the size of a doll bottle.

I didn't stay long. I still had school to attend.

On a beautiful autumn afternoon, I borrowed Dad's car to run some errands. Enjoying the drive, I stopped by Yvonne's for a brief visit. Yvonne, Wanda and Reggie were sitting on the couch wondering how they would get to the free food shelf and a second hand store.

"Just ask Beth," Reggie said gesturing toward me and laughing, "She never says no."

Yvonne turned to me and asked.

I suddenly realized Reggie was right. I had only meant to drop in for a minute. There were other things I wanted to do that afternoon. But as much as I wanted to say no, I didn't have the guts.

"Sure," I answered, "I'll take you."

Later I saw Lila. I had wanted to make my baby some moccasins, so I asked her how to go about it.

"I'll make them for you," she said. "Just give me twenty bucks for the materials."

Great. I gave her a twenty-dollar bill.

The next week, I told Annie about it.

"Oh, she'll never make those. She drank that money up as soon as you gave it to her."

I wanted to trust Roland's family. My own family looked down on me. I had no one to be close to. But I couldn't be close to Roland's family either, so I stayed to myself.

Alone in Roland's apartment, I had only my WIC and little else to live on. WIC, a voucher program for "women, infants, and children," is administered by U.S. Department of Agriculture and provides Federal grants to States for supplemental foods. It can be used from pregnancy up until your child is five years old and provides milk, eggs, juice, cereal and cheese. Established as a pilot program in 1972 and made permanent in 1974, it is open to anyone under a certain income.

I was glad for the food, but WIC vouchers can't be split up. When I walked to the store I had to lug the full voucher amount of milk home again, which was two or three gallons, along with whatever juice, eggs and cheese were on that voucher. At home, I ate grilled cheese sandwiches and tomato soup. At school, I could get a cup of chicken broth from the machine for a quarter. During my first six months of pregnancy, I lost 16 pounds.

At seven months of pregnancy, I began getting food stamps and a small amount of welfare. After paying some bills one afternoon, I put a twenty-dollar bill on my dresser and took another twenty to the store. When I returned, the twenty on my dresser was missing. I looked everywhere, but it was gone.

Later that day, Misty dropped by with a friend. "Hi," she said, "We were here looking for you here earlier but you were gone."

"Did you come down into the apartment?"

"Yeah, but we didn't take anything."

"How did you know something was missing?"

In mid-October I finished my second quarter of school and took a leave of absence to have my baby up north with Roland. Roland came down two days prior to buy a car and help me move our things out of the apartment.

Wanda was finally about to get her insurance settlement, so she rented a small house in a nicer neighborhood. We loaded much of Roland's stuff up in the car to store at her house. She could use it, but we wanted it back when we got an apartment again.

When we arrived in Cass Lake, I gave Annie my WIC vouchers and half of my food stamps to use while feeding us. I saved the other half of my stamps for after the baby was born.

"Let's get pumpkins for the girls and make Jack-o-lanterns," I begged Annie. I loved holidays and wanted to make the most of it.

"Well, I guess," she answered.

It's funny how lack of enthusiasm in other people, drains enthusiasm from oneself. We got the pumpkins, but carving them wasn't as much fun as I'd hoped. The apathy of the other adults turned my heart, and after a half-hearted attempt to enjoy the experience with Annie's girls, I abandoned the pumpkins. I even wondered why I'd gotten them in the first place.

"Come with me so you can sign up for commodities," Annie told me. Commodities, a federal food program, are available only on reservations. The program provides tons of canned meat, fruit, and vegetables, staples such as flour, oil, butter, canned and dry milk, pasta and cheese, and other various foods such as biscuit mix, potato flakes, and raisins. The list of foods is huge. The amount given a family is dependent on their family size. However, a family has to choose between food stamps and commodities. They can't get both.

"I'm getting food stamps in the city," I answered.

"They won't know that," Annie said.

So I climbed in the car and went along. However, the commodity office had recently developed a system to tell if you are getting assistance in another county, so I got caught. They didn't punish me, but it was very embarrassing.

By Halloween, the pumpkins were rotting by the door.

"You got them," Annie admonished, "you throw 'em away."

Roland and I were at Walter's when Dorothy came stumbling in the door.

"Roland! Troy says he's going to beat me up!" she slurred, "You're my favorite brother; Don't let him touch me!"

Troy walked into the house, a look of disgust on his face, "Come on Mom, get on home!" "Roland," Dorothy reached over and clung around Roland's neck, "Don't let him hit me! You're my favorite brother ever since Mike died!"

"I won't let him hit you," Roland said. "Troy, you leave her alone."

"I'm just getting her home!"

"Bring her home then. But boy, if you touch her, you'll feel my boot!"

Annie, Dorothy and I divvied up the cooking of the Thanksgiving dinner. I was the worst cook, so they didn't give me anything hard. I was responsible for corn and Jell-O.

I suppose having Thanksgiving with Indians on the reservation should have been some kind of great, novel experience. It wasn't. I wasn't home and this wasn't Thanksgiving. Sure, I knew ahead of time that there wasn't going to be a white table cloth or fancy silverware. That was expected. And I knew their food was made different and they didn't include all the things that I thought should have been there. That was also expected. But there was something else. The family didn't sit around the table, savoring good company. They didn't come together after dinner and play games. There was nothing about the day to make it special. No, everything was just put on the table and people ate - some at the couch watching TV - and then everyone went home.

The empty day held no meaning. It was a reason to enjoy turkey and pie just because everyone else was, and nothing more. But then, there didn't seem to be much about any day that made them excited.

"I-yie!" Roland yelled as he dropped a tiny spice drawer. As it hit the counter, dozens of cockroaches teamed over each other to get out.

.

A week later, Roland took a group of kids out to the forest to get Christmas trees. While we trudged through the snow, six-year-old Paul peed his pants.

"I-yie! You little girl!" he was mocked by adults and children alike, "I-yie! You peed your pants!"

A shamed look crossed Paul's flushed face.

"Here," Annie offered me one afternoon, "I took this twenty from some money Lila had. This is for your baby's moccasins."

Roland added, "And don't go giving people money like that again."

I was grateful Annie had cared enough to get the money back.

Later, I watched her as she laid a white towel on the table and bent her daughter's head over it. Slowly, gently, Annie ran the small comb through the little girl's black hair.

"What do they look like?" I asked.

""Here, look on the towel and you can see them," she answered. "See that there?"

"Oh." I bent, but not too close, to see the tiny bug. Remembering there were eggs to watch out for too, I asked, "So what do the gnats look like?"

"Gnats?" Annie laughed, "Did you hear that, Roland? Gnats! They're called nits! Here, look on her head, see those tiny white things? It looks like dandruff, but if you can't pull it out easy, it's a nit. Another way to tell is if they pop when you squeeze them between your fingernails."

I drew back, worried about the chances of getting them and glad the baby would be born without hair. I didn't think I'd stay around too long after it was born.

Roland was still drinking. One dark night in mid-December as we came back from Mission, he sped, drunk, at 90 miles an hour. I screamed at him to stop. Doesn't he care about this baby? As he slowed near a corner to make a turn, I made a move to open the door and get out. He hollered at me and sped the car up again. We careened around the corner and kept going. Finally, he slowed as we neared town.

A week later we lay in bed reading until well after midnight. It was cold and crisp outside. Light snow wisped around in the quiet night. I began to feel something, but never having been through this before, wasn't sure what I was feeling.

"I think I'm in labor."

"No you're not."

After a few minutes of silence, "Yes, here it comes back again."

"Just sleep for awhile."

I laid in the bed for a while longer. Finally, I got up and called the Bemidji hospital. Roland's brother, Glen, sat up on the couch in the living room and listened.

I returned to the bedroom.

"I really want to go. They said it was probably time."

Reluctantly, Roland got up to take me to the hospital. Outside, the fragile layer of new fallen snow crunched under our feet as we walked to the car, where I handed him the distributor cap, which I had removed and hidden a few days earlier.

Hard labor didn't begin until the very early afternoon. I was proud of myself for staying pretty stoic throughout most of the next four hours. Roland had said his sisters would have been mad if I yelled or cried. But when I heard Andrew's first cry, I couldn't help myself. I burst into tears at the sound of my own baby needing comfort.

I loved Andrew from the minute he was born. It was the best feeling, the best high I'd ever had. I couldn't believe I was really a mother. One minute, I wasn't; the next minute, I was. That baby crying was mine. I wanted the nurses to give him to me right away so I could stop him from crying. I was the mom. I wanted to cuddle and comfort him myself. Suddenly, I was crying with him.

Roland stayed outside the door during the actual delivery. A half-hour after Andrew was born, Roland kissed me and told me he was going back to his dad's to tell everyone.

"I'll come right back with Annie," he said.

"Okay" I told him, then asked the nurses to bring Andrew back to me as soon as he was clean. I wanted him in my room when Roland came back.

Andrew and I waited half the night for them to come. I finally allowed the nurses to take Andrew back to the nursery, and I fell asleep, broken-hearted.

I didn't see Roland again for two days. I needed him to sign papers so Andrew's last name could be Ward, so I called and left repeated messages with Dorothy, but she lied and said she didn't know where he was. All the while he was right there with her, drinking.

Although I didn't say anything, my doctor knew the situation and pitied me. I didn't want her to pity me. I wanted to tell her that everything was all right and Roland was going to come. I didn't believe that myself, but I wanted her to believe it. I didn't want anyone to know I was always being abandoned; they might guess how unlovable I was.

I kept Andrew with me as much as possible, nursing him and sleeping with him. I couldn't stand to hear him crying in the nursery. Waking up at one point, I was horrified to see that my chin had left a red mark and small indent on the top of his head. Not even a day old and I'd already wrecked him.

Verlin dropped by my room.

"Hi!" I exclaimed, flattered he'd take the time to visit me.

" Hi. Boy, I hurt my hand and had to come into the Emergency Room. You should have seen it; it was bad. I was...."

I lost interest in his chatter when I realized he was there only to have someone hear his story. He never asked about the baby or me and left right after his story was told.

Other than that, no one visited during the two-day stay.

Roland finally came just before discharge. He signed the paternity papers and we had our complimentary celebration meal offered by the hospital. I let Roland take my glass of wine, and he let me have his Boston Cream Pie.

We spent Tuesday night at Walter's. Walter was so tender; he kissed the baby and offered us his bed, "so the baby will be warm." Roland gently declined the offer.

On Wednesday we left for Minneapolis. Dale, his wife, Tammy, and their six-month-old baby, Wally, went along. It was snowing, but I wanted to be home for Christmas.

After dropping Dale and Tammy off with their family, we drove to Dad's. Chris, Steph, Tonya and Bobby met us at the door. They had a big "Welcome Home Andrew" sign in the living room and they all wanted to hold him at once.

On Christmas Eve we were called and told Andrew was jaundiced and needed daily blood tests, so we drove down to the hospital. Afterward, Roland dropped the baby and me at home and went back downtown by himself. He came back late, smelling of beer. I was glad most of my family was already asleep and didn't see or hear him.

Christmas day dawned with a terrible snowstorm. Roland slept while the rest of us opened presents. My family, always practical, had bought Andrew a car seat. Seeing that Roland wasn't going to be out of bed that morning, Chris volunteered to go with me to the hospital for Andrew's blood test.

The weather was terrible, so I first called to make sure they really wanted us down there. They did. So we bundled up the baby and placed him in his new car seat.

The snow had been falling all night and was still coming down. It didn't appear that many plows had been out yet that holiday morning. University Avenue was treacherous and slow, so we cut down 40th to try the new freeway. To get there, we had to cross a railroad bridge. Coming down the west side of the bridge, I knew we'd made a mistake. There was no traction at all and the car started sliding. I pumped the brakes and frantically worked the wheel to keep us from going through the guardrail. Suddenly, our car went into a spin. When it stopped, we were in the other lane, pointing up the bridge and east again.

Calmly looking at my sister, I suggested that since our car was already pointed back toward Dad's, we should just head home. She prudently agreed.

The doctors were overzealous with Andrew, but it was baby Wally that was really sick. He'd caught pneumonia and had to be hospitalized. While at the hospital, Dale called his 6-year-old daughter, whom he hadn't seen in ages. After he promised her that he would come see her, she said "Daddy, this is my best Christmas present ever."

Dale never did go see her.

For the rest of the week Roland continued to go downtown during the day and sleep with us at night. I searched for an apartment on my own. Late one night, Roland called me and asked for help. He'd lost his boots, he told me with slurred words, and wanted me to come get him. So I laid Andrew beside Chris on her bed and went to look for Roland. I searched for a couple of hours in the middle of the night, up and down the street behind the Indian Center where he'd told me he was, but I couldn't find him. I returned home about dawn. A day later he called again. This time sober, he was able to tell me where he was.

On January 1, 1983, I moved into a sunny one-bedroom apartment on the south side of Minneapolis. The landlord, glad to get someone he assumed responsible, waived the first months rent. Although an older building, it was well kept. It had hardwood floors and a small front porch. The back door out of the kitchen opened to an outside wooden landing with stairs down to the back yard. Dale and Tammy moved in with Roland and me, intending to visit for only a couple weeks. I finally took out my saved food stamps and stocked up on necessities.

It was a relief to be out from under my family's eye. Not that they ever said anything, but I knew what they were thinking.

Roland and Dale continued to drink, but it was usually on the weekends and most of the time at Wanda's. Tammy and I and the babies went with them. I didn't like sitting around watching them drink, but went along with it because being apart, not knowing what he was up to, bothered me more. I preferred to drive him to his parties than have him take the car himself or be wandering around for days. But I never drank with them out of fear of what could happen if I didn't have my senses about me. I didn't trust any one of them drunk, not even Roland.

Wanda's house was crowded. Her brothers Roger and Matthew, Matthew's girlfriend, and their children all lived with her. While everyone else drank, I took care of Andrew and listened to the women tell me how to care for a baby.

"Give him sugar water when he hic-ups."

"Give him some oatmeal so he'll sleep through the night."

"Don't hold him so much. You'll spoil him."

"If my grandma had seen you dress him in short sleeves, she would have slapped you." (This was not a threat, just advice.)

"Nicoa Myenga," Wanda said, "means 'Little Wolf'. That will be Andrew's Indian name. It's tradition for family to give the baby their Indian name."

I looked over to Roland and he nodded.

"Okay," I said, thinking it all sounded pretty cool. That night I went home and wrote the name in his baby book.

Wanda had gotten her insurance settlement: tens of thousands of dollars. The family went nuts spending it as quickly as possible on clothing, boom boxes, and a good time. Parties at her house quickly became orgies of drugs and alcohol. Not only shirttail friends and relatives were invited, but strangers, too. On more than one occasion, Wanda got up the next day to find her pockets had been lightened while she was passed out.

One night, she had a man and woman spending the night who she'd met just that day. They were all playing cards at the kitchen table. I sat next to Roland and watched. While they played and drank, someone passed around a small brown jar and everyone but me took from it.

A couple of hands were played and it was Roland's turn. They asked him to throw a card. He didn't respond. They asked him again. He sat, stone faced.

Someone reached over to take a card. Roland growled and clenched his fist to prevent it, crushing all the cards in his palm. Drool coming from his mouth, he spoke to us with growls, his words unintelligible. My God, I thought, What's wrong? What was in that jar?

Everyone started yelling at him, someone pulled at the cards and suddenly Roland stood up, his chair crashing over and fists flying as he began to fight. "Don't hurt him!" I cried, as Matthew and the stranger wrestled him to the floor. Suddenly Roland went limp.

"He's passed out. Carry him upstairs," Wanda ordered. They dragged him upstairs and laid him on a mattress in the middle of a room.

A couple of hours later, as I lay next to Roland while he slept it off, I could hear them talking downstairs. The strange girl asked, "Where's Beth and my boyfriend? Roger, go check and see if they're together."

Roger ran up the stairs, looked in the room, then ran back down, "No, she's with Roland."

When Roland woke in the morning we went home, but the party continued. A couple days later, we were told the strangers had taken a few hundred dollars from Wanda's front bib pocket while she'd slept, then disappeared.

One day on returning from school, I found Dale and Tammy alone in the apartment.

"Roland took off drinking," Dale reported as I was taking off my coat.

"He did not," I answered stubbornly.

"Sure he did. Just ask Tammy."

I looked at Tammy.

"Yeah. He said he was tired of baby-sitting and took off," she answered.

"D--- him!" I hollered and threw down my coat. "All I ask is that he stays sober during the week and watch Andrew for me..."

"A-waa!" laughed Roland as he climbed out from behind a chair, Dale and Tammy laughing with him. "You don't trust me at all, do you?"

I was finally feeling disgust for Roland and his drinking. Figuring I'd rather stay home, safe with my baby, than follow him and his friends, I no longer went with him anywhere.

My dad had given me one of his cars after ours had broken down. Two weeks later, Roland was arrested and jailed for drunken driving. His lawyer told me it was an act of God that Roland was still alive. He had driven straight into oncoming traffic. The only reason he wasn't killed was because the other cars had swerved out of the way. My problem now was that photographer friends Dave and Louise Nelson were expecting him to be at their studio for a photo shoot in three days. He was to portray the image of an Eskimo on the cover of a corporate report. I called to tell them where he was, and they were upset.

"His face was approved by a committee." Louise said, "it will put the whole project back if we have to find someone else."

Louise decided to post Roland's bond. The bond, fortunately, was equal to the amount Roland was to be paid for the shoot. Roland showed up for the shoot as scheduled, and Louise's clients never knew about it.

But I obviously couldn't trust Roland to always be there to baby-sit, so I put Andrew in a day-care home. I was able to get on a government program that paid for it. However once that was done, Roland felt even less responsible and increased his drinking. Dale and Tammy moved over to Wanda's, so I was pretty much on my own. I tried to keep Roland from coming into the house when he was drunk, but it wasn't always possible to stop him and I had no phone. One time he even cut the back door screen in order to reach the latch.

I tried to keep my car from him, but if he had been sober for a few days or a couple weeks, I let my guard down. One night, Roland went out to buy disposable diapers and didn't come back. Much later, Matthew appeared at my kitchen door holding a grocery bag. He gave some excuse for Roland, handed me the diapers, and disappeared. I knew he was lying. This was a nephew I'd trusted. It hurt that he'd play games with me, even if to protect and obey his uncle.

In the late hours of a frigid night a day or two later, Roland returned with a group of strangers, all having difficulty standing on their feet. This was the first and only time I'd ever met his brother David. They told me the cops had taken the car keys but had left the car in a no parking zone. Roland asked me for my key so they could go back and move the car home before it got towed. I knew he wouldn't come back, but I didn't want to go after the car myself and leave Andrew alone with those people. Even worse, if I didn't do something to get rid of them, they might try to hang out at my house.

While I was trying to decide what to do, David sat on the couch and beckoned me over. "You can't kick me out," he said with a slur, "I'm Roland's brother. I can come here anytime I want. I can stay here if I want."

That decided it. I gave Roland the key, anything to get rid of them.

Andrew was crying all night and I was throwing up. As I lay in bed, sick to my stomach, I wondered how long it would take for someone to find Andrew if I died. My brothers and sisters rarely came to visit. Andrew could easily be alone for days before anyone would notice. We had no phone, so there was no way to call anyone. Finally I got up, wrapped Andrew against the icy night, and took the bus to the hospital.

"He has an ear infection," the nurse told me. "But you are throwing up from stress."

I was disappointed. I wanted to be sick. I wanted to be hospitalized and have the nurses take care of me.

The next day I stared out the window at the corner grocery and wondered how I could get Andrew some more milk and juice. I had a WIC voucher, so money wasn't the problem. The problem was that it was freezing out and Andrew was finally asleep after our long night. I didn't want to bundle him up and take him to the store, but I didn't want to leave him alone in the house either. What if something happened to him?

Andrew would be hungry when he woke up, so I finally decided I had no choice. I threw my coat on, locked the door behind me, and ran to the store. Sure that my baby would wake crying in an empty house, I rushed, gathering my needs as quickly as possible, and ran back home. If someone found out I had done this, I'd be in a lot of trouble.

I rushed up the stairs to my kitchen door. Setting my bundle beside my feet, my cold hands worked the lock. The door swung open. I grabbed my bag and hurried in. To my immense relief, everything was quiet. Moving softly into the bedroom, I held my hand in front of my sleeping child's face, comforting myself with the fact that his warm, even breath was still there.

Roland came home and harassed me all evening, then passed out on the bed. About 3 a.m., a nephew began banging and hollering for Roland to open the door.

"Roland, open up! My mom kicked me out!" he screamed, and banged some more.

I knew the guy was probably freezing; the temperature was below zero that night. But there was no way that I was going to open the door. I lay still and hoped he would go away without waking Roland up. It seemed like forever that he stayed there, banging and hollering. Fortunately, Roland was completely passed out, and the nephew finally left.

Roland pulled himself together for a few weeks. Then I came home from school on a Friday at the end of May and Roland asked to use the car to run to the store.

"Go ahead and start dinner," he told me. "I'll be right back."

About 8 p.m., I threw dinner into the garbage can. The next day, after reporting my car stolen, I put Andrew in a stroller and walked the streets for about three hours looking for Roland.

Shirley told me to check over at her cousin Norine's.

"He's probably sleeping with her," she said.

But Norine's boyfriend came out on the porch and told me Roland wasn't there.

On Sunday I remembered old advice. So I called the jail, and sure enough, there he was. Why doesn't it surprise me that the police, who had received my stolen car report, couldn't locate it when it was parked in their lot the whole weekend? Apparently, Roland had crashed the car. This time, he wasn't getting out of jail so easily.

That evening I went with Bobby to the wrecking yard to get the baby seat. The car Dad had given me was totaled. I saw the look of disgust on Bobby's face. This car had been his car before Dad had given it to me. How could I be so stupid, putting up with Roland's stuff for as long as I have.

On Monday I went to the courthouse for Roland's court hearing. I watched with repugnance as he was brought into the courtroom with a line of other men. It turned my stomach to see him smiling and laughing with the other prisoners. He was acting as though it were all a joke. A few times during the hearing he turned to look at me, trying to catch my eye. I turned my head the other way, refusing to even acknowledge him. He was given six months in the workhouse and I was glad.

Beth Ward

CIGARETTE PAPER

she stood on the porch
watching as he was led
away by the cops, his
hands cuffed behind him
they pushed him in the
back seat of the patrol
car, a proprietary hand
on his head

passive, she watched
with a cigarette in her
fingers, nail chewed
fingers bitten til they
bled, faint red spots
on the white of the
cigarette paper

he looked back and
she turned her head
afraid she'd say
what she was screaming
silent in her throat

while deep in her belly
an empty fire of fear
burned with the cold
aching of a phantom
limb

© **By PHONACELLE SHAPEL**

Chapter seven:
Play it again, Sam

With Roland put away for six months, I considered moving out-of-state as soon as I finished school. But when it got right down to it, I was too scared to leave my family. So I stayed. I even installed a phone, which Roland then began calling on. He only had a few minutes to talk as there were many other inmates waiting their turn. But he begged me to stay with him and to please be around during the times that he had phone privileges. I didn't make any promises. He asked me to come visit. I agreed initially, telling myself I was only doing it for Andrew's sake.

The aged brick building, long and maybe three stories high, could have been a factory except for the barred windows. Walking through the big door into the tiled, room size entryway, the long line of women waiting for visitation had already formed. Only so many men at a time could fit into the visitation room, so the visiting women were allowed in on a "first come first serve" basis. The line progressed as each woman approached the barred door and gave the guard her name and the name of the man she was visiting. After registering for the visit, we were instructed to wait until our name was called.

One set of women was called at a time. Upon hearing our names, we lined up and were allowed into a narrow room off the side of the entryway. A row of chairs lined up in front of a row of windows. We sat down and waited for our men to appear.

Roland was glad to see us, but I remained aloof. I was only there for Andrew. I held Andrew on the ledge in front of the window so he could see his dad. After a couple glances Andrew noticed him, but for the most part he was more interested in climbing back into my lap and pulling on the shirtsleeves of the women sitting on either side of me.

Roland wanted us to come back again; but taking the bus to the workhouse was too difficult, what with putting the stroller on and off the bus and making the connections. On top of that, I was still mad at him. But Roland wrote and called daily. Sober in the workhouse, he was making promises.

"I'll never drink again if you marry me."

While Roland was in the workhouse, Wanda moved out of her house. This didn't surprise me; she and her family seemed to move every six months or so for various reasons. She called to tell me to come and get the things Roland had stored there. Not having a car, I called Wanda's mother, Yvonne, to ask if she would help me move Roland's things, including his mother's antique sewing machine.

"Get your white people to help you," Yvonne said, and hung up.

I wasn't going to call my "white people." Roland was in the workhouse for crashing up the car they had given me. There was no way I was going to ask them to come down to the south side to help get his things moved. So Roland lost his possessions.

In early June, when Andrew was about six-months-old, I borrowed a car and took him up to Cass Lake to get enrolled in the tribe. When I arrived at Walter's house, he was in the back yard. Seeing me, he smiled, walked over and gave me a hug. He was still agile and able to get around, but his mind was becoming forgetful. He would forget he had just bought bread or potatoes and would go buy more. Annie laughed about how many lemons were in the fridge.

We sat down with Dorothy on a blanket in the shade and talked. Andrew lay between us, his chubby legs waving in the summer air.

As the afternoon wore on, Andrew's bottle emptied.

"Paul," Dorothy called to her son, "go fill this bottle up."

It bothered me that Paul and the other kids were ordered around so much.

"No," I said, quickly standing up. "I can take care of my kid." I took the bottle in the house and filled it myself.

Later that day while unpacking, I kept Andrew's bottles in my bag and kept all our things in the middle of the bed. I didn't want to bring any roaches home.

After enrolling Andrew, I spent the next day with Walter, driving him 14 miles to Bemidji to buy tires. As we drove into the tire lot, Walter motioned, saying, "Oh, I forgot my money. We have to go back."

I pulled back out of the lot. When we arrived at his home, he got out of the car and began walking up the sidewalk. Halfway to the door, he stopped, turned, and fished in his pocket.

"Oh," he said looking into his wallet, "I had money with me all along."

We drove back to the lot. As it turned out, this was the last time he recognized me and the last time we enjoyed time together.

Andrew was baptized in early June 1983, at the same church Grandma and Grandpa were married in. I called Shirley to see if I could pick up Junior and Joy for Andrew's baptism. She liked having her weekends free to party, so it was fine with her.

Wanting both of Andrew's heritages to be represented in choice of Godparents, I asked Bobby and Roland's niece, Pam, if they would serve. They both agreed and attended the class.

However, on the day of the baptism, Pam didn't show up. I waited with my family for a few minutes, then, fearing she had forgotten, quickly drove to her house a few blocks away. No one answered the door. Frustrated, I rushed back to the church. There were other babies being baptized that day, so I couldn't hold up proceedings looking for her. Entering the sanctuary, I asked Chris to be Godmother.

Gerald Arrow, the Deacon and a tribal member, was officiating. In many Church rites that included tribal members in this community, the priests yielded to Deacon Arrow. In step this day with his reputation for irregular procedures, he asked that entire families come up onto the altar for the service. About four families along with ours mounted the altar for the blessing and stood in a circle around the font. Joy and Junior stood beside me while Bobby and Chris stood forward with Andrew. As Deacon Arrow spoke and prayed, Joy began to fidget. My attention was on Andrew and the proceedings, so I didn't notice when she began swinging her arms around. Suddenly, she jumped to the side and knocked over a large holy candle. The candle tipped forward, knocking the stand on which the oil tray rested, which in turn tipped, dumping the oil vessels into the holy baptism font. I watched it all happening as if in slow motion, but despite the disturbance, Deacon Arrow continued praying. When the prayer was finished, he slowly and carefully put everything back into place, first cautiously up righting the candle, then gingerly removing the oil vessels from the font. After changing the baptismal water, he paused to bless all the materials again.

A calm and quiet man, nothing seemed to frazzle him. After the ceremony, when other parents and babies left, he blessed Andrew with the name "Nicoa Myenga," and then blessed a pair of eagle feathers from Roland.

Later, Pam apologized, saying she'd simply forgot and had spent the day with her sister.

In mid-June I began working at a plasma center only four blocks from my home. "How come you're working here when you could stay home with your baby for the same amount of money?" a co-worker asked one morning while standing with our supervisor, Don.

"I don't want to raise him on welfare."

Don laughed. "See, she's smart! She understands it's better for kids if you work than to sit around on welfare."

But if it weren't for the no-income crowd, Don's for-profit plasma center wouldn't have anyone to draw from. Many regular plasma-givers were college students. But selling plasma twice a week for money was also common with alcoholics and drug addicts. Many of Roland's relatives and friends came in for that reason.

It was my job to 'stick' the IV into clients, monitor the blood bags as they filled, and stop the process once the bags had reached a specific weight. Leaving the IV tubing in place, I delivered the bag to a window where a technician spun it to separate the plasma from the serum. After it was separated, the serum was returned into the client.

While working with most of them was fun, having Shirley's brother show up in my section was unnerving. Sure, he would kid with me, but I knew the family's habit of being nasty to people behind their backs and I was afraid of giving them any reason to mock me later. Fortunately he had big veins and sticking him went smoothly.

There was a car for sale in the classifieds. They only wanted $175 or so. I called the owners, an Indian couple, and they brought the blue station wagon over for me to look at. A plump little girl with long dark hair bounced up and down in the back seat. It didn't take much to sell me the car; the price was right.

Later I drove the car out to visit Roland. After I told him about the car and the names of the people I'd bought it from, he said, "That had to have been Dale's little girl in the back seat."

"It was?" I'd felt so bad for her ever since Christmas when Dale had promised to visit her; I wished I'd known who she was when I was near her.

I took Junior and Joy with Andrew and me when we did things with my siblings. We took them to the fair, the fireworks, and even my aunt's farm. My brothers and sisters cared about Junior and Joy and enjoyed having them along.

Now that I had a vehicle, I also began visiting Roland about twice a week. Most days, in order to give all the women a chance to visit, the jailers limited the visiting time and allowed each woman in only once. However, on the few occasions when there weren't a lot of women waiting, some of the nicer jailers allowed us in twice. Roland really wanted the visits. He said there wasn't much else to look forward to, so I visited as much as allowed. It was hard to hear each other sometimes above the din. It was also oppressively hot. It must have been more so on Roland's side of the window though. Their shirts were wet under the arms and sweat dripped on their faces. When guards announced the time was up, the men left the room reluctantly, but for the women it was a relief to get out of the building and feel a breeze again. If it was such a relief for us after

15 minutes of being inside, what must it be like for the men after a few months?

My supervisor at work might have said going to work is better than welfare, but he wasn't going to bend any to help a person manage it. Andrew was sick and his regular daycare wouldn't take him, so I had to ask Steph to come down and baby-sit while I went to work. During my lunch hour, I came home to check on him.
"I can't do this," Steph complained, " He's been crying and screaming all morning."
I called work to tell them I couldn't come back that afternoon; I had to take Andrew to the doctor. One of the tech's answered. After checking with Don, she came back to the phone.
"Don says don't bother coming back at all then."
"I have to take him to the doctor. My sister says he's too sick for her to watch."
"I don't know what to tell ya. Don says you're fired."
I took Andrew in to the hospital and he was diagnosed with pneumonia.

Losing the job didn't really hurt financially. Welfare was actually better. The pay was the same, but the job didn't cover Andrew medically and welfare did. In addition, because I held the job from only mid-June to mid-July, my social worker decided I hadn't made enough money in either month and issued me full welfare checks for both.

Children were common during visiting hours at the workhouse. Andrew spent so much time at the workhouse that summer, he learned to climb stairs on the workhouse steps. It was sometimes difficult holding wriggling, chubby Andrew while talking to Roland through the glass. I brought his walker or stroller along, but he would get inpatient in them and start to fuss. Once I brought my playpen in the hope Andrew would fall asleep in the shade outside.

Many of the women would sit together talking and laughing on the steps or lawn as we waited for our turn to visit. It didn't surprise me that three of the women I met had husbands that were long-time friends of Roland. One was married to a man, who, at the age of two, lost his mother when his father stabbed her in the middle of a street. The wife of another had two little boys and was pregnant again. Life with the fathers of her children had been anything but easy.

We began sympathizing with and getting to know each other, even spending time together at home. I began giving those two women, and occasionally others, rides to and from the workhouse. We shared quite a bit on our biweekly trips.

During one trip I talked about how Deacon Arrow had blessed eagle feathers for Andrew.

"You can't do that," one told me, "You can't mix religions like that."

"The Deacon thought it was okay."

"Well he was wrong. Indian religion and Catholic can't be mixed."

"I don't see anything wrong with it. God is God."

"Those religions are two different things."

Not wanting to argue, I dropped the subject.

While walking from the car to the building one afternoon, the pregnant girl stooped down, picked up a clod of dirt and quickly popped it in her mouth. Seeing I had noticed, she sheepishly explained she doesn't know why, but she gets hungry for dirt. Later, as a nurse, I learned the craving for dirt and other strange material is called "pica" and occasionally happens in pregnant women with specific mineral deficiencies.

Another woman I met also caught a ride with us a couple times. Although married, it wasn't her husband she was visiting. It was her boyfriend. To the little girls sitting on her lap, she said, "Remember, keep this a secret from Daddy."

She quit going a couple weeks later though, after receiving a letter the boyfriend had mistakenly sent with some other woman's name on it.

I had originally planned to take only Andrew, Junior and Joy to the State Fair. I didn't like being around Misty anymore, and Cheri had left her mom and was living with her aunt. But as I picked Joy and Junior up at their mom's, I saw Misty walking past the bushes of her house, glancing my way, looking forlorn.

"All right, come on."

Misty ran to the car.

"I guess if I'm taking you, I'd better go get Cheri too."

We pulled up to their Aunt Laurie's duplex and went in. Although it was almost noon, Cheri was still asleep in the small, almost closet like room they'd given her. Clothes, empty beverage cans and ashtrays were everywhere. I had to shake her quite a bit before she awoke.

Stopping at the bank, I pulled out all the money I had, $75. After paying the entrance fee and buying the kids lunch, we had very little money left. None of the kids wanted to go see the exhibits. The girls wanted to go to the midway for the rides. Junior cried to go in to the monster trucks show. I argued that we hadn't enough money for both the truck show and the rides. Cheri argued for Junior.

"He don't get a chance to see that kind of thing everyday. Let me take him in."

"What are the rest of us supposed to do while you're in there?"

Cheri was adamant and I finally relented. Misty and Joy sat with Andrew and me in the park and waited.

While we waited, Misty told me she wanted to go to the Catholic school for sixth grade. Her best friend was going there.

"Well, it's a good school. I'll see if we can get you in there."

When Cheri and Junior finally came out, we all went home.

The next day I contacted the school. After listening to the situation, I was told they could enroll Misty and would even be willing to give her a scholarship.

Excited, I called Shirley and told her the good news.

"Mind your own f------- business," she snapped, and hung up.

I was confused. Why wouldn't she want this for Misty? In my naive mind, I had no idea how forward and meddlesome I must have been to this older woman. I had already taken her husband. Why did I think I should have anything to do with her kids?

Cheri called and asked if Laurie and her children could spend the night.

"Laurie's boyfriend's been beating on her," Cheri explained.

"Sure," I answered.

I had always felt uncomfortable around Laurie. She was a nice person, but because she was Shirley's sister, I never knew if I could trust her. But Cheri told me that ever since Laurie took her in, Shirley hadn't been speaking to either of them. Well, I didn't want to have her stay with the boyfriend, and as long as we're on the same side of Shirley, I guessed I could do it.

"He was trying to grab the baby right out of my arms!" Cheri complained when they came in the door.

Laurie had four children, two older ones by a Sioux and now two babies by this new boyfriend. The babies were only about a year apart, the youngest a newborn.

"I wasn't going to have this second baby," Laurie said, "I didn't want to stay with this guy. I don't like what he and his family do with babies. They give them beer in their bottles. And he's always beating on me. I was going to just have an abortion and not tell him, but one night he was after me and I hid under his pick-up. Then Shirley yells out the door at him, 'how can you beat on her when she's carrying your kid?' Well, after she told him, I had to go through with it. He'd never let me get an abortion."

She went on about Shirley. "My old boyfriend always said Shirley was going to drive her kids away. It don't surprise me Cheri don't want to stay with her ma."

After Cheri and the kids fell asleep that night, Laurie and I were still up talking. She told me that she and her younger brother Alvin had lived with Roland and Shirley after their mother had died. She said she couldn't stand living with them because Roland was awful to Shirley at the time. To get away, Laurie enrolled at Flandreau, an Indian school in Eastern Minnesota, but Alvin had called crying and lonely for her, so she returned to Roland's house.

Laurie also told me she and Roland's sister Lila had been in the Army together. "You two were in the service?" I asked, very surprised.

"But Lila couldn't quit drinking and got herself kicked out," she answered.

A week later, Cheri, who had returned home to her mother, ran away again. Shirley called and warned, "Don't let her stay with you."

But when Cheri arrived, I let her in. Her mother called and threatened. This time I wasn't going to let her intimidate me.

"Come on then," I challenged.

She never came.

Cheri stayed, enrolled at South High school and rode with me to visit her dad.

"I want to be an architect," Cheri told me one day while riding in the car. "Just like my dad. I'm not going to grow up and be like everyone else."

"I hope you keep that thought," I told her.

She also had begun going out with some big guy with a funny name. Neither Shirley nor Cheri would see it as my place to say anything about it, so I didn't. The guy was about 19 or 20 years old. The most I could do was tell Cheri about birth control.

Junior came with me to the workhouse once, too. His mother had told me before that she didn't want her kids visiting the workhouse, but I took him anyway... thinking Shirley was just trying to control everyone and Roland had a right to see his kids.

Later Junior told me his mom had found out he had been to the workhouse and had been really angry.

"Are you glad you went anyway?" I asked him.

"No," he answered.

Over the phone I told Laurie about Junior visiting Roland, and she replied, "The one smart thing I ever heard Shirley say was that Junior needed to be with his dad more. So I don't know why she got mad you brought him to see his dad."

In a park behind the Chicago-Franklin liquor store, men and women with glazed eyes shared paper bags under the bushes. Here and there, faceless men reeking of alcohol slept it off under a tree. And here, little Candis, curled up by herself, spent the night. Her dad had met up with some guys and told her he would be right back to get her. Little Candis, seven-years-old, curled up under a bush and spent the night alone.

In September, wanting a real home and a yard for Andrew, I found a three-bedroom house just four blocks away. Although much of the house needed work, it had hardwood floors and a beautiful built-in buffet. The owner wanted to sell. I didn't have money and she was desperate, so we agreed on a rent-to-own arrangement.

Back at my apartment I sat down with Cheri to discuss details, such as the need to find a refrigerator and get the utilities hooked up.

"I don't think this is the time to move," Cheri said.

Her remark irritated me. Who was she to tell me what I can and can't do?

"I do. I'm not raising Andrew in an apartment."

We moved in the end of September, making three or four trips between the two buildings with my station wagon.

Cheri and I were getting along on the surface, but inside I was feeling used. I came home to find her boyfriend at the house a couple times. Not liking him much, I felt intruded upon. Everything they did bugged me, such as wrassling in the living room, tipping over the couch, and making tea in Roland's coffeepot without cleaning it out afterwards.

Two weeks or so after we were settled, I sat across the living room from Cheri, who was lounging on the arm of an overstuffed chair. She had quit South High School and was now trying the Indian School. I asked how things were going there.

"Well, to be honest," she said, "I haven't been going to school."

"Well, to be honest, it's about time you were honest," I said sarcastically.

"That school isn't any good. All of the kids are jumping around and no one listens to the teacher. I can't learn anything there."

"Cheri, that's the same thing you said about South High."

Angry, Cheri moved out to live with her boyfriend and his parents. She stayed there only a short time though. After arguing with his mother, she moved back to Laurie's.

The phone was ringing.

"Laurie's dead!" Cheri cried when I answered, "Her boyfriend was drunk and they rolled over the pick-up!"

I called Shirley's cousin, Nova.

"Laurie's dead," I told her.

"No she's not." Nova responded. "I just saw her up at a funeral two days ago. You're thinking of that funeral."

"No. Cheri just called. Laurie and her boyfriend were drinking after the funeral and his pickup rolled."

Nova choked and hung up. The next day, I picked up Cheri, Misty, and Cheri's new boyfriend, Gene Peters, to go up north for Laurie's funeral. On the way, we had trouble with the tire. Stopping at a convenience store, I asked a couple men for help. While I watched them work, Misty changed Andrew' diaper and went around back of the building to throw it away.

"Hey!" the guy hollered when she came back, "Where did you throw that! You'd better not have tossed it on the ground!"

"I threw it in a garbage can!" she hollered back.

"There's no garbage back there!"

"There f------ is too!" she cursed and got in the car. My face burned. This man had been kind enough to help us, and here Misty goes and mouths off. Not knowing what to say to the man, I got in the car and pulled out.

Arriving at the funeral home, I dropped the girls with their relatives and I went to stay with Dale and Tammy. Laurie's funeral was brief. I didn't go to the dinner; Shirley wouldn't have liked it.

Laurie's older kids went to stay with their father. The babies were given to their dad, the man Laurie had feared.

Beth Ward

DARK WINGS BEATING

the city broods over
the shadows walking
the alleys and it
listens to the dark
wings beating through
airless rooms

while the mist flows
in from the river and
steals my breath in
white wisps

© By PHONACELLE SHAPEL

Chapter eight:
Crying in Indian Country

Roland's release date finally arrived, but he was unexpectedly taken from the workhouse to a county jail on a long-forgotten warrant. After a few hours of panic, I was able to get my dad to post the necessary bail to get Roland out of the second jail.

Andrew seemed to take to Roland quickly and within a few days, was learning to walk by crossing from Roland to me and back again. Roland stayed sober and did what he could to help me with Andrew and the house. He wanted to start doing upholstery in the basement, a skill he'd learned from Lila's ex-husband. I wanted to have a job that would let me stay with Andrew, so I started the process of opening a day care in my home. This process involved paying fees, undergoing inspections, attending seminars, and answering questionnaires. It would take a couple months to accomplish. While answering the questionnaires, I avoided mentioning Roland. His record might have disqualified us from obtaining the day care license.

After a couple weeks, Wanda called to ask if we wanted to buy her waterbed. Because she'd gone through tens of thousands of dollars in only a few months, her attorney had cut her off from the rest. Unable to touch her money for the time being, she was trying to sell some of the things they had purchased.

"No, we don't need a bed," Roland answered her.

That winter we found Candis and Annie on Franklin Avenue. Annie had come down from Cass Lake a couple months earlier. She had an apartment at first, but told us that after paying the landlord with a money order, he returned saying she hadn't paid it and wanted the rent again.

"Did you keep the receipt from the money order?"

"What do you mean?"

"Did you tear the top part off and keep the rest?"

"No, I didn't know I was supposed to."

Now they were on the streets, without a place to stay, and Annie was drinking, so I offered to take Candis home with us. Candis didn't want to come.

"You want to sleep on the street with your mom?" I asked. But I didn't need an answer. Candis was a little girl without a home or any belongings. All she had was her mother. Once her mom left her sight, who knew how long it would be before she saw her again. I felt sorry for this little girl. But Annie told her to go along with us. We kept her for a few days, then Verlin's mother came and took her from us. Roland figured they wanted to add her to their welfare check.

Cheri spent the spring at a detention center after having stolen a car. When we visited, she proudly bragged about her popularity among the other kids at the center.

Shirley called to tell us Misty had been picked up for stealing at Butler Drug store. The police had taken her downtown. Would we go get her?

We arrived at the courthouse. The officer spoke briefly to Roland and then released Misty to his care. Outside on the street, Roland and Misty laughed together. Disgusted that he wasn't mad at her, I walked a few feet ahead of them. Behind me, Roland asked Misty, "Why did you take those cookies?"

"I was hungry!" she said, as if Roland were stupid for asking, and then laughed.

Too mad to keep my mouth closed any longer, I turned and spat out, "Well why didn't you just walk the four blocks to our house and get something to eat then!"

Roland and Misty looked at each other and started laughing. I turned and kept walking.

Roland had been sober in the six months since his release. If you included his time in the workhouse, he'd been sober almost a year. In April, we began making plans for a June wedding. Roland bought me a wedding dress, and we had a portrait taken of Roland, Andrew and me together. After the pictures were taken, we stopped at Dairy Queen to get some cones and then went to a park next to the river. Roland took Andrew, on a short walk while I waited upstream. The weather was warm, the trickling water peaceful and the trees just beginning to bud. Roland showed Andrew the ducks, then turned and came back. We each took one of Andrew's chubby hands and swung him as we walked back to the car.

It felt like we were a family.

Andrew was happy and outgoing. One of his favorite games was running and hiding behind the living room chair as soon as he heard his dad's car pull up outside. Roland then came in and made a big deal about trying to find him. Andrew would squeal and laugh when his dad finally crept over and grabbed him.

When Andrew played outside, I had to keep an eye on him. Turn your back for just a minute and he'd be up on the neighbor's porch ringing their doorbell. On a Friday in early May, Roland and I worked all day penning Andrew in with a fence around the yard. Andrew and I then went to spend that night at my dad's. Cheri called me there the next day, upset. While we were gone, Roland had gone out drinking. Cheri's broken voice betrayed the strong mask she usually wore; she wanted me to do something to stop him.

"We were all over to Verlin's house," she told me, "Everyone was drinking, then my dad asked me to tie the tourniquet for him while he shot up. It was my 16th birthday and he was asking me to help him shoot up!"

"What happened? Why is he doing this when everything was going so good?"

"He said he felt under pressure." she answered without explanation, "He also plans on going to Texas on Monday."

I felt the color leave my face. Why would he want to go off and leave us? Not knowing what else to do, I called Elmer Dovetail.

"Don't be scared," he said, "God will watch over your family. Believe it, and thank God for already having helped you."

I tried to do that. I told myself that I wasn't scared about what Andrew would do without Roland; I wasn't scared that he wouldn't come home. I told myself that I wasn't scared that he would lie to me some more, that he didn't love me, or that I was going to lose my best friend, my son's father.

"God, please help us and Roland. Please save our family."

It turned out one of Roland's friends had a large amount of money in the bank and the possibility for fun and travel was too much to pass up. Two days later Roland gathered some things and left for Texas. With no one to talk to, I wrote a letter to Andrew:

"If he was having problems, I would have listened. He didn't give me a chance. He didn't give me any warning. Now it's too late, because once he starts drinking its almost impossible to get him to quit. I wish I could stop him somehow. I wish I could make him come back. I wish he wasn't an alcoholic. I do love him.

I pray, but he still drinks. So maybe prayers don't work. Maybe if I had more faith the prayers would work.

I haven't eaten since Sunday. I can't eat when I'm scared."

A couple days later Andrew heard a car across the street. He squealed with glee, and ran behind the living room chair, waiting. After several minutes, he peeked out from behind the chair and called, "Daddy! Come get me!"

"Daddy isn't here Andrew."

Andrew was silent a moment, and then stepped out, his lip quivering and eyes beginning to water, "Where's Daddy?"

They had gone to Texas, traveling through Arkansas. Roland called Elmer from Fayetteville, and Elmer was to come to meet them. But Roland's friend grew impatient, and they moved on before Elmer arrived.

The elementary school called me to come and get eight-year-old Candis. Her mother had left my number as a message phone and Candis's hair was infested with lice. I arrived at the nurse's office and found Candis with a scarf around her head.

Annie had her own place now. As we drove to her mother's apartment, I told Candis about the daycare that I was trying to start.

"Oh! I'll help you! I'll put a table by the door and take the money for you!"

I hadn't been to their apartment before. It was above a downtown bar. Candis led me through an old door and up a filthy flight of stairs. The stairwell stunk of stale beer and urine. In the hallway, wine bottles and dirty diapers littered the floor. At the end of the hall, the window was broken. I stopped to glance out and could see little children in dirty pajamas playing in the alley. One wore a winter stocking cap pulled almost over his eyes as he swung a stick around and threw it in the air.

Annie's apartment was bare. As I'd seen many times before, a mattress served as the bed and there was little other furniture. Annie smiled a greeting and we talked a few minutes. She was embarrassed about the lice. I felt for her. I loved Annie and in all the time I'd known her, had never sensed hardness in her heart nor felt maliciousness. Despite all the troubles and as mad as I got at others, she seemed to be honestly unable to turn things around. Despite all I'd seen in her life, I never condemned Annie.

And although I had seen hardness in Roland, for some reason I never believed that was really him either.

Roger asked if he could stay with me. A very handsome boy at eighteen-years-old, he was one of the few young people in Roland's family to have graduated from high school. In addition, he'd had a chance to go to visit Russia with the school and he took it. That was impressive. If anyone was going to make it, I was sure he would. I wanted to help him.

So I helped him fill out the admission form for the Community College and get a learners permit for a driver's license. In addition, I took him to the UPS warehouse to apply for a job.

Once he got the job, I drove to the warehouse daily to drop him off and pick him up. After two weeks of work, he got his first paycheck. Then he quit.

"Aren't you going to work today?" I asked him after he'd missed a couple days.

"Nah, I don't feel like it. I don't like the job."

Frustrated, I sat down beside him. I could lead him to water, but couldn't make him drink.

"Roger. I'm not your mom. I can't have you lying around here. If you want to lie around, maybe you should go back and live with Yvonne."

Roger left. He never did go to college. I don't know if he got his driver's license.

After a brief visit in Texas, Roland and his friend headed north again. Roland called once or twice from North Dakota. He told me where he was and how much he missed me. In the background I could hear music and commotion. "You're at a bar," I told him.

"No, I'm not in the bar. I'm standing outside of it. I don't feel like going in. I miss you."

They were running out of money and were staying in various missions.

In the middle of June, about 2 a.m., Roland came back. "I really do want you and Andrew. I love you and miss you," he said.

When Andrew got up that morning, he didn't seem to remember Roland. He looked at Roland, turned, ran to me and cried.

For two days I lived in a state of uneasiness and indecision; hearing Roland's words of love, but resenting his brazenness, glad to have someone near, but not wanting him to touch me; relieved to have him back, but scared to trust him. I asked Roland if he was sure he really wanted us. He said yes. I wanted to believe him. I decided to.

So I began to make plans again and he started to help around the house. We told each other that we were married in our hearts and were meant to be together.

"So Cheri, you're going out with your cousin's brother! Iye-Yie! For that matter, he was almost YOUR brother!" Roland ribbed her, "I used to live with Darlene, Gene's mom. His older brother was six-month's-old at the time. That's Dan Hunter's baby.

"You were living with your best friend's girlfriend?" I asked.

"Oh, Dan didn't care. He was in jail at the time."

Junior and Joy began coming over again. For Roland's birthday, we took them to a drive-in movie. I began to relax and trust Roland again, but Andrew continued to be scared of him and would come only to me. In the mornings, Andrew called me, not his dad, to get him out of the crib. When Roland tried to hold Andrew in my family's swimming pool, Andrew wouldn't let him. Roland, never good with rejection, turned it quietly back at Andrew. In my mind, the first bricks of a wall between the two were being laid.

To celebrate my birthday a few days later, we arranged to meet Chris and go to the Showboat Theater. Junior was to baby-sit. But around lunchtime, I told Roland that I wasn't sure we could afford to feed Junior and Joy if they came over next week.

"I'm leaving," Roland answered.

My blood drained. "You don't have to react that way," I pleaded. "Okay, I'll make things stretch."

"My mind is made up. I wanted to get drunk last Sunday night anyway."

I called Chris and canceled the show.

Beth Ward

I went to visit Roland in Cass Lake in late July. I couldn't stay long; my daycare finally had a child so I had to be back home on Monday. Roland was staying at Dale's apartment in town. I didn't tell him I was coming; I just showed up.

When I arrived, a lot of people were drinking on the dirt lot that served as a yard. They told me Roland was inside. The tiny apartment was dark and hot. I don't know how many people were there, too many to count in the dark. Roland was sitting in a chair by the wall, his chin resting on his chest. I walked over and plopped Andrew into his lap. His head snapped up, startled. It took a moment to realize it was Andrew on his lap, and then he looked up, grinning.

"Ohhh! Et's youu!" he slurred.

I stayed a couple of days. I didn't mind the partying. In fact, I felt comfortable. I had a purpose; I was there helping people. I bought fruit for the kids and toilet paper for everyone else. I felt needed. And during the day, Roland and Dale were sober, having a couple beers only to ward off the shakes.

Little Wally was old enough to be learning to pee in a coffee can in Dale's kitchen. Most of the day, he and Andrew sat in the cool black dirt outside the apartment and dug holes with spoons while the adults lounged in the shade of old elm trees. The little boys were filthy, but it didn't matter. They were happy and the adults were content to just sit and watch them.

Grandpa Walter no longer knew me. His dementia had worsened and he had begun forgetting people, starting with his most recent acquaintances. Naturally, I was one of the first he forgot. Because our relationship had died, I felt grief just as you would when someone dies physically. It's hard to know how to act when you walk into a room and the person is still physically there. I had to stop myself from speaking to him as I used to, because he would only look at me and then back to his children, as if asking them who I was. Our relationship was gone and I had to treat it that way.

Because of a car accident some time ago, Dale got an insurance settlement of $5000. I encouraged him to buy a house on the tract, which sold to tribal members for only $1000.

"If you buy a house, you won't have to worry ever about where your family will live."

"Nah," he answered, "I was born poor and I'll always be poor."

Dale took a whole carload of people to the go-carts and then to eat. After that, he and the others drank the rest of the money up.

Dorothy was driving around drunk. Stopping at Dale's, she slid out of the car.

"Would youse watch Paul for me?" she asked Roland and Dale as she leaned unsteadily against the car. Paul was in the back seat, staring out the window.

"I don't have no where to go," she went on, "and he needs a place to sleep."

Roland and Dale both shook their heads 'no'.

'Come on, bro, "she argued, "he can't be sleeping in the car."

"Well, sober up then and take care of him!" Dale admonished.

As she was leaving I pulled on Roland's arm.

"You should have taken him. What if she gets in a wreck?"

"But if we took him, we'd end up baby-sitting for days."

Roland took Andrew hunting for an afternoon with Dale and Wally. They all piled in the car and drove through the forest for a couple hours; Dale and Roland shared a six-pack between them. Tammy and I stayed home. Having no goals in life does have its advantages. There are no schedules to keep or deadlines to meet. Forget pressure; forget trying to pay bills. If someone comes after you for money you owe, just pick up and go somewhere else. In the meantime, don't worry about it. You can sit out on the worn, wooden stoop, feel the sun on your arm and the light breeze in your hair, and do nothing.

Well, I could pretend I had no responsibilities for only a couple days. I liked being at Dale and Tammy's and didn't want to go home, but I owned a daycare, so I finally left, driving home alone with Andrew.

My daycare, which I had worried would never get going, suddenly filled up. I had eight school age children. I couldn't believe I was getting $400 a week to go play in the pool at the park. Every month I filled out a form for the welfare office reporting how many kids were in the daycare and how much I was paid. My financial worker then worked out some kind of formula and either issued a welfare check for the next month or didn't. Usually we still received some kind of check, even if small, and Andrew remained on Medicaid.

Roland called, "Send me $100 for a bus ticket so I can come home." I wired the money right away. He received the money, but didn't come home.

When Roland finally came home a month later, he started outpatient alcohol treatment. Once a week I went along for a meeting with him and his counselor. I talked about how difficult it was to live with his drinking, and Roland complained about my poor cooking and cleaning.

Early one morning, someone pounded on our door. It was one of Roland's friends from jail. A couple of our day care children had already arrived and were playing on the living room floor. Roland told the guy to wait outside. Needing his shoes, Roland ran upstairs to the bedroom, where I was dressing Andrew. He was upstairs just a moment when we heard one of the children crying. Rushing downstairs, we found the man in the house. He was stoned on something and had tripped over a baby.

"Go on! Get out! Don't you ever come around here high again!" Roland hollered.

Later that week, Annie and others showed up on our porch with an empty bottle they wanted to fill using our outside lawn hose. It was a hot day, so I didn't see any problem with that.

"No," Roland told her, "We're running a day care here. You go somewhere else."

"Why couldn't they fill it?" I asked him.

"They were going to spray Lysol into the water and drink it."

A powwow was being held in the basement of Holy Rosary Church and the kids wanted to go. Roland stayed home. I think he had an upholstery job to finish. So I took Junior, Joy, and Andrew by myself. This powwow was different than most. It wasn't a contest and there were no cash prizes. It was a powwow to honor the elders and children and they did something I had never seen before. After the grand entry, gifts were given out to the people, courtesy of tribal government. Our kids stood in front of me watching in excited anticipation as the gift givers came close, then looked on in obvious disappointment as the gift givers passed them by. My guess: they weren't given gifts because the woman standing with them was the wrong color.

I was used to Indians hating white people, so it came as a surprise when I ran into an Indian woman who didn't. One morning I opened my front door to a tall, beautiful Indian woman. She had a five-year-old son who needed day care. I proudly showed her our play equipment and described the federal food program we were on.

"This is great," she responded, "but I'd like to visit one other house to be sure. Do you know of anyone else that has an opening?"

My neighbor had asked a day earlier if we could send a child her way. I decided to give the mother that number. I was sure we'd still get the child. After all, my neighbor was white. Surely this woman will decide we are the preferable daycare.

To my surprise, she chose our neighbor. "Your neighbor had only her own two children over there, so I felt my son would get more one on one attention."

But that wasn't the only thing that struck me about this woman. A career woman, she was educated and self-assured. At a later date, I had an opportunity to ride with her to a Pow-wow. During the drive, she described what she saw wrong in Indian country.

"A whole generation was sent away to boarding schools. While there, they were beaten if they used their native language. But most important, they lost the opportunity to learn parenting skills from their parents. Instead, they learned their parenting skills from institutions. So we are now raising children without the benefit of parenting skills. It is going to take time to heal. But the healing can only come from within the tribal community. No one can do it for us."

Roland began working at an upholstery shop on the northeast side. It didn't pay much, but he was glad for the work. I was surprised how little trouble he had getting up with the alarm.

We signed Joy up for ballet classes in the suburb near my dad's. Every Saturday that fall, I dropped her off at class and went to do laundry at my dad's. We also signed Junior up at a gym and paid for his and Cheri's piano lessons at the Park. In addition, Roland and I attended most of Junior's floor hockey games and were proud when Cheri won an award in tennis.

But Misty wasn't a joiner. She never asked to be part of any program, never indicated any special interests, and we, deep into our own problems, never thought to help her find some.

Misty, like Cheri, started her real trouble after leaving elementary school and beginning junior high. There were several elementary and junior high schools in Minneapolis and kids moving to seventh grade often found themselves surrounded by a whole new group of children. I often wondered if the pressure of a new school and the change in peer group at such an insecure age had anything to do with the troubles inner city kids had. Maybe junior high kids should be kept with the same group of children they'd gone to elementary school with, rather than shuffling the children as you would a deck of cards.

Misty basically refused to go. Because of Misty's truancy, the school district was now picking her up in a van every day from her mother's house and taking her to a special school. But the costly effort had no effect on her uncooperative attitude or interest in learning.

An Asian gang had jumped Savannah and Marci, who was Yvonne's girl. Marci had gotten away, but Savannah was left. She was gang-raped. Only thirteen, Savannah was already drinking heavily, had left school, been beaten several times, been stabbed in the throat, and had clap (gonorrhea). I tried to get Savannah into treatment – the same treatment center I had gone to as a teenager. The hospital was ready to take her, but no one in the family would help me to get her there. At the duplex Annie and Savannah were staying at with other people (Candis was in the custody of her dad at the time), I tried to talk Annie into helping me with Savannah.

"Well Savannah don't want to go, and if Savannah don't want to go, I can't do nothin," Annie said.

Busy at the kitchen table trying to hack a dirty cast off a little boy's arm, she stopped a moment to take a drag on her cigarette. I didn't know who the boy was. The son of the person Annie was staying with I guessed.

"Well, could we just trick her? Just tell her we're visiting someone?"

"Na-e, she won't fall for that," Annie said as she worked.

It was clear I wasn't going to get any help, so I gave up. After all, these adults were heavy drinkers and living homeless, transient lives themselves. Savannah was only a kid and wasn't near as bad off as they were, so in their minds, I was silly to suggest she needed help.

"By the way," I said gesturing toward the boy, "How come you don't just bring him down to the hospital and have them cut that cast off? It would be easier."

"Naa, his mom don't want to bother with that."

More likely she didn't want to sober up or was hiding from social services.

One day, as I came into Wanda's duplex, Julia jumped up from the table in confusion, looked frantically around for a place to hide, and then ran into the basement. She had been sniffing paint and didn't want me to know.

Roland and I began to talk about the troubles all the teenagers were having and wondered if there was something that we could do to make it different. For a little while, we even bandied around the idea of running a home for Indian kids. At the time, the Native American community in Minneapolis was predominately located within a two-mile radius. It was estimated there were approximately 15,500 Indians in the area. According to statistics, Native Americans had a higher infant mortality, lower education attainment, higher unemployment rates, greater incidence of poverty and disproportionately higher chemical dependency rate than other people groups in the state. Statistics said that 40% of this state's Indians had a serious problem with alcohol, as opposed to only 8.5% of the rest of the state population. It was considered the single most serious problem Indians faced because it contributed to the three leading causes of death in adults: cirrhosis of the liver, suicide, and homicide.

And too many youth were following their parents' path.

Beth Ward

THE ABYSS

she had the hands
of a supplicant
begging for her
death

to spiral down
into the abyss
of sparkling
stairs

© By PHONACELLE SHAPEL

Chapter nine:
Dying in Indian Country

Cheri moved in with us in about her seventh month of pregnancy. Both she and Gene were looking forward to the baby. They planned to pull their lives together and maybe even get married. Gene came over in the evenings and together they sanded and varnished a crib. He seemed like a sensitive kid, easily brought to emotion. I appreciated his tender heart.

I drove 16-year-old Cheri most any place she needed to go, from the launder-mat to the WIC office to the AFDC office. There is warped satisfaction in being able to walk a new mother through all the ropes and red tape of welfare, teaching them the ins and outs of public assistance, letting them know when and how to lie.

"In order to get the most food stamps, you'll need to tell them that you aren't sharing meals with us at our house. Tell them we keep our food separate," I told her during one trip to the welfare office.

As I spoke Cheri cried out, "Beth! This street is one way and you're going the wrong way!"

"It's okay. Not only do I have a driver's license, but I also have insurance now and all my parking tickets have been paid up. The most they can do to me is give me another ticket."

Cheri went into labor soon after her seventeenth birthday in May 1985. Gene started complaining of pain about the same time she did. Thinking his sensitivity was giving him labor pains, we teased him.

Beth Ward

At the hospital while waiting with Cheri, his pain intensified. The nurses suggested that maybe something was wrong and I walked him to the ER, where he was diagnosed with pneumonia. They admitted him and at the same time banned him from the birth room. Roland, never having attended a birth and having no intention to start, waited in a smoking room. I ended up being the one to stay and help Cheri through the delivery of the beautiful baby girl soon to be named Carrie.

Cheri and Gene moved into an apartment building and 15-year-old Misty moved in with them, though as far as welfare was concerned, she was still with her mother. We helped the kids as much as we could and visited frequently. I tried to encourage Cheri to feed the baby naturally, but after a few days she decided she didn't like it and switched to formula provided by WIC.

That summer a new financial worker called questioning the welfare payments I'd been receiving over the previous year. While it may have been true that Roland and I had defrauded the system on several occasions in other ways, it was not true in this case.

"But I've been reporting my day care income every month. You guys are the ones that did the paperwork and sent the checks."

"I'm sorry. Your other worker was mistaken. A person working over twenty hours a week is not to be getting any kind of welfare payment. Those are the rules," she said.

"I've got only one child in the day care right now. I work full time but make only $200 a month," I told the worker.

"That makes no difference. You'll have to repay the money you've received for the last year."

I let my one client know that I would no longer be running a daycare.

A rally protesting anti-Indian legislation was scheduled in the rotunda of the State capitol. I made a sign for Andrew to wear on his back – something about politicians taking away tribal land and rights and money or some darn thing. While we stood in the rotunda and listened to the speakers, a reporter took a picture of portly little

Andrew and his placard, which later appeared in the paper. After the speeches were over, the drummers began to sing and the group gathered for a circle dance. I had never participated in dancing before because I didn't want to seem like a "wanna-be." I also didn't want to stand out like a sore thumb in the crowd. But this group was relatively small and there were a few other white people. Andrew and I joined the circle and were quickly swept away.

A couple of weeks later, several of the family drove up to Taylor's Falls for a picnic. So many, with Annie, Wanda, Matthew, and several others, including children, that we took three vehicles. Roland and Annie barbecued while others went on a hike. Someone took Wanda in her chair down a path a little ways. Matthew talked about renting a canoe. I had something I wanted to tell Julia, but as usual, didn't get to talk to her much. She was still quiet and never got very near.

As we were finally readying to leave, I thought I'd better do it.

"Julia, do you want to get your drivers license? I'll help you get it if you want."

She smiled shyly. "Sure."

A couple days later, Matthew told us how excited she was, telling other people, "Beth's going to teach me how to drive!"

Arriving at Cheri's apartment one afternoon we found Misty alone with Carrie. Cheri had been away from the house for a few hours and Carrie's disposable diaper was so saturated with urine and feces that it was leaking out.

"How come you didn't change her?" Roland asked.

"There are no diapers!" Misty retorted indignantly.

"Well take the diaper off anyway and put a towel or something under her. You can't leave her with that soaked thing on!"

Another time Roland dropped by to find seven-year-old Joy baby-sitting and Carrie crying with hunger.

"How long have you been here with the baby?" Roland asked.

"Since this morning," Joy, near tears, responded. "Cheri and them went across the parking lot to the other building and told me to watch Carrie. They said they'd be right back. There's no milk for Carrie's bottle and I didn't know what to give her!"

There's not much even a government program like WIC can do if a parent doesn't bother redeeming the vouchers.

"What apartment are they in?" Roland demanded, then stormed across the lot to drag the girls out of their party.

A couple weeks later a detective appeared at our door. He had a notebook in his hand.

"Is this the home of Carrie Ward?" he asked.

"Uh, no," I answered, "This is her grandfather's house. Is she okay?"

"Well, I was told this is was where she lived. We have a report that she was drunk and smashed several windows at an apartment complex."

Roland, standing next to me in the door, answered, "That's not possible. Carrie is a baby. And she doesn't live here, she lives with her mother, Cheri Ward."

"Well, I have here that Cheri Peters is a baby living at the complex with her mother, Misty Peters."

"No! They messed you up on purpose. Cheri is Carrie's mother and Misty must have been the one that broke the windows and their last name is Ward."

The detective eyed us as though we were the ones trying to mess him up.

"They all live at that apartment complex," I informed him.

"All right then," he finally answered. Putting his notebook away, he turned and walked back to his car. Cheri was later evicted from that apartment, but as far as we knew, Misty was never punished for her crime.

We helped Cheri and Gene get another apartment near us and stocked them up on necessities. Misty moved in with them again.

"How come you're giving Carrie real milk instead of formula?" we asked. Carrie was still less than 6-months-old.

"Darlene says she don't need formula. We're feeding her already too. She eats real good," Cheri answered.

Cheri and Gene constantly struggled with money. We helped out when we could, but we didn't have much money either. At one point, we waited impatiently for Darlene to give the couple the $300 Cheri had said Darlene owed them.

Darlene phoned and asked, "Why am I the only one helping them?"

"What do you mean?"

"How come I'm the one that has to give them money!"

"We've given them money. But right now Cheri told us you owed her because you gambled their money away."

"She's a g-- d--- liar." Darlene hung up.

Roland decided to return to school to complete his Human Services degree and I decided to go back and become a RN. Being a Medical Assistant wasn't enough of an income. Cheri decided to join us and become a LPN. We were glad to see her want to go to school and were determined to help her any way we could. Driving to class in the morning, we stopped to pick Cheri up on the way.

Taking a language for one quarter was a requirement. I chose to register for Ojibwe because I wanted to understand Roland's language better and teach it to the kids. Cheri also signed up for the Ojibwe class, along with the remedial math and English she needed before she could begin the LPN course. That winter was my best time with Cheri. Although she still had people over every now and then for parties, it wasn't as often and she really seemed as though she was trying to become a strong woman and a good mother to Carrie. In addition, not living in the same house, we had no reason to pick on each other. Instead, as classmates, we shared homework and cafeteria lunches while joking about our teachers and sharing our ambitions. Finally we were peers as opposed to competitors.

"I really like that song about "Daddy's Hands," she told me during one lunch. "It reminds me of my dad. That other song about the little girl that gets beaten reminds me of the way my Mom treated me."

Roland bought himself a blue van with part of his student loan. As usual, due to Roland's traffic record and lack of a license we had to put the van in my name.

I saw an ad for night shift worker at the Sunshine Crisis Nursery and applied. This way, I could make money while Roland collected the welfare benefits for Andrew.

The Crisis Nursery, housed in what used to be a convent, was a facility that allowed over-stressed parents the opportunity to leave their children for two days - for free - in order to do what ever it was they needed to do to pull themselves together. The purpose of the nursery was to prevent abuse before it happened.

With tired and over-stressed mothers coming in constantly, some even as regulars, it was easy to see the need for this facility. Sure, it was true some women just came in to take advantage of the free service. We watched one woman in particular, after dropping off her children, climb into the back of a pick-up truck that carried several other people and a beer keg. However, this woman, whom I was told wasn't allowed to use the service again, was not the norm. One single mother had cancer and brought her son during the times she was in the hospital for treatments. Another single mother had newborn twins, along with several older children. Many others simply needed respite: time out.

My first night there my supervisor trained me. After showing me some paper work and kitchen duties, she told me to pick a bed and go lie down.

"The kid's are all asleep," she said with a blanket wrapped around herself. "If someone wakes up, we'll hear it. Besides, their parents sleep every night, don't they?"

This was going to be a great nighttime job for a daytime nursing student.

I loved the job. And while it was true that both I and the children slept through most of my shift, I loved working with the kids. After a point though, my co-workers and I decided against everyone sleeping at the same time. The two night shift workers now, after sharing the clean up duties, took turns sleeping, thus ensuring one adult awake at all times. We thought this was a good compromise, and still having the second worker available to wake if needed, we ran into no problems. The fact that we were deceiving our employer was irrelevant.

I liked most of the staff, but one man was particularly interesting. A tribal member from Cass Lake, he wasn't a drinker. When I asked him how he managed to stay straight up north, he told me that it's never been a problem. When he visits his family up there, he never encounters anyone drinking. That was hard to believe, but he didn't seem like one to make things up.

However, I'm sure life directly outside the nursery couldn't have been lost on him. The nursery was located right across from the tribal housing projects. The series of stucco apartments were run down and dirty. Garbage littered the parking lots and playground areas were hazards with broken glass and damaged play equipment. Drunks occasionally used the walls of buildings as a urinal. Children ran around unsupervised well into the night.

Through our second-story windows, open to catch the summer night air, I would hear loud voices at five in the morning. Looking out onto the orange lit streets, I'd see children as young as eight still running around. If they got close to our staff's cars, which had been broken into many times, or jiggled at the door of the nursery, I called the police. But I may as well not have. The kids were smart. As soon as the cop car rounded the corner, they ran in all directions. By the time the car arrived in front of our building, the streets were empty. Even more disappointing, if the cop was lucky enough to catch a kid, I would witness the same kid being dropped off in front of the projects an hour or two later.

One night a party was going on in a house kitty corner to the nursery. The loud music drew me to the window. Suddenly, a boy in a white shirt sprinted from the building chased by several other boys. They pursued him across the street to the grassy lawn of the projects, where they tackled him and started beating and kicking. I ran to the phone to call the police. When I returned, they were still at it.

I knew saying nothing would give the cops a better chance of catching them, but I couldn't just sit there while he was being beaten. So I hollered, "I called the cops!" to try to chase them away, then pulled back from the window so they wouldn't see where the voice came from. The boys quit and ran. The boy in the white shirt laid on the lawn a few minutes. I wondered if he were dead. Then he slowly got up, and, holding his arm across his stomach, ran down the street. He looked as though he were crying.

The cops made a slow drive-by, but not seeing anything, went on their way.

An hour later I heard loud voices again. Looking out the same window, I saw a large group of boys converge on the house, bats in hand. The next sound I heard was the sound of breaking glass as the boys surrounded the house, smashing windows. It only took a couple minutes, then they were gone.

What good would it have done to call the cops?

At Christmas time the Nursery was flooded with toys from the National Guard and other various community collection efforts. A department store chain also had an over-abundance of promotional teddy bears. I guess not many people were interested in buying them, so the store donated them 'to the needy.' My supervisor had more toys than she knew what to do with.

'Will you take some of these boxes across the street to the projects and give them away?" she asked me.

So Roland's nephew Matthew and I came to the nursery on Christmas Eve, rounded up the toys, and took them door to door. When we were through, I gave Matthew a few things for his kids and I took a couple things for mine. We saw no problem with this; our homes were no different than any we had just visited.

In fact, every house we'd been to had stacks of toys under the tree. Give-away programs are abundant. Cheri and I, in order to get toys for Andrew and Carrie, had also gone together to the Salvation Army give-away. I was amazed by how much I was allowed to bring home.

Despite our lack of need, my supervisor begged me to take the rest of the promotional teddies home. She had no idea what to do with them all. I took one for Andrew and one for Joy, the rest I brought up to the reservation.

"We don't need those," Dale told me when I got there. "The Tribe already gave us a bunch. See? They're over there in the corner."

"Well, maybe I'll bring them over to Elaine's."

"Don't bother. You won't find anyone around here that doesn't already have a ton."

Having watched the young dancers at the powwows for several years, I was impressed. I imagined Andrew as a fancy dancer. Wanting him to have a chance to learn, I called the Indian Center and was told about a child's drum and dance group meeting every week at the health center. Roland wasn't interested, so I took Andrew by myself.

The room was lined with parents sitting on folding chairs against the wall and their children sitting on their laps or standing near. I found a place to sit and held Andrew in front of me. I was surprised at the discomfort I felt. Having been with Roland for 6 years, I no longer felt conspicuous around Indians. But there was something here that wasn't right. I looked around for a familiar face, but my eyes met only hostile stares. I understood immediately I was not wanted. What I couldn't understand though was with all of the talk about the benefits of tribal culture, why would these people chase away a white person who was trying to make sure their child stayed connected to the tribal culture? We never returned to the class.

Candis was visiting Arnold's sister on the northeast side, and Annie asked if I would drive Savannah and her up there. Driving over a bridge on Cedar Avenue, I slid on black ice and rammed into the rear end of a nice little car. Unfortunately, I wasn't carrying insurance.

The owner and I both got out to look at the damage. His rear fender suffered only a small, inch long crack. I was relieved. No important damage occurred. However, he seemed to think it was important and asked for my name, address and phone number. In a panic, I lied and gave him false information.

At Arnold's sister's later that afternoon, we told them about the incident. After that, I put it out of mind.

A few days later Arnold paid me to taxi Candis and him home to Red Lake, a reservation neighboring Leech Lake. Candis was about ten at the time. Dorothy's son, Troy, was visiting for a few days and rode with us. It was a cold night. The snow fell softly and silently. It was late and we all were tired. We hadn't originally intended to stop anywhere, but we had gotten a late start, and the weather had slowed us down. I couldn't drive anymore, and was glad Arnold had suggested we stop at his other sister's house near Bemidji.

The house we stopped at, with shoulder high snowdrifts in the driveway, was an unexpected, beautiful, ranch style home. The owners were obviously employed. We weren't sure if anyone was at home at first, but their 15-year-old daughter finally answered the door. After she assured Arnold it was no problem for us to stay, she led me past the kitchen and down to the end of the hall where there was a room I could use to sleep with Andrew. It was a teenage girl's room. The twin bed had a fluffy, pink comforter and the furnishings and toiletries on the dresser were that of a bubbly adolescent. I guessed it was her room. I am not sure where she and Candis were to sleep that night. Arnold and Troy slept on the living room couches.

I don't know how long I had been asleep when I heard noises in the hall. I could hear a man laughing and talking in slurred, drunken fashion, and I could hear Candis laughing and answering, "No, no, leave me alone. Don't do that!" I heard a loud thump, and suddenly the door to my room flew open. In the darkness, the man pushed Candis onto my bed, onto my legs, and began fumbling with the zipper of her pants.

In horror, I sat straight up and screamed at the top of my lungs; "Get the H--- out of here!"

The man jerked up, turned to look at me, and then dashed from the room. To my surprise, Candis started after him. Quickly, I jumped out of bed and grabbed her by the arm, "No! Not you!" I slammed the door shut and pulled Candis back to the bed, putting her in between myself and Andrew, (who had never awakened). I wasn't going to let anyone touch her if I could help it. But I could hear the man moving around in the kitchen, getting himself something to eat. The kitchen was in between the living room and us. How will I get to Arnold and Troy for help? Who was that man? What if he comes back with a gun, mad, or scared I'll call the cops?

Candis fell asleep after a short time, but I sat in the room with the lights on for the rest of the night, too afraid to close my eyes. After a time, I could hear the man snoring, but I was still too scared to attempt to get past him. In my mind's eye, I pictured him sitting in a chair, sleeping with his head bent and his chin on his chest. What could I do? I was too afraid to leave the room.

Candis and Andrew slept peacefully beside me.

About 6 am or so, I heard the man, who I later learned was Candis' Uncle, get up and leave the house. I waited a little while longer just in case he came back in, then rushed to the living room and woke up Arnold and Troy.

Arnold listened to my story, but didn't react with the emotion I had imagined he would. He clenched and unclenched his fist and said the right words, but there seemed to be something missing.

However, when he said we would have to go to the police, I felt comforted. We gathered our kids and belongings and left. As we were leaving, the 15-year-old girl kicked the wall and swore.

At the police station, they recorded my story and commented that it is rare to have eye witness testimony to a sexual assault. They asked if I would be willing to come back to this county later and testify in court. I told them I would.

From there we drove to Arnold's home on Red Lake reservation. Crossing the boundary we drove down a long, desolate road which ran along the east side of the Lake. Every now and then HUD homes appeared beyond the snow-sparkled trees and brush. The area, beautiful and serene in its silent winter blanket, was nothing like I'd imagined. All I'd heard over the last few years was stories of chaos, violence and destruction. While I didn't doubt the stories, the fresh winter scenery certainly didn't reflect them.

Arnold's house, next to the lake, was a small one bedroom. He had custody of 10-year-old Candis and two younger children by another woman. To be polite, Troy and I stayed to visit for just a couple hours. I had felt okay driving him up, but didn't know him well enough to want to stay too long.

"Come up this summer and stay a couple days," Arnold suggested. "Youse can go swimming in the lake."

"Sure." I lied, "that would be fun."

Before we left, Arnold opened his closet door and pulled out two big boxes of government commodities.

"Here, we can't eat all this," he said as he sorted through and separated the cans of food. Troy and I packed as much as we could into the car.

Back in Minneapolis, I found Annie sitting on an unmade bed on the far side of the cluttered, unfinished basement of Wanda's duplex. I told her what had happened. She thanked me for telling her, but said little else.

Later, I wrote Candis and told her that all things considered, she was better off with her dad. I wasn't putting Annie down or anything, but was giving Arnold credit for having sobered up and taken responsibility for his three kids.

That spring, Annie went to visit Candis. While there, Candis showed her mom the letter I'd written. Annie felt hurt, but didn't say much to me about it. Annie warned though, "his family says if youse testify against the uncle they're going to turn you in for that hit and run."

"Well, they can go ahead I guess," I said, sorry we'd ever told them about the accident, "but I can't let that thing with Candis go."

However, the court never contacted me.

One year later, in a separate case, Arnold was charged and convicted of sexually abusing Candis. Candis was sent to live in a foster home.

.

In February 1986, because Misty was angry with her mother and didn't want to live there, and because Cheri wouldn't let Misty live at her place anymore, Misty moved in with us. We made it clear this was only on condition she straighten up and go to school. We did our best to help her. We first tried enrolling her in the Catholic high school her best friend was attending. We took her for an entrance exam, but she didn't pass.

"I'm sorry," the administrator told us, "we'd like to take her but her comprehension scores are way below our requirements. We simply don't have the necessary facilities to help her. I'd advise you to take her for testing."

At the Community College, Misty tested at the third grade reading level.

"Take her home and encourage her to read as much as possible. There are also some reading programs that you could enroll her in. They do cost a little, but if you can afford it, you should do it..."

Running out of options, we enrolled her in an alternative school down on Franklin Avenue. I encouraged her, told her she was beautiful and surprised her with a rose on her 16th birthday. I took her portrait to a modeling agency. Louise Nelson saw the portrait and told me she thought Misty was very photogenic.

But living with Misty wasn't easy. She wouldn't do anything she didn't feel like doing. The only time she would do the dishes without a fight was on my payday.

On Halloween I took Joy and Andrew with me to a party at the Crisis Nursery. I'd sewed Joy a "Strawberry Shortcake" costume. I made Andrew into Mickey Mouse. I found a ruffled slip for Joy and black tights for Andrew at the nursery. I was able to get all kinds of accessories for children at the Crisis Nursery, from clothing to diapers to baby bottle nipples. Some of it was given to me, some of it I stole. Funny how upset I was with Misty's thieving but thought nothing of my own.

Stealing from the Crisis Nursery at night wasn't hard. I worked with only one other person and all I had to do was wait for that person to fall asleep. Then during my normal duty of restocking from the basement, I would take extras out the side door to my car. Some of it I stored for my own use, other stuff I took up north and gave to Dale and Tammy for their three kids.

The small one bedroom tract house they now lived in was part of a quadroplex originally built to house an elderly person. Not being high on the list of tribal government cronies, this apartment had been given to Dale's family of five until another home opened up.

The house was usually littered with clothing and thick with cigarette smoke. They never had much food and the kids slept on the floor wrapped in dirty blankets. I brought them toothpaste and toothbrushes from the nursery every time I came, and then usually went out and bought other little things they needed such as toilet paper. Sometimes I'd help Tammy take the blankets and stuffed toys down to the launder-mat. At night, I curled up with the kids on the floor and slept.

While sitting on the hood of the car outside Dale's house one afternoon, Lila told me she would die soon and had already chosen her casket.

"There is no reason to live," she said while looking at the ground.

"What about your two kids?" I asked.

"No one needs me."

Back home, Roland called the alternative school Misty had been going to for a month or so now. He wanted to see how she was doing.

"She hasn't been here," the director answered.

"What do you mean? We drop her off every day!"

"She hides behind the door until you leave and then takes off."

After a particularly bad day with Misty, I urged Roland to go on a drive with me. As we went around a lake, I told him I could not marry him if I could not start saying no to his family. He wanted to get married, I guess, because he told me I could start standing up for myself.

Cheri's second child, Leon, was born in April when Carrie was 11 months old. I had the privilege of cutting his cord. Then Cheri took the rest of the quarter off from college. We could understand needing to do that with two small children, but we were afraid she'd never go back. Unfortunately, we were right.

In early June, Yvonne's son Bradley was placed with us as a foster child while she went to treatment. The very next day, Cheri and I got in a terrible argument. Two nights later, she called Roland and asked him to baby-sit the kids while she went out. Having been concerned about the number of times a week she'd been leaving the kids with sitters, he said no.
"I don't like watching the kids while you party."
I was glad he refused. I didn't want to see her anyway.
Sometime after midnight our phone rang. It was Cheri calling from the hospital. Leon had stopped breathing and they didn't think he would live. Roland rushed down. He found his grandson in the Emergency Room, tubes stuck all over his tiny body. Roland, at a loss for words, stood by and wept silently. Leon was declared dead a couple hours later, diagnosed with Sudden Infant Death Syndrome (SIDS).
The next day Roland and Cheri sat on her mother's steps while Shirley and Darlene planned the funeral. I felt terrible for Cheri and wanted to talk to her, hug her, somehow help her. But after having fought with her just two days earlier, I knew she wouldn't hear me.
At the funeral, Gene stood at the casket shaking with sobs while his mother held him tight. Cheri and her mother stood silently together.

As I was standing in the back of the room with Roland, he leaned over and remarked how uncomfortable he was. Yes, that would be expected at the funeral of your infant grandchild. But he went on, "I've slept with five of the women in this room."
Five? The casket scene no longer important, I counted Shirley, Darlene, Norine, and me. So who was the fifth? In the kitchen, I asked Norine but she laughed off the question.

After the meal, a pastor who had befriended Gene and Cheri in the months earlier said a few words. Then a group got together at the head table and began singing hymns in Ojibwe. They began with Roland's favorite, "Amazing Grace."

At the same table later, I saw Nova dig in her purse and give Cheri pills 'to ease the pain.'

Roland took Leon's death very hard. He felt guilty about not having taken the little boy that night.

"If I'd have watched him, I would have seen him stop breathing and he wouldn't have died."

Although Roland had started out very devoted to his grandkids, he realized now he could never change his children's behavior, just as they could never change his. As a result, knowing he had no control over his grandchildren's lives, he began to detach from them.

When Yvonne would visit, she complained about dirt on Bradley's neck and other minor things. In her eyes I wasn't doing good enough.

Bradley's sister, Sonya, lived in a nearby foster home and came to visit him every now and then. I was glad she could visit, but it was hard on Bradley. When she readied to leave, he broke down in sobs and clung to her. We'd have to pry him off. Once, laughing, she told another person, "Bradley was so mad about me leaving that he took Andrew beside the house and decked him."

On August 1st we had Bradley transferred to a different foster home.

The summer of 1986, Roland's nephew, Mickey, came down to stay with us for a couple of weeks. I was tired of taking care of all of the teenagers who wanted to live with us, so I wasn't happy about it. I was working full time and going to nursing school, and most of those kids really didn't want to listen to me; they just wanted me to spend money on them.

Roland and I were making plans for a California vacation. What we hadn't told anyone was that we also were thinking about getting married. I was getting vacation pay and some back pay from the Crisis Nursery.

To my outrage, without consulting me at all, Roland asked Mickey to go along with us. Whose money is this anyway? I had already agreed that Junior could go with us. How much money does Roland think I'm going to have? But I said nothing as we readied to leave.

We decided Misty would have to stay elsewhere while we were gone. While Misty and I watched, Roland locked up the house and put his battery charger under the back porch. I prepared a big box of food for Misty's Uncle Alvin, where we were dropping her off to stay while we were gone.

Still smoldering about money, I asked Roland if Dorothy shouldn't help out with Mickey's expenses. He agreed, and we drove to Leech Lake before leaving Minnesota. We found Dorothy at a cabin by the lake. It was just after the first of the month when welfare checks come out, so I was sure she should have some money.

She did, but was busy drinking it up. She gave me $40, and told me to have him eat potato chips.

"He likes chips. He'll be just fine with them," she said.

When we left, I was angry at Roland and Dorothy. But I wasn't going to just feed Mickey chips and nothing else.

Mickey and Junior, both about fourteen, were quiet and obedient most of the time. They spent a lot of time helping me with Andrew. The three of them seemed to get along pretty well. Roland and I, however, argued most of the time. Mickey, Junior and Andrew quietly put up with it. Despite the anger, Roland and I still planned to get married.

Elmer and Marcia Dovetail had moved out to a reservation in Montana. We hoped to find Elmer and ask him to marry us. But on arriving, we were told he was out of state.

Disappointed, we decided to spend the night at a campground down the road. Driving to a grocery later, I noticed how different this reservation was from ours. If the destitution was here, it wasn't as noticeable. The towns we'd driven through on the way down from Flathead Lake, although not luxurious, weren't as depressed as what we were used to. They resembled more the farming towns my grandparents had lived around, modest but well kept.

That night Roland and I argued some more. I left our camp and sat in the brick laundry building, crying. Roland left the camp, stepped through a wire fence and followed some cow paths up a small hill. But Mickey followed me into the laundry. He didn't say much, just listened. This fight was no different from any of the others. Roland and I both returned to the camp and made it through another night.

The next day we returned to Elmer's. He still wasn't there. I wanted to wait another day but Roland didn't. We packed up and headed for the coast to camp near the ocean. We didn't talk about whether we were going to go ahead and get married elsewhere.

Roland and I arrived in Reno, Nevada, in mid-August. We were almost out of money, so once there, I called work to have my check wired. That done, we found the "Heart of Reno" chapel in the yellow pages. It offered limousine service as part of the deal. I didn't have with me the wedding dress I'd bought a couple years earlier, but before the limo arrived, I did get my hair done.

The limo picked us up from our motel, drove us to obtain our license, and then took us to the small chapel. Once at the chapel, we purchased a minimum package and were quickly ushered into the service. The official was a heavy set, elderly woman and Junior and Mickey were our witnesses. The hasty service was unemotional. Maybe I really wanted to get married. Maybe I felt I'd gone too far to back out. Maybe I just wanted to prove something to Cheri and Misty.

Well, I can always get a divorce, I told myself as I walked down the aisle.

Before the trip was over, I had fallen for Mickey. He was really sweet and had a great sense of humor. As we drove home, he told us that he wanted to stay with us.

I decided I could handle Mickey, but Misty was another story. We found Misty in our house when we came home. Shirley had allowed Joy to stay with her there also. Misty's bedroom door had a hole in it where her boyfriend had smashed it, one of my brown towels had been cut up for unknown reasons and Roland's battery charger was missing. We were angry and let Misty know it. So she went home to her mother and complained about us. Her mother then twisted the issue. Angry, she claimed we didn't want the girls at the house at all, ever.

There's no reasoning with some people.

My sisters had arranged for a wedding reception to take place in my dad's back yard in October. Dad sent $300 to help pay for it, but let us know he himself wouldn't be coming. Over the next couple weeks Roland and I planned the party. With only $300 to spend, we had to think about what was really needed. We sent out invitations, went to the florist and rented a canopy.

It was delusional to even assume anything close to a normal reception could take place. But I'd lived in delusion for years now. There was no reason to assume anything resembling wisdom would miraculously blossom in my brain now.

In late August, Wanda, angry at Julia for not helping her down the stairs of her apartment house, tried to get down by herself and crashed down the flight in her wheelchair. Having re-broken her back, she was back in the hospital, facing new surgery.

On September 3, Roland and I came home to find a strange man standing on our porch. After confirming who Roland was, the man identified himself as the chaplain for the medical center. He had been sent at the request of Matthew Ward.

Beautiful, sixteen-year-old Julia... had hanged herself in the closet of Wanda's apartment.

Beth Ward

SLEEP

I wish I could retreat
into some dreamless sleep

where time would hang
suspended

and all the pain
was ended.

© By **PHONACELLE SHAPEL**

Chapter ten:
Gi-ga-wa-ba-min me-na-wa

After consoling Matthew at the morgue, Roland and I visited the brownstone apartment building. Death by hanging does not always happen quickly. In a situation where someone in a noose is dropped from sufficient height, the person may die quickly from a snapped neck. But without height, the person may strangle for several minutes, gagging and suffering before finally succumbing. As I stepped into the closet where Julia, who was taller then I, had hanged herself, the wooden rod from which the clothing hung just touched the top of my head. She could have saved herself simply by standing up. Did she hate herself that much? How could anyone hate themselves that much? How deep her despair must have been! Oh, why didn't any of us realize the extent of her suffering? That beautiful girl! Why didn't we visit her? Why didn't I just come and talk to her, be her friend, take her to get her license like I had promised? Something!

That evening, we got a call from a detective in the emergency room at the Hennepin County Medical Center. Roger had been stabbed in the chest. "Oh, No," I said. "His sister Julia just died!"

"Julia died?" The detective asked, "Do we know how Julia died?"

"Oh, yes. She was upset about their sister Wanda's accident and she hanged herself."

"Wanda?" He asked hesitantly, "And do we know what happened to Wanda?"

"Yes, she fell down a flight of stairs in a wheelchair and re-injured her back." The detective paused. "Do we know how Wanda fell down the stairs?"

I paused. "Yes. She was upset that Julia didn't want to help her down the stairs, so she threw herself down them."

At this point the detective paused. He must have been wondering if there were some kind of conspiracy against the family. I think, in some backward way, many of us hoped there was. It was too much to imagine that all this could happen to one family in one week's time. Worse - that they had all done it to themselves. It would have been a morbid comfort to have some other explanation.

The social worker in care of Julia's little brother Bradley released him into my care so that he could attend the funeral. I actually had to work that day and couldn't go to the funeral, but didn't tell her that because I figured it wouldn't matter whether it was Roland or I watching Bradley. However, as it turned out Roland volunteered to take Julia's body back up north to the reservation in our van and Bradley was shuffled into his mother's car. Roland fell apart up there and began drinking again and Yvonne did not return from the funeral on the day promised. When the social worker called looking for Bradley, I was alone at my house and had to confess I didn't know where Bradley was or when he would be returned. I was never allowed to take him again.

For the most part, I had learned to live with crisis in this family. But this week had been too much. Once I learned that Roland was drinking, I couldn't eat or sleep. My stomach churned constantly. I knew that Andrew and I were going to be on our own again. Because I couldn't eat or sleep, I didn't think I'd be able to properly care for Andrew either, so I called the Crisis Nursery to see if I could place him there for 48 hours. The on-call counselor, one whom I'd never gotten along with, suggested I put Andrew in a foster home. I hung up on her. I just needed help right now, for this moment; not forever.

To my relief Roland came back a week before our wedding reception. However, he told me he'd have to go back up in a few days to bring Dale and Tammy down. When he left, Cheri went with him. I was nervous about him leaving but couldn't change it. On their way out of town, Andrew and I rode with them as far as my sister's house where we were going to spend the night. On the way I told Cheri about my new pants, blouse, and white blazer that was missing.

"Misty was the last to wear them," I said.

"She probably took them," Cheri responded.

When Roland didn't get back on the day he said he would, my stomach again began to churn. I knew I should probably cancel the whole reception, but canceling would be so embarrassing. There was still a chance I was wrong and everything would be okay.

Of course, everything wasn't okay. Roland rolled his vanload of people into my dad's driveway the night before the party. The entire vehicle reeked of beer. Roland was drunk. So drunk, he'd allowed 16-year-old Cheri to drive.

"I don't want Andrew around all of these drunks," I told him.

Cheri answered, "Well, we grew up watching my dad drink and if it's good enough for us, it's good enough for your kid!"

"Yeah, but look how you turned out," I responded.

"Get in the car," Roland growled.

"I'll drive the rest of the way to our house," I answered.

"No. Cheri's driving. She drove this far and she'll drive the rest of the way."

I felt angry, but too embarrassed to go back into the house and let my family know everyone was drunk. Maybe things could still work out, I foolishly hoped.

Driving the open highway is one thing I suppose, but through the city is another and Cheri didn't have any idea how to use the side mirrors of the van.

"Look out!" I hollered as she tried to change lanes, "There's a car right next to you!"

"Shut up," she spat.

"I'm so sick of you and Misty. All you guys do is come and steal from me. Misty better get those clothes back to me, too."

"She don't have your clothes."

"You said she took them!"

"I did not!"

We made it home and people continued to arrive all that night. How was I to know that when I sent a couple of invitations to Roland's sisters, forty of his relatives would show up at my house to stay? And wedding receptions to this crowd meant heavy drinking. While Elaine and her crew were fine, many others I knew only by name and had to tell them over and over again that they could not drink at my house. Despairing, I stayed awake as long as I could, but eventually fell asleep about 4 am. The next morning, I found Paul sleeping on the floor. He was one of the children that I had given a bed to, but apparently James, now out of jail, and his wife, Gloria, had come in after I had fallen asleep and kicked him out of the bed. Sickened that Gloria – a woman who might have beaten her own child to death - was in my home at all, I told Paul never again, in my house, to give up a bed that I had given him. Sure, I could talk tough to Paul, but wouldn't / didn't say a word to James or Gloria.

Roland went to the store that morning with James. When he didn't return, I grew more desperate. The party was in just three hours, what happens if he's drinking again? What if he doesn't even show up? I had no way to go look for him. Then Gloria offered to drive me. My sickened feelings about what happened to her baby would have to take a back seat to my sickened dread about Roland. I needed help and I was thankful she was willing to give it.

After driving around a little while, we finally spotted Roland's van at Arthur's bar. Coming out of the bright sunlight into the dark room, It took my eyes a moment to adjust before I recognized Roland, his back to me, playing pool. His beer sat on the edge of the table. Walking quickly up behind him, I swung my purse and smacked it down on his head. He swung around. Seeing me, he started to laugh. The most frustrating thing was there was nothing I could say that he didn't already know. There were no words that could make any difference.

James got into Gloria's car and followed Roland and me in the van. Back at the house I didn't know what to do. I was supposed to go up to Dad's house to help my sisters get the backyard ready but I didn't want to leave my house to these people. No one was here to watch my things. Elaine was busy making a dish to bring to the party, but I knew I couldn't trust the others, including Roland. I was leaving my home unprotected. But my sisters were waiting for me and I couldn't call them and tell them that anything was wrong. So I thought I had no choice. I took Andrew and left for Dad's house.

Working with my sisters to ready the yellow canopy and set up the tables, my stomach was tied in barbed-wire knots. I wanted very badly for my relatives to believe my life was normal. I suppose I assumed that because I lived on the south side, they couldn't see my day to day life and had no idea what kinds of things were really going on. I wanted to preserve this illusion, which was obviously much more mine then theirs, that all-is-well.

My cousin arrived with the beautiful three-tiered cake she had made and set it on the white tablecloth. Everything looked beautiful. As nicely dressed people began to arrive, Roland still hadn't shown up. I welcomed my family's neighbors, friends and relatives and accepted their brightly wrapped gifts with a fake smile.

"Roland will be here soon," I told everyone.

Roland showed up an hour later, very drunk. Elaine, arriving in her own car, carried the chili and, followed by her children, went on down the slope to the party. Mickey smiled encouragement to me. Roland stumbled out and went on down. His four older children followed. Joy was wearing the pink dress and bonnet I'd bought her the Easter before. Dale was drunk too, but saw my shame and refused to get out of the van. I picked up Tammy's baby girl, the one Tammy had said she'd named for me, and took Dale's family down to introduce them. I was unable to even look in Roland's direction.

Suddenly Roland grabbed me and pulled me over to dance around the canopy.

"This is a traditional wedding dance," he told me, slurring his speech as he stumbled along.

I could feel my face burn hot as everyone watched. When he finally let me go, I hurried into the house, humiliated. Eventually, Roland and his crew left. Mickey had stayed. A few of the guests came into the house to say good-bye. Others just left.

Bobby took Mickey, Andrew and me home. No one was there when we arrived, but beer cans littered the floor and their contents stained the living room rug. The empty boxes they came in were stacked five feet high in the kitchen corner and Burger King wrappers littered the stairs.

I looked around; exhausted and distraught. I didn't have any energy left for anger. Bobby waited a few minutes, not saying much of anything.

"Look," said Mickey, "Roland's pulling up."

I looked out the storm door. Roland was trying to parallel park in front and not doing a very good job of it. He had a group in the van with him. Roland looked up and saw me in the door. He quickly turned his wheel toward the street and drove away. Now I felt angry - at myself as much as him.

"Fine then. The reception is done, and I'll be d----- if most of them are going to stay another night."

Bobby left and I started cleaning. Soon Elaine came for her belongings. I had no problem with her. She had tried to help with the day and had planned on driving back that night anyway. But Dorothy was with her.

"I paid $12 for the chili's hamburger," Dorothy demanded, "Pay me back."

"I didn't ask you to spend your money."

"Give me the $12 or I'm taking Mickey back with me."

I paid her and Dorothy climbed into Elaine's car and left.

Misty, Dale and Tammy stayed. I didn't mind Dale and Tammy, but I didn't want to take care of Misty anymore. Roland wasn't there and I didn't want him coming back, so she might as well go too. I was through taking care of his problems.

"Where's those clothes you took? I'm tired of you owning into my stuff!"

"I didn't take your d--- clothes!"

"Get out and don't f------ come back!"

She ran to the phone and called her mom. After speaking to her quickly, she hung up and came back.

"My ma's coming to get me and when she gets here, she's going to kick your a--."

"Let her come."

Dale, Tammy, and Mickey sat quietly in the living room and said nothing. After Misty threw some things into a bag, she stood at the door and waited for her ride.

As I stood at the top of the landing, Misty looked up at me and swore, "You dumb, f---- b----."

"Least I finished school," I said as I turned and walked into my room.

Misty's mother pulled up in front and honked. Misty grabbed her bag and left.

The next day Roland went back up north, taking Dale, Tammy and Misty with him. Mickey stayed with me and I enrolled him in a local high school and a karate class.

The first Friday after he began school, I woke Mickey up for breakfast.

"Do I have to go today? Can't I just stay home today as a reward for having gone the other four days?"

"No," I answered, shaking my head in amazement.

Through the grapevine we heard that both Roland and Misty were drinking heavily. Misty had even taken our van one night and tore up someone's yard. I called Tammy and asked her to hide the van keys. Later, I heard the vehicle wasn't running right anyway and they had parked it.

Roland called one evening, "Could you send me the title for the van?"

"Why?"

"I sold it."

"What? It's in my name. How could you sell it to them?"

"Well I did it and they need the title."

It was Roland's van; he'd paid for it. But I was mad he sold it for drinking money. I called the county sheriff's office.

"My van was sold without my permission."

Later, the deputy called me back.

"Look, I know the people that bought it. I used to go to school with the lady and they're good people. They've already bought new tires for it, so they said that if you want it back, they'd have to take the tires off. You'll have your car but it'll be on blocks."

Reluctantly, I sent the title.

Furious I was, but being a single mom was also lonely. Don't ask me why I kept wanting him back. I never could figure it out myself.

A month or so later, Roland called and asked if I'd come get him.

"Okay. I'll be up this weekend."

"And I hocked my tools. I need about $75 to get them back."

Everyone was drinking at Dale's when I arrived on Friday night. Roland greeted me.

"Buy us a twelve-pack, will ya?"

Misty, high on whatever, stumbled out the door with her boyfriend as soon as I sat down. A few minutes later, she returned. While I sat on the couch, she leaned over to her dad's ear, too stoned to know she wasn't whispering, and asked, "Can I get some of Beth's money?"

"I don't know," he answered, "ask her yourself."

Misty looked at me, then walked away. A few minutes later she came toward me.

"Can I get some money?"

"I need all the money I have to get your dad's stuff out of hock and then get home."

"You f------ b----," she swore. Turning, she pulled her boyfriend out the door.

After Roland and I made the rounds collecting his tools, we went back to Dale's to spend the night. Roland wasn't done drinking. He decided to go out to the bar with his nieces.

"I'll drive you," I told them. Wanting to make sure we could leave the next day, I figured I'd rather go with Roland to keep him out of trouble.

After spending about an hour at the bar, we were just getting ready to go back to Dale's when Misty came in. Her boyfriend was tugging on her sleeve, trying to pull her back out. Roland stood up and walked over to her.

"You only care for her!" she cried. "How come you always have to drop everything and do what she wants?"

Roland, with the help of the boyfriend, pushed her back out the door. The whole bar watched. As Roland walked back to our booth, Misty could be heard still screaming on the street. I felt satisfaction.

Before we left the next day, we drove up to the nursing home to visit Walter with Dale's family. Not finding him in his room, a nurse searched the facility for him. He was no where to be found.

"Oh darn it," the nurse announced, "he must have taken off again."

"Which way does he go?" Roland asked.

"Toward home," she said, pointing down the highway.

We climbed back into the car and took off down the road. After several miles, we saw the lone figure on the horizon.

"Man, can that old man walk!"

Roland pulled the car over in front of Walter. Walter looked up and, recognizing Roland, smiled.

"Ho! Wha'cha doing out here!" Roland asked, "You've got all those women at the nursing home worried about you!"

"Oh...gotta get home!" his dad said, still smiling.

"Your home's back there now. Come on," Roland said gently.

Walter came without a fight. After driving him back and settling him into his room, we had to go. We got in the car and counted heads. Wally was missing.

"There he is," Dale said, "by the little fir tree."

Two-year-old Wally stood on the trim lawn with his fly open, watering a tiny tree. A nurse watched from the door.

"Come on Wally!" Dale said laughing.

Cheri and Gene split up and Cheri, with Carrie almost 18-months-old, moved in with us. I did love Cheri and never stopped wanting to help her, but we walked a fine line with each other. As long as I smiled and gave her everything she expected, we were fine. We spent time together watching TV and teasing Roland. But again, I was the one that had to do the bending in order for us to get along. If I asked anything of her or refused her requests, I messed things up.

One afternoon after she had been with us about three weeks, Cheri went out with Misty and didn't come back. This took us by surprise. Although we had had our hard times with Cheri, we never expected her to walk away from Carrie.

Now Carrie was my responsibility. A few months earlier, Carrie had been diagnosed with anemia and a yeast infection. Cheri had gotten the medicine but had never really used it. Now with her gone, I wrestled with Carrie twice a day to get her to swallow the bitter iron solution and grappled to get rid of an infection. The infection had been going on for so long that the normal salve wasn't working. I took Carrie to the doctor, who gave me some stronger medicine, but that didn't work either. Something was still there. I took Carrie back to the doctor.

"The infection is gone," he said, "This is something else. I'm going to have to call child protection."

Child protection was called and a report was made. The doctor assured us that evidence was such that he did not suspect our home was the source of the abuse. However, we were told Carrie should not visit her other relatives.

Two weeks later, Cheri came back. Sitting on the couch and taking Carrie onto her lap, she asked "Carrie, do you love me? Did you miss me?"

I was surprised that her first words to her daughter after three weeks absence were self-centered, but those words were a reflection of the core problem. When we told her about her daughter's diagnosis, she said she didn't know how or when Carrie would have been abused. But she was willing to believe it might have been someone in Gene's family. This gave her an excuse to keep Carrie from them.

Not that she was passionate about taking care of Carrie, herself, though. Cheri left again without warning the very next day.

I could have insisted that Roland chase Cheri down, but I was happier having her gone. Besides, it was kind of fun to have a daughter. I picked up pretty dresses for Carrie at the Crisis Nursery, fixed her hair, and took her to the college day care along with Andrew.

At night, kneeling on my lap as I rocked in the rocking chair, laying her head on my chest and clinging to my neck as she liked to do, it would take only a few minutes for her to fall sleep.

At the Crisis Nursery, a new woman was hired. Initially, I liked her. But as time went on, I became increasingly annoyed. It got to the point where I couldn't stand being around her and only grunted replies if she spoke to me. For the life of me, I had no idea why I hated her so much. There wasn't anything I could see that she did wrong. She said she was a Christian, but never talked about it. She was just always smiling and kind all the time no matter how nasty I was. It made me want to scream.

That same month, Annie was in the hospital giving birth to little Shaine. I had worried about this pregnancy. She'd been drinking the whole time.
Bringing a gift to her room, we visited for a little while. Shaine looked good. I was relieved. Annie also looked good. Her long silky hair, washed and brushed, literally shined. Two days of being cared for, sleeping in a comfortable bed and eating three meals a day had been good for her. Or maybe it was the little boy. She held him closely in her arms and spoke softly to him. I hoped that maybe she would leave the hospital determined to stay straight for him - and herself too.

January 11, 1987, was the afternoon of a big football game. Matthew and Roland watched it together in our living room. Annie called a couple of times that day asking Roland to come over and talk with Lila.
"She's sick," Annie told him, "she's coughing up blood and won't go to the hospital. She wants to talk to you."
Roland was reluctant. He had been over there several times this week already. All they wanted, Roland figured, was to ask him to run to the liquor store again.
Lila had some money and a group had hung out with her all week helping drink it up. Lila hadn't moved from the couch the whole

time. Roland said the apartment stunk from the smell of alcohol, urine, and "some other strange smell" he thought he recognized but couldn't name. He really didn't want to go back there. So he told them he'd come, but then settled back down to finish watching the game. While he and Matthew watched the game, I opened one of my nursing books and tried to look up the symptoms the family had described to Roland.

After the game, I went with Matthew and Roland. I usually didn't go with him anymore, but I was worried about Lila. We pulled into the alley behind the brownstone building, the same building Julia had died in four months earlier, and parked. There was an ambulance parked near the back door. Roland got out and moved quickly toward the steps. I was slower; I had to help Andrew out of the car. As Roland began to go in, two men carrying a stretcher came out. Roland stepped aside to let them pass, glancing only a moment at the body with its sheet covered face, then started up the stairs. I also looked. The belly of the person was huge, as if it were a pregnant woman. The way my mom's belly had looked when it was filled with fluid just before she had died. I hesitated, then turned to the two men now loading the corpse into the ambulance.

"Is that Lila Hunter?" I asked them.

"Yes," one responded.

I called up the stairs, "Roland! Come back! It's Lila!"

He turned and looked down at me, "No it's not."

Up in Wanda's apartment, Annie sat. Her newborn, settled in the seat of the baby swing I'd lent her, swung quietly back and forth.

"I knew she was dying. We even called an ambulance the other day. But when they got here, she wouldn't go. She said she was going to die anyway and didn't want to die in the hospital. They said there was nothing they could do if she didn't want to go."

Later, Roland struggled with guilt for not having gone to Lila when he'd first been called. Questions tormented him. Could he have talked her into going to the hospital? Would it have made a difference? What was it that Lila had wanted to tell him? The last question haunted him the most.

He also finally recognized the "other strange smell" that he had noticed in the apartment. It was the same smell he's noticed when he'd had gangrene. The smell of rotting flesh as Lila sat on that couch drinking and dying. In medical terms, she died of acute pancreatitis and severe fatty metamorphosis of the liver. In my terms, she died of despair.

Roland drove her body home to Leech Lake. She was buried at the family plot in Mission, near the grave of a tiny baby girl laid to rest seven years earlier.

A month later we hurried to get up north as quickly as possible. Unfortunately, as we arrived and ran up the steps to the Indian Health Service hospital, Roland's sister opened the door and told him he was too late.

There were few people Walter knew near the end. Roland, during Lila's funeral the month before, was grateful to be among the few whom his father was still able to recognize. However, because of Walter's confusion and poor health, Lila's funeral was kept secret from the old man.

His wake was held in the Community Center, which was packed with people. Grandpa or Uncle to most of the reservation, Walter had been a well-respected elder.

Sitting on some steps at the far end of the room, I held Annie's baby and tried rocking him. He was crying non-stop and couldn't be comforted. His face and hands were dirty and he wouldn't eat.

"Let me take him to the hospital Annie."

Pointing to her dad's casket with her lips, Annie moaned through her tears, "Go ahead. I'm not worried about him. I'm worried about that old man over there."

Savannah and I walked through the snow carrying baby Shaine. At the hospital, the doctor admitted him with an ear infection and impetigo.

"It's not that serious," the doctor said, "But this is a better place for him to sleep than the floor of the community center."

At Dale's that evening, I spoke to Candis, whose foster dad had brought her down for the funeral. After what had happened with both her father and uncle, I was worried about what she must think of men.

"Do you remember when you were little, when you cried at night and Grandpa Walter would take you into his bed and comfort you?"

"Yes," she answered.

"That's the good way ... the way daddies are supposed to be. He never hurt you; he just comforted you. That's the way daddies are supposed to love their little girls, not like what those others did."

She was silent.

"Your grandpa really loved you, Candis."

The next day someone from the hospital called Annie and warned her that Child Protection was coming and if she wanted to keep Shaine, she'd better get over there before the worker did. Annie didn't go. Social services removed Shaine from the hospital and put him into foster care. A couple months later he underwent heart surgery secondary to Fetal Alcohol Syndrome. He was never returned to Annie.

Beth Ward

BARS

You have yours
and I have mine
the bars on the
windows that we
all shine

I placed them
there, one by
one, fear by
fear, till the
deed was done

My jailer laughs
and weeps with me

My jailer expresses
deep sympathy

And late at night
he plots with me

And feeds me bits
of reality

© By PHONACELLE SHAPEL

Chapter eleven:
Dying in the Heart

Carrie had been with us now for only about three or four months. It seemed like it had been much longer, but that was only because so much had happened in that short period of time.

Child Protection informed us that although there was proof Carrie was abused, there was no proof as to who did it. It could have been any of the many people her mother partied with. Without proof, they couldn't hold anyone accountable. We were told Carrie's father and his family were allowed visits again.

Darlene, anxious to see her, took Carrie home for the weekend. On Sunday evening, they returned. Setting the baby out of the car onto the sidewalk, they handed her the overnight bag and gave her a nudge. Having heard the car drive up, we had come out to receive her and were surprised to see 18-month-old Carrie by herself, climbing the steps to the door dragging the little bag behind her.

They watched from the road until they saw us pick her up, then drove off.

When Cheri finally came back a week or so later and took Carrie, I laid on my bed and cried for a couple hours.

I returned to the Ojibwe class in the last semester. I still felt it was important for the children to understand their culture, so I took Andrew and sometimes Joy with me to class. Pregnant again, I even considered wearing headphones on my belly so the baby could hear the language.

Mickey's brother Troy, whose head was shaved by friends during a drunk, moved in with us, too. I wanted the boys to learn to speak Ojibwe as well, so I wrote the Ojibwe names of household objects such as door, lamp, and window onto slips of paper and stuck them around the house.

It seemed like a good idea, but no one was really interested. Those slips of paper remained stuck to our furniture for a good year, little noticed by anyone.

The boys weren't interested in the language, but we did make progress in other areas. While staying with us, Troy obtained his driver's license, had his chipped front tooth fixed, and worked on getting his GED. Mickey worked on getting his driver's permit and attended high school.

One day Mickey came home an hour early from class.

"What are you doing home?" I asked him.

"My advocate let me out."

"What do you mean, 'let you out'?"

"Well, I didn't like my art teacher, so a month or so ago my Indian advocate let me drop the class and go to study hall in his office instead.

"What did you study in his office?"

"He'd ask me a couple questions and stuff, but …I wasn't really doing anything there …so now he just lets me come home instead."

Are you kidding me? I called the advocate. "In the first place," I told him, "I don't agree with letting him drop art. He has to work out his problems with his teacher. But in the second place, Mickey got two 'F's' last quarter! How come you're letting him cut out of school?"

"What are you worried about?" the advocate, also a tribal member, responded, "He's got three years of school left. He's got time to catch up."

Talking to this guy was a waste of time. About ready to blow my top, I called the principal instead, who agreed Mickey shouldn't be leaving school early. It was too late to get Mickey back into the art class, so he placed him into the real study hall instead. Unfortunately, the principal didn't have the cojones to fire the advocate for being the idiot he was.

The following day, Mickey confided that the advocate had told him "Don't listen to Beth, all white people talk like that."

What a jerk. Doesn't that 'so-called advocate' think Indian kids are capable of hard work? HE's the racist! I figured if anybody dared treat Andrew that way when he got to school, expecting less of him just because he's Indian, I'd knock their block off!

Right - it's easy to blow up at all the fools outside the family. But to open my mouth and say something to family members? Not so much...

For three weeks we struggled to rid our house of lice. Every time I had thought they were gone, I'd look on Andrew's head and there they were again. Fortunately, the Crisis Nursery was well stocked with lice shampoo and even an upholstery spray. I helped myself to the products, putting them into the car as my co-worker slept, and went through our home washing every head, stitch of clothing, and stuffed animal in the house more than once.

And as I went throughout pulling out every piece of clothing I could find, I came across a pair of pants, a blouse, and a white blazer that had been missing for quite some time. Whoops.

Not wanting the clothing to be found by anyone else - and my false accusation of Misty discovered - I stuffed the clothes in a bag and gave them away at the first opportunity.

But as for the lice, despite my cleaning efforts, scarcely a week later the pests would be back. The mother of Andrew's friend called one day and asked if we were having trouble with bugs.

Reluctantly, I admitted we were.

"So are we. But I think it's been coming from that new family that just moved in from Red Lake. I went and asked her about it, and she acted like she didn't even know what lice were. I told her I'd wash her kid's heads for her."

"I'll keep Andrew away for awhile."

The lice problem disappeared.

In order to pass the Ojibwe class that spring, I had to stand in front of everyone and give a short speech in the language. Family and friends were invited to the event. Roland and the kids came, along with Roland's sister Yvonne. After we had all given our speeches, we shared a potluck lunch that included venison, wild rice and fry bread.

I was given an "A" for the class, but even more important, Yvonne said I did really well. Yay! That felt really good.

The small man who owned the corner store was a friendly fellow, but unless I needed a last minute item, I avoided his store. His food was old. Previous purchases had included freezer burned ice cream and milk that was so outdated it plopped out like pudding into the glass when poured.

I don't know why I went in this day with my WIC vouchers. I must have been in a hurry.

"You have WIC?" he asked, "here, I let you get pop with your WIC instead of juice. You can get anything. It's okay. I do this for my good customers. You are a good customer."

"No thank you. I'll get juice," I said, while thinking to myself, 'why would I want to get pop when juice is more expensive?'

Returning, I met Andrew in the alley. He, along with some other boys, was racing around with a stick in his hands.

"Look, Mom! I'm part of a gang!"

At fourteen, Savannah had a baby girl. I called the hospital and told them she was homeless, truant and addicted. I told them that her mother was homeless, too. I asked them to place Savannah and the baby in foster care. But someone showed up at the hospital and claimed them. I suppose all they had to do was tell the hospital that yes, they did have a good place to stay. The hospital released them.

On Savannah's new welfare check, she and Annie got an apartment together. I brought over some clothes and diapers taken from the Crisis Nursery.

"Just take good care of the baby and everything will be okay," I told Savannah, "Don't start drinking again. Use your check to get five bags of diapers and a case and a half of formula every month. If you stay out of trouble, social services will leave you alone."

A couple of weeks later, one of Verlin's sister's called me.
"Do you have Savannah's baby?" she asked.
"No," I answered, "is the baby missing?"
"Well," the caller said, "Savannah was drinking and doesn't know where she left it."

She went on to say the baby had been missing for about ten days. As I hung up the phone, I was horrified. The baby could be lying dead in some alley. After a few moments of panic, I paused and called St. Joseph's Home for Children. 'Misplaced' children often turn up there.

"Yes," The woman on the phone said, "we did get an unidentified Native American baby girl this last week."

I hung up the phone in relief, but I didn't call and tell the family. The longer the home kept the baby, the better. Unfortunately, the family eventually called St. Joseph's and the baby was returned to them shortly thereafter.

Why does Social Services keep putting Savannah and her baby back on the street together? Why isn't anyone stepping in to protect these two children?

Roland had been doing well lately, staying sober and helping me. While we were visiting up north, Wally did something wrong and Dale got angry. Taking a stick, he smacked Wally on the butt and sent him to the bedroom. Tammy got up to go after her crying boy.

"Don't you go baby him!" Dale hollered, "You're always going and babying him!"

I felt for Tammy and Wally, but knew not to interfere.

Back home, Roland and I visited Nova and I noticed how harsh she, too, was with children. Her 11-year-old, overweight granddaughter was always being hollered at. Why are so many people so mean to their kids?

I never asked; I just wondered.

I was seven months pregnant when I finished nursing school. My father, siblings, Andrew, Roland, and Mickey and his brothers all came to the graduation. Afterwards, Roland took the whole bunch of us out to a restaurant. It was the first time he'd ever done anything like that. While at the restaurant, he surprised me with a wedding ring. We hadn't had the money for one up until then. It was a fantastic evening, bolstering the hopes and dreams I still lung to.

Not only was Roland sober, but he had a job. Roland was working for a traveling painting crew now and making good money.

Tired from working and going to school and in the third trimester of my pregnancy, I looked forward to resting. Because Roland was doing well, I hoped that I'd be able to spend the summer taking it easy with Andrew. So I put in my notice at the Crisis Nursery. For the first time ever, Roland would be taking care of me.

But nothing ever seems to go as planned. Two weeks before my resignation took effect, other night workers and I wrote a letter of complaint to our boss. The man being trained to take my place had us all worried. But in order to explain our concerns, we admitted in our letter that we all had been taking turns sleeping on the job. I suspect that she knew all along that we were sleeping, but the fact that we were foolish enough to confess it in a written note gave her no choice but to take action. As a result, the administration fired us all.

I was upset, thinking it unfair. But since I had already stolen everything I needed for my new baby; including a large stash of diapers, wet wipes, and other paraphernalia, I accepted it. The nursery's decision just gave me more time with Andrew sooner than expected.

Although I complained a lot about the amount of deceit in my husband's family, the hypocrisy of my own stealing never occurred to me

Getting fired was one change in my summer plans. The other change was much worse. The men Roland worked with were drinkers and the long trips away from home with them were too much. He called from the motel one night, drunk. A few days later, he went off on a binge again. As Troy was up north, and Mickey and Paul were visiting their dad in Texas, Andrew and I were on our own.

Good. It's about time. I was finally so angry at Roland that it didn't matter to me he was gone. I hoped that none of them would ever come back. I was tired of everyone. In fact, when anyone tried to come around or call, I chased them away.

Rats – and then you want to know what that stupid Christian woman at work did, after I had already been gone a couple weeks? That lady I hated so much and wouldn't talk to - she sent me a birthday card! The nerve of that stinking woman!

My disposition showed during a prenatal check. The nurse practitioner asked what was wrong.

"My husband's drinking up north. I don't think I'll let him come back."

Without hesitation, this woman, a complete stranger who knew nothing about me, asked, "Would you like an abortion?"

I was stunned. Outrage flooded me. How dare she! What an idiotic thing to say! I couldn't believe the stupidity of the question! How was it the baby's fault? What makes her think I'd want to kill my baby! How would killing my baby change Roland? How would it change how I was feeling? How dare she try to make things worse by suggesting she kill my baby! Would she ask that question so glibly to an upper-class woman married to a white man? I extremely doubt it! I was so insulted, so outraged and so flustered by the question, words couldn't come out. For heaven's sake I was almost eight months pregnant! I could have slapped her!

"OF COURSE NOT!" I finally spit.

I got through the appointment saying little else to her. As soon as I was out of the room, I told the woman at the desk that there was no way I'd ever let that woman examine me again, let alone deliver my baby, even if she was the only one on call. Anyone that stupid and thoughtless had no business near my baby.

My nursing boards were scheduled to take place at the Civic Center over a two-day period. I asked Marion if Andrew could stay with her over those two days. I'd do better if I didn't have to worry about him. The first day of the test, the staff ushered us into a large room. We weren't allowed to bring anything in with us and we weren't allowed to leave the room. It was a long and stressful day. That night I went to bed early, my body drained.

Around midnight the phone rang. "Beth.... This is Dorothy," came the slurred voice, "I'm over at a party.... Will you pick me up...and take me over to Franklin Ave?"

"No!" I barked and hung up.

That weekend, the nursing boards finally over, Andrew and I actually began to relax. Having nothing but welfare, money was now tight. But it was okay, Andrew and I didn't need much. We went to fairs, the library, and to visit my family. We went to the beach twice a week and spent the whole afternoon doing nothing but play together in the water and lie on the warm sand. If I had loose change, I bought each of us an ice cream bar at the refreshment stand. It was a beautiful, wonderful time.

Unfortunately, it ended too soon. I came home from an overnight stay at my sister's one day and found Troy and Matthew sleeping in the house. They'd gotten in through the upstairs porch door.

I was angry, but didn't show it. Not wanting them to hate me, I didn't want them to know how I felt. I scolded them and then let it go. My quiet time was over.

The phone rang just as I was falling asleep.
"Tell my dad Cheri had her kid," Misty snapped.
"Tell him yourself," I snapped back and hung up.

Mickey came back from Texas, but Paul stayed with his aunt and dad. I went into labor in September and Troy drove me to the hospital. I didn't call Roland. Why bother? He knew when I was due. I'd packed my overnight bag for Andrew also, intending that he stay with me. Troy dropped Andrew and me at the hospital door.

Around 5:30 p.m. the next day, Andrew tried to cut his sister's cord. The doctor helped.

Haley's initial color at birth was dark and her face was squashed, accenting her Indian features. My initial reaction to the way she looked was fear. My thought; "I've given birth to an Indian girl who will become a teenage Indian girl."

I was barely out of the shower when Steph arrived half an hour later from work. She very lovingly combed my wet hair out. Erik, Bobby and Chris arrived soon after. All of them took time to hold Haley. I was tired, but so touched and grateful to have them all there. What a difference this was from the time Andrew was born. When they left they took Andrew and his belongings with them.

"I'll pick you up and take you home when it's time," Steph offered.

I fell asleep that night comforted by my brothers and sisters. Alone with Haley, my feelings of fear passed.

She was beautiful.

Haley was already three days old when I called a nephew up north to leave a message for Roland.

"Just wait," his nephew said, "I'll go get him."

"No, I mean, don't bother. I just called to tell you so you can tell him. I don't need to talk to him."

"No, I'll go get him," he said, and hung up.

Strange. All the times I wanted to talk to Roland and no one would help me. Now, I don't want to speak to him, and someone is rushing to get him.

Roland called back almost immediately.

"I'll come home."

"Don't bother."

"I'm going to detox tonight then come right down tomorrow."

But of course, he didn't go to detox. He went to celebrate that night. The following night he went to detox.

Beth Ward

I took Haley in the stroller to the park when she was five days old. After opening her blankets so she could get sun on her slightly jaundiced face, I sat down to read. I wasn't there long when Troy rode up quickly on his bike.

"Roland and Elaine are here."

My stomach knotted and I looked away. Taking a deep breath, I slowly stood up.

"Okay. Tell them I'm coming."

Troy took off on his bike. I slowly put my things away and got ready to leave. Haley's face looked pink.

Darn it, I thought, I sunburned Haley's face a little. I hope Elaine doesn't notice.

Moving slowly, I made my way up the sidewalk. What was I supposed to do or say to him? I had no idea how to act. I didn't want him there.

But in a small way, I did.

In a small way I did, but I never fully warmed up to Roland those following months. I rarely looked him in the eye and we no longer touched each other, even while lying asleep in bed. I changed my phone number and - even though he <u>lived</u> with me - wouldn't give it to him! I didn't want him to give it to his older daughters.

I hated to see Roland alone and lonely, especially when I remembered how he used to be. But I couldn't trust him anymore... and love involves trust.

I found a job as a charge nurse at a nearby nursing home. I didn't want to leave Haley and start work at Cedar Pines, but the job was just weekends and it was close enough that I could come home during break and nurse her.

Andrew asked Roland to play with him with the train set Uncle Bobby had given him for his birthday. I knew Roland and Andrew couldn't play together for more than three minutes, and they didn't. Andrew said something and Roland got mad and walked away. Andrew cried and begged Roland to come back and play, but he said, "No." Andrew finally quit crying and started to play alone with his legos.

Dying in Indian Country

Just before Christmas, Roland and Andrew each received about $400 from the tribe. This was the first and only tribal disbursement I'd ever seen. Andrew's money was automatically deposited by the tribe into a special savings account to be held until he turned 18. Haley didn't receive a check at all because she hadn't been enrolled yet as a member.

Cheri, who'd also received her money, had been staying with us. Roland and I began to argue about her again. I had been supporting everyone, but Cheri was refusing to use any of her money to help out. I wanted her to go.

"Well if she goes, I go," Roland hollered.

"Good-bye," I yelled back.

For a moment, Roland seemed stunned. But then he packed up and, with Cheri and all their money, left.

Some time later, Savannah killed her mother's boyfriend. He had been verbally abusing Annie, and Savannah got angry, went into the kitchen, returned with a knife, and stuck it in his back.

I didn't hold Savannah to blame, though. I couldn't. So many people had abused her. I blamed all the adults who could have – should have – helped her, including Roland and the social workers. I was disgusted with them all. Why didn't anyone help her?

After the murder and Savannah's arrest, I called her defense attorneys and told them how she had been living. I wanted her lawyer to know what she had been through – the alcoholism in the family and the abuse, neglect, and gang rape she'd endured. I wanted him to be sympathetic. But I also called the prosecution. I wanted someone to finally do something.

I don't think anything I said had any affect on anything, but her first baby was taken away from her, and Savannah went to a group home. And that was great.

Wanda was admitted to Bridgeway Treatment Center. Wanting to encourage her, I went to visit. Once there, I felt I'd better explain my absence from the extended family. It wasn't just because Roland

and I were separated or because I didn't get along with his oldest daughters.

"Wanda, I haven't come around you guys for awhile because I care about you all and just can't keep watching all the bad things going on. I just can't keep watching everyone get hurt and die."

Wanda didn't take offense. Instead, she felt touched by the idea someone cared. 'No one's ever said anything like that to me before," she answered quietly.

My sister Steph moved in with me in January. When she came, I was excited. I had visions that we would shop together, do each other's hair and in general, be sisters together in a way we never had before. But neither of our schedules ended up allowing it. I was working the 3-11 shift and at times even back to back or doubles, and she was working two jobs. We rarely saw each other.

Troy and Mickey were my babysitters, not because they were good but because they were convenient. Some mornings I'd find Haley soaked in her crib because they hadn't changed her before putting her to bed. Later, I learned there were times girls stayed over while both Steph and I were gone. Steph was especially angry when one of her heirloom coffee tables was broken.

Troy came home one day and told me something Misty had said about me. That was it. I'd had enough.

"I'm going down to kick her a—right now."

Matthew stopped me. "She's pregnant. You better not go over there."

"I don't care. I'm sick of her!"

I was afraid if I stopped now, I'd never do it. I jumped in my car and drove over to Cheri's place. Standing in the snow outside, I called Misty down from the upstairs duplex.

She hurried down the stairs and opened the screen door. "What?"

"I'm so sick of you and your mouth! If you don't cut it out, I'll kick the s--- out of you!"

"Wait a minute." She turned and ran back up the stairs.

I stood for a minute. What did she do that for? I waited. What's taking her so long? I felt stupid just standing there. How long am I supposed to stand here?

Finally, after what felt like forever, I turned and slowly started walking to the car. If she came down, I didn't want it to look like I was running off but I wasn't going to just stand there either. I slowly crossed the street, opened my car door, and sat in the car. Now what do I do? I looked up to her window to see if anyone was watching. I saw no one.

Well, I'm not going to sit around here all day, I thought. Moving slowly, I started up the car and left.

Roland came back down in February. I wouldn't let him stay with me, so he stayed at Cheri's house. But he came over to see us often. I was dropping him off one afternoon when Cheri passed my car and walked up the steps of her sidewalk. Sitting in the driver's seat, I could see her through Roland's passenger window. Roland, with his head turned my way, had his back to her. She turned at the top of the steps and silently mouthed a curse at me.

"Did you see that?" I asked him.

"See what?"

"I can't take this crap anymore, Roland. If I have to get away from you so I can get away from them, I will!"

Roland turned, got out of the car, and went upstairs. I drove off.

After awhile, I couldn't take Roland hanging around anymore. I wanted to start a new life with new friends, so I decided to talk him into going far away.

"Roland, I talked to Elmer last week. Why don't you go out west to visit him?"

"Nah."

"Why not? It'll give you a break. Some time to yourself. I'll buy your ticket."

I'm not sure why he agreed to it, but he did. He wasn't going to leave for a couple days though and I was afraid he'd change his mind. So I did everything I could to pamper him and make him think everything was fine between us, including having him stay at my house.

The night before he was to leave, Misty's newest boyfriend, Wesley Redwood, came to the door for Roland. They spoke quietly for a few minutes, then Wesley left. I knew without seeing it that he'd brought Roland some weed for the road. I was glad this was all going to be over soon. I was sure Roland would never get enough money together for a ticket back.

At dawn Andrew and I brought Roland down to the bus depot. Andrew hadn't had a chance to get breakfast, so he was surly. Roland teased him about going along, but Andrew just scowled.

Roland boarded the bus. As the bus slowly backed up to leave, Roland waved from the window. Andrew grabbed my arm and began pulling me to the car.

"Wait a minute. Your dad is leaving! Wave good-bye!"

"Come on," he glowered without even looking at the bus. "I want to eat!"

I waved weakly at Roland and left. Andrew's rudeness made me feel sorry for Roland, but I also felt relief that this permanent separation probably wouldn't bother Andrew much.

The truth is, I wanted to start going out with my staff after work. As long as Troy and Mickey were there and I knew the babies were already in bed, there was no one that needed me and no reason for me to go home. I'd never been a person to go to bars before. I didn't even know what to order when I finally went. But having been a good student of TV commercials, I tried to appear knowledgeable and simply ordered a "lite." Being with the crowd was fun and I was able to relax. After a few nights, I didn't even want to go home at closing time. Some of my staff didn't either, so we began going to different houses. After all, the kids wouldn't need me until breakfast time.

While smoking weed in one house, an aide started laughing.

"I just can't believe it!" He said, "Here I am getting high with my charge nurse!"

Everyone laughed with him.

I liked the family atmosphere at Cedar Pines, but I learned that Bridgeway Health Care, the facility I was working at when I met Roland, was paying more. So I switched. The night after my final night at Cedar Pines, I was supposed to go back there about 10 pm with a pizza. Afterward, we were all going out. Stephanie had come home just as I was leaving to go get the pizza.

"Here," she said, "I've got us some munchies and a movie! Let's spend the evening together!"

"Sorry, I'm doing something with people from work."

"Okay," she said, and sat down in front of the TV by herself.

I felt guilty as I left. As I should have; co-workers come and go, but sisters are meant to be forever.

At Bridgeway the following week, I was disappointed. At Cedar Pines, I was charge nurse and had a position that gave me responsibility and freedom. Now at Bridgeway, I was nothing more than a pill pusher. The atmosphere at Bridgeway, which had changed corporate hands over the years since Roland was a patient, was also different. It was no longer 'laid back;' it now had very strict rules for quality control. Stepping just inside a door to hand a resident his pills one day, I turned around to find the quality control supervisor slapping my med-cart locked.

"Never leave it unattended!" she snapped.

One night an aide was having difficulty getting a resident with dementia to take a shower. The aide got rough while handling the patient. The next day, I asked my supervisor about it.

"I haven't been here very long," I said, "and I don't know the patients as well as this aide does. Was it necessary to get rough in order to get the patient to take a shower?"

"This is a 'vulnerable adult' issue," my charge nurse responded, "You should have stepped in and stopped that aide. I'll have to report you."

I hated going to work. It was hard leaving my babies, but leaving them to go to this place was all the worse. Halfway through a shift one day, I was trying to teach a diabetic woman how to give herself an insulin shot. I drew the insulin into the syringe and attempted to tap it. As I did this, I tried to explain the purpose, but couldn't think of the word "bubble." I couldn't think straight at all. Struggling to concentrate, I stumbled through the rest of the lesson. As soon as I was finished, I went to the director's office. I had no idea what was going on with me, but I knew I had to leave.

"I can't do this." Tears rolled down my cheeks. "I have to go home." She let me go.

At home, my neighbor suggested I go to her psychologist. I called for an appointment. Because of the apparent crisis, they squeezed me in late that afternoon.

The psychologist rushed around the waiting room. Her hair was disheveled and her face wore a scowl.

"Come this way."

In her office, she informed me that she and her husband were leaving on vacation that evening, but she had twenty minutes or so to spend with me. I quickly summarized my situation.

"Well, it sounds like you're suffering from post-partum depression. We'll have to get you on some medication."

I squirmed in my seat.

"The main thing here is to keep you working. I'll send you across the hall to my husband. He'll take care of the prescription."

I crossed the hall to his office. Although I knew I was happiest when I was with Haley and I doubted I had post-partum depression, I didn't mind getting medication. Anything to make me feel better. I left the office with a prescription – and never returned.

That evening, I got drunk with my neighbor and Troy at the home of another neighbor. Her husband, having to work in the morning, stood on the landing and begged us to go away. We stayed until the early hours of the morning.

For the short time I knew her, I thought this woman was a great friend. She professed to be a Christian, but I didn't hold it against her. More important was that she listened to all my problems and commiserated with me. In support of a person's right to have whatever they desire, she gave me permission to let go, get drunk, be promiscuous, and have a good time. So I began an affair.

A week later Elmer called, 'Roland is on his way home. He's hitchhiking."

"No! Tell him not to come home."

"Well, he's already left! How come you don't want him home?"

"I just don't want him. You shouldn't have let him leave."

"He's a Christian now you know."

"Yeah, right!"

Roland arrived a week later. Knowing what I was going to tell him, I hid my kitchen knives. I was afraid he might get mad.

Not being allowed into the house, Roland stood on the porch staring out across the street. He wore a tan jacket in the cool spring air. His hands were in his pockets.

"I don't want you to stay here," I told him. He turned to look at me. His eyes were soft and moist. He looked away, said nothing for a moment, then quietly responded.

"I'm Christian now. I can't live like I was living anymore. I want you, Andrew and Haley to move with me out to Montana."

"I've got a job and I'm buying this house."

"I'll wait for you a little while, but whether you come with me or not, I'm going back."

Roland went to stay with Misty. Well, that would be that. Shirley, remarried, had recently left her husband and was homeless as well. Not only were she and Joy living there, but Cheri, her little girls and Junior too. Roland would be under the same roof with his ex-wife and *all* their kids and grandkids. A remarkable situation; they were one big happy family again. He wouldn't need my babies and me. Also, with the amount of drinking and smoking going on there, it wouldn't be long before he got started and that would be the end of his talk about sobriety and Christianity.

Roland not only stayed sober but he kept coming around. He told me that he couldn't hang out at his daughter's house because of the drinking. He said even the smell of alcohol now made him nauseous.

"When I started hitchhiking back from Montana, one of the first cars I got into gave me a beer. I tried to drink a little but it made me sick to my stomach. I threw it away." He wondered if the nausea was a gift from God to help him stay sober.

I started letting him watch our kids while I was at work. For two weeks he courted me. One night he picked me up from work and took me to our old restaurant - just like we used to. When he dropped me off and drove away, I felt as though I'd been on my very first date ever with him.

One day I called home from work. 'Roland, I forgot my medication this morning. I just don't feel like I can cope. Could you bring me my medicine?"

"Sure, I'll bring it right over."

But the medication didn't help. It was my life I hated. How could a drug change that?

After just two months, I left Bridgeway and went back to the family-run nursing home where I had felt more comfortable.

"Shirley is going back to live with her husband in Detroit and Joy wants to move in with me," Roland said one day.

I sat down. How could Joy "move in" with Roland? He didn't have a place. I knew I was asking for trouble again, but I really did love Joy. "Well, I guess you both could come here."

Joy and Roland moved back in with me on March 16. I explained to Steph that I had to do it for Joy's sake, but she didn't buy it. We argued and Steph moved out. Troy also went back to Cass Lake and stayed there.

I enrolled both Joy and Andrew in swimming lessons at the YMCA. While they were in class and Haley was in the nursery, I worked out in the weight room. I was there partly to get back into shape after having a baby, partly to build myself up in case of another attack by Shirley.

Joy reported that the family from the Red Lake rolls joints on their coffee table. Four- year-old Andrew joined in, "I stole some cigarettes from 7-11 for them. They wanted me to smoke one."

"And Mom," he confided, "Rose is Louis' girlfriend. They were in the garage and she told him to put his hand in her pants."

I felt sick. Rose and Louis were both nine-years-old.

Standing on our sidewalk with Andrew, I pointed from one house to another.

"I don't want you to play over there or that house either. They do bad things over there. You are not to go inside the house across from them, or play with the kids over at the red house. And stay out of that green house, too."

"But Mom," Andrew objected, "then there's nobody left to play with!"

Elmer and Marcia came to visit relatives in Cass Lake, then came down to the city to spend a couple nights with us. Having them physically in front of me was reassurance that they really existed. Seeing them was like nourishment.

"Why don't you move on out west?" Elmer cajoled.

"I'm buying this place. Where would we live out there?"

"There's plenty of places."

"Well, if we did go, Roland would have to find us a nice house first."

"Well, don't be so high on the horse. Sometimes you have to accept something not so good for awhile if you want to make a better life. You might have to accept living in a trailer or something."

Later, I spoke to Marcia. 'What happens if I quit my job, drop this house, go all the way out there and then Roland starts drinking again?"

"He really is a Christian now. I know; I saw him crying on his knees on my living room floor. I was there."

I still didn't think I loved Roland and didn't trust that he was really going to stay sober. And I most definitely didn't believe he was really a Christian. But I knew I wasn't happy being a single mom trying to buy a house I didn't like in a neighborhood I hated. I also knew that because there were no openings on the day shift, I'd have to be evening charge nurse for awhile. When Andrew started school in the fall, I'd never see him.

I also knew I was an angry, bitter woman and if I kept going that way - my heart filled to the brim with hate - I'd end up like some of the bitter, old women I had worked with in the nursing homes. I decided moving couldn't be worse than living here.

We sat around the dinner table with Mickey, Joy and my kids. We made a commitment to each other that we were going to stick together and move as a family. Grandma and Grandpa were having their 50th wedding anniversary and later that summer was my class reunion, so we decided to wait and move in late August, before school started. I'd have to prepare the house for sale and hire a realtor.

Roland loved powwows and never missed them if they were close, but I had never seen him dance. For two days we visited a powwow in the park. A circle dance began and because I had enjoyed it so much two years earlier, I begged Roland to dance with me. He finally gave in. Together, we took Andrew and Joy and joined the circle. By the time we were done, we were all laughing and smiling. It was our first and last time dancing together.

Joy's mother came back from Detroit just a couple weeks later. She wanted Joy back. Roland and I decided to fight it. I took $1000 of the money my dad had given me for new gutters and hired a lawyer. I knew it was wrong, but felt there was no choice. Joy needed a better life. But the lawyer didn't serve the papers to Shirley properly and the judge wanted them served again. That was going to cost more money. We couldn't afford it and Joy told us she wanted to be with her mom anyway. Around the end of April, Joy moved back to Misty's with Shirley.

Two weeks later, in mid-May, I took the rest of the money Dad had sent to prepare the house, took some vacation time from work, and we drove to Elmer's with Andrew and Haley to see if we could find a home. Mickey was still in school, so he stayed behind.

At Elmer and Marcia's, I was able to spend time with my babies without any pressure. I felt free and relaxed. Roland and I picked up the classifieds and began looking around for a place to live.

There was a house in the Moiese valley that was for sale. We drove out there to look at it. Coming over a hill, we beheld the beautiful valley for the first time. Parking in the driveway of the home, we should have known it was out of our financial reach. But being dreamers, we spoke to the renters living in it anyway. They were moving out in two weeks, they said, "But the owners don't want to rent it again, they want to sell it."

A preacher friend of Elmer's knew someone with a small trailer for sale. It was run down, but it was a place to live. We bought it for $1500, then left for home a few days later. Andrew thought it so neat how, although it was warm and sunny at Elmer's house, he could throw snowballs at the highway rest stop in Homestake pass.

Andrew and I were on my porch when Misty and Wesley pulled up in front of our house in late May.

"Where's my dad!" she yelled.

"He's not home.'

"Come here, Andrew!" Misty called.

Andrew stood up hesitantly, then looked at me. "You stay here," I told him. To Misty I said, "Your dad isn't here. Go on."

"Come on over here, Andrew!" Misty hollered again.

Andrew moved toward the steps, then looked at me.

"I said stay here." Then I turned toward Misty. 'Roland isn't here, Go home!" Wesley started the car. Misty stuck her head out the window of the moving car and bellowed curses at me until they were half way down the road.

When Roland got home, I complained, 'That's it, Roland! I can't stand it anymore! I'll give my notice at work and let's move week after next!"

Roland looked up at me, surprised. "I'm ready when you are."

We called Elmer and Marcia and told them we were coming, but the trailer we'd bought needed too much work to move into right away. Besides, we had no land to put it on. So, still having their classifieds, we called the owners of the house we'd seen in Moiese and asked if we could rent it. To our surprise, they agreed over the phone. I packed everything up. Roland and Matthew got a U-Haul and moved a load of our things while I disposed of everything unneeded in a rummage sale. Roland and Matthew then turned around and came right back so we could drive out together in our car.

During my moving sale, Dad called. As I spoke to him, someone came to the door and wanted to know if I would sell an item for just a dollar. I agreed. Dad was disgusted.

"They won't pay you a good price. I will buy all your things. Will $300 cover it?"

"That will be fine, Dad." And I gave him our address in Moiese to send the check.

When Roland returned with the truck, I realized that I had miscalculated the amount of money needed to rent the U-Haul. I had forgotten to double the mileage for the ride back. There was no way we were going to be able to cover it.

So Roland returned the truck to the lot at night and Mickey, he and I hurriedly got ready to leave early the next day. But once the wagon was packed, Andrew was no where to be found. We split up covering the neighborhood. I stopped next door.

"He isn't here," they told me, "but you better make sure he's not at the neighbor's next door. We just found out their 12-year-old kid's been molesting our little boy."

We fanned out, found Andrew playing with a friend, quickly got in the car, and left.

None too soon, I thought to myself. What a horrible neighborhood – I am so glad to be getting our kids out of it.

Roland drove our wagon and Mickey and I traded off driving the small hatchback I'd bought from Bobby. Along the way, we stopped frequently to let the radiator of the dying wagon cool.

Beth Ward

SAFETY LINE

Give me a line
To tie down my mind.

It's drifting away
It's wanting to stay.

© By PHONACELLE SHAPEL

Chapter twelve:
Freed: Living in the protected place

Moiese was a small hidden gorge within a bigger valley. A wide river bordered it on the north and hills all but encircled it, enabling it to remain more protected from the weather than some of the adjacent areas. The local Indians named it "the protected place." There were only two entrances into the valley; one way was a county road that came in under the train trestle, the other a back way through tribal land along the river. There were also only about eighty families in Moiese. Most were ranchers with extended family, living in clusters, who had lived there all their lives.

I'd never been inside the house we'd rented, so was surprised at how nice it was. Only about twenty years old, it was fully carpeted, had five bedrooms, two bathrooms, a dining room, porch with sliding glass doors, and a workroom downstairs. It was perfect for us. By far, the nicest place we had ever lived.

But it had taken all we had to move out and for the first few days we had no money to hook up the electricity. Without electricity, we weren't able to run the pump and have water. We realized now how vital this utility was when there is nothing at all to drink.

Now that we were living on another reservation, Marcia drove me over to get commodities. What a blessing. The variety of commodities here was more than I'd seen before. And most important, we were given several cans of ready to drink apple, orange, grape and pineapple juice. I also signed the children up for

WIC. I wanted all the help we could get. The next day Dad's check for $300 arrived and we got our electricity connected.

In the meantime, Roland, Elmer, and Elmer's son Kirk left for Canada. Elmer had been offered a job salmon fishing with a friend and they hoped that Roland and Kirk would be able to get on the boat, too. Marcia and Kirk's wife, Gayle, cried as the men left. I didn't.

Within a few days, Kirk and Roland were back. Unlike Elmer, they weren't able to get on a boat.

Marcia, apologizing for being such a bother in her loneliness for Elmer, came over almost daily. That was okay. I was lonely for friends and welcomed her visits. With the warm sun and quiet company, I found myself relaxing as I hadn't been able to do in years. My responsibilities were to the children now and I cuddled and played with them. In fact, my medication from the psychiatrist now went untouched. I had no need for it.

I applied for and got a job with a home health agency, traveling two or three days a week around the valley taking blood pressures and clipping toenails of patients in their homes. Roland picked up work where he could, plowing fields for our landlord or changing irrigation pipes. He also put an ad in the paper to do upholstery.

Mickey helped Roland where he could. Years later, he recalled the comfort and peace he felt with Roland, whether it be just sitting together on the porch in the mornings drinking coffee and smoking cigarettes, hiking to the top of a hill and watching the sun set, fishing an afternoon away at the river, or working with Roland on a car. He said that at the time, he felt we treated him like another adult and he appreciated the trust we had in him. He said he felt like he was equal to us, and he really liked that.

Not more than a month after we arrived, July 15, 1988, word came that Roland's brother Charlie had been found dead. He had been stabbed in the chest, aorta and heart while drinking in the Cass Lake city park the night before. He also had multiple bruises on his head, neck, upper extremities and torso. I watched Roland as he walked out onto our porch. With his back to us, his head hung down and his shoulders shook with sobs.

Marcia called the Coast Guard to let Elmer know his cousin had died. The next day, because Marcia didn't have a phone, Elmer called Roland.

"What's wrong? Is Marcia and Lyndi all right?" he asked anxiously, 'The Coast Guard came out to get me and said someone in the family had died."

"Oh, Elmer, it was Charlie Hunter."

"Oh," Elmer said, saddened by what had happened to Charlie but relieved it wasn't Marcia or Lyndi. "Well, I'll be home in a day or so."

"You don't have to come home. We just wanted to let you know."

"Well, it's too late now. They took me off the boat. I can't get back out there."

We couldn't afford to go back for the funeral, but a few days later, Elmer and Marcia came over to help us hold our own funeral and dinner for Charlie. Although Roland felt some guilt for having pulled Elmer off his boat, he felt comfort having his cousin next to him.

In a farming area like Moiese, it's not easy to just drop in on people for coffee. Farmers and ranchers are busy. Sure, they'll stop and chat with people for a little while if they've got some time. They're not rude. But they are busy. What with the whole family working crops and cattle and many women weeding their vegetable gardens and baking home-made bread, they certainly didn't have time for entertaining strangers from out-of-state.

I still didn't want anything to do with Christianity, but starved for company and because the Dovetail's were the only people I knew, I went along with Roland when he attended their prayer meetings or revivals. Sitting on someone's living room floor one evening, I watched as the roomful of people burst into what they called "speaking in tongues." With their eyes closed and heads lifted, they rambled incoherent syllables. Beside me, one woman, seemingly lost more in thought than prayer, recited her syllables in lazy fashion while staring at her fingers.

Another evening at a friend's we were shown the film "Thief in the Night." It was a pretty dumb, poorly made movie…but at the same time, I identified with the heroine. It was a seventy's movie – and she was a blond, middle class girl who, like me, believed that she was already a "good person" with no need for Christianity. Unfortunately, the movie went on to show how wrong she was and how she suffered for it.

"I guess it can't hurt to be a Christian," I decided, after viewing the movie. After all, "If it's not true, it won't matter that I called myself a Christian. But if it is true, I'll be protected."

That fall, we enrolled Andrew in kindergarten at the public school and Mickey in the local Indian school. If Mickey's school had had a kindergarten, I would have enrolled Andrew there, too. I'd heard a rumor the public school was racist. But the Indian school didn't have elementary grades, and the other was our only option if we wanted bus service.

Well, bus service in the morning anyway. Being a rural school, there was no money in the budget for a noon kindergarten bus. Fortunately, there were five other families with kindergartners in Moiese that year - a real fluke in this small valley. The six families, including us, got together and organized a noon carpool. This was fortunate not just in that it relieved the daily pressure of driving, but it also allowed Roland and me to get to know several families. They were very nice, not racist at all.

Living in Moiese was fascinating. Huge irrigation pipes crossed the fields and sprayed water in every direction, creating misty splendor and enchanting rainbows. Ranchers hired people to move those lines twice a day all summer. If a pipe mover was lucky, his line was on wheels and could be moved by simply starting a motor. Other pipelines were flat on the ground though, and had to be taken apart and moved section by section. This was heavy, exhausting work.

Sheep and cattle were also all over the place. We learned quickly that barbed wire fence and cattle grates aren't perfect answers to keeping livestock penned. In fact, there didn't seem to be any such thing as an impenetrable fence.

Looking out the window one morning before school, I saw the road was crowded with a couple hundred cattle all moving east. At first I thought it was the largest group of escapees I'd seen yet, but then I saw several people herding them on horses. It was a beautiful sight. I had no idea people still herded cattle.

"Look, Mom," said Andrew. "It's Billy on that horse!"

Looking closer, I could see he was right. Billy, a tribal member, was one of Andrew's classmates and only six-years-old! How could he be riding a horse let alone herding cattle! But watching him, it was easy to see he knew just what he was doing.

"Wow, he must have got up pretty early to be working like this before catching the bus for school."

"Kyle and his sister work, too," Andrew told me, 'They change irrigation pipe before school. Sometimes Kyle comes to school smelling like cow poop."

I was amazed. Kyle, a non-Indian, was also Andrew's classmate. Billy and Kyle were both really nice kids, happy and full of energy. Kyle's mom said he loved helping out on the dairy farm so much that he hated to waste time sitting in front of the TV. He didn't even know who the cartoon character "He-Man" was. That was hard to digest. A kid who would rather work than watch TV? I was so used to fighting teenagers over such minor jobs as dishes and taking out the garbage, it was hard to believe kindergartners could be so happy with these heavy jobs. But this was something I began noticing in kids of all ages all over Moiese, from the dairy family to the ranching family to the potato growers. The families all seemed to work hard and happily together, even the teenagers.

Mickey began bringing home a friend from the tribally-run school. They had both joined the high school football team that fall and we had been enjoying going to the games and watching them. The friend, quiet and polite, was another tribal member that lived in Moiese. He was also an example of a teenager who seemed to enjoy and help his family. What was it that made the difference here?

Whatever it was, it wasn't the Indian school. I was bothered by the way the students were allowed to run around, constantly disrupting. There didn't seem to be much organization. I also spoke to the English teacher about the lack of homework.

"Mickey is terrible with spelling and punctuation. How come you aren't correcting him?"

The teacher, a kind and gentle man, was apologetic. He said he was mainly concerned with getting the kids to write creatively. He feared constant correction would intimidate them.

"Are prospective employers going to be concerned about intimidating them?" I asked.

As the weather got colder and snow began to cover the fields and trees, I became homesick for holidays with my family. We made plans to take time off from work and go home at Christmas. I promised my family I'd bring a real 'Western Christmas Tree" back with us for my dad's living room. That wasn't a hard thing to promise. Beautiful trees, lush and full, could be bought for only $5 in our area. We purchased two and decorated our house with one and laid the other in the snow to await our trip.

As it turned out, Roland decided our car wasn't good enough to make the trip. But Elmer and Marcia didn't hesitate a moment in offering us their van. With that and my family paying for our motel, we were on our way. Unfortunately, in our rush to get on the road, we left the Christmas tree behind.

Roland and I decided before we arrived that except for Christmas day, which he wanted to spend at my dad's, we wouldn't feel pressured to spend time with each other's family. I stayed with my family; he went to the south side to visit his. Mickey was free to go with either one of us. We came back together in the evening at the motel. Joy spent a few nights with us in the motel. Roland's granddaughters, Carrie and her little sister Angela, also spent a night, but other than that, it was a relief for me not to have to see anyone else. I didn't want to.

On Christmas Eve, there was no tree in my dad's living room. Although we'd told my family when we arrived that we had forgotten the tree, none of us made an effort to go to a tree lot and get one. I guess none of us knew who was supposed to do it so no one did. At any rate, it was Christmas Eve, already dark outside, and the tree lots were probably all closed by now.

So Bobby took the initiative. With a couple of others, he got in his car and went to a nearby tree lot. The lot, of course, was closed and all the trees were locked behind an eight-foot chain link fence. So he climbed the fence and grabbed a likely tree, as likely as any in the dark. He hoisted the tree to his comrades, but before leaving the enclave, he taped a twenty-dollar bill to a window.

Proud of himself, he brought his tree home. And a Charlie Brown tree it was. After he got it into the light, not only could we see the scant and stripped branches, but also the red tag, which begged someone to take the tree for only $5.

It was a special tree for a special Christmas; After having missed my high school reunion, Grandma and Grandpa's anniversary, and the funeral for three of my cousin's children killed in a fire, I was so glad to be back home with family.

But our separate family visits, as typical, brought separate results. After hearing about our vehicle troubles one evening, Dad offered to buy us a new car.

"Are you serious?" I excitedly asked.

"Go home, find the car you want, and let me know how much it will be."

However, on another evening, Roland returned from the south side with a different kind of acquisition.

"Junior wants to go back with us."

Immediately I panicked. 'What if he drinks? What if he doesn't listen? What if..."

"You always have to worry about what might happen! Quit second guessing and give him a chance."

I didn't want Junior to come. It wasn't that I didn't care about Junior. I did care about him. I was just afraid and didn't want to be hurt by Roland's older kids anymore. Junior hadn't done anything to me yet as his older sisters had, but I was afraid he would. Roland was right. I wasn't giving him a chance.

Taking Junior back to Montana, we laid out rules for him and in fairness, applied the new rules to Mickey as well. We then enrolled Junior at the tribal school with Mickey and were promptly sickened by how the tribal school transferred his credits. He had taken basic math two years in a row at South High School. The first year, he had failed. The second year, he had gotten a "D" in the very same math class. But the tribal school now went ahead and accepted those two grades as fulfillment of their two-year math requirement.

It also bothered us that the school seemed to be playing an attendance game with the government; giving kids reward incentives to show up to school during the week that head counts were made for funding.

Then Mickey, who up to this point had been so good, began to get in trouble. He was picked up twice drinking with Elmer's sixteen-year-old daughter, Lyndi. Two months later, he ran away with the hatchback we'd given him a couple weeks earlier. We looked for him all over the valley and even put an ad in the paper with his picture.

I was sick for him. I imagined that if he were suddenly to come walking into the driveway, I wouldn't know whether to hit him or hug him.

Two weeks later, I called my old neighbor back in Minnesota and asked if she'd seen him. She had. Mickey and his girlfriend were staying with Matthew at our old house. We called the police and they were picked up as runaways. The tribe flew Mickey's girlfriend home.

My sister, Chris, without hesitation, took Mickey to stay with her at my dad's house. Looking back, I could see how time and again through the years, she'd been there to help. I appreciated how quietly she'd always stood behind me, always there to lend a hand when we needed it.

Chris looked into getting financial help from the state for Mickey, but when told that the Indian Child Welfare Act (ICWA) requires that the tribe first give its okay, she decided to support him on her own.

Later, Mickey told us, "I figured I was causing problems between you and Roland. I wanted to leave before things really fell apart, before I was asked to leave." I tried to tell him that wouldn't have ever happened, but Roland, feeling betrayed by Mickey and angry that he had taken off with the car, felt it best that Mickey stay where he was.

Many years later, Mickey admitted that his reason for leaving was the new rules and apparent sudden lack of trust. His sense of being an equal was gone - and it pained him.

I was glad Mickey was safe with my sister, but grieved over having lost him. Elmer told me to get over it and take care of my family in Moiese. It took me about three months to get over it. I involved myself with Andrew, Haley and my gardening.

Unfortunately, my feelings for Mickey kept me from opening my heart to Junior. Junior was a good kid. He stayed out of trouble, did what Roland told him to do and was showing signs of being a great artist, but I wasn't going to involve my heart anymore. It wasn't Junior's fault; I just couldn't. My heart was starting to callous.

That spring I took Andrew, Haley and Junior on a week long retreat sponsored by the tribe. I did it for Junior's sake. I wanted him to be able to express his emotions as well as have some insight into what was happening in the family. I thought a week of free counseling would be good for him.

The cabins on the lake were both beautiful and comfortable. The meals were delicious. The actual counseling, however, was feeble. Monica Reneau, who counseled the young children, including Andrew, was quite pleased with herself for having taught them all to say, "I am special." The exercise, to me, seemed shallow and presumptuous. I knew Andrew, outgoing, assertive and very popular in class, had no trouble feeling good about himself. I mentioned that to her, but she explained all Indian children have trouble with self-esteem. Although I knew that was an insulting and racist statement, I didn't argue with her.

The male counselor was just as weak. His brand of counseling was simple feel - good games and nothing like the hard-hitting stuff I was used to from my experiences and wanting for Junior. In addition, the counselor had little insight into people. After Junior had borrowed my car and was gone for longer than he was supposed to be, the counselor explained to Junior that the reason I had been blown up about it was because I was worried about Junior. The counselor was wrong. I was worried about the car. But not wanting to be honest and hurt Junior's feelings, I went along with it. Again, it wasn't Junior's fault. He was okay. It was me that was messed up.

The remark from the counselor that made me the angriest, however, came at the very end of the week as the last group session finished and people were giving each other final hugs. The counselor put his arm around me.

"You have an Indian heart," he said warmly.

"What?" I responded, surprised. "What do you mean?"

'Well," he explained, "I mean you have a heart that is open and loving, like an Indian heart."

He had obviously overlooked the fact that I hadn't been totally open or loving to Junior. But there was something else about his statement that bothered me. Unable to move on, unsure of how to respond, I stood for a moment trying to figure out why I felt so deeply offended. Finally I stuttered, "What's wrong with a white person's heart?"

He was the one looking stunned now, so I went on, trying to explain feelings I wasn't sure how to explain… "What's wrong with my heart being white? What's wrong with having a heart like my parents?" I paused, then said, "My family is open and loving, too."

The guy gave me a sickly sweet smile and tried to hug me, "Oh, I didn't say that as an insult, you're taking it all the wrong way…"

"Take it the wrong way? Wait a minute, I'm a white person! If I have an open and loving heart why would it come from some other race? Doesn't the fact that I have an open and loving heart mean that white hearts are good, too?"

The man looked perplexed and walked away.

Frustrated, I had no idea if I'd gotten across what I was trying to say. Why is there always an assumption that one heritage is somehow better than others? What an insult to any other ancestor a person might have! No race has a cornerstone on being good; no race has a cornerstone on being evil. Hadn't I seen cold selfishness in many Indian hearts? You're darn right I had - selfishness just as deep and hateful as any other heritage. Where do people get these silly ideas about one heritage being better than another?

Roland came only for the final celebratory meal. At one point, they passed burning sweet grass around in a circle, waving the smoke onto themselves in prayer. Roland refused to wave the smoke and passed the grass on to the next person. Later he explained to me that he isn't doing traditional Indian spiritual rituals anymore. He didn't like the spirits that went along with them. I wished he'd told me that before I took the sweet grass.

Shirley was moving back to Detroit that summer, so Joy again asked if she could move to be with us. I still loved Joy so I agreed and my brothers and sisters brought her out when they came to visit over the Fourth of July. It took a few weeks for her to calm down, but for a short time we worked well as a family again.

Our landlord, who wanted to sell the house we were renting, asked the Housing and Urban Development program (HUD) to look at it and consider purchasing it. I loved the house and was distressed at the thought of it being sold to someone else.

"If you buy it, can we apply to live in it?" I asked the HUD inspector.

"No. Only tribal members will be allowed to apply for it," the man answered.

"Well, my husband is tribal. We're low income too.'

"No, only tribal members from this reservation can apply."

After they left, I called the regional HUD office and asked if it was true that HUD programs could discriminate like that.

"Yes. Reservation programs are run by the tribe and their members get preference," I was told.

"Wait a minute. Isn't HUD a federal program supported by tax-paying citizens? We've paid taxes."

"This is how the program was set up."

Unable to believe it, I called Washington DC. This particular house was no longer the issue. What disturbed me was that government officials were telling me that this racism was both legal and acceptable.

"Anywhere else," I told the woman on the phone, "HUD is open to everyone that's low income, no matter their color. This reservation is mostly white. Where do all the low-income non-members go for HUD if they can't use the program here?"

"I'm sorry. The program has been set up for the benefit of the local tribe. Your husband would have to return to his own reservation if he wanted to obtain the benefit."

She didn't say what white people who grew up within reservation boundaries were supposed to do.

"What are you saying, that tribal members aren't free to move around the country? They're supposed to 'stay put' inside the boundaries made for them?"

I hung up, unable to believe discrimination was so 'matter-of-factly' condoned. Using federal funds to boot.

In August, I began working at a local hospital. When I was interviewed for the job, the Director of Nurses told the Supervisor that although I had only been a nurse since 1987, was only a two-year nurse, and had only worked in nursing homes, she thought I would be a good investment because I was fresh and could be trained the way they wanted.

I began working there three days a week, Fridays, Saturdays and Sundays, for 12-hour shifts, and spent the nights in an upstairs bedroom rather than go home.

While I was gone, our Pastor told Roland about a children's bible camp that Andrew could attend. Later, when they had trouble finding a camp nurse for it, they asked if I would be willing to help. They told me I could bring Haley with.

That was neat. I could bring my kids to camp and get to stay with them. However, when we arrived at the camp, we learned that it was a segregated camp. This particular camp was only for Indian kids. The kids were all nice; that wasn't the problem. I was offended because our family wasn't told there were several camp dates we could have chosen from. We were told only of this camp. Why? Why were we given only one choice? And why did they think all people of Indian heritage need to be segregated? Why can't everyone camp together? Did our pastor see our family as "Indian" first, rather than a Christian family no different from everyone else in his church?

The camp itself wasn't even fun. I had expected some fellowship among the adults – in fact, I was starving for it - but there was none. I was left totally alone in the nursing trailer. Why? Even Andrew was uncomfortable. He decided he didn't want to stay in the tent with the other boys. He wanted to sleep in the trailer with Haley and me. My pastor objected.

"Andrew, if you sleep there, I can't have you participating in the camp activities."

Andrew chose to stay in my trailer anyway. I was fine with that. I was feeling a strong need to draw my kids close to me - and away from the staff.

After a time, a young staff woman befriended me and gave me some answers. She agreed that the staff seemed cold, but she said they were being cold to her, as well.

"And most of them are from my home church!" she added, "We came here the day before camp started. We were told during our first staff meeting that Indian people are different and that we have to be careful when ministering to them. The counselors told us not to hug the kids because Indians think white people are dirty and don't like being touched by them."

I shook my head. "Talk about offensive. Where do people come up with this stuff?

After putting Andrew and Haley to bed that night, I prayed;

"Dear God, I feel awful. The staff hasn't been open and sociable. I feel very alone and pretty much doubting everything. Dear God, please come into my heart and make it strong. Please strengthen the hearts of my children. Please allow the Holy Spirit to work in everyone tomorrow. Including me."

My kids asleep, I wandered out to the deserted camp circle and sat on a log. A lone man appeared and sat down next to me. It was the evangelist, the man who had been invited to speak at the camp. I told him how badly I felt at the camp, and how surprised I was by the lack of fellowship and warmth.

"I've noticed it, too," he said. "There's something real ugly at work here."

We spoke together for awhile and prayed. I told him about my growing doubt and questioned whether I was even a Christian. To encourage me, he read the message of Salvation and God's promises for those who believe, including Romans 10:9. He then asked me to tell him whether I honestly believed or not.

"Yes," I responded, "I do believe Jesus is Lord and that God raised him from the dead."

"Then, yes," he assured me, "you are a Christian."

Feeling comforted, I went to bed. But the camp itself couldn't end soon enough for me. There was no improvement during my stay, and we never returned.

Roland and I began talking to an elderly couple about buying their forty acres only a mile or so from where we were presently living. The husband told us that we could easily make our monthly payments by renting out land to neighbors.

In the middle of August, the manager of the Credit Union called my Nursing Supervisor to see how my job was going in order to approve our loan request. The supervisor told her that I was doing quite well, and would be working there awhile. My loan was approved on the basis of her remarks.

In the meantime, Shirley was asking us to send Joy back to her again.

Dear Chris;

...our neighbors also wanted to buy this piece of land when they heard it was for sale. But we got there first. I hope they don't hate us. We can't move for awhile though. Roland has to put the trailers on blocks and remodel.

Guess what? Joy and her mom have changed their minds again. Surprised? We're not. But we haven't decided exactly what to do about it yet. What's Shirley going to do if we ignore her? What's Joy going to do? Joy just wants to protect her mom I think. Well, more on that boring soap opera some other day.

You know what? I clear at least $1600 a month working here three days a week.

Wow!

Back at the hospital, Dr. Brown treated a patient very badly. The woman had brought her little girl into the ER because she thought she might have been sexually abused. For some reason, Dr. Brown lashed out at the mother. In the hall outside, the mother cried in my arms and told me how she herself had been abused as a four-year-old. I couldn't understand or condone the doctor's behavior, but I also knew I'd get in trouble if I told the woman she was right to be upset with him, so I said nothing while she cried. The next afternoon,

Dying in Indian Country

I went to Dr. Brown's office and politely asked him why he had done what he did. I sat in his office and listened as he told me that Indian people "are not as intelligent as you and I" and need to be treated sternly at times. He obviously didn't realize I was married to a tribal member. I didn't know how to respond – was I hearing what I thought I was hearing? So I sat there and again said nothing.

A few days later, I brought my family to a hospital function, and co-workers, including the doctor, met them for the first time.

Meanwhile, on the nursing floor, I offended some nurses with some of my own comments. I hadn't meant to be critical. At times, I was just kind of startled seeing things done contrary to the way I'd been taught.

At any rate, I began to experience more and more stress from some of the nurses. I'd never been a slow learner, but learning so many new things took time. In addition to being criticized over my skills, I was being chastised for inconsequential things, such as the way I sign my name. Another time, as I was reading the Bible on a Sunday morning during my off hours, a nurse told me that I should be reading a medical text instead.

Things were beginning to feel uncomfortable; so I tried even harder to do everything right. There was a car accident and a woman and baby were killed. All the nurses left the floor and went to the ER. I was going to go too, when a staff nurse turned and said, "No, you aren't to go down to the ER anymore."

This was contrary to our supervisor's previous instructions, so I was confused. In addition, I'd never been in charge of the medical floor on my own before. Unable to argue, I remained on the floor, frustrated.

It was a particularly bad accident and there was a lot of commotion and activity. Nurses were coming and going for supplies. I was eventually allowed downstairs to feel the back of the baby's head, which was crushed. It was an emotional evening for everyone. A five-year-old girl had survived, unscathed. She was sitting on a gurney outside the ER, crying for her mother and brother.

The baby was brought up to my floor and placed in a patient room for the relatives to mourn, as was common with the tribe on this reservation. We put a newborn hat on him. He was small, his face so sweet. Crying for him, and probably for my children back home, I picked up the baby and held him.

I was already in bed that night when another nurse knocked on my door.

"Did you give out the 9 p.m. medications?" she asked.

I sat straight up in bed; my face burned. The medications for the five or six patients weren't mine to give when the shift began, but because I ended up being the only nurse on the medical floor, it had become my responsibility.

"No," I finally answered, "I forgot all about it."

The nurse closed the door and left. I sank back into my bed with lead in my stomach. I knew they had real reason to fire me now.

Beth Ward

there
isn't
much
use
for
a
woman
who
cries

sometimes
I
wonder
why
it's
me
I
despise

© By PHONACELLE SHAPEL

Chapter thirteen:
Are we ever really protected?

Just before Labor Day weekend, about three weeks after the Supervisor had given a good report about me to the loan officer, the tension was thick. I knew I was probably going to be let go. That week I called a lawyer and explained what was happening. I had an agreement with the hospital and I knew they were about to break it. The lawyer listened, then said he'd get back to me. A little later he called back to say he couldn't take the case because his firm represents the hospital. I gave up.

After the Labor Day shift ended at 11 p.m., the Director, not normally at work at that hour, walked quickly past and told me to come to her room. There, she asked me to sign a resignation. She said they would fire me if I didn't resign and I would never get another nursing job.

After it was all done, I left the hospital in tears. The truth in my heart was that I had really been trying as hard as I could. I had put everything I had into it. Usually, when I have done things wrong in my life, I know exactly what I had done to blow it. But this time I didn't. I had no idea what I had done to make things turn out so bad.

Although I'd lost the job, the land deal was ready to close. We didn't tell them I was no longer working and went ahead with it. We hoped I'd find another job and everything would be okay.

So we took out a loan for about $20,000 from the Credit Union to make the initial payment and costs, and signed an agreement to pay the balance through monthly installments directly to the owner.

We moved our $1500 trailer, along with a second one we'd bought with money from the loan, onto the land and sandwiched the small house between them. Not having the money to continue renting while we waited for Roland to remodel, we moved in right away. What we bought that September was a very, very tiny house and forty acres... with a very dry, useless well. But according to Roland, every tribal member is entitled to a free well and he hadn't had his yet. So he went to the local tribal health department. To his surprise, they turned him down because he wasn't a member of the local tribe. Nevertheless, he knew he was right and went over their heads to the Bureau of Indian Affairs office in Portland. He must have known what he was talking about, because they agreed to have a new well dug for him. The BIA put us on a waiting list for the well, so until it was dug we hauled water from the homes of friends.

Our neighbors to the north agreed to continue renting the land at the rate they told us they were renting it from the old owner, $1200 a year. In addition they agreed to take care of the field's electric and water bills.

We struggled all fall to make ends meet. Pregnant again, I went to work at a nursing home 60 miles away, working 32 hours between Saturday afternoon and Monday morning every week. The nursing home put me up at a nearby motel for the few hours I had to sleep. Restocking the supplies at night, I fought off the urge to take things home with me. I was a Christian now. I wasn't going to act the way I used to at the Crisis Nursery.

At home, Junior got angry with me and went to his dad to complain. I expected Roland to turn on me as usual, but to my surprise, he stood up for me. Neither Junior nor I knew what to say.

In November, Junior decided to go back home so we gave him a bus ticket for his birthday. Ten-year-old Joy became upset. If Junior could go back, she wanted to go, too. But while we knew we couldn't help Junior much longer, we still hoped Joy was young enough to work with. We hoped that if we could keep her away from the drugs and violence of the city, she'd have a different life than a lot of her relatives, so we refused to let her go. We even approached tribal lawyers to see if we could get legal custody.

However, stress was building within me. I didn't get along with my nursing director and the job didn't pay enough to cover our expenses. Faced with a mounting pile of bills and not wanting to lose our 40 acres, I re-applied for my Minnesota nursing license and planned to go back there to work.

I didn't want to leave my children; I felt I had to. I counseled myself that many women in Mexico have to leave their children and work as maids in order to make ends meet. It didn't even occur to me to expect Roland to support us fully.

To get my license renewed, I first had to complete some continuing education credits. As I came closer to finishing them, the angst in my heart about leaving my children increased. I made up for it by sewing soft, black edging onto the wrists of Haley's grey cloth dress coat, painting little plaques for their walls, and reading children's stories aloud into Andrew's tape recorder so he could hear my voice while I was gone. I promised myself that once this baby I was carrying was born, I would spend the summer sitting on a blanket spread under a tree on our front yard, doing nothing but enjoy my three beautiful children.

Our pastor's wife came to me after church, "Haley was crying in the nursery. She said you were going to leave her." I didn't think Haley even knew. But thinking I had to go and not knowing how to talk to her, I ignored what the Pastor's wife said and pretended it didn't happen.

Because Joy was still fighting to go back to her mother, we decided to let her. She could ride back with me. We knew that in the big city it would be only a matter of time before Joy also became involved with drugs, alcohol and sex, but we were told that unless we had proof of what was going on in her mother's home, there was no way the courts would listen and give us custody of her. The only thing we could do was pray that she wouldn't get killed.

A few days before we were to leave, Cheri phoned Roland, "I want to clean up and have a new life. Can I come out on the bus this week?"

Well, with Cheri here, it's best that I go, I thought. Roland can help her better if I'm not here.

The day before I left in January, Cheri arrived by bus with her daughters Angela, 3-years-old, and Carrie, age 5. Angela now had shoulder length black hair and plump Carrie, with dimples when she smiled, had wavy, long, auburn hair. But they were a mess. Angela had thrown up on herself during the bus ride. Her mother had fed them nothing but candy and chips for the last twenty-four hours. And Carrie had open sores on her hands, oozing with green pus. I recognized the mess, (having seen many of Roland's relatives struggle with it) as eczema that had been neglected. I took her right away and placed her hands into a bowl of betadine. I didn't want her to touch the toys (which Haley still tended to put in her mouth).

Carrie cried and asked her mother if she really had to do this.

"You don't have to do that. I got medicine for you."

"You can't put a topical medicine on these hands until you've cleaned them first," I argued. Roland jumped in, "Put your hands in the bowl, my girl."

Before I left, I took many pictures of my babies. I had a foreboding feeling that I'd never see them again. Joy, happy to go home to her mother, jumped in the car. On the way, wanting to prevent the inevitable, I explained to Joy that there would be boys who would want to use her but who would not love her. I asked her to promise me that she would not sleep with anyone until she got married. Only 11-years-old, she wouldn't promise.

Staying at my dad's house, I worked seven days a week as a night shift nurse for a temporary service. I got paid up to $20 an hour going to nursing homes and trans-care centers all over the city. I was in charge of hundreds of patients along with staff. Although five months pregnant, I worked every night of the week, sometimes even additional shifts back to back and double, taking on different nursing homes, unfamiliar staff and patients at the drop of a hat. Because that responsibility was something I really did not want to do - but forced myself to do - it haunted me. Although I didn't show it, I was terrified of the job. It's too easy to make mistakes. On top of that, I was suffering from the separation from my children. I thought of them constantly. I drove my siblings crazy continually talking about Andrew and Haley. Every other day I was either calling them or writing them and dropping quarters or candies into envelopes for them. Every week I wired Roland most of my money.

One night, the agency didn't have a placement for me. By midnight, everyone else in my dad's house was asleep. Not wanting to mess up my sleep schedule, I looked for things in the quiet house to do to stay awake. Finding a Bible study that our pastor had sent me, I settled down on the couch to go through it. I can't remember which verses he had sent, other than that they had something to do with Peter or one of the books of Peter. But sitting there, alone without distraction, the words finally hit me. For the first time, I truly got it.

On Valentine's Day I sent packages to the kids as well as a wooden, barn shaped mailbox I had made for the house with the help of Bobby. Roland, to my surprise, sent me a bouquet of flowers. Although I knew it was probably purchased with money I'd worked for, I was still touched. He had never made that kind of effort before.

Around noon a few days later I called home. After several rings, Haley answered the phone. "Hi baby, how you doing? Where's Daddy?"
"He went to the store."
"Where's Cheri?"
"She's sleeping."
"Who's with you?"
"Angela. We're hungry. Can we have something to eat?"
"Where's Andrew and Carrie?"
"With Daddy."
Panicking, I told her, "Run to Cheri's room and ask her to come to the phone."
"She won't wake up. I'm hungry."
I hung up and called back a couple times, hoping to wake Cheri with the ringing, but the girls always answered. Angry and helpless, I called back several times until Roland finally answered. Then I let him have it. Why was I working so hard to support that house with Cheri and her girls eating there and enjoying my money, yet she couldn't even drag herself out of bed long enough to feed my baby?

We planned for me to return to Moiese for Easter. As the holiday drew near, I bought material for a pretty Easter dress and pink spring coat for Haley and spent all night sewing it. I also shopped for Easter baskets and other gifts for both children. In addition, I sent extra money for Cheri and asked Roland to find her a place to live. I didn't want her to be there when I got home.

Roland helped her move into a trailer park 30 miles north of Moiese.

At Easter time, I packed the car with gifts for Haley and Andrew. Roland called to let me know Junior had contacted him asking if he could ride back with me and live with Cheri.

"All right, maybe he can help me drive."

I had to pick him up at Shirley's house. I stood by my car while he packed his things into the back. While he was packing, Misty drove up and sent a tiny little boy across the lawn to say good-bye to his uncle. This was the first time I had seen Ross. I turned and looked the other way while Junior hugged him. I didn't want to have anything to do with Misty's kid. I wanted my own. Junior and I drove straight through to Moiese, speeding most of the way.

Easter Sunday, Junior, Cheri and the girls came for dinner. Angela was mischievous and full of energy. Carrie was quieter but kept up with Andrew. After dinner the adults sat in the yard while the children played. Cheri, seeing Angela coming from around the house, hid behind Roland's pick-up truck. Angela, not seeing her mother, panicked and began to cry. Cheri, enjoying the game, smiled big and giggled from her hiding spot. Unable to bear the cruel joke made on a little girl whose mother was prone to leaving her, I pointed Angela toward her mom.

A few days later, as Roland and I were leaving Cheri's trailer after a brief visit, Haley wanted to stay and spend the night.

"No, you're too young to spend the night here," I told her.

"Her and Andrew have already been spending the night here," Cheri retorted.

"Well, I think she's too young."

Roland glanced at me, disgusted, but I was just as disgusted with him for having let them stay there. I pulled a protesting Haley into the car and we left.

Later, Andrew told me about staying the night at Cheri's trailer.

"She got up and left at night. I heard the door close and I woke up. She didn't come back for a long time." In fact, much later her neighbors told us that sometimes she'd be gone days at a time and they'd have to take the girls in and feed them.

My Easter break was over and I returned to work out-of-state, this time taking two-year-old Haley with me for the two-day drive. We stayed with my cousin Marion, to whom I paid $100 a week for room, board and baby-sitting. Marion watched Haley all night while I worked and most of the day while I slept.

Staying with Marion and her husband was fun. If I woke up early enough, Marion and I went shopping or to rummage sales. We also played cards with Marion's brother most nights before I went to work. Not only did they teach me Canasta, but they showed me how to cheat at it. While they couldn't fool each other, they got a kick out of how easy it was to trick me. I hadn't had that much fun in a long time.

I had hoped to have enough money to help Roland open an upholstery shop in Ronan. I reminded myself again of the dream to rest with my children on a blanket in our shady lawn while Roland supported us.

However, for some reason no matter how hard I worked, we still never had enough. So I went back to Dad and asked for about $2000 more. I waited patiently while he chewed me out, knowing that when he was finished, he would give me the money.

At the very end of May, 1990, I had only a couple of weeks left before my baby was due, so I returned to Moiese. Roland's hunting partner, Don Burgess offered us the use of his house until the BIA could dig a well at ours. Roland was reluctant at first, but I begged him. "Please, I don't want to have a baby in a house without water."

Two days later, we moved our essentials to the house located only a quarter mile from Elmer. I packed boxes and Roland drove them over. After packing a particularly big box with blankets and clothing, I asked for his help moving it.

Sitting in the driver's seat of the pick-up, he snapped, "Move it yourself," and then drove off.

That night as I put away dishes in the new house, my stomach cramped so badly I had to stop working for a moment. The pain passed and I started working again, but a few minutes later, the cramp returned. My due date was still a week away, so it took awhile for me to realize I was in labor.

Hard labor began around noon the next day. Our little girl was born just before 4 pm. In truth, I wasn't ready for her at all, physically or emotionally. As I lay in bed with my tiny girl, I couldn't help asking aloud, "Where did you come from? What's your name?" I had never slowed down enough through the pregnancy to take time to emotionally or physically prepare for her. Roland and I had never even talked about a name. I hadn't even packed a bag of clothes for her to wear home.

I felt like such a terrible mother. She was a beautiful baby. She deserved so much better.

In addition, Roland and I weren't getting along. His upholstery shop still wasn't doing well enough to support us. Furthermore, we'd spent the better part of six months separated, making our own decisions. We weren't used to having to work together as a team.

On his way to pick us up and take us home, Roland decided on the name Heidi. He also dug some of Haley's old clothes out of a bag and brought them for Heidi to wear home. The nurse insisted on carrying Heidi to the car. I felt so ashamed; the clothes she wore smelled of dust. I really was a bad mother. I had meant to wash and hang the clothes in the sun before she was born, but with working as I was, then moving to a different house, then her coming early - there just wasn't time.

Once home, Elmer came almost nightly to hold her. This was the only child of mine that Elmer did this for. Maybe he knew how much she needed him. She and I wouldn't end up spending the summer together on the lawn.

Bad enough that I wasn't mothering my own children as I should have, I also felt guilty about not paying attention to Cheri. What did I expect from her? She needed someone straight and responsible to take her by the hand. I was wrong for continually pushing her away and not trying to help. So I tried to spend more time with her and took her and the children to the beach one afternoon for a picnic. We were pleasant with each other but the conversation, mostly about other people, was strained and uncomfortable. Cheri had heard from family that Dale and Tammy had lost their fifth baby to SIDS (Sudden Infant Death Syndrome). Tammy had awakened one morning to find the baby dead on the couch. After that, Dale started drinking again; everything fell apart for them and they broke up.

Cheri also talked about wanting to have two more babies; boys this time. Oh, Cheri, I thought to myself, please don't do that.

We made plans to go on a picnic with Cheri and the girls for the fourth of July. When the day came and we stopped at her trailer to pick them up, Cheri motioned her dad inside. A few minutes later he came out with the two girls and put them in the car.

"She's going to the Powwow with her friends instead."

"What? So we're supposed to take care of her girls?" I asked, bewildered.

"What did you want me to do? She's probably going drinking."

We took the girls to Glacier National Park, but I resented it so much I couldn't relax.

Returning to Cheri's trailer that evening, we found no one at home. Roland had no choice but to keep the girls over night. In the morning, not wanting to be forced to baby-sit for a few days, I insisted he bring them home. Cheri was still gone when he got to the trailer, but a man answered the door. Knowing I didn't want the girls to come back to our house, Roland left them with the man.

"They cried to come back with me," he barked when he got home. "How do you think I felt leaving them with some strange guy?"

Roland was right. It was terrible to leave them there. I should have told him to go back and get them. But I couldn't. The anger within me from being constantly 'used' was close to erupting. I just couldn't take it anymore.

"If we keep taking them every time she feels like drinking, she'll just keep doing it."

When Heidi was six-weeks old, I decided to take her and Andrew back with me to work. I was still very tired but we needed money and all Roland and I did was fight anyway. Andrew was old enough to play on his own while I slept, and Heidi would spend a lot of time sleeping with me, I hoped. I wanted to take Haley along, but was afraid I wouldn't be able to find a sitter for her. I waited until night to leave so she'd be asleep and I wouldn't hear her cry. It was a very selfish, bad decision.

Just before I left, Roland and I had another big fight. I hated to leave with that between us, but he hollered, "Go on, get out of here!" So I did. Later he confessed, "I never wanted you to go, but I figured you wanted to. Maybe you had a boyfriend there or something."

And I didn't really want to go. I thought I had to. Thinking he didn't love me, I cried most of the way to Missoula. I also ached for Haley from the moment I backed out of the driveway. An hour away, I passed what I thought of as the last possible exit to turn around at before heading east. In my blinded mind, there was no way I could turn around now and go back to my husband and little daughter.

After a couple of weeks of working, I took Andrew, Heidi, and Marion's son for a drive. I had told Roland I would show Joy the new baby. I parked my car in front of Nova's, got out, and asked one of her kids to run and get Joy, who lived down the street. My kids stayed in the car. A few minutes later, Joy came running down the street toward us. Lifting Heidi out of the car seat, I handed Joy the baby just as she ran up to me. Joy had just started smiling and cooing at our beautiful Heidi when over her shoulder, I spotted Shirley running straight for us.

Quickly taking Heidi back to protect her, I warned Joy, "Your mom's coming."

I bent down to place my baby safely in her car seat and kept my eyes on Heidi as I securely buckled her so not to appear worried. But my senses knew just where Shirley was. As her fist swung at my head, I shot my arm out and blocked it, then turned and started swinging. I was not going to let her humiliate me this time. Grabbing hold of the top of Shirley's head while she grappled to hold me, I pulled on her hair and pushed her head down toward the ground with one hand so that she was bent forward at the waist, and swung under with the other fist at her face as hard as I could. I know I hit her at least twice, but her arms kept getting in the way so I couldn't tell if it was hard enough to hurt. She'd knocked my glasses off. Without my glasses, I felt like all my senses were dulled but I wasn't going to give up or give in. I pushed her onto her back on the sidewalk and got on top of her. Her arms were still free, but so were mine and I was swinging. I could hear Joy crying.

Nova hollered, "You're scaring these kids!"

I ignored her. Scaring these kids? How could I be the one scaring them after all they've grown up with!

Someone grabbed me from behind and pulled me off. I could hear Misty's voice. Was she the one who pulled me off? I couldn't see.

Shirley got up and did some more hollering but didn't try to touch me again. I hollered back at her blurred form, unable to see her face to know if I had successfully damaged her. She left with Joy and I turned to stare at the sound of Nova's voice. Not wanting them to know I couldn't see, I called behind me, "Andrew, get my glasses for me."

Andrew scrambled out of the car, grabbed them and handed them to me, then scrambled back in.

Trying to keep my voice from cracking, I told Nova, "I wouldn't have come but Roland wanted Joy to see the baby."

"I know."

I got in the car and left. I drove around for a little while, not wanting to return to Marion's until I was all done crying. I was so ashamed, I wasn't even sure if I was going to tell them about it at all.

But the boys answered that as soon as they got out of the car.

"We should have called the police as soon as you got home," Marion later said as I nursed my scrapped knees. I hadn't thought of it.

I began falling asleep on the job and I wasn't making enough milk for Heidi. In her first three months, my baby had gained only six ounces. Suffering from exhaustion, I had to go home.

The Bureau of Indian Affairs had finally finished sinking our well and putting in a new septic tank, so we moved back to Moiese. I struggled to get to know my husband again and learn how to take care of my two children plus an underweight Heidi. Our upholstery business in Ronan was failing and it was all Roland and I could do to manage. I didn't visit Cheri at all.

We were watching TV one evening when a car pulled into our driveway and Junior got out. He had his bags with him. "I can't live with Cheri anymore. All she wants me for is to be her baby-sitter."

We let him stay.

On a late October night we got a call from social services. Cheri had been arrested. They said something about a disturbance at the trailer park and Cheri driving a car drunk. Social services had placed the girls in a home for the night. Would we come get them tomorrow? We agreed.

The park owner later told us that Cheri had been drinking for quite a while. Going into her trailer to get clothes for the girls, we found garbage strewn all over, the beds we'd loaned her broken, and dirty clothing lying in heaps everywhere.

Three days later, after she was released from jail, Cheri came into the upholstery shop, leaned into the playpen and hugged Angela. Roland wasn't there, so she said she'd come back later to talk to him. She didn't come back that day, but when we closed up shop, we found a note to Roland on the steering wheel of his car. In it, she said that she was offered a chance to go to the coast with a friend and she was taking it. Good-bye.

If she'd asked me to watch her kids, I would have told her I couldn't. I would have told her that I was already on the edge of insanity and ready to fall. But she didn't ask. As far as she was concerned, she had asked her dad to watch them, not me, and it didn't matter whether I liked it or not.

I hardly even knew Angela. I tried to handle it for a few days, but then fell apart. Roland stood at the kitchen sink, with his back to me, and sobbed because he knew I couldn't take care of them. He also knew that, trying to keep his business afloat, he couldn't stay home and take care of them either. He didn't want to call tribal social services to come and get them, but he knew he had no choice.

He called, then left the house so he wouldn't have to watch them be taken.

But Roland didn't abandon them. He was faithful and went after them every weekend. We took them to church and occasionally kept them overnight. I could handle it, I guess, as long as I knew it was just a night or so and I was being asked, not forced.

In December, it was evident that the upholstery shop wasn't even meeting its own expenses, let alone family expenses, so we closed it. Roland decided to try to do what he could from Moiese, instead, where he wouldn't have any overhead.

Elmer's daughter Celeste had moved to Ronan with her family. Her husband, Kirk, had been hired to pastor a local church. They were also interested in fostering Carrie and Angela.

"That would be great," Roland responded. They began the paperwork and even took the girls for occasional short visits.

In late January we went to the foster home to see about getting the girls that weekend. The foster mom met us outside and was close to tears. They were gone, she told us.

"I thought you guys were mad at me and had them moved."

"We didn't move them. We didn't know anything about it," we told her.

"Tribal social services just called me yesterday morning and told me to get their stuff together and have them to the office by 11 a.m.! Then another foster mom took them."

Kirk and Celeste hadn't finished the paperwork yet, so we knew they didn't have the girls. It took two weeks for the Tribal government to finally tell us where the kids were. When Roland drove up to that house, the girls ran out to hug him. They were crying.

"Grandpa, we thought you forgot all about us!" sobbed three-year-old Angela.

Roland asked for an explanation from the office as to why the girls had been moved like that. He was given no real answers. However, a staff woman - who had recently quit - told him that a foster mom was about to move into a HUD house but had suddenly lost her foster kids. Without the necessary number of children in her household to warrant the number of bedrooms in the HUD house, HUD wasn't going to let her move in. So social services went looking for another two kids for her.

Carrie and Angela were chosen because their parents were from another tribe and weren't around to complain. Roland was angry and wanted the girls out of the hands of tribal social services immediately. He wanted them back in our home.

By then, I had gotten stronger. Over the last three months, I'd gotten back into a pattern with my own children and had also gotten to know Cheri's girls a little better through their weekend visits. I also agreed with Roland. Foster Care shouldn't be using kids as pawns.

Putting them into foster care had taken one afternoon, the process of getting them back took over a month. The girls were in our house for just six weeks when Cheri finally came after them around Easter, 1991.

In tribal court, Roland testified that Cheri hadn't called the girls more than once or twice in her six month absence and that he didn't believe Cheri, who intended to take them back to Minneapolis, would straighten up and take care of the girls. But Cheri promised the judge that she would go to treatment and even told the court that unless the girls were living with family back home, the court was out of compliance with the Indian Child Welfare Act. The tribal court, which apparently either didn't understand ICWA or simply wanted to be rid of the girls, agreed. As we prayed with Angela and Carrie outside the building, Angela kept glancing furtively in her mother's direction, afraid of losing her again. Cheri took them immediately afterward and left town that same day.

I didn't cry when they left. It wasn't that I didn't care; I cared very much. I just wasn't going to let myself feel it. I couldn't let my heart get hooked anymore.

Not long after, we were told Cheri was drinking again and the girls were living with their grandmother, Darlene.

Beth Ward

I've taken all the questions
with their empty answers
and build for them
a keeping place,
with walls of
yearning glances.

I've taken all the pain
that was never ended
and built for it
a keeping place,
with walls
so carefully tended.

I've taken all the grief
that I never shared
and built for it
a keeping place,
with walls
of lonely airs.

I've built a keeping place
and no one knows
it's there,
and sometimes I wonder,
as the walls repair,

"How long before
the walls grow thin,
or before
the walls grow thick,
and which is the
worse,
the isolation
or the
collapse?

© By **PHONACELLE SHAPEL**

Chapter fourteen:
March 1991; The Eye of the Storm

The upholstery shop closed and we began looking for a buyer for our land. In March 1991, I began traveling 45 miles to work in another nursing home. Deeply in debt and barely able to keep food on the table, we prayed God would help us out of the financial mess we were in. One neighbor offered to buy the land, but after a few months of negotiations called to say they were backing out. Roland wasn't home when he called, so after I hung up, I cried to God for help.

A few minutes later, another neighbor drove up in his jeep and asked how I was doing. He wasn't a person we knew very well, so it wasn't like him to just drop in and talk. He told me he wasn't sure why he stopped; he'd just felt like it. I wasn't sure why he stopped either, but I began to tell him everything about our land problem. He pondered the 40 acres, then said he might buy it and let us rent the house. I couldn't believe it. Negotiations began again.

That same summer, a friend told us about a non-denominational Bible camp that her family attends every year. People came from many different churches from all over the United Sates and Canada. It even hosted speakers from Germany and Romania - men who had smuggled Bibles into Russia before the Iron Curtain fell. Not only was it an interesting and diverse camp, but there was no charge. In imitation of 19th century evangelist George Mueller, the camp depended totally on donations. Cabins and meals were provided -

we were told to just bring bedding. Best of all, it was nearby, under the shadow of Glacier National Park.

Roland didn't want to go. He had upholstery work to do. So the kids and I went by ourselves that first summer. Later in the week, Roland came up to stay a night. Nestled in the pines near the foot of towering mountains, the morning air was sweet and cool. And while we didn't totally agree with every doctrine endorsed by the camp's leadership, that wasn't a problem. The leadership wasn't intrusive and there was no pressure to agree with everything. The families there were friendly and easy to talk to, totally unlike the camp I had been a nurse at a few years earlier. A person could sit on a bench and strike up a conversation with just about anyone. But at the same time, a person could walk away and be totally alone, or off sight-seeing with their family if they felt like it. In addition to the national park, there were waterslides and various tourist attractions nearby.

During the time Roland was with us, we visited the park and explored the Hungry Horse dam. Roland enjoyed the Bible camp so much he wished he'd been there all week. I enjoyed the atmosphere and teaching so much, I decided to join a family Bible study that was meeting in Moiese. The study included people from three different churches, some of whom had been with us at the Bible camp.

In late September, after our neighbor had taken over our land payments, he came over to talk again. We stood at the edge of the field and asked him how much it would take for us to eventually buy some of the land back. He said $10,000 for the two acres we lived on, because it had a good well and septic. Not understanding this was a reasonable offer, my legs went out from under me and I landed on my knees. He didn't pay anything for that water and septic! I don't know what I had expected. He was a businessman and business is business. Still, I had hoped for a price within our reach. Trying to hide tears, I went immediately into the house. Roland stayed a while longer talking to him.

We still had our initial land loan to pay off with the co-op. Even with my work at the nursing home and Roland's upholstery in Moiese, we still couldn't make ends meet. Roland tried to start Ward Construction and bid on tribal housing jobs for the reservation. Elmer was also trying this, but they both had to quit because for all their effort, bidding almost to the point of making no money at all, the jobs consistently were given to members of the local tribe. This was legal in the eyes of Tribal officials. "Tribal preference," a legal form of discrimination, gives first choice of jobs to enrolled members of the local tribe, then first generation descendants of the local tribe, followed by enrolled members of other tribal reservations, and finally non-Indians.

Roland picked up other odd jobs here and there, building a bathroom or porch. But we weren't making it. Collectors were calling constantly. The credit union refinanced us, but we struggled even with that and all we were doing was paying interest. The money pressures had us arguing more and more often.

In January 1992, I began waking up in the middle of the night, unable to sleep, praying as hard as I could - crying and begging God to help us.

I realized that as the wife of an alcoholic, I had become controlling as a way to protect myself and my children, and I was still trying to control everything even two years after he had sobered up. The stress was way too much and was wearing me out. I needed to step back, stop arguing with Roland, and simply let him make decisions for the family.

Concurrently, Roland had gotten comfortable with just standing back and letting me make many decisions. So when there came times when he did want to make a decision, I, rooted in anxiety, wouldn't let him. We needed to reverse that. So to remind myself to step back and close my mouth, I started wearing a scarf for a few months. It was really rocky for awhile there. Roland actually got angry sometimes when I wouldn't say anything or make a decision. Friends had to remind me that it's okay for a married couple to talk through things and make a decision together. When Roland did make a decision he felt was important, and it wasn't the decision I would probably have made, I needed to just suck it up and go with it. But after a couple months, we both began to feel more comfortable. The most wonderful thing about it for me was that when I had a financial issue or some other stressful thing that I didn't know what to do with, I could remind myself that it wasn't my problem. Let Roland handle it. What an amazing relief that was.

We still had a long way to go and it would take a few years working on our marriage to get there, but we were started in the right direction.

The next month, while driving the nursing home van, it occurred to me that I'd never seen a medicab service in Montana. Back in Minnesota, I had called the Medicabs all the time to pick up nursing home patients for appointments. But here, the facility van was used for all transports. By the time I got home, my idea for Medicab was bubbling over. We would use the mini-van Dad had given us to transport patients to their medical appointments all over the valley.

Our neighbor, who according to our contract was to give us $6000 if we moved off the land in order to pay for improvements we had done on the property, agreed to give us $5000 immediately in order to start the new business.

Within two months, we were on the road. Roland continued to do upholstery on the side, but I let go of my nursing job so I could mind the Medicab phone while Roland drove the cab. Although we couldn't afford to run at the price most private-pay patients could afford, it didn't take long before more than enough Medicaid clients were using our service.

A couple months after we began Medicab, Roland told me to stop getting WIC and commodities. The whole concept of welfare was bothering him. He had been thinking about how, when his other children were growing up, he knew it didn't matter if he got drunk every day because his wife could get welfare and his kids wouldn't starve. He said that as long as he knew his wife could get government housing, fuel assistance, medicine and food, he knew he wasn't needed.

Roland figured that men need to know they are important to their families or they end up feeling useless, and government programs were part of what was holding people down instead of helping them up. Now, in this new life, he wanted to break away from government and take care of his family on his own.

I understood that, but I wasn't happy with it. I was sure there were lots of things we couldn't do without. During my visits to the commodity warehouse I'd been trying to take only those things we thought we needed. We didn't have room to stock all the food we were entitled to – that they wanted to give us. And there were some products I rarely took because most of the family didn't like it so we never used it. Like the canned meat. (But sometimes when we had no money for dog food, I'd get it and - as many people did - feed it to the animals.)

But if he wasn't going to let us go there anymore...

"Well, let me go back to commodities one more time to stock up," I pleaded. "I didn't get everything I could last time."

"No. We're done. We have an income now. We should be using that instead of expecting other people to support us."

Are you kidding me? I couldn't believe it. How were we going to afford that biscuit mix and fruit juice on our own? And cheese! Cheese was so expensive at the store; we'd never be able to afford it on our own. We'll never have cheese again!

A woman we knew tried to talk to Roland.

"There's nothing wrong with getting help. Everyone does it now and then," she said. "My husband gets unemployment. Are you trying to be better than everyone else?"

"I'm not comparing myself to everyone else," he told her. "I'm doing what I need to do for me and my family."

With two children under five and another on the way, I was aware how much free WIC milk and juice we were passing up if he did this right now. Holy Cow! Does he know what he's refusing?? However, deep down I knew he was right, and although I argued initially, I was proud of him.

We began considering other ways to meet needs, such as raising chickens, goats, or maybe a cow. Roland was right. We could find our own way to feed the kids and at the same time, help them to learn responsibility by having chores. So we bought chickens and goats. The girls were primarily responsible for feeding the chickens and gathering eggs and the goats were Andrew's. Heidi, our little lover of animals, was enthralled by it all.

Required to write a senior paper in order to graduate, Junior put together an essay on the dangers of cigarette smoking. To do it, he copied directly from two or three health clinic pamphlets but didn't tie the thoughts of the separate articles together, use correct punctuation or spelling or write a thoughtful conclusion. He even stapled one of the pages of his composition upside down. After twelve years of state and tribal schooling, he was still unable to write a good paper. Even more distressing, the tribal school gave the paper a passing grade.

Nothing about his academics kept him from graduating. However, the school surprised us by holding back his diploma due to his poor attendance (this from the school that bribed kids to show up for attendance week). We had required him to go to school daily, but he had begun hanging out with a drinking crowd and sometimes took very extended weekends. We wouldn't see him at all for four or five days. We figured the school cared more about attendance records than academics because they get paid for kids showing up, not learning anything. Heck, maybe the longer they took to graduate, the more money the school got.

More and more things were bothering Roland and me about the reservation. Maybe Junior couldn't write, but I could. Writing was a way to sort out thoughts...

"Dear Grandpa:

In the paper, Roland and I read that the mayor... had written to a senator asking that the reservations be dissolved. He's right. But now the Tribal Council is threatening to take back land they'd leased to the city... It all seems so childish. I'm always afraid people might assume that Roland is a member of this tribe. I want to write a letter to the editor and say what I really think and feel but I'm afraid to. The Tribal government is very capable of retaliation. It's not our water well I'm worried about. If they refuse to ever fix it again, we might be better off paying a real company. But I'm worried about Roland being a businessman in this community. I think I'd best keep my mouth shut. For now anyway. I have so much to say and it's burning inside me. Number one; it's not good for my kids, their kids, or any people to grow up believing that they are owed free housing, food, medical, no taxes and welfare on top of it. What does that really do for someone's character? I want my kids to learn to work for their living. But enough of that, I'll bore you."

Our family Bible study group had a picnic at the National Bison Range. I was glad Roland had come along. Still tending to withdraw from social situations, he hadn't attended the Bible study yet. I was glad to see him come and play softball, getting a chance to meet these men in a non-threatening environment.

In the group was a thickset, blond man named Will Stanley. He came to the study with his beautiful wife, Judy, and five tow-headed children. Initially he had intimidated me. He never seemed to look directly at me (kind of like Roland's buddies on the Rez) and there were times during discussion that he would get upset about issues and talk heatedly. In all honesty, he first looked to me like a red neck. But he was really intelligent and kind. As time went on, he grew on you.

Will's homeschooled kids, along with a few other families from our church, fascinated me. I remember my cousin Marion having once said, "our kids are going to try drugs and have sex anyway, so we might as well accept and not fight it." It was really disheartening to hear her say that, but watching this group of children, I was encouraged that she might be wrong.

From the time I'd first met these "Christian homeschooling" families, I watched them closely for tell-tale signs of overly domineering parents or physical abuse – the kind of stuff one suspects when one hears of Christian homeschooling families. I'd seen enough abuse in the last ten years to know what I was looking for. But I never saw abuse in these families. Instead, I saw happy, well- mannered, intelligent kids, (even teenagers!) joking with and teasing their parents. Additionally, most of the teenagers were interested in and skilled at sports, gymnastics, hiking, science, computers, music, drama, and dance. You name it.

They were EVEN enjoyable to sit down and talk to; they had no fear of adults. They also seemed to have little problem accepting their parent's strict rules in relation to chores, dating and drugs. The conflicts they did have with their parents, such as whether or not they could spend the night with a friend on a school night or whether it was their turn to do dishes, were trifling compared to the kinds of problems I was used to.

I remember one mom trying to tell me that all families have problems. She used some kind of example like... children not doing their homework or something like that. Oh, what a Blessing that would be if that was the extent of a person's problems!

I had to ask myself what it was that made these children - these families - so different from all the others I'd known. It wasn't just because they were Christian. I'd seen many "Christian" families that were just as messed up as any other. It also wasn't all about a single church or doctrine. These families came from several separate churches.

After watching them for a period of time, I decided the significant difference between these families and others was:

1. The absolute dedication the parents had to God and each other;
2. The absolute dedication the parents had to the health of their children, physically, emotionally, spiritually, and academically;
3. The absolute dedication the parents had to honesty, principle, and character;
4. And finally, they all had a very strong father figure.

At a church 'singspiration' our kids sang with several other children. A 'singspiration' in our valley was an event where various Christian churches (Catholic, fundamental Protestant, Evangelical and charismatic) got together to worship Jesus without concern for doctrinal differences. Andrew had a fun part. He was told to take the mike and mouth the final words of the song while our pastor, hidden with a different mike, did the real words, giving Andrew the appearance of a very deep voice.

Refreshments were served afterwards. Roland later remarked how surprised he was that he knew so many people. It had been awhile since he'd gone to a singspiration, and the last time we'd hardly known anyone. Since then, we'd met, through various intermixed studies and get-togethers, people from many denominations.

When Haley told an older couple she had no grandma, they adopted our kids as grandchildren. Every year on Easter and Christmas Della and Marvin remembered our children with gifts, just as they did their own. The character of many people in this valley was surprisingly open and friendly. When first moving here six years ago, we were surprised by the number of people who brought over garden vegetables, used clothing, or home-canned goods. Since then, we'd treasured the way people wave as you drive past, hold benefits to help the sick in the community, and pray for you when you need it.

When accidents happen and strangers have been rushed to the hospital in critical condition, we have been called through the "prayer chain" and been asked to pray. I had never experienced this kind of community love and attention any other place we had lived.

Praise our Lord. I was so glad that we had these friends the Lord had given us. The baby I was carrying was covered in prayer on several occasions. I was so grateful to have so many people around that cared so deeply.

"And Lord Jesus, please thank and bless that Christian woman at the Crisis Nursery for me - the very kind, patient woman who put up with so much from me. I am certain, without a doubt, that she had been praying for us during that very difficult time in our lives. Please let her know that everything worked out."

While there were many good things for us to learn from our Church friends, our Church friends were also able to learn many good things from Roland. One white man asked Roland if he would join an all-"Indian" church that he was organizing. "We need strong Indian men to preach there," he said.

Roland wondered what the purpose for such a church was, and responded that creating an all-Indian church would only increase and encourage racism. "After all," he said, "Heaven isn't segregated. We're all going to be there together. Mark my words, that church won't last." He was right, after only a few months, the all-Indian church folded.

Another time, he was asked to hold the chalice of grape juice at communion time. Standing at the altar while the congregation passed by one by one, he began to feel extremely nauseous and was afraid he was going to faint. He made it through, and later, when telling the pastor's wife how strange it had been to feel so sick while standing at the altar, but just fine again when he sat down, she quickly apologized. They had discovered just before service that they were out of grape juice, and in a hurry, substituted real wine from someone's kitchen. They hadn't thought twice about how it might affect Roland, our living proof that miracles still happen.

Timothy was born just before 4 pm in September, 1992. Because Roland was still not comfortable with the birth process, my friend Ann came down to be with me at the hospital. Roland came down to visit us afterwards, as did our pastor and his wife, who recited beautiful scripture for us from the book of Timothy. The next day, Roland drove 500 miles for Medicab before he was able to come get us in the evening.

Timothy was given two different baby showers; not to mention showered with attention from friends. People dropped in all week with gifts for the baby and food for the family. At our Bible study, Will Stanley's girls jockeyed with each other to be able to hold him.

It was one of our most peaceful and happy times. Medicab was busy enough to keep Roland moving, but not busy enough to take up too much of my time with paperwork and phones.

We homeschooled that year. I spent a lot of time with the children going over their schoolwork while nursing Timothy. We chose to do this for several reasons. First, we didn't believe the public and tribal schools were doing a very good job and we thought we could do better. Second, we wanted to be able to teach our children about Jesus Christ throughout the day, as well as teach them that certain standards are important. We did not want to teach them the world view that the public schools were teaching. Third, we wanted to avoid the pressure within public schools on the reservations to placate tribal government. "Indian Week" is one example. It is hard when you are teaching your child that Jesus is the only way and truth to have the school telling him that because some of his ancestors honored a different spirituality, he should, too. Complaints to the principal the year before hadn't helped. In general, all children were expected to participate during this "Indian Week," including the "River Honoring" and the powwow, even though Roland objected to the river honoring and hadn't participated in a powwow for five years.

How can schools across the country deny children the right to carry bibles or pray to Jesus, but go ahead and promote other religions? We understood that some people thought they were making up for past atrocities to Native Americans by hosting and participating in these types of things, but what appears to be happening is that children, most of whom have more than one heritage, are getting an unhealthy sense that this particular heritage is significantly different and more special than others.

Our homeschool work was so well organized that year that we managed to finish Andrew's math book by January and had to start a new one. Haley, only a kindergartner, learned to read, add and subtract. I was also able to enroll Heidi and Haley in a ballet class that fall. We went to the library weekly and Andrew participated in 4-H, cub-scouts, soccer, and baseball. I was so incredibly organized that year that I even had monthly menu plans with corresponding grocery lists.

Little Heidi, too young yet for school, would sit nearby enjoying our kittens or playing with toys while Andrew and Haley studied. One day, after Andrew and Haley had been practicing a song all week for a church event, Heidi, who hadn't appeared to be paying any attention, stood up and started singing the song and dancing the steps that went with it. She performed steps almost perfectly, then sat back down and resumed playing with her dolls.

In our usually disordered and agitated family, this was truly a unique period of time. Perhaps it was a God given rest stop, an eye in the storm.

Medicab grew and prospered. Social services told us constantly that our Medicab was a Godsend. I was very good at getting people's transportation needs met no matter how convoluted the situation. We took on more counties and hired contract drivers who drove their own vehicles, kept their own records, and worked directly from their own homes. Some of the drivers, referred to us by Christian friends, we met in person only once or twice; but some we never met face to face. Most of the drivers were struggling with families just as we were, so we paid them a good percentage of the fare received for each trip. Medicab was taking care of people, both clients and drivers.

One of our tribal clients, a woman with severe arthritis, said to Marcia Dovetail, who was her driver, "I don't know why, but I always feel at peace in the Medicabs."

In the spring of 1993, Medicaid had us audited. The auditor spent a couple of days at our house. After the first day, he confided to us.

"When I was driving over here, I'd expected to find a hornet's nest. From what the supervisor at Medicaid had told me, I thought I was going to find some fraud. I changed my mind after meeting you though."

He said he could see we were honest and trying our best. He could tell we weren't experienced business people and needed some advice on how best to document our work, but he could also see that we were not making a lot of money. It was clear most of our money was going to pay expenses.

"I thought I'd be here going over your books for a few days, but there's no problems here. I'll be done after just another half a day."

He went back to the state capitol with a good report.

Roland was down at the river fishing in late May when fourteen-year old Joy called. Roland's family phoned so rarely that I knew it had to be important. My guess was Joy was pregnant. Maybe it crossed my mind only because I myself was pregnant again, as was Misty. At any rate, it's what I guessed.

"I'll go down to the river and get him," I told her. "Give me an hour."

Later that evening when Roland got off the phone, he confirmed my guess. Fourteen-year-old Joy was expecting her baby about the same time I was expecting mine.

In early August, 1993, I got out of bed and immediately began packing some of Timothy's newborn baby clothes.

"I need to get these sent to Misty. She's going to be having her baby soon." I said.

Later that evening we found out that her third child, Caleb, has been born that very same morning.

Interesting, considering that within three years, he would become my son.

Joy's little girl, Ashley, was born January 1st, 1994. I had thought ahead and already sent a special baby gift with the Christmas package. Our Rosie was born two weeks later.

Beth Ward

Down in the darkly depths
of me,
sweetly plays
a melody.

There I dance
most wild and free,
and laugh at life's
hypocrisy.

© By **PHONACELLE SHAPEL**

Chapter fifteen:
The work begins

Up until now, my hard labor had always started after lunch time and I had all my babies before dinner. But here it was, after 6 pm and I still hadn't even started the hard labor. The doctor came in, checked, and said it would be quite awhile yet – I was only at 3. She told the nurses she was going to go to a party and would check me again in a couple hours. I was so disappointed. It had never happened this way before. I should have already been well into hard labor by this time of day. I should have been almost done and getting my dinner soon.

All the staff left and I was alone with Roland and Ann. Ann, seeing I wasn't handling the disappointment very well, began to pray.

Suddenly, the worst contractions I had ever had began. My entire body felt an extremely intense pressure from the tips of my toes to the top of my head. Worse, there was no rest between waves. Even my lips felt like they were buzzing. Ann rushed to get a nurse. The nurse ran in to check, and then ran out again to catch the doctor. The baby was already crowning. The doctor rushed back with a white coat over her street clothes. The infant warmer was pushed into the room, blocking Roland's exit.

Rosie was born at 6:20 pm, and Roland witnessed his very first birth.

Now I could have dinner.

Roland and the kids picked us up from the hospital after church that Sunday. We now had five children, two of them babies. The nurses couldn't see how I'd manage. It was chaotic, that's for sure. We were glad to get them all into the car and on the way home. We stopped at a McDonald's drive-thru to feed the kids. At home, everyone fought over holding the baby. Elmer and Marcia Dovetail dropped in within a half hour.

Roland wrote in Rosie's baby book:
"I wish to see you grow up as the Lord would want you to and that your life would be dedicated to the Lord, first. And as you grow up to womanhood, your life will always be a happy, good natured life and always having your eyes looking to the Lord for guidance and happiness."

Later that spring, Will Stanley decided to run for a State House seat. I was excited and begged him to let me help. It felt like old home week to play politics like my mother did. With zeal, I organized a successful fund-raiser for him and helped him make signs. In the summer and fall, I went door to door for him. But campaigning in this area wasn't anything like campaigning at home. For some reason, although many turned out for the fund-raiser, I was the only one helping him with the footwork. I wondered if this was because many of our Christian friends felt they needed to remain out of politics.

We found out later that wasn't the reason. The apathy for politics was pandemic to the area. While dropping literature one afternoon, I ran into his opponent. He was a nice man; I held no grudge against him and we spoke for a moment. He was surprised to see me out and admitted ruefully, "No one's stumping for me."

On September 1, 1994, the State hired a company called 'Integrated Transportation Management' (ITM), a "managed care system," to administer Medicaid transportation throughout the state. From the moment it began, I found myself tied to the desk trying to arrange and fix appointments for our steady flow of clients. I cried the first day. The confusion for everyone and constant mistakes of the ITM staff were unbelievable. After the first week of non-stop deskwork, I thought that this couldn't possibly go on for long.

After two months, it became apparent that ITM had no idea what it was doing and maybe never would. But our Medicab had 14 people contracting to drive for us in four counties. A transportation consultant told the director of the Council on Aging that we had the "Golden Egg" of transportation in this area. I didn't want to just give that up.

In November, exhausted from the amount of paperwork required and number of mistakes ITM was making, I began contacting taxi companies around the state. When I asked them if they were having trouble with ITM, they laughed to keep from crying. Taxi companies and passengers all over the state were having major problems. Encouraged by Will's victory at the polls, I asked the companies to meet and form a committee to address the transportation problems in the upcoming legislature. They were more than willing. Another company president had been in the process of trying to organize us anyway in an effort to get better rates for the wheelchair vans.

During this time, I read an article in the paper about a family in Idaho that was trying to keep their five-year-old boy. The child was half-Indian; his adopted family, the only family he had ever known, was white. Although the white mother had given the child to the family as a newborn and the Indian father had never shown any interest in the child, family on a South Dakota reservation was now trying to get custody of the boy through the Indian Child Welfare Act.

According to a House Report on the Indian Child Welfare Act (ICWA)

"The intent of Congress in passing the Indian Child Welfare Act was to protect Indian children from removal from their tribes and to assure that tribes are given the opportunity to raise Indian children in a manner which reflects the unique values of Indian culture."

I have to admit that when Roland and I first read that – knowing our own experience with how relative children were being raised - we had to wonder what "unique" values Congress was referring to. We didn't mean that in a mean way, but the truth was the only culture we saw most young and middle-aged people practicing was a drug and alcohol culture. So...if Congress was referring to something else, we really wanted to know. They used the word "Unique." So, exactly which values do American Indian Tribes currently have that very few, if any, other cultures have? How are we supposed to know and assure that children are raised in a manner which reflects those unique values, if we don't know which values are being referred to?

In a 1989 case called <u>Mississippi Band of Choctaw Indians v. Holyfield</u>, the US Supreme Court declared that Congress had enacted ICWA to protect Native Americans. The Court concluded an Indian tribe and an Indian child have an interest in maintaining ties <u>independent of the interests of the birth parents</u>, and, thus, "*Congress determined to subject (voluntary) placements to the ICWA's jurisdiction ...even in cases where the parents consented to an adoption, because of concerns going <u>beyond the wishes of individual parents</u>.*"

The Act itself states:

"*An Indian tribe shall retain exclusive jurisdiction over any child custody proceeding that involves an Indian child...*"

And there is

"*a requirement that the cultural and social standards of the Indian community be applied by the State court when it applies the placement preferences.*"

Seriously? Is our federal government mandating that the social standards of Cass Lake be applied in any court that would be considering custody of our children if Roland and I died? Which cultural and social standards of the community are being referred to? The ones everyone wishes and pretends still exist, or the tragic standards that actually exist?

We couldn't believe our government had virtually signed away our rights as parents. Knowing the reality of the 'social standards' on Roland's reservation, that was the last place either of us wanted our children to go if something happened to us. Furthermore, what right did Congress have to decide that our children's traditional Native American spirituality was more important than their Jewish or Catholic heritage, let alone the evangelical spirituality Roland and I had chosen to raise them with? Does Congress honestly have a right to pass a law like this?

ICWA also says;

"Indian tribes have the authority to define their membership..."

Most tribes say a quarter blood is the requirement for membership, but some go down to *1/64,* and some require only that a child's heritage can be *traced back to the Dawes Rolls*. Therefore, most of those who are eligible have much less than 50% heritage. Further, most eligible children DON'T live on a reservation and don't participate in Indian tradition. In 1990, there were 1,878,285 American Indians and Alaska Natives in the U. S., and 554 federally funded tribes. Only 437,079 Indians, or about 23%, lived on reservations[1]. Approximately 77%, (1,441,206) lived outside the reservation, with 56% residing in metropolitan areas. How many children of negligible descent does this law affect?

This isn't an exaggerated concern. The ICWA pertains to not only enrolled children, but to any child the tribe deems eligible for enrollment. This means that even if a parent lives far from the reservation, hasn't ever participated in tribal events, and chooses not to enroll their child in the tribe, the tribal government still has the right to intervene and have a controlling say in certain custody cases involving that child.

The Idaho father was quoted as saying, *"the intent of the act was to protect Indian children within a reservation. It wasn't meant to try and force a child onto a reservation who... never would have been there otherwise."*

Roland and I agreed. Tribal governments do not "own" tribal people. Despite Congress's claim that they have the right under the commerce clause, our children are not commerce and tribal members

---
1 1990 U.S. Bureau of Census, Department of Commerce.

should have the right to choose their own lifestyle for their families. The United States government, in our opinion, did not have the prerogative to give away our constitutional rights or our freedom to have our children raised in the religion of our choice. In our case, we'd chosen Will and Judy Stanley as our children's guardians should anything happen to us. We didn't want tribal government interfering with that choice.

What parents need to realize, as many who have miniscule amounts of heritage through the Cherokee Nation have come to realize, is that this law could include their own children or grandchildren – even if they are 99% Irish, Latino, or African American.

Appalled that our country had made this kind of racism legal, I wrote a letter to the editor and sent it to a few papers, including the Idaho family's home paper. A week later, the editor from the Idaho paper called to tell me they had printed the letter in a special column.

At the same time, retrocession was a big topic in our valley. At issue was a state agreement with the local Tribes to cross-deputize, allowing tribal police some jurisdiction over non-Indian residents. The non-Indian population rose up against the agreement. Non-member residents felt strongly that without a voice or vote in tribal government, they should not be subject to the tribal government jurisdiction.

Nationwide, as of 1990, Indian reservations had a total population of 807,817, but as much as 45%, or 370,738, were non-Indians. On 30% of the reservations, the number of non-members was equal to or greater than the number of tribal members. Further, tens of thousands of members live on reservations other than their home reservation.[2]

Even most foreign countries give immigrants the option of becoming a citizen with the right to vote. That is not the case in Indian Country, areas totally within the United States and subject to will of Congress. You can't become a member simply because you live within the boundaries – even if your family has lived there 100 years. Many families in western Montana homesteaded in those areas before the federal government declared them to be

---

2   1990 U.S. Bureau of Census, Department of Commerce.

reservations. In some cases, families moved to the Polson area in the early 1900's when the land was advertised by the federal government as *"former...Reservation."* These families did not homestead with knowledge that their descendants, still living on their family farms, would be subjected to tribal jurisdiction 80 years later.

Prior to a 1993 legislative hearing on the retrocession agreement within this valley, the county commissioners attempted to sit down and talk it out with the tribal council. The tribal council came to the meeting but was not willing to hear the non-member concerns. One tribal council member sat through the entire 45 minute meeting with his back to the commissioners, refusing to recognize them as a legitimate entity.

Later, after the majority of the population of the county voted against the agreement in a referendum, the Tribal council called for a boycott of white-owned businesses. However, many tribal members, embarrassed by their council's antics, refused to honor the boycott and it failed. That is, the boycott failed to break the non-member population. However, neither the Tribal Council nor the state needed the agreement of the people in order to enforce the cross-deputation. Retrocession commenced.

Non-members became increasingly distressed and frustrated, resulting in resentment and animosity. Pro-tribal government groups then falsely label this anger as "racism" and effectively shut off any chance at communication.

We were also concerned about tribal jurisdiction over non-member Indians such as Roland. In particular, we were concerned that all reservations have a right to try ANY person of Indian heritage, whether they were part of that reservation or not. Again, the issue is all about not having voice or vote in the government trying you. How does one reservation have the right to try a tribal member of another reservation - a separate government - without it being all about race? An out-of-town attorney, after reading one of our letters to the editor on that issue, wrote to us in agreement:

"In 1988, in the case of <u>Greywater v. Joshua,</u> the 8th circuit court of appeals held that tribal criminal jurisdiction did not include non-member Indians.

Non-member Indians are United States citizens. The United States Constitution should pertain to all United States citizens, no matter their color. Non-member Indians should have access into the Court system into which they pay taxes, and be able to appeal into a court in which they have voice and vote.

The U.S. Supreme Court ruled in a case called <u>Duro v. Reina</u> that Tribes do not have the power to try non-member Indians for criminal offenses. Although the court hinted that there are constitutional reasons for this concerning the rights of individuals, it did not make its ruling on a constitutional basis.

Consequently, soon after the ruling [a Senator] attached a one-sentence amendment to a defense appropriations bill temporarily overriding the Supreme Court's decision for one year. The next year, [the Senator] managed to have Congress pass a bill permanently overriding this ruling. This effectively subjects non-member Indians to the jurisdiction of the Tribes because Congress has almost unlimited power over Indian Affairs.

However, Congress cannot pass a law that violates the constitution. If the Supreme Court, in the <u>Duro</u> case had based its ruling on the constitutional rights of the non-member Indian, Congress could not overrule this decision. Thus, it appears that the only remedy left to nonmember Indians is to claim in court that tribal criminal jurisdiction over them is unconstitutional, no matter what Congress says."

The attorney offered to represent us, or any non-member Indian, if cited into the tribal court.

That same month, Roland gave Junior an ultimatum: stop drinking or leave. Junior decided to leave. Roland had also heard that Misty was using crack and neglecting her three kids, so he took time out from work and drove Junior back to Minneapolis at Thanksgiving time to see what was going on.

Hoping to catch Misty off guard, he didn't tell anyone he was coming. Nevertheless, while he was there he couldn't see anything wrong with Misty's household and came back to Moiese satisfied, figuring that gossip had just gotten out of hand again.

But he had an interesting story on returning home. Six-year-old Ross had been telling his family all week before Roland arrived that his "grandpa was coming to get him." But Roland hadn't told anyone he was coming. Six-year-old Ross just knew.

In January 1995, after hearing that Misty's newest baby, Dewey, had been born with crack cocaine in his blood, Roland drove back to get the four children. Not knowing if the parents would also come, I went along to care for the children on the trip back. On our way, we stopped to visit the Stanley's, who were at the capitol for the start of his first legislative session. Judy, unable to have any more children of her own, was aching for another child to hold and love. As we spoke that evening, she said in what I assumed to be a kidding way that she and her girls wanted little Dewey and were daydreaming about where they would put his crib in their house. As we left their home to go back out on the road, she called after me, "Bring me back a baby, Beth!"

She seemed almost serious, but I knew that if Roland took custody, he wouldn't be willing to give the child to someone else. I felt sad for Judy.

Once there, we spoke to Misty and her boyfriend Wesley Redwood about straightening up and starting a new life. They seemed willing.

"No one around here helps us anyway," she said.

So they came, along with their five young children, little Ross, five-year-old Brooke, eighteen-month-old Caleb, and Dewey, only about 4-weeks-old. Roland's oldest granddaughter, Carrie, cried to be able to come along, but Cheri wouldn't allow it. Cheri also begged to be able to keep Dewey.

"Misty's let me take care of him since he was born. In fact, when she was in labor she told me I could have him. Please just let me keep him."

"No," both Misty and Roland answered, "the family stays together."

Misty was hard on her kids the whole trip. She'd holler at them for little things and slap Ross and Brooke in the back of the head. She was particularly hard on Brooke. At a rest stop, while Misty was in the restroom with the kids, Wesley spoke to us privately. He said he'd always had trouble with the way she would treat them, especially Brooke.

"I know how you feel," Roland answered. "My ex-wife was the same way with my girls. That's where Misty gets it from."

However, despite their agreement, neither man tried to stop Misty when she hollered at or swatted the kids through the rest of the trip. That was understandable though. We all knew how her stubbornness could quickly escalate into rages and I didn't much want to tangle with it during a road trip either.

We arrived home and went about fitting the family in. We let the Redwoods take our girl's room, and we moved the girls to another area. For some reason, I never thought twice about taking the family in. Both Roland and I really wanted to help. I guess I was ready this time.

Two days later, Roland and I returned home from a meeting with the Passenger Carriers Association, the newly formed group of taxi companies. They had just elected Roland to the board and we were pretty happy, but upon entering our house, our excitement was quickly doused. We found Misty angry and determined to leave. She'd already called her mother and arranged to have a bus ticket sent to the depot. I tried to talk her out of it. As she stomped out of the living room, she hollered at me,

"Oh, I'll pay my dad back for what he spent getting us!"

"It's not the money he wants," I hollered back, knowing she'd never pay it anyway, "it's you!"

Misty stopped. No one had ever said anything like that to her before. She slowly walked back to the living room and sat down.

"Well," she said, "I didn't really want to come anyway."

"Why did you get in the car then?"

"I didn't want my dad to get mad at me."

"So coming out here and then leaving is better?"

"Well, I want to go."

That evening, Misty got a phone call; her ticket was paid for and waiting.

"Well, take us down there to get the ticket," she said to her dad. "We'll wait there for the next bus."

"It's 9 p.m." Roland said. "It'll take an hour to get there. The bus terminal closes at 10 p.m. and the bus doesn't come until 4 a.m. We'd have to wait all night in the car."

"Well, I want to go."

Roland didn't respond.

When we were out of earshot, I begged him, "Roland, you can't take them down there tonight! It's winter! These kids can't sit in a car all night - Dewey is 4-weeks old!"

"I know, I'm not letting her go tonight."

Roland went back to Misty and told her truthfully that it was too late, with this weather, to get to the station before it closed. As long as they couldn't pick up their tickets, they might as well stay the night and take the 10 a.m. bus tomorrow. Misty and Wesley sat on the couch together, disappointed. Caleb sat between them with Misty picking at his hair every now and then for the rest of the evening.

When it came time to leave the next day, little Ross wanted to stay. But Misty wouldn't allow it, and they all left on the bus. Later we were told that as soon as they got back, Misty and Wesley got someone to watch the kids and went out to party.

Judy Stanley's arms, heart and home, longing to hold that little baby, were left empty.

Two weeks later Timothy was sitting on my lap when I noticed something in his hair. It was a bug. Quickly checking the heads of the other children, I found all were infested with lice. It took a couple months of repeated washing of their heads, clothing and bedding to get rid of them. I asked the pharmacist if maybe there was a variety of louse that was getting immune to pesticide, but he didn't think so.

We joined the Passenger Carriers Association in testifying in front of a legislative committee that winter but were not successful in ridding the state of ITM.

Also that session, Will Stanley introduced a bill addressing the controversial state/tribal hunting and fishing agreement. The State had signed an agreement with the local Tribes a few years earlier giving the Tribal Government jurisdiction over all land within reservation boundaries – including private property - and the right to sell permits to hunt and fish on that land. The non-member residents within the reservation boundaries were not allowed input to that agreement. Negotiations were held behind closed doors, although it directly involved non-members and their personal property rights. Will's bill would remove personal property from tribal jurisdiction.

The bill failed in committee, but Will wanted to try pulling it out on the House floor anyway. In an effort to support it, I told a friend to call me on our 1-800 number and I would fax their support to the Capitol. To my astonishment, word spread quickly and in the next 24 hours, over 300 people called to our house asking to have their support faxed. Some people assumed we were a government line and attempted to speak about other tribal issues also. The emotion was overwhelming. Roland and I had no idea so many people felt this strongly.

While talking to one of the callers, the upcoming trial of a reservation resident was discussed. Orval Johnson had been fighting the State/tribal agreement with civil disobedience for about three years. His disobedience consisted of annually hunting pheasants on his own property without purchasing a tribal permit, and annually being cited for doing so. His disobedience stemmed from the fact that when a person purchases a tribal permit, they are essentially paying a tax to tribal government without the benefit of representation. In addition, they are signing away legal rights by agreeing to be tried in Tribal court if they inadvertently break a hunting law. (The tribes hunting laws differed from not only the State's but from other tribes within the State.)

Orval's annual trial was coming up. The caller suggested that we have a rally at that time and address all the issues that people were upset about, including the National Bison Range...

(Yup – there were a lot of issues people were upset about.)

Under the Tribal Self-Governance Act of 1994, the Tribe had recently requested a contract with the Department of Interior to manage the National Bison Range (NBR), arguing that the Range is a place of historical, cultural, and spiritual significance to their people.

Lots of people were totally against the management transfer and believed the real reason the tribal government wanted management of the Bison Range was for money. The Tribal Council would be able to administer the NBR's federal budget and an unknown amount of matching funds without having to submit to any federal audits.

People were also against it because the management transfer would allow the Tribal government to use 'tribal preference' in hiring on federal land with federal funds. In other words, they would be able to discriminate in hiring while using tax-payer funds. Some of the current employees who could lose their jobs had volunteered for a year or so before getting hired.

Lastly, there wasn't a lot of local respect or agreement that the place was of historical, cultural or spiritual significance to the tribe. It didn't even exist until the American Bison Society decided to preserve the buffalo in 1908. They raised the funds to buy the land in 1907 and chose this area because the government was about to open the area up and offer land for sale. This was the same period of time that homesteaders were told this was a "former" reservation.

The lands were reserved from mostly unallocated lands within the reservation's former boundaries and $50,700, the fair appraised value at the time, was paid to the tribe by Congress. The ABS then purchased thirty-four head of buffalo from a family estate and donated it to the Federal Range. The tribe claimed historical ownership over those buffalo because an individual tribal member, in business, had originally sold them to the family years earlier. However, other animals were donated by the Boone and Crockett Club of New York, Yellowstone Park, and the Canadian National Parks Service. How could the local tribe claim to have historical ownership to those animals?

Later, in 1972, when the Tribal Government said they wanted more money for the entire reservation land, including the Bison Range, U.S. Claims Court agreed and Congress paid the Tribe a second time. This time, it was over 6 million dollars plus interest. The judgment specifically noted that the Bison Range was included in this payment. The tribe both accepted and spent the millions.

Beth Ward

In April of 1995, we held a Bison Range/Orval Johnson rally on the courthouse steps and with the help of three men, a range employee, a local writer, and the former director of the National Bison Range, we began a petition drive that garnered over 3,000 signatures in just 4 weeks.

Beth Ward

SHADOW BONES

he crouches on the
rim of tomorrow, shadow
bones reflected on the
canyon walls dancing
in the winter winds

with eyes like molten
glass going cold and
brittle in the evening
of the world

shattering on the
sands in the emptiness
of the ending

he reaches out his
hand, fingers spread
wide toward the stars
and weeps

© By PHONACELLE SHAPEL

Chapter sixteen:
One Day at a Time

That June, Misty's social worker asked Roland to care for the children while Misty went to treatment. Again Roland went at his own expense to bring the four children back to live with us. The arrangement wasn't by court order. It was termed a "voluntary" placement because after being warned by the worker that the kids would be taken anyway and her parental rights permanently severed if she didn't comply, Misty chose to comply.

Cheri also asked if she could come. Carrie and Angela, after begging to leave Darlene's house and live again with their mother, had been with Cheri for a few months now and she had been taking care of Dewey for the last six months. She assured us that she wanted to change her life. At the time, after having lost her apartment because of drug activity and not paying rent, she was living in a motel and the county was supporting her. She told us that the social workers wanted her to give Dewey back to Misty because they didn't like Cheri's lifestyle, and Darlene was threatening to take Carrie and Angela back with her. When we tried to ask why, she became indignant, so we didn't push the issue. We correctly assumed she was leaving town as an effort to keep her children, but hoped that once she was with us, she would straighten out and become a good mother.

Roland and Misty had agreed with the social worker that Roland should care for the children while Misty went to treatment. However, when it came time to leave, Misty wouldn't give Roland 22-month-old

Caleb. He stayed with her. So with Cheri, her boyfriend, Cheri's two children and Misty's three, Roland brought seven people home.

Knowing the problems Medicab was having, we probably shouldn't have even considered taking people in, but Roland was raised to help family whenever they needed. In addition, with the amount of new Medicab paperwork keeping me in my office 10 hours a day, we hoped God was putting extra people in our house to help with all the work.

Our Medicab business was dying. In mid-May 1995, the state announced an administrative rule change that said it would pay Medicabs only 63 cents a mile after July 1st. Our expenses were $1 a mile. A representative from Human Services was quoted in the paper saying that SRS really didn't want to charge 63 cents a mile, but that they wanted to get rid of Medicabs. (We were the only Medicab really running in the state, but others were talking of starting up).

We opened our home to the families, but not wanting to struggle with lice again, I insisted Roland stop on the way out and wash everyone's head. Then, as soon as they arrived, I washed heads again. The results were horrible. Bugs were practically dripping off the combs, some still alive even after the second washing.

We began chopping hair on the girls and shaving heads on the boys, including those of my children. We hated to do it, but we knew if we didn't we'd be fighting the pests for months. Anyway, after it was done, I had to admit Timothy's heart shaped face looked cute without hair.

In order to deal with all the children, I hired a neighbor to help by doing a little vacation Bible class for all the kids. Daily, she came to read Bible stories to them on the front lawn and do art projects on the picnic table.

To the thrill of all who were lucky enough to see it, Andrew's goat gave birth to triplets. Some of the hens also had small broods of chicks trailing them. This was as exciting to our own kids as it was to the city kids.

But the summer was expensive. Our grocery bill skyrocketed. We bought clothes, shoes, medicine and even had Cheri's tooth extracted. Roland took Andrew and Cheri's boyfriend to a Christian

Men's convention called Promise Keepers, and we took the entire group up to our annual family Bible camp. When the social worker learned later that Caleb was still in Minneapolis, she asked Roland to come back for him and he made another trip at his own expense. While there, his nephew, Jerry Ward, asked him if he and his family could also come out to stay with us.

Jerry, raised in a foster home, had struggled with his temper and alcoholism all his life. Just recently out of prison, he wanted to try to make a new life for his little family. So Jerry, his wife, and their two kids followed Roland back to Moiese. With Caleb and the four from the new family, our house now held nineteen.

Caleb, almost two-years-old, didn't speak much (except to swear), still wore diapers, carried a bottle, and cried wherever he went. When he got angry with the other kids, which was frequently, he quickly struck out. We spoke about him to a member of our church who was a child counselor. He told us to hold Caleb snugly during temper tantrums and help him feel safe.

"Overall, you guys are doing a good job. This is probably the best place for him."

But I was in the office all day arranging transportation between drivers and clients, taking care of the paperwork mess ITM required for billing, and writing legal briefs. In addition, I was trying to put together a non-profit transportation business to replace Medicab. Even if we couldn't save our income, I wanted to make sure our clients were still cared for.

We signed ten of the children up for crafts at the Junior fair, but unfortunately, Roland and I didn't have time to help them prepare and no one else in the house wanted to organize the kids and their projects. A church friend helped Carrie finish a pillow, but all that the other kids accomplished were some drawings.

Cheri, left with the children and housework, felt I was sloughing my responsibilities off onto her, so began nagging and pushing. She never really understood what a tremendous burden having everyone there was. If not for all the people in our home, my job would be much easier. I was also fighting to save out business, which was currently the only thing feeding everyone. Due to ITM, I had been overworking myself for over a year without much sleep. We were under a lot of pressure and I was very forgetful. I needed her to help if she was going to be staying there with us.

Further, when we tried to teach Cheri about God and the necessity to live a clean life, she'd throw up her hands and say "my way works fine." She also thought we were too hard on her kids because we corrected them so much. She felt the kids needed time to learn to be Christian. We understood they needed time to learn, but my own children were telling me that Carrie and Angela were teasing and insulting and doing whatever else they could get away with behind adult backs. I couldn't just let Cheri's girls do whatever they wanted.

Cheri's frustration grew deeper, as did mine. She began to treat me as though I owed her something. While she was right that there were times I ignored her and should have paid more attention, she didn't realize that my efforts to help were from my heart and not something I was forced to do. But time and again, she took me for granted, which only increased my urge to ignore her.

Cheri also criticized us for not "minding our own business" when it came to politics.

"No wonder everyone hates you," she said.

"If you care about people, standing by and doing nothing while they get hurt is wrong," I answered, "Did Jesus mind his own business?"

Good statement in theory. It did seem to be easier for me to confront big issues outside of our home than it was to confront people within our home. I didn't know what to do when Cheri time and again took her shoe off and hit Carrie with it. I knew she'd never listen to me, so I hoped Roland would step in and say something.

Cheri's boyfriend did some farm work for neighbors and got paid and Cheri, who had worked in bars and casinos back home, received her tax return. Neither offered their money to buy groceries, pay utilities, or even to get their own place. They spent most of their money on this and that, although they did listen to Roland on one point and bought themselves a car.

Jerry and his wife stayed out of our fighting, but also refused to listen to anything we said about working hard for a new life. They didn't refuse openly or with hostility, they just didn't want to hear about Jesus or get up the energy to help Roland or me with the household - or find their own place. They spent most of their time keeping after their son, who was medicated for hyperactivity and attention deficit disorder. Finally, they got up one morning and left for home. They didn't tell us why and they didn't even say good-bye. We learned later that soon after he got home, Jerry got in trouble again and was returned to prison.

About a week later, Cheri allowed Carrie to be rude to Roland and I hollered at Carrie. Cheri, Roland's first child and the one closest to him, had always been a wedge between Roland and me, so when she started yelling, I thought Roland would be right next to her. To my shock, he stood by me instead, defending me and our lifestyle.

Cheri said, "You always used to understand me."

He answered, "No, I always used to side with you."

Stunned, I left the house quickly so he and Cheri could be alone. I hoped they would talk it out and I knew if I stayed, I'd only get in their way. I didn't want to be blamed for anything he was saying. But a few minutes later Roland came out into the yard where I was standing. Cheri had gone to bed. They hadn't talked it out.

The next day, Cheri announced that she wanted to move out with her girls and baby Dewey. We didn't mind them moving out; in fact we wanted them to. But the social worker, who was upset that Roland had initially left Caleb with his mother, had said Roland must take care of all four kids, so the baby had to stay. However, the more Roland resisted Cheri, the angrier and more manipulative she got. She yelled and screamed and then called Misty and told her we were abusing the kids.

"Misty said to give him to me," she told us.

"If I let you take him, the social worker will take all her kids from me," Roland answered.

"Dewey doesn't know anyone but me!" Cheri wailed in tears.

We all knew this was really about Leon, the baby boy Cheri had lost years earlier. Our hearts broke for her. Roland shared her pain over the baby and didn't want to see her hurting again. But he couldn't budge. He didn't trust yet that she would stay straight and care for Dewey the way he needed to be cared for. Seeing Roland wasn't going to listen to her, she lost control and threatened us.

"I'm going to kick Beth's a.... and you'd better watch your house, too!"

"Do that and I'll call the cops after you," Roland retorted.

Angela ran crying out to the car where Cheri's boyfriend stood. "Grandpa won't give us Dewey."

He said, "Who does he think he is, God?"

Cheri had been so used to Roland giving in to her all her life that she didn't know what to do when he didn't. She kept pushing a little farther and farther until the situation was way out of hand. If she had calmed down and listened to her dad, it would have softened him. It wouldn't have changed his mind about giving her the baby, but he wouldn't have been as mad. But she didn't, and they both remained stubborn and angry. She finally gathered her things and left Moiese without Dewey.

Dewey must have gotten used to us in the two months, because he didn't react at all to her leaving. With the responsibility for the children totally on my shoulders now, I started teaching Ross his ABC's. Caleb and Timothy played with the baby goats and Brooke and Heidi played dolls together on the stoop without fighting. It was amazing to see the sudden change in everyone's temperaments.

But once back home, Cheri convinced Misty we were mean to the kids. Misty got the social worker to call and tell us to bring them back.

"Misty hasn't gone to treatment yet," the worker apologized, but she placed them with you voluntarily, so she has the right to move them.

We thought about insisting that social services pay for the return this time, since they were the ones asking Roland to travel. But Roland decided to heck with it. A week after Cheri had left, we returned the kids.

Roland told me later that when he dropped the kids off at Misty's, Caleb waved good-bye to his mom and tried to follow Roland out. Then Dewey started screaming. Dewey didn't know Misty at all. It broke Roland's heart to turn and go out the door.

Medicab as a business had shut down on July 1st. In its place we were running the non-profit Valley Missions. However, because donations weren't coming in very well and volunteer drivers couldn't be found, we had to limit the people we could help. While Medicaid still paid the 63 cents a mile, that didn't cover costs. A diabetic widow in need of dialysis three days a week was one woman we continued to help. As Medicab we had been transporting her for months and knew her poverty and loneliness ever since her husband's death a few months earlier. We didn't want to add to her problems by letting her know that the money we spent on gas was all the money we had.

Medicaid now carried two accounts for us: one in the name of Medicab, which we were still trying to collect payment for several runs on, and Valley Missions. The ironic thing was that Medicaid, for some reason, began overpaying us on Valley Missions for some runs already paid for on the Medicab account. Here we sat in poverty; with about $10,000 in overpayment checks in the one hand, and an undetermined amount of money still owed to us by Medicaid missing from the other hand.

My old self told me to just cash the overpayment checks. The state owed us anyway. But Roland and I knew, after working with government bureaucracy this long, that it didn't matter if the state still owed us money. They would come looking for these checks as soon as they realized the mistake.

So we put the checks aside. We knew we weren't going to cash them, but I think I had some silly idea that we could hold them hostage until we received what was actually owed us.

It was quiet now, with just our five kids, and I had mixed feelings about it. On the one hand, I missed the other kids. On the other hand, it was very nice not to have 19 people in the house anymore.

At church we really felt the children's absence, especially when they sang songs Brooke and Carrie had liked. We also felt sad when we were told that some of the "Promise Keepers" men were having a breakfast on Saturday and the whole family was invited. The men were to serve their families; Ross would have enjoyed that. He and Angela also missed the treasure hunt and barbecue their Sunday school class had after church at the pastor's house.

But Andrew was happy to be back as top dog – our numero uno helper. He really didn't like Cheri there, telling him what to do. Although only 12-years-old, he had recently developed his deep voice and grown taller than both Roland and I. Once that happened, he started to think he was an adult. It was a rocky adjustment for all of us, but we loved having him big enough to help Roland. With Medicab totally gone, we decided to focus on upholstery.

That wasn't the only change happening though. Our landlord sold the land we were living on to his son Harland, our church brother, on January 1st, 1996. "Don't worry," they said, "Nothing will change for six months or so." We weren't worried. After all, he was our brother.

My sister Tonya decided to move out of the city, so in February she sent Roland gas money to come get her and her things. While waiting for her to tie up some loose ends, Roland visited his family every day. For the first few days, although Cheri and Misty knew Roland was visiting at their mother's house, they wouldn't come see him. When they finally did, Ross told Misty that he wanted to go back with his Grandpa.

"I kept telling my mom I wanted to go with you," he said to Roland, "but she wouldn't come over here and I was afraid I missed you."

Misty finally agreed to let little Ross go. He told us later that because his mother had continued her drug use, he didn't want to live there anymore. Tonya, however, was unable to leave for an undetermined amount of time. So about mid-February, Roland packed up Tonya's things and Ross and came home. Tonya was finally able to come about a week later.

Around this time Medicaid began making noises about the checks we were holding. Their noise included threats. Although we were no closer to getting paid for runs we'd legitimately done, I was too tired of the paperwork to fight any further. Even the thought of filling out the Medicaid billing forms nauseated me. Tonya tried to help me obtain some of the money, but she became just as frustrated and both of us gave up.

In frustration, I sent all the overpayment checks by restricted certified mail directly to the Governor's office with a letter – no longer hoping to ever be paid the final amounts owed us.

A good friend wrote to Roland and asked him if he really believed politically the same way as I did. The friend stated that he is "all for the Indians," and would like to see the reservation system continue because diversity is so nice, Indian tradition is so neat, and it's great to be able to come and see how they live.

This friend was a very kind, loving person, but we wished people in general would realize how condescending that type of thinking is. Sure, many tribal governments encourage people to think that way. But not every tribal member wants to be a national pet. The reservation isn't a zoo, or a museum, for white people to come to for entertainment and to watch pow-wows. Not every tribal member wants to wear a head dress anymore than all men of Scottish heritage want to wear kilts. Tribal members are humans, and there are a lot more people in despair and death on many reservations then there are people contentedly and happily practicing traditional culture and spirituality.

Further, many tribal governments aren't helping matters. Some are, in fact, purposefully hurting their members. A friend, a tribal member, confided to us that he had been essentially sharecropping with his white neighbor. The tribal member shared his tribally leased land; the neighbor shared his tractors and other heavy equipment. Together, they both benefited. However, the tribal government found out about it and was angry. Without warning, it revoked the tribal member's lease on the land, threatened to revoke other land he leased, and threatened him with forced eviction from his HUD home. The government eventually allowed him to keep his home and other land, but permanently revoked the land he had shared with a non-member. Our friend, having a large family and afraid of retribution, had no intention of taking a chance by speaking out.

In several letters to the editor, tribal members had complained about how they are being treated by the Council:

"They (Tribal Council) throw us peanuts, and we live like a pack of dogs," wrote one member.

"It makes my heart sad when I get treated negatively by my Tribal Council...This insensitivity for people has been displayed right

before my eyes in tribal court chambers. I have also been denied freedom of press by my own tribal newspaper," wrote another.

"...the accumulation of all the power in a few, be they elected, appointed, or self-appointed will only pave the way for tyranny within our tribal structure. We must make it impossible for a single group of people to exercise such powers," wrote a third.

For ten years, the three commissioners in our county attempted to get tribal representatives on the various boards for County solid waste management, weed control, park, and land use planning. The Tribal Council had not appointed anyone in all that time. The spirit of cooperation did not exist.

"I want to add though, said one commissioner, "when we have had tribal government employees work with us, they've been helpful. However, when they go back to the tribal council with a report, nothing happens. The Council doesn't appear to allow employees to represent the Tribe's interests. For this reason, we've asked for actual Tribal Council members to be appointed to the boards, but have gotten no response."

The County Commissioners then tried to set up monthly meetings between the Tribal Council and themselves. The commissioners were showing up 100% of the time, but the tribal council less then half. The Commissioners couldn't even get cooperation with animal control.

"If we pass an animal ordinance, it won't do any good without the Tribal Council's cooperation," another commissioner said, "Tribal members don't have to pay any attention to an animal ordinance if the Tribal Government doesn't pass a similar ordinance. This same problem affects planning, zoning, even the use of billboards."

"What we need," added the third, "is mirrored ordinances, with each jurisdiction enforcing their own. But we need to get them to work with us in order for that to happen."

Some non-members called us and, after complaining that the current State Representative in House District 74 had not been paying enough attention to our county issues, asked if Roland would run against him. A couple weeks later, a man showed up from out-of-state. He, too, asked Roland to run and said he'd help as an advisor. Surprised, Roland thought and prayed about it for over a month. While he was trying to decide, the advisor called a couple more times.

"The incumbent is too liberal. We need someone to run against him. I've heard from a few people that you are well-liked among the conservative community."

I wanted to see Roland do it, although I didn't know much about the current representative beyond what Roland and I were hearing from friends. And while it would have been exciting to win, we knew the chances weren't good. Moiese wasn't a part of the district Roland would be running in and we really didn't know very many people up in that area that was. Also, Montana prefers home-grown representatives and many candidates in this state proudly advertise that their "family has been here four generations..." Roland's opponent was born and raised in the area. He had gone to high school there, had a legal practice there, and his father was an influential businessman in that district. In addition, the incumbent had been in office for ten years - and was Speaker of the House.

Despite all that was against him, Roland decided to try it.

Roland spoke at forums and I went door to door for him. At his first forum, his legs seemed to be shaking just as much as his voice was.

The issues most people were upset about in the valley were tribal issues. Non-members who didn't have any vote on the reservation were feeling increasingly voiceless and helpless. The out-of-state advisor didn't understand that though and continually tried to steer us away from the tribal issues. He insisted we address high taxes and big government. He said those were the catch issues of the year. We didn't disagree. Property taxes, in particular, were a strong issue in this valley. So Roland, thinking the advisor knew best, agreed those issues were the important ones to address. As time went on, our advisor added gun control and abortion to our list. Again, we didn't disagree. However, our original issues of importance, the tribal issues, were ignored.

Roland was invited to give his message on a radio talk show. We went there a little afraid. The Governor had been on the week before, and despite his media driven popularity, we were told he had been hung out to dry on this show. But surprisingly, Roland didn't get any flack at all. He stuck to speaking about the tribal issues because that was what the people who called in wanted to talk about. When asked about his childhood, he told about living with his grandfather and how much that relationship meant to him. Speaking of his grandfather's death, his voice became emotional.

"I can tell you really loved your grandfather," the host said.

The callers were very supportive and later we received letters and calls from people that had heard the show and were impressed.

Shortly before the election, I was asked to host a public meeting where Roland and Will were to talk. No one else in our "hate" group wanted to; they feared tribal members would show up and harass us. And they did. Before the meeting had gone far I was in tears. But the emotion of the meeting charged Roland, and he went in there and (according to Will; I didn't hear it because I was still crying outside of the room) gave his best speech ever.

The Tribal Council-run newspaper then ran an article condemning me and the other white people involved, but said nothing about the speech Roland gave.

A week before the election the advisor gave us letters to mail with a statement about our opponent in relationship to his record with abortion. After the letters were mailed, we were told by an acquaintance that the information was wrong. We immediately called the advisor to ask about what he had written. He claimed the letters never said it was true, only insinuated the opponent *could* be doing this because it was possible for him to do it. What twisted logic! My throat went dry and my stomach felt like lead.

The advisor went on to say, "Don't worry about it. Everyone writes this way. Besides, no one will question it."

"Someone already has. Roland says he's going to get on the radio and retract it."

"Now don't go do that! So one person knows! So what? If you go on the radio everyone will know!"

Ashamed to have sent those letters, Roland wouldn't listen to him. Too bad it took so long for us to stop listening to him. Roland, disgusted by the dirty politics, made a public apology on the radio, broadcast several times in the last couple days before the election. I got on the phone and spent hours calling as many of the voters as

I could, to apologize to those who might not have heard it on the radio.

All things considered, we were grateful to have received 35% of the vote.

Tonya, by this time, had settled into a job as a paralegal and moved out on her own.

Harland, our brother from church and now our landlord, sent us a letter stating we would have to get rid of our goats, chickens, some cats and grandson it we are to remain on the property. He also asked that we put new siding under the trailers and build better steps. We had no direct neighbors and his family lived a couple of miles from us. How was our trailer's appearance hurting anyone? Also, he and his wife knew we had very little money ever since we lost Medicab. They knew we needed the chickens and goats to feed the kids milk and eggs. He was a rancher himself, why would he want us to get rid of the animals?

I tried calling the man, but he wouldn't talk to me. He said he would speak only to the man of the house. Roland went to speak to him, and he gave Roland until July to move out.

Roland and I were trying to sort this out when Misty's social worker called again. Having gotten reports about Misty's neglect, they asked Roland to come after the rest of her children. Roland didn't answer right away. Harland had made it clear he didn't want extra family members living in our home. In addition, we could barely support ourselves. How could we handle additional children?

But the children needed help. One of Misty's social workers told me over the phone, "If Misty was white or black she would have lost these kids a long time ago," the worker said, "Most social service workers are too afraid of or confused by ICWA to want to mess with it. And the Tribal government wants the kids to stay with family as much as possible. As a result, Indian kids stay in terrible homes much longer than other kids."

"As a social worker, why don't you say something about it?"

"I'm the most conservative person in this office. Few here will consider or admit that ICWA is hurting kids."

In prayer, Roland put out a fleece to the Lord. 'If it is God's will the kids come out here again, the money to get them here would be provided.'

To our surprise, the social worker called back and offered transportation money from a special fund. They'd never done that before. So, Roland decided to trust the Lord to help with all the kids.

Not only that, but a couple days before Roland came back with the kids, a grocery truck overturned at Palmer corner. The driver had decided that certain things were unsellable and allowed our friends, who had run over to help clean up the mess, to stock up their cars with boxes and bags of necessities. These friends had no idea that Roland had left to pick up four grandkids, but they arrived at our house with six bags of large boy's (blue) pampers, 15 boxes of cold cereal, a case of Ramen noodles, some canned food, a bucket of laundry detergent, bleach, fabric softener, 36 rolls of toilet paper, and 9 rolls of paper towels, among other things. It was like the Lord was preparing us for the kids, because we sure wouldn't have been able to afford all of that on our own. It was a real blessing. We had not only enough food and paper goods to keep a large family for a few weeks, but a summers worth of pampers that were just the right size for baby Dewey.

Brooke, Caleb, and Dewey returned to us in June 1996. Before the children even arrived, they were already being prayed for. Before they even got here, people were helping.

Their first week here, the school age kids made beaded scarves at Vacation Bible school. They really enjoyed the class, which ran from 2 to 4 p.m. every day for one week. Brooke would start asking me at 10 in the morning if it was time to go yet.

While picking the older children up one afternoon, I left the babies buckled in the car. Glancing out the school window while the older children gathered their things, I saw Caleb, who must have released himself, standing over Timothy and Rosie, who were still strapped in their seats. Looking closer, I could see he was punching them both in the face.

During the trip to get the kids, Roland had picked up the June 7, 1996, issue of the Native American Press/Ojibwe News, a tribal newspaper published in northern Minnesota. I had never seen this newspaper before, but not wanting to read the usual rhetoric about how terrible white people are, I wasn't interested in looking at it.

"No, look," Roland encouraged, "There's an article in here about the Leech Lake Tribal Council being indicted for millions of dollars in fraud!"

That piqued my interest. Sharing the paper, we read a lengthy article about the allegations of corruption, intimidation, bribery and ballot box stuffing against both the Leech Lake Council and the White Earth tribal council. It surprised us that a tribal newspaper would be so upfront with allegations like this. Usually tribal papers, funded and controlled by tribal government, painted only what made the reservation look good.

Defense overwhelmed by vote fraud evidence in week 4 of Chippygate
By Greg Blair,

The enrollees came from all over the country, many of them full- blood Indians, while some had blonde hair and blue eyes. However, not one of them hesitated when asked by prosecutors if they were eligible to vote in the White Earth reservation's elections. "Yes," was the answer jurors heard from nearly one hundred witnesses who testified this week that they were denied the exercise of this right by the fraudulent practices of Darrell "Chip" Wadena's gang. Some of the witnesses reported that they had never lived on the reservation or voted in tribal elections. One of the witnesses was a doctor, another was a former Twin Cities radio personality, one was a minister and yet others were successful businessmen and women. Some were raising families, others were retired elders and some were also struggling in poverty.

Many said they had left White Earth as young children or older adults. Others said they had voted on the reservation, but not by absentee ballot. Yet others said they had voted once, but prosecutors showed them two sets of signed ballots for verification. Still others insisted that they had never voted in the reservation's 1994 general election, but that they had voted in other past White Earth elections.

By day's end, the federal courthouse in St. Paul, Minnesota resembled a White Earth reunion more than a federal corruption trial. The get-together was even larger than during the reservation's founder's day Pow-Wow held in mid-June each year. A common sentiment was expressed by one witness, who said after testifying, "That's the reason my parents left the reservation, there is too much corruption and I guess it's still going on."

Leech Lake members, residents played key role in White Earth vote conspiracy
By Jeff Armstrong

White Earth Reservation officials used funds from a public assistance program with a $1.1 million annual budget to compensate Leech Lake arid White Earth members who helped them obtain and certify fraudulent ballots in 1990 and 1994, according to testimony in the federal conspiracy trial of White Earth's top officials.

Indicted White Earth election board chair Carley Jasken also directed the assistance program, but despite the federal charges, Jasken will be responsible for overseeing next Tuesday's balloting. Eleanor Craven testified that she and fellow Leech Lake member Leo Gotchie, then a district RBC (Reservation Business Committee) candidate, were campaigning for absentee votes on May 25, 1994, when they stopped at Peter Peqette's south Minneapolis home. Craven said Gotchie suggested the stop in hopes of obtaining gas money for their return trip by using her notary seal to validate White Earth ballots.

Shortly after their arrival at Pequette's, Craven testified, Jerry Rawley showed up at the residence with an *attache case full of "hundreds" of signed absentee ballots in sealed envelopes. Although the Minnesota Chippewa Tribe's election ordinance requires absentee voters to sign the "affidavit envelope" in the presence of a notary public - who must then verify that the voter actually cast the enclosed ballot - Craven said she and Pequette proceeded to notarize the invalid ballots.*

...Craven said Rawley then collected the votes and handed Gotchie an apparent payment. "He gave something to Mr. Gotchie and he said, "here, take care of your notary,"

...Among the "votes" delivered on May 25, 1994 were those of Cheryl Boswell and her brother Neil. Ms. Boswell, like more than three dozen witnesses in a single day, testified that she never voted in the election and that the ballot envelope in her name was a forgery. Boswell also caused a subdued stir in the courtroom when she told the court that she knew her brother's vote was false because Neil Boswell had died six months prior to the election.

...An employee of Harper's at Leech Lake maintenance, Terry LaDuke, received two payments of $400 each from the White Earth general fund in 1994. LaDuke testified that it was a common practice at both Leech Lake and White Earth to gather ballots to be notarized, with or without the voter's presence.

Money is at the core of court queries
By Pat Doyle

The question drew a response that startled some in the courtroom: How much money do you make in a year?

When Darwin McArthur, executive director of the White Earth Band of Chippewa, replied that he made $59,000, a tribal member in the spectator section gasped. By standards of the White Earth Indian Reservation, McArthur's salary is extraordinary - but not close to the income of his bosses.

...Jurors...listened to testimony of how council members tapped tribal accounts to buy themselves vehicles or to pay their taxes.

"If they tell you to issue a check, that's what you do?" a prosecutor asked McArthur.

"Yes," he replied.

In 1993 tribal funds provided $240,122 for Chairman Darrell (Chip) Wadena, $209,507 for council member Rick Clark and $187,237 for Secretary-Treasurer Jerry Rawley.

Prosecutors say those figures include tens of thousands of dollars that the officials embezzled from their tribe by creating gambling and fishing commissions that provided them with checks for work they didn't do. Additionally, Wadena and Rawley are accused of accepting bribes or gratuities of $428, 682 and $21,500 respectively from Clark to assure that his drywall firm would land a contract to help build the tribe's Shooting Star Casino in Mahnomen.

...In their questions to witnesses, defense attorneys have suggested that tribal officials deserved the money because they built a casino that employs about 1000 people, most of them Indians, on a remote reservation in northwest Minnesota. Moreover, they say the officials were operating in the belief that treaties and federal statutes over the years gave them the authority to do what they did.

And defense lawyers have tried to convince the jury that overzealous federal investigators singled out Wadena, Rawley and Clark for conduct common among Indian officials. Whatever its outcome, the trial exposes that a tribal government operates without checks and balances, in which council members typically avoid scrutiny by their constituents or non-Indians.

Council members made decisions about their pay at meetings they routinely held without notifying White Earth members. McArthur said they did so to "avoid opposition."

Beth Ward

Life is like
a book
sublime

Adding pages
to my
mind

© By PHONACELLE SHAPEL

Chapter seventeen:
The Mission is Clear

Two weeks later we went to our annual bible camp and stayed in the dorm style housing. The boys: Andrew, Ross, Caleb, and Timothy, got one room, and the rest of us were in the room next door.

Initially, we thought that our large number of kids would bother the elderly people in the rooms near us. We told the kids not to run in the halls, but the babies, a one-year- old, two two-year-olds, and a three-year-old, did it anyway. Dewey, giggling while he ran, was especially a problem. But everyone was so nice and seemed to enjoy the kids so much. They treated the kids like their own grandchildren and said they weren't bothered by them a bit - even the time that Rosie had to go to the bathroom so bad that she took off down the hall naked.

After one hot day, while Roland took the five older children to church service, I tried to bathe the sticky, dirty babies. I was tired and needed to get them all clean as quickly as possible so we could all go to bed. There weren't any tubs in the bathrooms, only showers, and the sinks were too small for even Dewey, so I put them all into a shower together. Timothy went in first, and started singing and dancing. Then Caleb decided he'd try it, and when Rosie saw they were having fun, she joined them. Soon all three of them were singing, laughing and strutting around. I had to keep them from getting too wild so they wouldn't fall. Dewey just stood next to me and watched cautiously for a little while, then laughed and went in too. I wished Roland could have seen them or that I had a camera. I finally had to make them come out so we could go to bed. Getting four slippery, squirmy, jumping babies dry, brushed and into pajamas isn't easy, either.

Roland couldn't stay at camp the whole time though. He had to go home and work on some furniture. But before he left, friends put together a birthday cake and ice cream for his birthday. Our landlord, there for the camp along with other church friends, pulled Roland aside and said, "Promise Keepers is having a big gathering in Washington DC next year. They suggest everyone try to bring a minority with them. Would you go with me?"

Having been given grace by the landlord to stay a little while longer on the property while we searched for a home, Roland initially agreed to go with him. But a year is a long time, and the offer and acceptance was later forgotten – probably with relief by both.

After Roland had gone back home to work, several neat people at camp helped me with the kids. One morning our pastor was waiting for me when I came to breakfast and helped get the kid's food, then cut up their French toast. Another time, a lady saw that I was way at the end of the line and grabbed my arm, pulled me to the head of line, and stuck me in to get my trays.

"You've got too many babies to wait to eat."

No one in line got mad. They all smiled and said, "Go ahead."

Another friend helped once by watching all of the kids at a table while I went after trays, then she got our drinks for me.

The kids went to the Lake to swim three times while we were up there. I tried to keep all the kids playing within the boundaries of my single line of vision, with Dewey at the edge of the water right in front of me, but he was a terror to watch. While I was eyeing one of the kids, or pulling Caleb up when he slipped, Dewey would waddle over to someone else's blanket and try to take their pop, chips or beach ball. People didn't seem to mind. He was pretty cute. By the last day of camp, Dewey was running down the hall and into old people's arms to hug them. One lady I didn't even know had us all sit together up on the stairs so she could take a picture and remember us.

Back at home on the fourth of July, Roland took the older kids to see the fireworks while I put the little ones to bed. He wasn't gone a half-hour when they all came back. He had made it halfway to Charlo when a deer had jumped out in front of the car. He was able to drive back because he wasn't far away, but the car's front end was smashed, the radiator full of holes.

"On top of that, the deer was too smashed to use for meat," he lamented.

The kids did see fireworks by standing on the roof of the root cellar in our back yard. Ross was excited by all the color.

Throughout the summer, various people came by with gifts of garden vegetables and butchered meat. The kids played games on the trampoline, swam in the little pool, and made forts in all kinds of strange places.

The 4-H Junior Fair was in August and we were better prepared for it this year. All of the kids entered things they had made. Ross won a blue ribbon for his chocolate candy. Andrew's goat was Grand Champion at the 4-H fair for a second year. Admittedly, there was no competition. His was the only goat. But hey, he did a very good job taking care of that goat.

Meanwhile, Congress was looking at changing ICWA again, so we were doing our best to be heard. I was new to the issue and didn't understand that some of what I thought was part of the new bill and found upsetting was actually already in the law since 1978. But no matter, it was still wrong...

August 26, 1996
Dear Representative Gingrich;

>I have not heard a thing about the progress of the ICWA amendments in over a month. Please send me a letter explaining what is going on and what your position is.
>
>I am the white mother of children that are 50% Native American. My husband is 100%. The last I had heard, Senator XXXXXX was proposing language that would allow the tribes to decide who is Indian and require social services to notify the tribes within 6 months if child custody is being transferred.

#1) 1 hope that you can see that if Tribes are allowed to set the blood quantum, social services will be required to do a literal "title search" on every child they work with. If one tribe in the country decides that children that are 1/64 are under their jurisdiction, social services will have to check the lineage of every child, or face the chance of future lawsuits.

#2) This would deny me as a person. My heritage is considered less then valuable compared to my husband's heritage. My family is suddenly unimportant and expendable. The government would be making a decision that there is a race in the United States that is better than others, and more worthy of having its culture taught.

#3) The Government would be deciding that one religion is more important and worthier than any other religion. It would be deciding that even if my husband and I decide to raise our children as Christians, the Tribe will have the right to take the children if we die, and teach them a religion that we as parents consider to be pagan.

Please sir, see past the idea that this is about tribal sovereignty and see into the actual stripping of parental rights, the denial of religious freedom, and the destruction of families.

If it is about keeping families together, please support the Congressional Parental Rights and Responsibilities Act. That act should cover all family rights, no matter the race. If this is not about keeping families together, but is in reality an effort by Tribal Governments to control the children of families that are trying to leave the cover of the reservation, please recognize that and protect us. Thank you,

PS. By only allowing social services, tribal governments, and lawyers to testify about this issue, Sen. XXXXXX is ignoring the most important voice. The families themselves. We exist, we have our own minds, and no government should be allowed to take away our parental rights.

Newt never answered, but others did. One Senator's staff told us that unless they see large numbers of Tribal members protest, the Senator will continue to assume most members are happy with ICWA. But:

- Many tribal members don't understand what ICWA actually says and does, let alone feel they can do anything about it.
- A law that infringes on the constitutional rights of even one person should be reconsidered, no matter how many people do or don't point it out.
- Everyone seems to forget that this law affects ALL people groups in the United States; not just tribal members. Tribal governments have a right to determine their own membership and some have made the requirement quite broad. The Cherokee Tribe, in deciding that any child whose lineage can be traced to the Dawes Rolls is eligible, has sought jurisdiction over children of extremely minute heritage. One little boy was less than 2% Cherokee heritage – 98% Caucasian. A baby girl was 50% African American and the rest primarily Latino. In other words, children of EVERY heritage are included in this law – and <u>all parents, of any heritage, have a right to protest.</u>

Dear Mr. and Mrs. Ward,
    I read your "letter to the editor" in the (paper) last week and am so glad someone would dare to tell the truth. You did and I applaud you for being "politically incorrect." My husband and I listened to your conversations (on the radio) and you, Mr. Ward, are a remarkable individual. If your wife picked you, she is, as well, a remarkable

woman! We were so sorry that you didn't earn the chance to go to the legislature - there will be another time for you to try.
God Bless you both.

A sister from the church, in an attempt to be helpful, told me that maybe we were being kicked off our land because we allowed the kids' toys to lie scattered around the yard all night. Maybe if we had the kids clean up the yard every evening, the other family wouldn't be upset with us anymore.

Maybe if I quit politics, she also said (still meaning well) and took better care of the home and family... and in essence, baked bread and made a better pie crust... I'd be a better Christian woman and life would improve...

But I had more on my mind than getting neighbors to like me. I needed to get my husband to like me again. I had spent over $1000 faxing Congressmen about ICWA at a time when Roland and I had absolutely no money. The reason it cost so much was because calling just about anywhere outside of Moiese was long distance, and our computer fax was very, very slow. I had hidden what I was doing from Roland by turning down the screen light and sound, so he couldn't tell that the computer was faxing all night.

The phone was shut off and I had to sell my ceramics kiln and molds to pay the bill. Now the propane was running out and we had nothing left to sell.

I couldn't speak to Roland when he was this mad at me, so I wrote a letter. But I wasn't honest with him or myself. Not willing to admit I had been impulsive and wrong to fax Congress all night long, putting us into deeper financial trouble without asking him, I cajoled him to 'have faith.'

This behavior, obviously, was more to the point about me not being a responsible wife and mother than baking bread and picking up toys. My kind neighbor was correct in the sense that I didn't have my priorities straight. She was just mixed up on what the priorities should have been.

August, 1996
Roland;

We ARE in horrible shape financially. We've never before been like this because in the past when we had no income, we'd gone ahead and got welfare. Now, we are essentially destitute. So do we give up, or do we take hold and start a slow crawl back? Elmer, Boots and Norm prayed for us last week. Now we have to stand on that and fight the battle.

I think you misunderstood about the propane. I realize that if the propane gauge says "0", there is no propane. I wasn't questioning that. I was saying that if it was God's will, he could keep it going on fumes. Remember that we aren't supposed to jump ahead of God, but give him a chance to bless us. I was asking you to pray and see if God would indicate his desire. Maybe he wanted you to buy propane, maybe not. But I haven't mailed those bills yet. If God wants you to buy propane, go buy it.

But I do not think you are mad about the propane. I think you are mad about the phone bill. I realize I used the fax too much. I think my kids, in relation to the Indian Child Welfare Act are worth it. When will another chance come up to fight ICWA? I sold my ceramics kiln and molds and paid the last bill in full. Now we have to figure out this bill.

Many of our creditors have been angry that we haven't paid anything in two months. You should have read those letters. We need to make an effort every month to send something to our creditors. And don't forget, we also have to make a payment soon to (the) bank. That is why I questioned the propane. It is summer; we only need it for cooking. We have a microwave and an outside grill. And there is nothing wrong with peanut butter for lunch. I can get creative. What are our choices for making money? There are three: #1) Continue to work at the upholstery, #2) find outside jobs, or #3) get welfare.

We both know welfare isn't an option. Outside work is an option, but that is up to you and the Lord. But you are so good at upholstery, love it so much, and so many Christians have encouraged you to keep doing it, I wonder if that's where God wants you. I want to fight through it. I want to just continue with the work and referrals that we have right now and work at eating away at our debts slowly. We have no choice but to go forward, slowly mending our financial problems.

About our home: Please pray deeply about this. We have no financial way of making a move. Even if we rented, where would we get the money for first and last months deposit? It would be at least $1000 just to move. Again, we have three choices: #1) Continue to pray for a financial miracle. #2) sleep in our cars. #3) go talk to Harland

I leave this decision totally in your hands. I will do what ever I have to do to support you by spending as little as possible, praying, baking as much as I can today to prepare for whatever happens, taking care of the kids, and tearing apart whatever furniture you want me to. I can do that if you want to go out and see your upholstery referrals. Our neighbor will allow you to call them, just give her some phone money.

Also, if you have chosen the furniture for the commercials, is there other furniture that you have fabric for already that we can fix up and sell in a week or two at a rummage sale? Maybe we need to go through the house again and get rid of even more stuff.

Please stand on the promises given us during that evening of prayer in our house. We can overcome anything with the help of our Lord God and by sticking together.

Beth

A few days later, our propane tank emptied and we ran out of hot water. Now was the time to get creative as promised. The children all needed baths and their hair washed. How was I going to coax them into cold water long enough to clean them? Well, I figured that when they play with their wading pool in the yard, they don't seem to mind hose water. So I filled the little pool up and let it set in the sun for a couple hours. Then I herded the crew outside, (with swimsuits, of course) and let them play. It was still on the cool side, but it was working. While they played, I took them one by one to shampoo their heads and soap their bodies. This only added to the fun, as they now had piles of soapsuds to play with too. Of course, they hated the rinse off, which I did with the hose. But once rinsed, they were back in playing.

Elmer Dovetail drove up just as we were finishing. "Ooh, will you look at that!" he chirped, "can I get in?"

Harland gave us another deadline of Sept. 1. Because we had to move and had nowhere to go, I wrote to Misty and Wesley and asked them to come out by bus and get their kids. I also asked if they could send money for Dewey's diapers; my summer supply had run out. We got no response from either of them. Indirectly, we'd heard that both were still drinking. Misty hadn't even entered treatment yet.

It had been a year now that we'd been trying to make Ward Upholstery work out of our trailers, but out here in the valley, we just couldn't get enough business to support us. Maybe moving into Ronan where Roland could get more business would be good. We went to the bank for help. However, because of our debts they couldn't give us a loan. In mid-August, with nine children in the house and no money, we didn't know what to do. The deadline for moving was just around the corner.

Although we were broke, we went searching. What could we do but try? Unfortunately, trailer parks didn't want to rent space to nine kids and home rentals were financially out of reach.

Roland and I visited some realtors. We had to find something. Maybe there would be a small, run down house somewhere that someone was desperate to rent. Paging through a realtor magazine, we found a building for sale in Ronan. The asking price was only $50,000. This included two storefronts on a Main Street and an apartment in back with two bedrooms. The upstairs, although there was no access to it, had a potential of 4 bedrooms. The building had been empty for some time. We wondered if we could negotiate with the owners…but the listed realtor said their contract had run out and they couldn't give us a name.

Undeterred, we decided to stop in Ronan on our way home and look at the outside of the building. It wasn't encouraging. There didn't seem to be a foundation, water was standing beside the building, and there was buckling in some of the outside walls. At that moment a carpenter friend drove by and stopped.

"$50,000?" he said, "This place is probably worth no more than the lot it is on."

Roland decided to offer the owners $35,000, contract-for-deed. But who were they? A neighbor down the street told us they also owned the Yellow Bay store.

We drove up to Yellow Bay the next day. The owners immediately drove back down with us. Roland walked through and silently noted the dirt, weak floors, and mildew smell. But it wasn't as if we had any other options, and both the upholstery and the family would fit. In addition, the library, park, school, and church were all within walking distance. We prayed that they were as desperate as we were.

Surprisingly, they were. The husband made an offer, "The Realtor contract is expired," he said, "We'll take $32,000." We agreed, then asked if it could be contract-for-deed.

"No" his wife answered. They had had a bitter experience with a contract and weren't willing to try it again.

We went back to the bank and were turned down again.

Now what? On the way to tell the owners about the bank's denial, Roland pulled the car over to pray. It was only a few days before Sept. 1, and we had no other options. After praying, Roland said, "we will offer them $500 a month in rent. If it is God's will for us to have the place, they'll accept the offer."

The wife was alone at the shop. As we walked toward her, I told her we had been turned down by the bank. Without missing a beat, she quickly asked: "Would you rent the place for $500 a month, then?" Without hesitation, we accepted. We didn't have any money, so Roland asked if he could postdate a check.

"Fine," she said. The next day we cleaned the building and began moving in.

The blessings continued. We weren't able to cover that check, but because we found four feet of water underneath the floor, they weren't concerned about the money!

"No problem," they said, while filming the mess made by a neighbor's water line, "pay us when you can. Hey, and maybe we can do a rent-to-own."

The next week, the city dug a hole and fixed the water line. Well, we figured, if the Lord put us here he's not going to allow the place to fall down around our ears.

Andrew, Haley, Ross, Brooke and Heidi all went back to school at the Christian Academy. Roland would drive school bus every afternoon and I would clean class rooms at night to pay the tuition. Sometimes one or two of the kids went with me and helped. Ross was the best worker. He just jumped in, doing everything he could. We still had to pay for books and uniforms, but the headmaster gave us time to do that. Our school kids also joined fall soccer and Ross and Brooke quickly became team stars.

And... the younger ones also played as a team. While I was working in the front one morning, two-year-old Rosie opened the back door and led the boys outside and onto the street. Fortunately, Celeste was driving by, saw them and stopped. When we were in Moiese, surrounded by wheat fields, the children were free to go in and out of the house without fear. We were going to have to get used to the difference.

Another big difference between town and country was that people were now dropping in almost every day of the week. I liked visiting people, but I hated for them to see my messy house. So I told the kids that coats, shoes, bookbags and toys all belonged in their rooms and no where else. That rule didn't last long.

One morning when the older kids were all at school and I was unpacking moving boxes, a woman from the school came by to set up my classroom-cleaning schedule. Seeing how busy I was, she took the three littlest for a walk to the park in order to give me some time. Once there they fed the ducks and played on the swings.

Throughout the week, other people came by to give us meals, fresh milk, or bags of vegetables. Throughout the month, various friends helped out by taking two, four, or even eight children at a time over to their homes. I could get used to living here!

The blessings were real, but I was feeling overwhelmed with the move, our financial situation, and all the children. After confessing my depression to the children's headmaster, he encouraged me to call Will and Judy Stanley for help. They came over immediately, taking Caleb and Dewey from me. Judy still wanted to adopt a baby boy and they talked about keeping these two. Huge stress lifted from my shoulders.

> Dear Joy:
> Tell us as soon as you get your GED. We've been waiting to hear. And Good luck in the office classes! The classes you want to take will be great. There will be a lot of good jobs for you. Computer keyboard especially. (I could have used that kind of help when we had Medicab!) <u>You are so smart for doing that</u>. I hope you like it. It'll be hard going after the baby is born. But you are strong, smart, and have guts. You can do it. I really like the computer. I never took a class though, so you'll end up knowing more than I know!
>
> I can't believe Ashley and Rosie will be three in a few months. They aren't babies anymore. Hope you are feeling okay. The last month pregnant is usually the worst for me. But you're still young, so maybe it doesn't bother you as much.

We still needed to pay our rent and deposit to the landlords, not to mention the upcoming rent for the next month. We needed to get the upholstery shop open in order to make money, but we couldn't open the shop without money. I prayed to God for some miracle. We had only one thing of value to sell: Our Medicab license.

"Please God. All I want for Christmas is to have that license sell."

A little while later, a retired business man called us and asked to meet with us about Medicab. He wanted to start Medicab back up again in Missoula. As long as the cab was just in the city, the price Medicaid was willing to pay made more sense because there weren't all the dead miles that had to be traveled. He said he was willing to give us $5000 for our license.

His wife looked directly at me and said, "How is that for a Christmas present?"

What a strange thing to say in September. Thank you, Jesus.

Very stoic at age 6, Heidi rarely complained of pain. After mildly complaining about a sore ear for a couple of days, her ear broke open on Sunday. I was combing back her silky, dark hair after church and noticed the gunk in her ear. I asked her about it, but she denied any pain or any knowledge of it breaking.

Then I noticed small sores around the ear and a couple of places on her face. Realizing she had a serious ear infection and fearing impetigo, I decided to keep her home from school on Monday. But I didn't know how I would pay for an office visit. We had only about $60 in the checking account. How much would a doctor and medicine cost? I went to bed wondering how we would manage getting her well, as well as other needs. The first $1000 we were expecting for the sale of our Medicab license wasn't to come for another month. We had expected it sooner, but apparently the Public Service Commission had to post the sale in the papers before they could give their blessing.

Expecting to have had the Medicab sale over with, we had also ordered business cards with a new phone number (reserved for us by the phone company) for Ward Upholstery. Monday was supposed to be our opening day. But without a $200 deposit, we couldn't get the phone hooked up either. How can we open a business without a phone? But we couldn't postpone opening the upholstery shop; the family had too many needs. We needed to get working.

Monday morning we woke to a very chilly house. I got up and moved straight away to turn up the heat, but nothing happened. Apparently, the oil had run out in the middle of the night, as well. We had wondered how long it would last. We were only using what had been left over in the tank from the previous renters of this building. So I put thick socks and sweaters on Heidi, Timothy, Rosie, and myself and sent the others off to school.

Not knowing what else to do, I went about the business of opening the shop. Praying to Jesus, I also went ahead and made an afternoon appointment for Heidi. Roland, while working on last minute needs of the shop, took the problem of fuel and phone to prayer.

At noon, the mail came, and with it, $600 from Aunt Charlotte. God Bless her. Our phone was hooked up, oil tank filled, and Heidi saw the doctor and got her medicine (which she couldn't stand). We opened the shop and Roland sold an antique couch from our showroom right away. God Bless Aunt Charlotte. She and the Lord must have a direct line to each other.

The Stanley's had wanted to keep the boys, but after we gave them a copy of the ICWA, they realized it was probably not possible for them to adopt and if they were going to keep them, they wanted it to be permanent. So they brought them back after just two weeks. Still, for those two weeks I was able to rest a little and spend time with Timothy and Rosie.

The headmaster from the Christian school had once commented that he would like to operate a bookstore. Now that we had two storefronts, we asked if he still wanted to do it.

"Sure," he said, and immediately proceeded to load us up with new and used surplus schoolbooks that we could make available to homeschoolers.

We then remembered a conversation we had had with the manager of a Christian resource store a few years earlier. We had discussed bringing videos up to Ronan from their store in Missoula, but we didn't have a good place to put them at the time. So Roland and I went to ask if he still wanted to do it. Roland had an errand to run first, so he dropped me off at the store.

But it wasn't the same manager as the one I had remembered, and this one was a little uneasy. He didn't know us and didn't want to get involved with people who might not have the same goals and objectives in Christ. I started to explain what we believed, but he held up his hand and said, "No, God will tell me before you leave here."

He then went on to explain his ministry, describing it as "pure and totally non-profit." He said, "God is the owner," and there was nothing to be sold under their banner. The videos and books were for library use, reaching out to both the churched and unchurched. He said that money is not an issue here; God's ministry is.

"Don't worry whether or not people give to the donation box," he said, "when you do that, you allow anger and bitterness to enter your heart, and that squeezes out Love and Ministry."

After going on to tell me about his vision for the future, he told me about how strangers had come in last month and put up shelves for him. While he was talking, Roland walked in. He stopped speaking and looked at Roland.

"I know who you are," he said, "you used to run Medicab!"

Roland nodded yes.

"Well," he said. "The Lord had put it upon my heart to pray for you a long time ago! Hey! I know your hearts! You can have those videos!"

He loaded us up with 50 videos and the sign from his front window. Maybe the Lord had more than just shelter in mind when He gave us the shop.

> Dear Theresa:
> I know God has been good, and I know half of me wants to keep the grandkids with us. But in honesty, only half of me.
>
> We are afraid of the ICWA; that if we don't keep them, it will put the kids into the hands of relatives that drink. In my head, I know there aren't any other options. But in my heart, I don't want this. I am tired and can't handle it. I don't want to take care of other people's kids anymore. I want to be alone with my five. Isn't that selfish?
>
> I don't feel right. I don't feel at peace. Maybe it's the kids, maybe it's the loss of our business, or maybe it's the bill collectors calling. Maybe it's the move from Moiese. I can't settle into this house and feel like it is really home. Well, we haven't been able to pay the rent, so of course I can't feel like it's home.
>
> And yes, I am angry at our church. Whether my personal need to be cared for is good or right or acceptable, I don't know. I am sure a lot of people in our church

think it is not. But even if it isn't good, it's still there. I'm desperate. I'm on the edge. When I allow myself to stop being busy and think about it all, I feel that I might go crazy. Of course I've prayed for God's help. Half the time all I'm doing is hating myself and crying out to God for help. But when most people in our church sense my need, they go running as fast as they can in the other direction.

But some don't run from me. For some reason, they aren't scared of me. At least not yet. I know they aren't a permanent answer or even a complete answer to all that is going on in my life. They can't be. And I don't expect anyone else to have an answer either. I know that I have to learn to get my needs met from God. But right now, I thank them for being there.

On Joy's birthday, she gave birth to a son, Jordon Jr. That very same day Misty also gave birth to Kelly.

Joy, Jordon Jr. and Misty were ready to go home within a day or two. Kelly was not. Kelly, born with cocaine in her blood, had surgery at four days old and was hospitalized for another month.

Misty and Wesley called the day after Kelly's birth. "We think it's time the kids come home. A hospital social worker here said she'd help us get a house. My mom says she'll pay for your gas to get them back. She'll send it next week when she gets paid."

Calls through the week indicated Shirley was really planning on wiring the money on Friday. From what we were told, Shirley would rather the kids be in a foster home than with us.

"Roland," I asked him, "Misty's baby is in the hospital because of her drug use. You're not really going to take the kids back, are you?"

"You've been complaining you can't handle the kids. Now you want them to stay? Besides, I prayed that if the money's provided, they will go back. I'm sticking to that. If God wants them to stay, the money won't come."

Roland was right that I wasn't handling things well. But my feelings were mixed; I still didn't want them to have to go back to living with neglect and abuse.

Thursday night, Shirley called and confirmed the plan. Roland was to pick the wired money up at 4 p.m. the next day and take the kids back that weekend. On Friday afternoon I packed clothes, preparing for Roland's trip, all the while hoping Shirley wouldn't call and go through with it. At 3:45, Shirley called. Disappointed, I handed Roland the phone. He spoke to her a few minutes, then hung up.

"They aren't sending the money. The Child Protection worker told them the kids would go straight to a foster home the moment they arrived."

"I thought that's what she wanted."

"I don't know. Don't ask me to figure it out."

On October 24, 1996 the county Juvenile Court ordered the five Redwood children into out-of-home placement, further ordering that the four older children remain with Roland. The grounds for removal included reports of heavy use of crack; selling furniture, food stamps and baby formula for drug use; lack of clean clothes and food for the kids, and babies born with cocaine in their blood. The parents also failed to follow through with treatment care plans. Brooke and Ross had also, at only five and six-years-old, been held back in school a year because of lack of attendance. Brooke had only attended 51 days one year, and 58 the next – meaning that in two years, she had not yet had a full year of kindergarten.

The county, having taken custody of the kids, began to send us child support.

Haley, at 9, was growing more beautiful and mature every day. I depended on both Haley and Andrew a lot as I wrestled with all the babies and the business. It was helpful to know they were mature enough to sit in the front of the shop if I had to be in back making a meal, doing laundry, or tending kids. Andrew, who was now 14, didn't mind as long as he could play the computer, and Haley didn't seem to mind as long as she had a good book. They also helped

Roland in the upholstery side of the shop, tearing down furniture for him.

Heidi, at 6, had beautiful dark eyes and features. Our neighbor had once described her as having an exotic beauty. Still shy, she enjoyed being alone reading or drawing by herself, though having extra kids in the house was helping her come out of her shell. Rosie, at 3, was going on 20-years-old. She was one headstrong, determined princess. She ran the house and everyone knew it. When the boys had first moved in, I had been afraid for her. I thought Caleb, Dewey and Timothy would trample my baby girl. I should have known. After all, she was tackling Timothy and holding him down when she was only nine months old. She holds her own, no need to worry about her.

One night at a Bible study, I told friends of some of the things from the past and cried for the first time about little Candis being left in the city park by herself all night. Can you imagine being 7-years-old and alone in the dark? I wonder where she slept. Or if she did. I never asked at the time.

Candis, now grown, had her own daughter removed from her two years earlier.

And now we were called and asked to take Savannah's children. Already having nine, we weren't sure if we should. But Annie said there was no one in the family but us that was sober right now, and if we didn't move to take them, they would be placed with family members that weren't as stable.

The ironic part is that three different families, including the Stanley's, had indicated interest in adopting some of the children we already had, but knew they couldn't because of the Indian Child Welfare Act. Why can't Congress see that by leaving children in unhealthy families, they are just perpetuating the problems? If kids stay within a dysfunctional extended family, they continue to learn unhealthy methods of coping. But tribal governments have motivation to try to keep kids under their jurisdiction. According to Oklahoma Choctaw member and Attorney S. Kayla Morrison:

"Each member is worth about $5000 to the tribe in federal aid. And this begins when children are born in Indian Health Service hospitals to the time they die in the same hospital. With more members, we get more money, so we have a vested interest to keep swelling our membership with NBQ (no blood quantum) members... For every dollar allocated by Congress, 89 cents goes to support the Bureau of Indian Affairs administration. Of the 11 cents that finally comes to our tribal headquarters in Durant, Oklahoma, one-half, or 5.5 cents, supports the tribal administration, which is only one percent of the tribal population. The 99 percent compete for the remaining 5.5 cents. We have a tribal membership of over 110,000. We receive $150 million each year in federal aid. By the time it comes down to me, I receive $.00005 as my share. What can I buy with that? Nothing. And, since I am a dissident, I receive nothing. The health care is so bad, I refuse to go to our hospital because I am afraid they will kill me. So what do I benefit from all the federal aid pumped into our tribe each year? And I am not alone. The majority of our tribal membership is cut off."

That same year, an 86-year-old elder from the Reservation wrote a letter to the editor saying:

"I have seen Indian people, who were once strong in the Indian way, turn against their own because they can not afford to stand up for their rights or they'll lose their (tribal) jobs. Many of our councilmen have lost their Indian tradition and no longer look after their people. When the chieftain system was abolished and the tribal council created, it was with the understanding that they were only to be messengers for their communities. Now it seems they make decisions for the over 7,000 membership without ever asking or informing the people. Creating ordinance 96 (granting immunity from suit to tribal employees) is a law that greatly impacts the people and is as unfair as the council being able to grant executive clemency... The inequities have continued for so long that it seems only the lighter-skinned, acculturated Indians predominate over all of us, continuing to impose their law and beliefs on to us. I'm calling for all tribal members to come forward and tell their stories. We need to quit waiting for someone else to solve our problems. We are our greatest oppressors when we sit back and allow this to happen."

In one month, four people we didn't know told us they had read our letters in the newspaper and liked them. Two came into the upholstery shop.

"Keep it up," one said.

The other, a tribal member, asked Roland to do his couch, then told Roland that he wishes he could write letters like we do, but right now he is negotiating a land lease with the council, and so...

If it weren't for these constant comments, we probably would have quit a long time ago.

Beth Ward

ASHES OF BEFORE

Now comes the burning
of the mind, past all reason,
past all time.

Leaving ashes of before,
dying embers on this shore.

Sudden sparks that only char,
the clearness now is smoky,
marred.

© By **PHONACELLE SHAPEL**

Chapter eighteen:
Joy

In January, Joy and her boyfriend, Jordon, came out with their two kids. We only heard they were coming about a day earlier. We were glad to see Joy, but not knowing her very well anymore and not knowing the boyfriend at all, (except having heard bad stuff in the last few years), we were nervous. But the Lord blessed. Roland had become swamped with upholstery work, and Jordon jumped right in to help strip and sand furniture. He wanted to learn all he could about the business. In addition, he joined me at Bible study and was touched to his heart. Praise God. He was crying with happiness and so was I.

"I want to take care of my family properly," Jordon resolved. "I want to marry Joy."

A small house right next to us opened up for rent. Joy moved in right away with their kids; Jordon waited until after the wedding. They were married on Valentines Day at our church. Roland needed to have 50 chairs done for a restaurant by Valentines Day. He and Jordon stayed up all night doing the order, not sleeping at all until 3:30 in the afternoon, two hours before they had to begin dressing for the wedding.

Roland was walking on air. He had prayed for so many years for his older children. Now, not only was he able to walk his daughter down the aisle, but he had the relief of knowing she and her husband were interested in Jesus. We prayed this wedding would be blessed by God. To Roland, it was like celebrating the prodigal son. We didn't have much in the way of a fatted calf to slaughter, but we did everything we could to make it beautiful.

And it was. Little things fit into place so perfectly. The dress I'd bought to be married in years ago, (but never wore), fit Joy like a glove. The cake top decoration that we had saved from our wedding was a heart, (valentine) with bells. Many people offered to help and purchased or made various parts of the reception dinner.

Graham Kendrick's "The Candle Song," which in the rush of the week Joy and Jordon had never gotten a chance to practice, went off without a problem and was so beautiful with Joy and Jordon lighting the candles in the semi-dark that people were crying.

Jordon spoke as though he were on fire for the Lord. His prayers and enthusiasm amazed me. I was even afraid that Roland and I would dampen his spirit because we have gotten "burnt out" in certain ways.

After their honeymoon, Jordon worked hard helping Roland. They worked together late on several nights. The new jobs continued to come in at a rate of one or two a day. Primarily small jobs but still work. One Saturday Roland bid on and won four jobs.

Roland was also working two days a week for the local paper. He had been driving hundreds of miles on Tuesdays and Wednesdays, delivering bundles of papers to grocery stores and post offices all over the valley. But with all the upholstery work coming in, Roland decided to take a risk and back away from the newspaper job. So he trained a friend of ours to take his place while he remained on call only for back up.

Joy began helping me with the kids. With her two kids, there are now 6 preschoolers in our household. I paid her to take the babies to her house and do arts and crafts with them. I still had some problems with Joy. She sometimes hung around in our house while I was making dinner and then when I called the children to eat, allowed Ashley to slide up to the table with the others. I understood that in her family this was okay. However, I had nine children to take care of already and I knew Joy had plenty of food at home to feed her children with. This is what I explained to Roland, who was reluctant to tell Joy to go home and cook.

"In Indian families it's considered rude to turn people away from the table." Roland said.

I knew that. But this was a night when I had very little meat to stretch, and Joy had been pulling the "hanging around" thing about three times a week. I had half a mind to send our nine children over to her house to hang around HER table for an evening.

"Roland, let's cut to the chase. I'm not Indian and I don't want to play by Indian rules anymore. I'm white, I'm the cook, and in MY family, it's rude to invite yourself to dinner."

Ashley and Joy went home angry.

Joy didn't stay angry though. While visiting with her in her kitchen one day, Joy confided, "You remember that guy on Franklin Avenue that looks just like Dad? He was trying to ask me out. It was weird. He was following me all over the place." Joy was full of stories that afternoon. "Carrie wants to come out here now. Did you know she's drinking and smoking?"

"How old is she now?"

"Twelve. One day she was at a crack house and walked into a room where this girl was tied up. The girl asked her for help, so she just closed the door and got out of there. Carrie's been running all over the streets. Darlene can't control her. Cheri beat Carrie up for what she's doing, and then Darlene called the cops and put Cheri in jail. Cheri has a restraining order keeping her from going near the girls now. So Carrie wants to come out."

"Not if she's drinking already. It's too late. I've got too much going on with all the other kids to spend time fighting with her."

"I can control her. I'll make her listen."

"She'd have to live with you totally, then."

Joy switched the topic to Misty. "Social services gave her a bunch of Christmas presents for her kids, but her and Wesley decided the kids didn't need them so they sold them. Misty and Cheri were both stealing from me too, like a boom box and other stuff. They were stealing Ashley's Christmas presents and everything so they could get high. I'm sick of her. Once when Misty's social worker showed up to take her to treatment, she hid and cried and told me not to open the door."

Jordon came in from working with Roland.

"Yeah man, straight up. Them people are bad. I'd be working hard, man, and come home and there ain't nothing to eat cause they ate it. But that's the way it is, I guess. They bring their gang friends around, too. I mean, I got my gang but they understands I'm a family man. My girl here, Joy, she and my ma wanted me to get jumped into a different gang. They says, "that gang'll take care a-you better." So I goes out in back and I get jumped in..."

"What's 'jumped in? I don't know what that is."

"Oh, man, that's when the gang takes you out and beats you up. You don't know that? And if you can stand it, man, if you can show them you got what it takes, then youse in! Man, if yo boy Andrew had stayed, man, he woulda been jumped in a long time ago! Man, he's a big kid!"

After telling me more, he agreed to sit down and write about it. I left it just as he wrote it:

> "Man homey you is hitting that weed too much. That ain't the problem little man, I need some lute in my pocket. Why don't you ask RoDog to go hit that store tonight. That way I don't need to be broke. Man homey Ro-Dog gonna hit that store with or with out you. So Noonie want to put in some work tonight huh? Yeah homey, I'll bring you with on this mission partner.
>
> What I'm about to tell you is the starting of my story that is true. This is how it goes back in the day. I was about fifteen and I had alot of problems. So I took it upon myself to live a life to be ruthless and loyal to the underground world of crime. I smoked weed tremendously not caring about nothing but homeboys and homegirls. I didn't go to school just crime school. This was taught by finding out on my own and the dedicated thugs that surrounded me. My problem was I wanted rank and I wanted love. All the fools I kicked it with called me Noonie a nickname my grandmother gave me. My boy Tuggie was selling dope and all the homies would be at his house. We skipped school and made money. The ride we had was A nice little sunbird on some five star rims. Ro-dog is a good friend of mine. Tre-duce is my little brother. Us three were like the best of homies for years. We use to go to school and be all the student we could be. But that was then and we was on

our mission to be college students. Some how life turned around on us right in front of our eyes.

Our thing was to hit a store at night and take all the cartons of cigarettes we could grab. The next day we would work together getting the money for them then we would split the lute. The white bars would buy the Marlboros and camels. The Arab stores in the ghetto would by all the Newports. For instance this how we would set it up. The plans we made were important. That way less things would go wrong. This is organized crime no snitching, no telling people how we came up on lute unless they was there. We took turns switching the jobs on our missions. At times we would need to steal a ride cause the store was out in the suburb or on the other side of town. At times police would roll right passed us on our way home. Things like this would make us laugh. It was a game. More then a few times I was so brewed I went and did a store by myself. That would get Tre-duce and Ro-dog mad cause we might have planned it out for two weeks and I went and messed things up. I was happy I got lute but they came up short. So for awhile there we wasn't cool like boys. During this time I spent time with homeboys that were smoking weed. That was one thing I liked doing. Hittin that weed like it was no thang. Could make me forget about my home life which, I just wasn't there. My mom is an chemical dependent person who would have relationships with abusive men. This chased me away from home. I was too little in size to fight the men that were being mean to her and us kids. One time my mother told me she would die from a drug overdose. She was drunk when she told me this. I took it serious and my grandma got her into treatment. My brother Tre-duce and I went to a foster home for a short period time of three months. During this time I grew into a state of mind that was to defend my self cause my mom isn't always gonna be there. Knowing when I was younger she had let are grandmother take care of us for a long period of time.

Homeboys loved me mainly cause I made us laugh and I was an outgoing individual. There was a rumor my friends were telling each other I wasn't all there. Meaning I was looney. This really hurt me but I didn't let them know. Two friends of mine were shot when I was in this halfway house. Ro dog was one of them and I spoke with him. He told me it was over some other Indian dudes that wanted his jacket. This is the time my homeboy Ro dog started carrying heaters. Man, when someone close to you gets popped you really start thinking. That could of been me and from now on it's gonna have to be different. A friend of mine pulled this sawed off pump out right on the city bus. Something there that night made me look at homeboy like he was the man. The situation was these drunks from back of the bus started pushing on him saying things like you think you bad now. After that about three of us started to push on these dudes like you wants some you gonna get some. Then when the pump came out the whole bus turned quiet. Tell you the truth the thing that made me nervous was what if these drunks hadn't got off the bus. The bus driver was kicken us all off, cause we was drinking on the bus. But my friend told the bus driver they started messing with him first. See the driver didn't see the pump so he let us stay on. Then my brother Tre -duce says if any niggas talk shit we gonna buck them. My friend asked me why your brother gonna say that. Why don't you go check him. Look I said, "he all drunk anyways so who cares.' After that dudes my brother was sitting by just start getting off the bus. I knew that was a dumn thing my brother said but we had got jumped by black kids as we was growing up. So we older now and we drunk. Feelings run high when you buzzed up off some malt liquor you know. Anyways I met this female at this youth program. Her names Joy and my little brother was telling me about her. He knew I liked her so he asked me, why you want to hook up with her? I did but I told Tre duce keep his mouth shut. I wanted to get to know her before I asked her out. I never wanted a girlfriend to come between my homies and I. The way I saw things was a girlfriend will come and leave. A homey will always be there. This was why Joy and I started out being friends. She had boys asking her out so I got a jealousy in my heart. This is when I knew I had feelings for her. In my mind she was happy and I started to want true happiness as her boyfriend.

Around this time the police caught me at my grandmothers house. My grandma raised me so there for she was like my mommy. I had this warrant from auto theft and fleeing the cops. Thats when I sat in juvenile center for a couple weeks. My brother Tre-duce was in there and he has been there more then I. I remember throwing this basketball hard at this other kid right in the face. My little brother looked at me with a surprised look. To represent as an older brother and let others know not to mess with you. That was taught by my mom and grandma."

Jordon

"Go ahead and use this," he told me, "people should know what it's really like."

In March, Tonya married Dusty, the postmaster, in their home with a Justice of the Peace. Roland, our three oldest children, a friend of Dusty's and I were the only ones present. They planned another wedding later for relatives.

During a meeting with supporters the next week, (the same supporters that some human rights organizations accuse of being a "hate-group"), I told them about the wedding. Someone responded that in the old days, a wedding was always accompanied by a good "shivaree," a surprise housewarming for newlyweds.

"We haven't had a shivaree in years," Orval said, "at my shivaree, people drove right up into the yard at midnight, honking horns and a-hollering. Why, some of 'em got out of their cars and even came right up into the house!"

One woman laughed. "Do you remember that time we hooked up George's camper trailer while they were in there sleeping and hauled it into town?"

Her husband added chuckling, "I was pulling it. They were in there trying to get dressed while the thing was rocking back and forth down the road. You should have seen the looks on their faces when we finally stopped and opened the door, half the town there to see them. Can you imagine! But they were okay once we broke out the food and drink."

"That was our last shivaree," someone else lamented.

"Oh! Let's do it for Tonya and Dusty then!"

From Indian Country Today: March 1997

> To the editor:
>
> By act of Congress approved Oct. 25, 1972 the Secretary of the Interior was to pay claims judgment funds to certain Americans Indian tribes and lineal descendants of the Sisseton Sioux Tribe, with interest thereon. The American Indian tribes involved had previously approved of the division of funds. Now 24 years later only the tribes have been paid their share and the lineal descendants have not been paid a cent. Sen. Dorgan of North Dakota introduced a bill (SB391) in the Senate on March 4, which would pay out the original amount, or principal, <u>less any interest</u>, to the lineal descendants and pay all the accumulated interest to the tribes. Sen. Conrad of North Dakota, Sen., Daschle and Johnson of South Dakota and Sen. Baucus and Burns of Montana are co-sponsors of the bill.
>
> The Secretary of the Interior has an approved list of 1,968 lineal descendants of the Sisseton Sioux Tribe who are scattered throughout 36 states. Since the descendants have no organization or leaders they apparently have little or no voice and little standing with the U.S. government. Some of the lineal descendants are currently enrolled with American Indian tribes other than the Sisseton Tribe, some are not enrolled with any tribe, and some have died.

> The lineal descendants of the Sisseton Sioux Tribe hope and pray that fellow Americans will be sympathetic to their plight and will contact their senators and congressmen urging them to kill SB 391, and order the Secretary of the Interior to pay all accumulated funds to the rightful owners -- the lineal descendants of the Sisseton Sioux Tribe.
> (A South Dakota tribal member)

On April 28, 1997, the Redwood children were adjudicated in need of protection or services and continued out-of-home placement.

Aunt Charlotte called and began asking about the building we lived in. "Do you like the building? How much would the Landlord settle for? Has there been a title search? Has it been inspected for termites?"

I answered her questions. We were still praying about the owner's latest offer. If the landlord would wait a little bit longer, maybe we could show the bank that the upholstery business was good.

"The owners have changed their mind and want only $25,000 for the whole building,' I told her. "Remember it was originally listed in the real estate ad for $50,000. Then the guy offered it to us for $32,000. Joy joked that if we wait just a little longer, he'll give it to us for free. The building does need work. Having lived here for nine months now, nothing is hidden to us. But Roland has done construction on and off in the past and can handle it."

We went on to discuss Tonya's upcoming wedding and Charlotte's plans to come out for it.

In May, Roland, Andrew, and Jordon went to Promise Keepers. The following weekend we shivareed Tonya and Dusty. The "hate-group" had decided to be nice and not give them a tough time. I arranged to meet Tonya and Dusty in the park for a picnic. In the meantime, the Shivaree-er's met at Orval's place. The plan was for them to roll their gift-bearing parade into town honking.

When the partying parade was fifteen minutes late with no sign or sound of approach, I went into the senior citizen center to call Orval's house and see what was wrong. While listening to the phone ring, I heard honking and hollering outside. I rushed out to catch Tonya's reaction, but where was she?

"Haley! Where is Tonya and Dusty?" I yelled while the line of cars passed and turned to park in the lot.

"Oh, they're not here. They went to the store."

I guess this time the surprise was on the partiers rather then the newlyweds!

Jordon and Andrew were in the backyard digging post holes. Will had given us two truckloads of wood with which to make a fence. Joy and I watched as they worked.

"Why aren't you telling the kids they're Indian?" she asked.

Surprised, I wasn't sure how to answer. "Well...we don't tell 'em anything. I mean, we just don't make a point of one heritage over another. They know they're Indian. They hear it. It's not as if our older kids have no idea that their dad is Indian and Mom's white. But they know they're German and Irish, too."

I tried to explain that we try to teach the kids they are humans first; there is no difference between people and that race doesn't matter. To make an issue about differences between people is what creates problems. We want the kids to be comfortable with who they are, no matter their color or heritage.

We'd really like the world to stop making an issue of race, but it seems like government policies do more to make sure everyone remembers the differences and to separate people than to bring people together. The differences between Roland and me are obvious, but who cares?

However, that doesn't mean that diverse culture shouldn't be shared and taught. Roland has said many times that yes, he is Christian first, but he is also Indian, and while he doesn't choose to honor traditional religion, he still respects other various cultural aspects of daily life taught to him by his parents and grandfather. For that matter, we're not against teaching the kids to make sauerkraut either. All cultures have unique and interesting cultural aspects to share.

Roland flew to Washington DC on June 4, 1997. He sat on a panel discussing Federal Indian Policy and met with various Senators and Congressmen. In addition, he met with an advisor to Secretary of the Interior to discuss the National Bison Range.

June 10, 1997

Mr. James Pipkin:

Thank you for taking the time to see me and giving me the opportunity to discuss the National Bison Range with you.

#1) and very important; The National Bison Range has been deemed "Inherently Federal." In general, a lot of the major decisions can't and shouldn't be turned over to another entity. With the Tribe unable to take over these decisions, these programs can never truly be considered self-governance. And so the NBR, among other National resources deemed "Inherently Federal," should not be considered transferable under the Indian Self-Determination Act.

#2) We need you to realize the true nature of the Flathead Reservation. If the purpose of turning over the National Bison Range is to benefit the local community, we would like to remind you that 3/4 of the population on the reservation are not Confederated Salish & Kootenai tribal members. The CS&K Tribes are a minority. Please do not turn over a program of national interest to this local political body.

#3) In a January 1996 letter to a county resident, Former tribal Chairman Mickey Pablo is quoted as saying "basic funding will not change under tribal management of our National Bison Range. Our Federal Government funds the management now, and will under the tribes' proposal." He goes on to say, "hiring will occur according to tribal practices which falls wholly within the bounds of federal law."

Tribal practices legal under Federal Law are the following:
ORDER OF PREFERENCE:
1. Enrolled members of the (governing) tribe.
2. First generation descendants of the (governing) tribe.
3. Enrolled members of other tribal reservations
4. Non-Indians.

In other words, 'Preference in Hiring" will happen on Federal land with Federal dollars. At the present time, the NBR is an equal opportunity employer. Please don't change that.

#4) In 1972, the Indian Claims Commission paid CS&K Tribes 6 million dollars plus interest for all lands within the Reservation boundaries, including the National Bison Range. Although we don't know the actual amount, with interest tabulated over a 60 year period the actual payment may have been as much as 70 million dollars. We believe this payment is further evidence that the United Sates Government has tried to be fair.

#5) Accusations by the Tribe that their opponents are racist is a smoke screen. What is going on is opposition to the politics, attitude, and heavy-handedness of this Tribal Government. This is not an issue of White against Indian, but an issue of certain Tribal members against all non-members. (Bear in mind not all CS&K tribal members agree with this tribal government)

#6) This year, State moose hunting permits were reduced dramatically. Evidence shows that off-reservation hunting allowed by the Tribal government has not been done with "stewardship for the good of all" in mind. If the CS&K Tribe is currently not willing to exhibit good resource management for the benefit of the rest of Montana's citizens, (not to mention the benefit of the resource itself), by limiting off-reservation hunting by its members, can we expect them to manage the NBR with all citizens in mind?

Thank you for your time and consideration.

Roland Ward

Rosie missed Roland terribly while he was gone, and cried on the phone when he would call.

Our upholstery business had slowed down some, and we couldn't afford to keep giving Joy and Jordon work. The two of them had begun to fight, and Joy chased Jordon down the street with a knife. Although Jordon had just been hired to work full time at the grocery store, they abruptly took a bus back to Minnesota soon after Roland returned from DC. Their landlady's final bill for electricity and oil came to $361. The landlady left the bill on our counter. Andrew had been watching the shop when she came in.

"She's giving you the bill," he reported, "but she said she won't rush you to pay, just pay it when you can."

Beth Ward

MATCHED STEPS

with matched steps
they walk the meadows
behind the barn,
blackberry sweet on
the wind, a taste of
summer on their lips

he holds her hand as
the years slip away
and the path grows
dusty down to the
barn

and on moonlit
evenings she still
walks the meadows,
his memory lying
sweet on the wind

and she matches her
steps with his

© By **PHONACELLE SHAPEL**

Chapter nineteen:
Misty

I started the kids back on some school work over the summer. I hoped to move Ross up into the third grade. But when I started Brooke on the same math book she'd been using the previous year, she got every answer wrong. She was also unable to count change. So I decided to start from scratch and gave her some simple problems, like 3 + 4, or 7 - 1. Stuff like that. But she had no idea what to do. She looked at the problem and asked, "What is it?"

So I sat her down with a bunch of paper clips, and asked her to count out seven. Then I told her to take away one, and count how many she had left. We did the same thing for every problem.

I called her teacher, who confirmed that yes, Brooke has trouble. She can be taught something one day, but by the next day, she can't remember. That's why she sent her back to the kindergarten to work one-on-one with that teacher.

"Start at the beginning and just repeat and repeat to Brooke over and over every day for the rest of the summer," Roland advised.

> Dear Joy, June 17, 1997
>
> Here is your driver's license. Also, here is the final bill for electricity and oil. The landlady says the total is $361. Please look it over for accuracy…did the oil get filled twice? …I owed you for that last week; the day you baby-sat, and the day you did laundry for me, ran errands, and keeping Dewey over night. I'll just give her $50. I'm

sure that should cover what I owe you. Let me know if I am forgetting something....I'll make it $61.02, so it will leave just an even $300. I can't give her any more than that...

...There is one thing I was concerned about, and we never did talk about it much;
Rosie is my third daughter and my baby, just like you were for your mom. There's no way a mom can get away from how she feels for her baby. You know your mom has always had that special place for you in her heart, and you have a special place for your babies. So I hope you don't hold it against me that I treat Rosie for what she is...my baby.
I was never sure if you understood why I couldn't do or be for you and Ashley the same way your mom does.
Last year we were asked by Misty to take her kids for a couple months. We talked about it, and then decided, "Okay, we'll put aside some of our plans for a little while and help out." We agreed to take Misty's kids, and then in January we also offered to help you, but that has never meant that I can or should set aside my own feelings for my own babies. That would be impossible. And it would be wrong to my kids. I owe them my Love.
But we do the best we can to do what is right for everyone. We're not out to hurt anyone. Sometimes we make mistakes, but at least we are trying.
And maybe I could have done more for Ashley if I didn't have five kids of my own plus Misty's kids. I know that Roland wishes he had had the strength to do more, too. But a person can only do so much and when there are so many people that need attention, a person just ends up exhausted at the end of the day.
So I guess that is what I was hoping you understood. We do our best, but with so much to do, it's hard to be perfect. We Love you and we Love Misty's kids. We are trying. Maybe you already did understand. I hope so, and thank you if you do.

I apologize for mistakes I made while you were here.

Beth

Due to a court ordered and county financed visit, Misty and Wesley arrived by Greyhound bus on July 6, 1997. Dewey was the only child in the yard when they arrived. Misty asked him to hug her. Not knowing who she was, he was hesitant, but does after she asks him a couple of times. Brooke saw her dad and ran to him, excited.

Ross and Caleb were across the street at the basketball court when they arrived. We went out onto the sidewalk while the boys crossed the street to greet their parents, walking, not running. As Ross came down the sidewalk, he had a sheepish look on his face. Caleb looked nervous and played with his hands. He didn't appear to know who they were. When they got to us, they stood in front of their parents, who reached out to hug them.

Back in our yard, we barbecued.

"Joy and Jordon are drinking again," they told us, "The only reason they came out here was cause they were in trouble back home. Someone was after them." Roland and I glanced at each other. Although we knew Joy hadn't been totally up front with us, we also knew better than to listen to anything Misty had to say. After they talked a while about family back home and we talked about the kids here, Misty asked Roland if the kids could spend the night at the motel. Roland told her the social worker had said 'no' to the kids spending the night.

"How will she know?" Misty questioned.

Wesley quickly added, "She told us it was okay because the motel is so close. She didn't know when she talked to you that the motel was going to be so close."

"Yeah," said Misty, "When she found out it was close, she said it was okay with her if it was okay with you."

Roland didn't say anything right away, but when Misty asked again later, he told her that he would call the social worker Monday morning and confirm it. Misty looked the other way and angrily puffed on her cigarette for about ten minutes.

Later, while Wesley and Roland did some work on Roland's pickup truck, Misty was overheard telling the kids that she will be finished with her treatment plan in eight weeks and will be able to have them back then. Brooke spent some time brushing her mother's hair, and ran to get her mom's cigarettes, purse, or pull-up for Dewey when asked to. The boys played in the yard. Misty, sitting in a lawn chair, hugged them as they came and went.

After dinner, Misty said she was going to take the kids to her motel for an hour. Over two hours later, they finally brought them home again.

The next day, the parents were an hour late coming to pick them up. Roland called the social worker, as promised, who confirmed that there were to be no overnights, but allowed the parents to keep the kids later – until 10 pm. But even with that, they were late coming home, with Misty claiming they were already asleep so we should just let them stay. The kids, of course, told us later that none of them had been asleep. Brooke returned angry with us, though, and Caleb was a little distant, but Dewey asked for kisses good night. Ross reported that his mom is moving them to a Minneapolis foster home.

The next day, Dewey didn't want to go with his parents and put up a fuss before they arrived, refusing to even get out of bed. After being assured he could stay home, he started to smile and gets out of bed. But Misty and Wesley weren't going along with that and argued that they didn't come all this way for nothing. They then began accusing us of misusing money and abusing the kids. I stopped talking and left it to Roland to handle.

Roland spent about two hours in the back yard talking to them. He gave them our views on spirituality and how we work together as a family. They asked about our finances, but Roland didn't respond. Our finances weren't any of their business. I, on the defensive, reminded them that groceries for a family this size cost about $800 a month. The kids are also enrolled in a private school, take piano lessons, and have sports fees and accessories. In the end, they told Roland that they understood and it was okay.

Later, Wesley worked on Roland's truck for money and Misty wandered from room to room as the children played. Wesley commented to us, "Joy and Jordon fight all the time. They were too young to get married. That's why we aren't going to get married. So don't even ask us."

I looked at him, not ever having considered asking him to get married, and thought to myself, 'Joy and Jordon are too young to get married, but not too young to have two babies, carry guns, and rob stores?'

The day came for the parents to go back. After dropping them off at the bus depot, Roland said that Brooke cried quite a bit, but the boys didn't show any emotion. When they got back to the house, Caleb told me that his parents are going to buy him a bike, and Ross said that they are going to buy him some soccer shoes.

Dewey and Caleb were a little difficult after Misty and Wesley left. They ran through the house, purposefully bumping into people. Caleb even tackled his siblings despite having been told several times not to. They seemed to totally ignore us, where normally one or two scoldings would be all that was necessary. In addition, Dewey refused to take a nap. He cried the whole time he laid in bed, until I finally gave up because it was getting too late in the day. Brooke also ignored us several times when asked not to hang out in the store. Just before dinner, Caleb was aggressive toward Dewey in a way that we had not seen in a year. He gritted his teeth, punched Dewey, shoved him and threatened him. I stood him against the wall for ten minutes.

Dear Joy, July 11, 1997

I just finished paying last month's phone bill, and feel very sad and betrayed. You have made over $100 in long distance calls on our phone bill...In addition we have learned from someone here that you were drinking with Susy B. You had told us that you weren't drinking the night Haley baby-sat. And your landlady, who is a friend of ours and who we still have to see around here regularly, told us that Jordon had lied to her about when he was getting paid and when he was paying her.

We did our best to help you in every way that you asked us to. You have to understand that I was/am very busy with all kinds of things; nine children, an upholstery shop, library, and Roland's politics.

However, despite the fact that we have so much going on, we took time to make room for you in our home, help arrange your wedding, help arrange a house for you, bring you up to Polson several times for your driver's license, talk to you when you wanted someone to talk to, and arrange a potluck for you. All this took time and energy from my other responsibilities.

In addition, we gave you both jobs even when we couldn't afford it. You know for a fact that there were weeks when you and Jordon received money at the end of the week, but we did not. That is because we are loyal to our promises and we never wanted to go back on you. And so despite the fact Roland also worked all week, you made money but we did not. (as a matter of fact, the kids are asking why we have so much food now. They don't realize that it was $1000 a month we'd been paying you, and that that money is now available for our own use.)...

It seems that our upholstery slowed down about the same time Joy had become tired of the straight life.

In a note written July 17, 1997, our dentist informed Minnesota social services that Dewey and Caleb needed to see oral surgeons to take care of the neglect they experienced while younger. Caleb, the doctor wrote, "has extensive decay caused from 'baby bottle' syndrome" and he will be referring Caleb to a specialist because of his age and "the severity of the decay."

It has been almost twenty years since that bruised baby girl was buried. Most of the small children we knew then have several children of their own now. But we see these nieces and nephews doing just as they'd been taught by family all their lives...destroying themselves and their children. Why? Among the many obvious reasons, there are also some questions:

1. How does it feel to be constantly pitied and told that you are a forever victim? Real racism is horrible, but pity

destroys people just as much as hate does. It's not the same as empathy or compassion.
2. What is taken away when one loses the satisfaction of earning money to support your family? What is taken away when one goes to a warehouse to pick up food instead of going out to the woods, smelling the fresh air, moving through the grass, enjoying family and the outdoors as you hunt or fish? Due to lack of awareness, the general public supports laws that superficially seem to help troubled tribal members but in fact worsen the situation.
3. How does it feel to be victimized by not just one, but two governments? Millions of dollars in federal funds are spent by tribal officials on lawyers, lobbyists and campaign contributions for the purpose of obtaining and retaining power and more money, rather than invested in reservation growth and economy.[3]
4. Is Fetal Alcohol endemic to communities with high rates of alcoholism? The SAMSHA[4] survey and Indian Heath Service reports have found American Indians exhibit higher prevalence of heavy cigarette, alcohol, illicit drug use and need for treatment than the general population. Do we have a generation of fetal alcohol victims raising a generation of fetal alcohol victims?
5. How does it feel to be under pressure to be a 'cultural artifact?' …To be told that unless you be and act a certain way, you are not a "real Indian?"

---

3 In 1996, Tribal entities gave over $1,200,000 to National Party Committees. The Mashantucket Pequot Nation gave over $400,000 in soft money alone. During the 1997 calendar year, lobbyist spending topped $5.5 million, with Mississippi Band of Choctaw Indians topping the list with over $1 million. The National Unity Caucus, a tribal Political Action Committee, reported over $200,000 in contributions from various tribal entities in the year 1996. This money was distributed directly to candidates across the country. *Native American Press, 10/98.*

4 SAMSHA – Substance Abuse and Mental Health Service

That summer we worked to get a newsletter out. After the newsletter was distributed across the county, we received encouraging responses.

"Good job you folks are doing. ...thanks to you all."

"To Pres. Roland Ward- I wrote to Sen. Gorton. He certainly has the right idea. I hope his legislation succeeds...You are doing a good job...."

Late in the afternoon on August 12, I ran into a woman who harassed us at a public meeting and again at Cosco in the spring of 1997. As I was coming out of a shop, the woman quickly approached me.

"Can I have one of your fliers?" she asked smiling.

Recognizing her, I answered, 'no,' and kept walking to my car.

She followed, still smiling, "Why? Are you discriminating against me?"

I opened my car door and started to get in. "Yes."

She grabbed my car door to keep me from closing it. "Give me one of your flyers."

"Get your hands off my car."

"Give me a flier. Are you discriminating against me because I'm an Indian?" I pulled on the door. "Why would I? I'm discriminating against you because you're yourself."

"Who am I?" she said, smiling and pulling at the door, "Do you even know who I am?"

"Monica Reneau."

"You can't even pronounce my name! She laughed. "How can you know me!" She pulled again to keep the door open. "Give me a flier. I'll get one myself," she said, and tried to reach past me.

"Get your hands off my car" I said, and pulled again on my car door.

"Are you discriminating against me because I'm Indian?" she said again, with a grin on her face.

"No. I'm discriminating against you because you're a mean woman. You make trouble."

Dying in Indian Country

She again tried to reach in, but I stood in her way. She attempted to push past me but I held my ground.

"I make trouble?" she asked, "Do I make trouble in the neighborhood?"

"Yes," I answered.

She went on; "Do I write letters and...

Looking straight into my eyes, she suddenly shoved her body into mine. I looked around quickly to see if there was anyone near by that could call the cops. No one was around.

"Are you drunk?" I asked.

"No," she said, "I just came out of the restaurant."

"Get your hands off my car," I said again. "Or I'll call the cops."

She made one more attempt to get past me. When I still stood firm, she smiled again and said, "I'll just go to where you got them." and marched off, smiling, to the YMCA.

I closed my car door and drove home.

Rosie, who had been in the front seat watching, repeated over and over again the whole way home, "That's a bad woman. She wouldn't get her hands off our car. That's a bad woman."

We drove over the mountains to stay the weekend with some friends on the Blackfoot reservation and whom we had met at Bible camp. They, like us, had an interracial marriage; the husband was Indian, the wife, white.

The main street in this reservation town, although longer than one in Cass Lake, looked just as worn out and dead. Sure, there was some business. The usual fare for a small town. But there were also a number of boarded up buildings. Driving into the tract area, where our friends lived, it was as if we were driving through Cass Lake. The same simple BIA designs, the same littered and dirt packed yards.

The wife greeted us, but things weren't okay. The husband was at a bar, drinking again. After first making certain my children and I were comfortable, she asked Roland to go with her to bring her husband home.

At the bar, she told her husband, "Roland and Beth are here. Please come home."

Roland, feeling ill, also tried to talk to him, but later told me that he could feel the man's unwillingness. There was nothing that could be done.

The wife was embarrassed. The poor woman struggled to hide her shame and busy herself making dinner. Watching her fighting to keep her "everything will be alright" face, my heart broke. I knew just what she was going through, and I wanted to tell her that she didn't have to do that in front of me. If she wanted, she could just let go and say what she's really feeling. She could tell me that she's scared he's not going to come home, that she's scared he would lie to her some more, that he didn't love her, or that she was going to lose her best friend, her daughter's father, her husband.

I wanted to tell her that I knew just what it felt like and take her in my arms and hug her and tell her it was okay, neither I nor Roland blamed her.

"Don't be scared," I told her, summoning up Elmer's words to me so long ago. "God will watch over your family. Believe it, and thank God for already having helped you." She agreed. Together we prayed, "God, please help us and save our families."

After we left, Roland said, "I felt the oppression in that town as soon as we arrived. Like a black cloud, the same as when I drive onto my reservation."

I agreed, "I didn't want to say anything, thinking you'd get upset if I compared the two towns. But it felt just like that to me, too."

Aunt Charlotte came for Tonya's 'family' wedding in August. While here, she met with our landlord and confirmed her intention to purchase the building. To celebrate Aunt Charlotte and her kindness, the children and I put on a play. Andrew got to perform as the evil "Risky Rat." Charlotte enjoyed the show and was impressed with Andrew's ability to act.

"I'm not acting," he told her with a smile.

During a Child Custody hearing in early September, 1997, Misty and Wesley told Roland's lawyer that as a Christian, Roland was in defiance of ICWA. They told the lawyer that Roland would not allow them to send Native American gifts to their kids, such as jewelry or dream catchers and that Roland refuses to take the kids to powwows. We told the lawyer that the parents have never asked about or attempted to send the kids anything at all, whether Native American or not, in the whole time they'd been with us. In addition, we ourselves had given Brooke an Indian beadwork set for her birthday.

But is this what the law is policing? Is it meant to be used to mandate and enforce a certain religion on children, and prevent a grandfather from teaching his grandchildren what he really believes? Further – is it written down anywhere the official and legally acceptable way a tribal member is supposed to teach about God or tradition? What is the measure of tradition and who measures it?

As an adult in the 1970's and 1980's, Roland took his older children to powwows and took them up north during ricing season. During ricing, Roland would parch, jig, and fan the rice the old way. He would invite his children to help; but none of them were interested, preferring instead to spend their time with friends. They weren't interested in dancing at powwows, either.

In the winter of 1986, while taking Ojibwe classes at the Community College, we attempted to interest the kids in the language. Cheri attended classes for a short time, but dropped out. None of the others showed any interest in that either.

In the last few years, Roland's most obvious connection with the past had been to take the kids hunting and fishing. During these outings, as he identified a bird in the air, spied an animal in the woods, or started a fire from scratch, Roland taught tradition without even always being aware of it. And by making sure we had venison and wild rice to eat, Roland taught the kids to appreciate these foods. He also taught them to like fry bread; (although he wasn't totally successful in teaching me how to make it).

And there are many other not-so-obvious ways he has taught the kids the old ways. For example, he taught children to honor their elders, not talk back, and to get up and give an elder their own chair if it is needed. These are important parts of the old way that many have forgotten. Roland felt strongly that children learn to respect elders as he had been taught to. During the last few years, he also taught chastity, honesty and the work ethic, which are traditional values everyone ignores. He stressed how important those virtues are if one wants a healthy, happy life.

Finally, He taught the children to love, honor, and respect God. How can those lessons be weighed and judged?

And how can two young people like Misty and Wesley, both only part Indian and not at all familiar with or personally practicing any kind of tradition, get away with accusing a full-blooded elder of violating ICWA?

Also in early September, 2007, Aunt Charlotte, after taking out a personal loan of her own, sent $25,000 for the purchase of our building.

"$5000 is a gift," she told us, "and you can pay the rest back at $500 a month."

"We'll leave the building in your name until we have it paid off."

"No, I'm 70 years old. Put it in your name."

The building, we felt, was a gift from God through our wonderful Aunt Charlotte. As such, we felt our Christian Library was just 'giving back to God' a portion of what he had given us. And the library was growing. People had been dropping off donations of books, videos, audio tapes, various magazines and materials, and even shop furniture for library use. Some have been anonymous. At times, we have been in the back rooms for a few minutes, only to come out and be surprised with books or videos sitting on our counter. Or at times donors left the material with one of our children, who unfortunately couldn't tell us who the benefactor was.

The upholstery shop was also busy, and Andrew and I helped out where we could. When Roland, who still felt nauseated near the smell of alcohol, would get a call from a bar, he would have to be the one to go make the bid. He stomached the stench and got the job done as quickly as possible. But when the job was finished and it came time to deliver the furniture back to the bar, he would ask either Andrew or I to do it.

The state flew the Redwood parents out again for a visit with the kids. The social worker, saying there was no evidence from the last visit to show the parents unfit, had given permission this time for the kids to stay in a motel with their parents the entire week.

When I told the kids their parents were coming, Ross showed no emotion at all. Brooke began to cry.

"I miss sitting with my mom. She would give me hugs and stuff. Sometimes she let me curl her hair. I liked when she spent time with me, like taking me to the park and pushing me on the swing."

Caleb didn't seem to know who we were talking about.

Misty and Wesley were very friendly when they arrived. They both appeared to be trying hard to do their best. In speaking to them, Roland learned the county had purchased the airplane tickets at the last minute, costing taxpayers $2600. In addition, the county had paid for the parents' motel and given them cash for groceries and what ever else they needed. Altogether, the county must have spent almost $4000 on the trip. Lastly, the county was paying for both an apartment and phone service back home for the couple. All this in effort to reunite the family. Kelly, the couples third crack baby, was still less than a year old.

On Monday, the first day, Wesley got Ross and Brooke to school on time. After politely introducing himself to the headmaster, he walked them to their classrooms. It was raining that day, so Andrew brought Ross' rain jacket to him at school. When Ross saw Andrew, he asked him for a big hug and told him that he missed him.

Wesley was the one to bring the kids to school on Tuesday as well. In the afternoon, they called and asked for a pan to cook with. Andrew brought it over. The room was filled with cigarette smoke. When Dewey saw him, he shouted "Andrew!" and ran to him. Then he and Caleb then pushed past Andrew to run around outside before they were called in again.

Later, Wesley came over asking for work. He said he was bored in the motel room and they were out of money. Roland told him he could come over the next day to help.

On Wednesday, a friend attempted to visit with Misty at the motel but was rebuffed. Wesley came over about 10 am and sanded furniture for Roland most of the day. We gave him lunch. He was good natured, helpful, and did his work quickly. He laughed and told Roland how angry Brooke was Sunday night when they wouldn't buy her 'lunchables' and pop for her school lunch. I was glad he hadn't given in to her. Maybe he wasn't such a bad guy.

That evening, Ross came over and said his mom wanted to have a couple of quarters in order to finish the laundry.

Roland asked, "What happened to the money I just gave your dad?"

"Spent it at the grocery store."

Roland wasn't sure what to think, knowing that not only had he just paid him, but the county had also given them money.

"I don't have any quarters in my pocket, my boy."

Wesley worked again Thursday. He was friendly and worked quickly and quietly. We gave him lunch and Roland paid him again before he left. At 4:30 p.m. I picked Brooke up for ballet class. She was in a good mood. The rest of her family was walking over to the bowling alley. Because the lawyer and social worker had told us that Misty and Wesley were bringing late birthday gifts, I asked Brooke what she had gotten.

"Nothing," she answered, looking surprised.

"Oh," I back-tracked. "I made a mistake. Don't worry about it."

On Friday, Wesley arrived to work about 10:30 am. He worked until about 4pm, and we again gave him lunch and paid him.

Saturday morning, Roland picked the family up from the motel and they went to Brooke's soccer game. A teacher reported that Brooke burst into tears at the sound of her father, in attempt to encourage her, hollering at her from the sidelines. Brooke told the teacher, "My dad is yelling at me. I can't do anything right!" After the game, they came by the house to say good-bye. The kids were supposed to go with them to the airport, but Ross wasn't with them.

"He wanted to stay at the soccer field with the other children. He said good-bye to us there," Wesley said.

Later, Ross told us that his parents had taken them all to the movie 'Conspiracy Theory.' He said that it had lots of blood in it that he didn't like, nor did he like the sandwiches their mother had made them for school because they "tasted like cigarette smoke." Their mother had gotten up to get them ready for school on Monday and Tuesday, but had stayed in bed Wednesday, Thursday and Friday.

He said that they never had breakfast before school, even when she had gotten up.

His dad had walked them to school the first two or three days, but had stayed in bed the last two, saying that he couldn't walk them because he had to go to work. On Friday, no one woke them up for school and Ross barely got Brooke and himself there on time. For most of the week, other than going to school, Brooke and Ross said they stayed in the motel room. The couple times they did go to the grocery store, the number of people they waved at or spoke to had surprised their parents. But Brooke said her mother told her to "shut-up" and "quit waving."

Still, Ross was happy that his parents had promised him his own VCR, Stereo, and cable TV when he moves home with them.

Rosie was very glad to have the kids back and fixed Caleb's plate to sit next to her at supper.

Roland and I had enjoyed the week alone with our children. I had a great time with Rosie and Timothy. Also, it was a lot easier to keep on top of laundry and housecleaning. I could clean a room and it actually stayed clean for the whole day.

Roland and I didn't know whether we wanted to keep the kids or not. It was easier for us to live with just our five kids. But on the other hand, we still didn't trust them and didn't want to see the kids get hurt again. We didn't want the kids to go home, but at the same time, we knew God had changed Roland's life and could very easily change Misty's.

So we prayed.

Beth Ward

TROMBONES

on the bridge
trombones play
the midnight blues,
a retrospective
desolate as a rusted
mirror reflecting
nothing, a dim
monochrome on the
underside of his mind
his hands are shoved
deep in his pockets while
the distant trombones riffle
the air and a moaning starts
in his soul, shattering his
bones into polished fragments
shiny as rain on new iron

and he walks the black
ragged edges of the city,
his shadow lost in the neon
smears of light, philosophies
crashing to dust under his feet

© By **PHONACELLE SHAPEL**

Chapter twenty:
The First People.

From a man in Canada with an organization similar to ours, I received this e-mail:

"God be with you. It is so important for your voices to be heard and it seems there are so few opportunities. Let's keep in touch. I would still like to run a short article on your point of view in our newsletter."
Greg

I received this message from another:

>Hi Beth
>I just caught the discussion on reservation jurisdiction and your post therein. I too made a posting just now at that site. If you get a chance please review the discussion on "spearfishing on (the reservation)" Sports>Outdoors>Spearfishing. I have been discussing "tribal sovereignty" with...others there and would like to get your thoughts. If possible I would also like to meet you and your husband one day. I am a friend of Bill Lawrence, Judge Jim Randall, and Roland Ward. Perhaps you may know of these men. If not you should. They are fighting hard for you. I hope to hear from you.
>
>>Frank

I showed the letter to Roland and we both had a laugh. Roland had met him in Washington DC a year earlier.

> Frank;
> Thanks for your note!! At first I didn't know if you were pulling my leg or what. Well, I've heard of Judge Randall and I've spoken to Bill Lawrence a few times on the phone; they sound like pretty good guys. You also said you'd like to meet my husband and me. That sounds fun. You've already met half of us though. I'm married to Roland Ward! Thanks for the kind words! Roland says he had a good time with you. Roland does remember you warmly. Keep up the fight! It's good to hear from you!
> Beth

Another person Roland met in Washington was a lively Oklahoma Choctaw woman by the name of Scott Kayla Morrison. She wrote her story down for us:

"My first up-close and personal experience with tribal governments was my first job after law school. I was staff attorney at the East Mississippi Legal Services (EMLS) on the Mississippi Choctaw reservation. I was the first Choctaw attorney to work there. I got crosswise with the government when I took my job seriously and challenged the practices of the tribal government... My truck was shot sitting in my driveway at my home on the reservation. It was just a shotgun and it was just my truck, I rationalized, so [I] stayed another six months. EMLS was kicked off the reservation because they wouldn't fire me. Chief Phillip Martin told EMLS manager that he could not guarantee my safety if I came on the reservation. Since almost all of my practice was in tribal court, staying away from the reservation was impossible and still do my job.

"When the tribal attorney asked the EMLS manager if I would be fired if I was arrested, not convicted, for a crime. At this point, EMLS manager told me not to go to the reservation alone. But it was too late. That day, Custer's troops came for me, only they were wearing Mississippi Choctaw tribal police uniforms. Without a warrant or a legal document to bring me to the reservation, the tribal police sent a county sheriff to my home, sent a Miss. Narcotics Bureau officer to search the homes of my friends in Jackson, broadcast a description of my truck and tag number, and rounded up my friends on the reservation for questioning my whereabouts. No one knew, but I was on my way back to Daisy, Oklahoma, when all of this was going on. I heard later, the plan was to arrest me for criminal defamation and I would have committed suicide in tribal jail or been shot while escaping.

'When tribal sovereignty can kill me, I can't support it. That was exactly my thought when I realized how cavalier Chief Martin was in his attempts to get rid of me. Nothing would have been done if they had found and killed me because the tribal police would be heading the investigation. Tribal sovereignty insulates and protects tribal leaders. This gives them the authority and power to do anything they…please.

"I went to law school to protect and defend tribal sovereignty. I believed all the [BS] Professor Robert Clinton taught me at the University of Iowa. He had written a textbook on Indian law… What he did not have a clue about was what the theories he was preaching and teaching were doing to tribal people on the reservation. He, like other academics who did not have to live under tribal governments…

"The tribe, as defined by the federal government, is the chief and council, not the tribal membership. We were merely pawns in a money game. When a chief has the power and authority to kill a person and expect no retribution and federal money is used to facilitate such a murder, something is dreadfully wrong. Yet that is exactly the situation on the Mississippi Choctaw reservation, and other reservations across the country. There is no police force without federal dollars, yet the force is only accountable to the chief. Hence, we have a federally funded goon squad at the beck and call of the tribal chief. My experience in Mississippi clearly laid that out. And Professor Clinton and other NARF Mafia legal scholars were off the scale when I survived. What if I told my story and the general public began looking behind the façade? …That was unacceptable. Moves were made to paint me a black sheep and an outcast among those who were my peers a year ago.

"I was groomed to be a part of the problem. Professor Clinton had contacts to place me in a position where I could go represent tribes and defend this sovereignty that he had helped create over the years. I clerked a summer at Native American Rights Fund (NARF), the oldest non-profit legal organization to represent tribes. NARF did do good work at one point, but their philosophy became corrupted along the way. The NARF Mafia mentality is a philosophy of tribes can do no wrong. Tribal sovereignty is upheld at all costs even to a point of sacrificing tribal members. NARF has a policy of not representing tribal members against tribes. "With the per capita income of tribal members being the lowest in the country, they can not afford to pay attorneys, and even if they could, who would represent them? Most law students were taught like I was, to represent tribes, the Bureau of Indian Affairs or tribal entities. We were not encouraged to help tribal members with our law degrees. After Mississippi, I never looked at Indian law the same way. . I was proud of my black sheep reputation. You bet ya. If I have to defend the power to kill me, I can't do it, folks but thanks for asking.

"...[The Oklahoma Choctaws] have no blood quantum. Our membership is based on ancestry traced back to the Dawes Rolls of the turn of the century My grandmother was a child when she was enrolled in the mid 1970's when it became important to be enrolled to receive federally funded benefits, such as health care.

"Now, with much experience under my belt, I look at interracial marriages from only a blood quantum perspective. With the Oklahoma Choctaws, we have members who are *1/4000th* Choctaw and now have NBQ (no blood quantum). Now how can these people claim to be Indian? What part of them is 1/4000th? How do you even measure it? It is mind-boggling to me that we would even enroll them. The reason is money...With more members, we get more money, so we have a vested interest to keep swelling our membership with NBQ members. But are we culturally, racially, traditionally Choctaw? I don't think so. Tribalism used to mean what you contributed to the community defined your membership. With only your ability to contribute federal poverty aide money by the very fact that you are walking around breathing, you have no ownership interest in the tribe. We become a mobile country club with no land base but a membership roll. That is not the definition of a tribe...

"And let's add another layer to the blood quantum issue. Twenty percent of us are one-quarter or more. That means 80 percent is less than a quarter blood quantum and the majority of voters. Candidates have to appeal to them to get elected. So the 20 percent of us who are full-blooded or identifiable Choctaws are pushed to the edge of the herd. Is that what Congress intended when it allocated that [one dollar]. No. It was intended to benefit Indian people, not NBQ Choctaws. Does this cause dissension among the ranks of the tribe? You bet ya.' Can we do anything about it? No, not internally because of the election fraud. Our only hope of having the federal money equally distributed among the true Choctaw people is that Congress will regulate that the money be spent on one-quarter blooded or more, Indian people. That will allow us access to programs intended to benefit us.

"There is a cultural, spiritual bankruptcy among Indian people today, regardless of where they live. The corruption and violence on reservations today force many Indian people to move away from their land. Those who stay live in a violent state of siege, physically and spiritually. We are so far removed from what our Creators intended us to be. We have become soul-less people, the walking dead. We are also dysfunctional people...The death rate of Native people is staggering. On small reservations, the obituaries will run on for pages and pages in the tribal newsletter. These deaths will be from violence, natural causes, alcoholism, and homicide. The evil is eating its young and it is us. Why? We have stopped being human ourselves. We have no souls...

"...Reservations behave as a dysfunctional family. The classic is Oklahoma Choctaws as an incestuous family. Our chief, Hollis Roberts, was convicted of sexual assaulting tribal employees who were tribal members. The council voted to pay his legal fees as a way to resist federal interference in Choctaw sovereignty. The women employees signed a petition saying what an honorable man Roberts was. The entire tribal administration structure denied any wrongdoing on his part. It was all political, according to the party line. Well, this is the same as a father sleeping with the daughters.

The mother denies it is happening and disbelieves the daughters. The entire family rallies to protect the offender. The Choctaw tribe behaved as an incestuous family in that situation.

"Also, the sheer rate of alcoholism in Indian communities has an impact in the tribal power structure. If an alcoholic is elected chief, the entire governmental structure acts as an alcoholic or addictive organization. Anne Wilson Schaef has done marvelous work on addictive organizations. When you compare the characteristics of an addictive organization to the characteristics of a tribal government, they are the same, as any rez Indian will tell you. Some characteristics are: confusion, dishonesty, control, ethical deterioration, crisis orientation and abnormal thinking processes.

"We see how these characteristics play out, even without knowing whether the tribal leader is an alcoholic, in how many leaders are in federal prison on corruption charges. Darrel Chip Wadena is a classic example. He was convicted of money laundering and other charges of corruption and his defense was sovereign immunity. 'I am a leader of an Indian tribe therefore, the federal government does not have jurisdiction to prosecute me,' he said. The classic stereotype of a bullet proof alcoholic. This can happen when there is dishonesty and ethical deterioration in tribal leadership. This type of leadership creates an environment of confusion, chaos and crisis among the membership.

"Indian politics feels like my alcoholic family. Being around Indian politics makes me feel the very same way as growing up with an alcoholic dad. The conspiracy of denial is the same. "We don't air our dirty laundry in public" mentality insulated an alcoholic family from public scrutiny. (Or so they think until the alcoholic is arrested for drunk driving for the 15th time or for beating up his wife in a drunken rage.) The same thing is said about talking about our dysfunctional tribal governments. The fear is that if the public knew that Indian leadership is not any better, and in most cases, far worse than federal administration of Indian affairs, we would lose what little administration we have. All energy is spent covering up our dirty laundry instead of trying to clean it up. That is typical of an alcoholic family. But you can't white wash (excuse the pun) dysfunction forever. It catches up with alcoholic families and tribal governments, the same way it did with Chip Wadena.

"...Federal Indian policy also encourages dysfunction. We are sovereign nations and wards of the federal government at the same time. How is that possible? Two diametrically opposed ideas co-existing at the same time is not possible yet congress, the courts and tribal leadership act as if it is. Opposing ideas run through virtually all aspects of Indian law and policy creating schizophrenia in law and among Indian people. No wonder our leaders act dysfunctionally and we are dysfunctional. The environment created by the law dictates that we are dysfunctional.

"We are given federal aid for poverty programs yet we are also encouraged toward self-sufficiency. Tribal leaders have a vested interest to keep their members poor to keep the steady stream of federal aid coming in each year so there is a vested interest in sabotaging tribal businesses. If they are a success, the federal aid will stop, as Congress is considering with the wealthy casino tribes right now. But the purpose of tribal self-sufficiency was to get tribes off the welfare roles. Congress has pumped billions into Indian Country to accomplish that. Tribes have been busy accepting the money then misusing it or abusing it without creating a successful financial infrastructure. Congress has pumped billions into Indian Country to raise the poverty level among tribal members. Both Congress and the tribes feel betrayed when either side complains about it. Neither side bothers to THINK about it and realize the system was set up to fail. There is no way the system, as it currently exists, can work...

"This entitled mentality is what drives the above. Indian leaders prey on the collective white guilt each year when they go to Congress begging for money. We are effective beggars, and they soften Congress up through the media. Take pity on us mentality. Or, I think a more accurate description is the Munchausen Syndrome by Proxy. A parent will make their child sick in order to get sympathy. This is a recognized illness. Well, isn't that what tribes do each year when they beg for more money? They trot out the elderly, infants, staggering socio-economic statistics so Congress, burdened by collective white guilt, will give them more money to address these issues. The next year, Congress doesn't say, "what about all the money we gave you last year to alleviate these problems? Did you spend it like we wanted you to?" Instead, Congress gives more money. The sympathy received for tribes is the dollar. Tribes have to keep their members in a state of illness to keep receiving sympathy and as in all dysfunctional situations, they accept no personal responsibility for creating the situation. Tribes are responsible for keeping their members sick by misusing or abusing the money Congress allocates, but screams like a stuck pig if anyone calls them on it.

"When I hear that we deserve it because of treaties, I want to ask what article in what tribe? Where is it written we will be a burden on the federal taxpayer forever? Where is it written that we must remain poor and sick forever? This treaty entitlement is really a mask for a perpetual welfare state with no personal responsibility on the part of the tribe. When are we going to get our pride back and say, 'yeah, bad things happened but it is time we stood on our own two feet and pulled ourselves up by our bootstraps?' I don't see that at all. The media falls for the touchy-feely articles of the poor End of the Trail silhouette Indian. That is what we have internalized. We should begin putting the red circle and slash over that symbol. We are not a beaten, defeated people. We are/can be as smart, educated, savvy as the next if we were to get our pride back. We can't do that as long as we are pawns used by our tribal leaders to get more money. In an article in the April 1998 Harper's magazine, a Navajo cop was quoted as saying, "Congress should stop loving us to death. Don't send money. Send mortar and steel so we can do it ourselves." That struck a cord with me because that is exactly what should happen. Stop loving us to death, Congress!

"…With tribal sovereign immunity that absolves tribal administration from all accountability, it is hard to set an example. You can't very well expect tribal members to be personally accountable for their actions when tribal administrations don't have to be. And you can say that tribal governments merely mirror larger societal ill, and I will say so what? If all we have become is a mirror of the mainstream society, then why are we a tribe with separate lands and separate laws? The purpose of sovereign immunity is to stop being unique and become just like everyone else, the sad, sick people who can't get out of this morass of molasses we're all stuck in , like flies stuck to fly paper. You can squirm but you can't get out.

"And what would you do if you did get out? You can't be healthy and happy in that situation so you have to leave. When you leave, you leave your family, your land, your everything. But you can't stay and be sick, so that brings up more of a dilemma and you squirm around the goo but you just get more stuck. It's a cycle. You just can't win.

"The government is merely a mirror of what is going on in Indian families. More and more tribal leaders are going to jail for, oh, pick a corruption crime. Some argue tribal sovereign immunity to get out of criminal accountability. It worked so well to get out of criminal accountability, why not try it on the criminal side? Luckily, courts aren't buying it but it is being argued. A strong people have a strong government with honorable men as heroes. We have no heroes today.

"With no leadership, ethical deterioration through dysfunction, and a legal system that encourages such behavior: No wonder we are in a world of hurt. Tribal members cannot be healthy in this environment. Can't happen, and we are just nuts to think we can be healthy in such environment. Until the legal system changes for tribal leaders, we will continue to be in this mess. When the role models for our kids are tribal leaders who are not accountable to anyone, including those that elected them, what can we expect for future generations…

"We are like most addicts. It's their fault we are an addict. If the Euro-trash hadn't come, we'd be healthy. If the BIA weren't such jerks, we'd be wealthy. It's so easy to look externally for excuses for us being sick. And there may be some valid reasons to look externally, but we have to get well internally. Blaming will not do anything but keep us sick. So what if the Euro-trash came? So what if the BIA are jerks? We can't change it. Accept. Accommodate. Move on.

"Mass media plugs into the pity, not realizing that it just re-enforces our dysfunctional behavior. Get over it. Go on. Get well. That's all I have to say."

Roland left on Oct. 17, 2007 to attend the custody hearing. After a random urinary analysis had shown drugs in Misty's system, she accused Wesley of partying with her. They then fought with each other and separated. In court, different lawyers represented them.

Roland called us after the hearing,

"The decision on custody has been postponed until December 15th. Misty said she didn't want to give her okay for temporary custody to us. She wanted to go to actual trial. Everyone told her that she'll run the risk of losing all her rights, but she wouldn't listen."

"It would've been good for everyone if she had taken the deal,' I said, just wanting it over with and a decision made.

"They're also going back to treatment again. I told the judge it had better be long term in-patient, but I don't know if they're going to have them do that. But the judge said he got lots of letters from the community and needed some time to study them."

"Good. At least that means he's taking them seriously."

His voice lowered on the phone. He'd seen Cheri while driving down the Avenue that day and stopped to pick her up

"She's on heroin now. She asked me for help, but I had to tell her not until she began cleaning up on her own. Then she asked me for money to get something to eat. I told her that I couldn't give her money, but I'd take her to get some food. She said 'No, I have to go meet someone. Just give me some money.' I told her, 'No', and she just got out of the car and left. I feel terrible. I almost went back and got her."

"You feel like you did with Lila?"

"Yeah."

"Will you feel guilty if she dies?"

"Probably."

He couldn't talk any further right then, but when he got home from Minnesota, he sat on the couch and told more about the trip. He said he couldn't find anyone up in Cass Lake; they were all out drinking. But he talked to one of Elaine's grandkids and asked about Dale.

"Dale walks around like he's in a daze now, I guess."

Then, quietly, Roland began to talk about Cheri; "No one lets her stay with them anymore because she steals from them. So, she's on the streets. She looked terrible. I wanted to take her home with me, but something inside me... I just knew I had to tell her 'No'. And the way she looked. She doesn't take care of herself anymore," Roland said, his voice breaking. "I told her she never used to walk around like that. She would have been ashamed. But the way she looked when she got out of the car. The look on her face when I drove away..."

Putting his hands over his eyes, Roland began to cry. "It was the hardest thing I've ever done. I was abandoning my child."

Autumn was hard on Roland. His older brother Buck died alone in a boarding house. Roland and Andrew drove to Cass Lake for the funeral. Despite the fact a Bible was found among Buck's possessions, his children wanted the funeral to be traditional.

"How do we do it Uncle Roland?" they asked.

"If you've never had interest enough to find out what tradition is before, why are you pretending now?" Roland answered, "I'm not going to tell you how to do it."

Other young relatives came to him complaining about his political activity. But older ones - Elaine, her husband, and a few others - stuck up for Roland.

"I'm glad you're standing up like you are," Elaine said.

As Roland talked to Annie, explaining the things he was trying to do, she nervously looked away, pleading, "Don't stare at me! What did I do?"

"Oh, sorry,' Roland explained laughing, "I've been learning to live 'in the white man's world', looking at people when I talk to them."

In mid-December Roland was granted sole legal and physical custody of Misty's children. The findings of fact stated that the children's mother had not addressed her chemical dependency that led to the neglect of her children; specifically that she had not attended treatment or made attempts on her own to visit her children. Instead, she had continued her cocaine use. The father had agreed to a case plan and parenting services, but had also failed to follow through.

Interestingly, not once during this entire period of time did any social worker do any kind of home study or ever even step foot in our home. They had no idea that we only had two real bedrooms in the back apartment of this decrepit building. They had no idea that some kids were sleeping in store rooms meant for the shop area, or that Dewey and Caleb were sharing a bed. In truth, they didn't even know for a fact that Roland and I were sober and never did drugs. After all, Roland had a documented history of drug use and jail time, and didn't even have a current driver's license due to past DUI's. Yet, they put the children into his car and allowed him to drive away. As far as we could tell, the only thing that Social Services cared about was that Roland met the criteria for ICWA.

Neither parent put up a fight, although both asked separately if they could come live with us. A couple weeks later, because they didn't get the children and because they had been allowing drug activity in their tax-payer sponsored apartment, they were evicted.

Social Services hadn't contacted us anymore about Savannah's children, but Roland learned Annie had been awarded custody of Savannah's oldest boy. He wasn't sure where the other children were placed, perhaps with their father's family. Later during a phone call in which Annie was asking if we'd take in Elaine's 14-year-old granddaughter, she mentioned the boy.

"He's hard for me to handle. He needs a father figure."

"I know Annie, but I'm so burnt out right now by the nine kids I already have."

"Yeah, I was wondering how you do it."

"Not very well."

Timothy, 5-years old, was rushing past me when he suddenly stopped, reached into his pocket and dug out a few coins.

"Here," he said. "Give it to the homeless."

"What?"

"I don't need this money. Give it to the homeless." Then off he rushed again.

It was interesting to note during the uproar about Democratic campaign financing, in which hundreds of thousands of dollars were donated in the hopes of buying votes, that people were upset with China for trying to curry favor, while the $100,000 donated by a western Tribal Council hoping to regain land was viewed with sympathy. The general public blamed party leaders for having tried to swindle the poor defenseless Indians. A tribal leader spoke on television and supported that thought, insinuating that the Tribal government had no idea that they were doing something wrong.

How pathetic that tribal leaders play this game when caught with their hand in the cookie jar. To pretend they had no knowledge and that the bad white man was at fault again is an insult to the intelligence of all tribal members. Further, that kind of propaganda fuels the racist attitude that Indians are perpetual victims who can not take care of themselves.

Then there's the other kind of propaganda - the kind designed by tribal officials to draw media attention and frighten people. Senator Burns, introducing a draft of a bill concerning tribal jurisdiction, had arranged a public meeting to discuss the bill. But there was no 'discussion.'

Several tribal governments arranged a huge powwow prior to the hearing and organized "caravans" from all seven reservations. A friend reported that before boarding the bus at the tribal college, he was asked if he was going to testify for the tribe. When he answered, "No," he wasn't allowed to board the bus. Another person reported that tribal kids were given the day off at the high schools in order to attend.

Once at the convention center, the tribes gave everyone free food. After they had everyone dancing and having a good time, they began a series of vengeful speeches.

Roland and I unintentionally walked through the pow-wow near its end. A security guard, seeing Roland was Indian, had "redirected" us over to the powwow side of the parking lot when we had tried to park near the entrance to the hearing. We had no idea what we were walking into until it was too late. We heard a part of one of the angry speeches and saw signs and banners with accusations of "racism" and "genocide." We walked on through the powwow hall quickly to get to the auditorium for the hearing.

When we finally arrived at the auditorium, there was a small smattering of people waiting, maybe 20, and half of them were Burn's staff or security. We quickly signed the list for open mike. We were told open mike would be "first come, first served." Good. We would say our piece and leave. Roland was the second on the list, I was the third.

Then the tribal governments finished their powwow and marched the charged crowd of about 1000 over to the hearing. The auditorium was packed. All the seats were taken and crowds lined the walls and back of the room. Senate Aide Dwight McKay announced there were others outside waiting, but because of fire precautions, the doors were closed to them.

Senator Burns wasn't there, but the meeting opened with his video-taped explanation of what he was trying to do. This should have been our first clue that this wasn't a genuine hearing.

Despite efforts of senate staff to explain this was a 'discussion,' hoping everyone would listen to each other and come to some understanding of jurisdictional problems; the crowd was hostile and unwilling to listen at all.

Roland and I knew a handful of people that were there to support the Burns Draft. But that small number I could count on one hand. They were all good, kind people who were truly concerned about things that were happening on the reservation.

The scheduled speakers were arranged so that a council member from one of the seven tribes would speak, followed by one of the supporters of the senate draft, then back to a tribal leader, etc. Open mike was to follow after that. We watched as the tribal leaders were thunderously applauded, with hooting, whistling, and war cries. CS&KT Chairman Nolan Ricco stood up to his applause, grinning from ear to ear. He told the Chairman that, yes, there are jurisdictional problems on his reservation, but they are limited to a few malcontents. Most people, he said, were fine with things as they are. He went on to describe the number of tribal permits sold and the number of vendors they patronize. Loud supportive hooting interrupted most of his comments.

Our friends, on the other hand, got up to hostile jeers. Sitting near the front, we could hear the heckling and snide comments. One man, a resident on the Crow Reservation, stopped speaking and asked the chairman to have the crowd not interrupt. The chairman good naturedly asked everyone to keep it down so that everyone could speak.

I was close enough to see the hands of men shaking as they tried to hold their papers and speak to the chairman. Their voices cracked. Two tribal women next to me traded nasty comments back and forth.

Open mike began, but we weren't called in the first set of people. We weren't called in the second set either. Nor the third. And there didn't appear to be any tribal members besides Roland that were there in support of the Senator. If there were any, they probably did just what we did after an hour and a half of listening to heckling and jeers. We gave an aide our written testimony, slipped out the door and never did testify. It would have been pointless.

As far as we were concerned, Senator Burns' 'hearing' was nothing but a sham, probably coordinated with the tribal governments (as evidenced by the lack of effort to control the event) and put on solely to give pretense to non-tribal members that he was trying to do something. He was trying to keep the votes of the non-members while at the same time submitting to tribal government.

We did stop and speak to two colleagues before we left. Both had been with the scheduled speaker list. They encouraged us to go ahead and leave. Hey, if they were shaking, what would it have been like for Roland? It would have been a lynching.

"One elder that night at the hearing looked just like my grandfather," Roland said while tearing apart a chair a few days later.

"Did you feel grief?" I asked.

"Yes, tremendous grief. It wasn't even so much what the elder had said, but that I'd been taught not to contradict my elders. It's hard to explain... I disagreed with him, but getting up to contradict him in public wouldn't have been right. Young people don't listen to elders anymore. I bet a lot of elders would have been embarrassed by the way those people were acting."

He was quiet for a few minutes, then said, "Elders are disrespected. I want to go to Washington and talk about the need for change, but I don't want to be in spit fights anymore. I want to go speak my heart, but I want to find a way to do it that's respectful."

Beth Ward

We fantasize and fool ourselves
with delusions big and grand.
All of life's a mockery
and reality be damned.

Sugar-coated shams
we swallow every day,
to make the living bearable
and, to keep the truths away.

Delusions tailor-made
for all our vanities,
hand-crafted on the looms
of gullibility.

All of life's a mockery
and reality be damned.

© By **PHONACELLE SHAPEL**

Chapter twenty-one:
Human Rights for all?

At some point, every person must come to grips with two important facts:

- One: People are the treasures on this earth, not money, not power, not entitlements, not things. As individuals, we need to care about others – no matter their background - and try to help when we can. At the very least, we need to make the decision not to maliciously hurt others.
- Two: The world has never been a safe place to live and intolerance, greed, discrimination and persecution are realities that men can't eradicate. That doesn't mean that injustice should be tolerated by society. <u>Society needs to categorically forbid and come against it</u>. But in each of our personal lives, we need to get beyond it. If we decide we are going to be angry and vengeful over things that have happened to us or to those we love, then the horror is perpetuated and more and more innocent people fall victim.

Should I hate others for all that happened in our family? No. First, I could go back through various people who had hurt us, but what good would it do? Many of them had been hurt at some point as well. Pain and evil exist; no person will get through life without being hurt by them and their domino effects. My father might not have been the most attentive and nurturing dad, and I could blame him for my subsequent choice in an alcoholic older man. But he, himself, was a child in Nazi Germany. He escaped while many of his relatives didn't. Two died at Auschwitz and two more at Camp Theresienstadt in the Czech Republic. There is no record of several others following the 1943 Berlin census, including a woman who had my same maiden name and who, like me, was a nurse. These people once lived, loved and were loved - and were senselessly murdered. Nothing remains of their lives but short notations in a seventy-year-old census...and my father's memory.

The world has rightfully captured and punished many of the murderers; it was society's job to do that, not my father's. Yet he was hurt in Germany and the effects of that hurt have lasted a lifetime. Should he hate others for all that happened to his family? He, himself, would say 'No.'

Second, is anyone to blame but me for my personal reactions and behavior? No, it is not my parents' fault, the governments' fault, nor anyone else's fault. I chose my behavior and I am accountable for it. Roland showed us this when he accepted responsibility for his life and changed.

The reason God tells us to turn the other cheek is because <u>it can't work any other way</u>. The only way to bring an end to the hurt people inflict on each other is for every individual to say "it ends here, with me."

"Do not seek revenge" and "Vengeance is mine; I will repay," says the Lord through Deuteronomy 32:35, Leviticus 19:18, Romans 12:19 and Hebrews 10:30.

Through the Lord Jesus, Roland changed his behavior and in doing that, changed all of our lives.

Together we wrote:

> "What cannot be denied is that a large number of Native Americans are dying from alcoholism, drug abuse, suicide and violence. Some die quickly, others die slowly. Some live most of their years dead in their hearts.

Dying in Indian Country

The ICWA, the Act of Congress that reversed the Duro decision and other pieces of politically correct legislation in fact give rights to the tribal governments by stripping individual Native Americans of their civil rights.

Current Federal Indian Policy is hurting not only non-tribal members, but tribal people themselves. Many treaties were meant to last only twenty or so years – (NOT 'as long as the grass grows' as is commonly believed.) It has been Congress that has been stretching it out longer. If this is so good for Indian people, why are the rates for suicide, alcohol dependency, and spousal and child abuse on the reservations so high?

Government dependence is killing people. Tribal Governments are in love with unchecked power and money though, and it is the tribal governments who are keeping their own people in bondage.

It is time to forgive and move on. Christ went to the cross blaming no one, without self-pity. If we are to come together as people, we must follow his example of forgiveness:

"But I say to you, love your enemies, bless those who curse you, and pray for those that spitefully use you and persecute you..." Matthew 5:44."

An end to the "victimization complex" would mean an end to the mind set that Native Americans are more "needy" then everyone else, an acceptance of the fact that Native Americans are just as good, just as productive as any other people group, and the beginning of treating each other as co-equals..."

Clyde Harms, director of the Montana Human Rights Network (MHRN) asked Roland for an interview. We didn't feel good about it, because this was the same group that claimed State Rep. Will Stanley was a racist. They'd also held seminars on the "dangers" of "extremist Christians" (i.e., those who take the Bible literally, have in-home Bible studies, homeschool, etc.)

We believed the real purpose of the meeting was to find a way to discredit Roland. So Roland wrote to the MHRN board of directors and said that although he welcomes a chance for open discussion, he does not believe Harms will be coming with an open mind. Roland cited articles and newspaper reports quoting things Harms and the Human Rights Network had said about Christians, homeschoolers, "Focus on the Family," the Christian Coalition, and other Christian entities. Roland told the board of directors that he will not meet with Harms until Harms apologizes to Christians, Homeschoolers, and Will Stanley.

"Should that happen, communication may be considered possible."

We didn't expect him to apologize. We expected he'd just drop the idea of meeting. However, Harms used the letter itself to attack Roland. His newsletter reprinted Roland's entire letter, and an accompanying article accused Roland of being just a figurehead for closet racist organizations; "The Christian Right will find a "rabbi" to make its case, the militia will find a black "patriot," and now, the anti-Indian movement has found its Indian spokesperson," the article said.

This newsletter was mailed to not only the MHRN membership, but also every state legislator. We heard about it from Will Stanley.

So we were right, the only intent of the meeting was to hurt Roland. They went ahead and tried to do that even without the meeting. Isn't it amazing how nasty a group with a name that includes "human rights" can be?

In early March, we received an e-mail:

> My name is Alex. I read your web page "Dying In Indian Country." I don't know the answers. I myself am seeking. I am almost half Cherokee. Even though I am not full blooded Indian, my Indian heritage runs deep within my blood. I feel for American Indians. I think without hope, we have lost. With hope, there is a chance. I try to do my part to keep my heritage alive and remembered truthfully. God has given me the talent to put my thoughts

on paper. So I draw and sketch my history. I want to show people our proud spirit. For what it is worth, I try to do my part. I have hope. I just wanted you to know that I agree with what you say, and tell you to have hope.

Alex

Later we received other mail;

Dear Mr. Ward Sr.,
"(I) am currently incarcerated in the . . . Reformatory, ...I had just read your article in the Native American Press/Ojibwe News and was touched by what you had to say in the March paper. I am a 19-year-old Native American man that feels "unneeded."

I am only serving around 15 more months, and I would like for my time to go good as possible. I believe in everything that you had to say to Senator Burns and Chairman Stovall.

I have 3, (going on 4) kids, and I am going to change my life of drugs and alcohol around for them. I don't want them to go through what I did with my C.D. (chemical dependency) problems. I lived a "rough" life, with a great family. I lost friend and family to Alcohol & Drugs. My Res. is losing our youth to the same, and I feel "unneeded" because there is no one I can find to talk to . ..I guess all I ask of you is to maybe write back as a penpal.. .I don't have many to write to about my concerns for our "youth of tomorrow." Can you please help."
Respectfully yours, Kent

Roland responded:

Dear Kent,
Thanks for writing. I found your letter touching. I know how it is. I've been in that (reformatory) myself. Stay strong and have hope. Life will get better if you strive for it.

About our youth; I am glad you want to help. We need people that want to change how things are. But first let's get you yourself rebuilt in spirit and strength. You have 15 more months; that time can be used in the best possible way for your inner self to take the time to grow spiritually, emotionally, and physically, in effort to take on the task you desire on your release.

And remember, you have four youths that God has given you direct leadership over as their father. Don't ever forget those children or turn away from them, as they are the very youth of tomorrow that we speak of. Part of what is happening with many of our young people is a tremendous sense of loss at having to grow up without their fathers. One of the evils of welfare has been its subtle encouragement that we men are not needed in our children's lives. This is a lie. Our children need us desperately. I have made the mistake of not being a full part of my older children's lives. Now I am reaping the results and watching these older children endure pain and suffering.

Please don't make my same mistake. Listen to elders even if they sound stern. Don't fall for the younger peers because you want to change your lifestyle. Most of all, don't give up hope, because there are more people that want to help you than you know, if you will only give them a chance to make things real.

Bro in Christ;
Roland Ward

Riding in the car on a shopping trip, I asked Roland why I've seen so many tribal members so harsh with their kids.

"Why do some people give their kids the silent treatment? Why do so many laugh at them and put them down all the time? Why don't they act like they care if their kid is hurt?

He answered, 'There is a spiritual emptiness, but we are also talking about people that up until 150 years ago lived in groups living off the land. They needed children to be brave and help as much as possible. And when they were twelve, children had to spend three nights alone in the woods without being scared. Parents sent their boys on this trip, knowing they may not come back. How many children today could do that and how many parents would let them? Survival of the fittest was not cruel; it was necessary. Children knew they had to grow up and take care of the tribe. And they wanted to; it was a sign of being grown up. Then society changed. Treaties were signed and wars were over. The U. S. government began providing commodities. Indians didn't have to fight with the neighboring tribes or go on hunting trips anymore. The child isn't watching his father and uncles ride off on horses, wishing he could go along, so he doesn't understand why he must grow up fast and tough.

"But family parenting is still the same. Most people learn to be parents from their parents. Children are still raised with toughness. Then when boarding schools came, people learned cruelty on top of harshness. Now some people think it's the way children are supposed to be raised. And with hopelessness and alcoholism, neglect started.

"But you can't tell people how to raise their kids," he lamented, knowing that his older daughters and some others would never listen.

Caleb had just finished a math and a reading workbook that we had purchased for him at Barnes and Noble. So with his completion of them, I filled out the "Honor Roll Awards" in the back of the books. He was so excited, he ran around showing Roland and the other kids his awards, then stopped and asked, "Do we give these to the Barnes and Noble man now?"

Eight-year-old Brooke had been making slow progress in her first grade class, but five-year-old Timothy was quickly gaining on her. Fortunately, her class was quite small, only four children, and she had been blessed with a very patient and nurturing teacher. Her progress was slow, but she was progressing.

She was also struggling in her piano lessons. While Heidi had learned her lessons and was growing in skill, after a year of effort, Brooke was still unable to read simple notes or remember simple patterns. In the last month or two, her teacher reported, she was goofing off at the keys instead of trying. On reflection, I realized the problems she was having in math and reading were naturally going to show up in other areas as well. She was probably goofing off during lessons to hide the fact she did not know her lessons and could not compete with Heidi.

But I realized something else as well. Her mother, Misty, testing at only the third grade reading level, had left school in the eighth grade. At the time we were angry at her stubbornness, it hadn't occurred to us that maybe she was 'goofing off' in an attempt, just as Brooke had, to hide the fact she was struggling with her lessons and had no idea how to compete.

Thinking back, I wondered how Misty had gotten to eighth grade with nothing more than a third grade reading ability. Was this another example of not expecting much from Native American children? I, an inadequate teaching assistant if there ever was one, had been assigned to help Junior as a child. Was I the best the system had to offer him? And even at that, why was no one assigned to help Misty? If she had gotten the help she had needed at the time, would she have been saved from the trouble she eventually fell into? The stress that all the children have gone through in the last few years - her children uprooted and my children having to deal with their uprooting - could that all have been prevented? And how do we help Brooke so history doesn't repeat itself?

In April we received some e-mail about our web site;

> Hi Roland,
>
> This sounds all too familiar. I write novels about prehistoric America, and because I know a little about the web, I put up a page for another Native American writer .. who also published her book ... I read her story and it sounds very similar to what I've read at your site. . . .You'd be amazed (or not) at what she uncovered, particularly about why the federal government and the BIA are ignoring corruption on the reservations and have been purposely doing so since their creation. Thanks, Guy

And another:

Hello Roland:
Please come to my site and tell me if you would like to be on my links page? I am not Native. My husband is part Cherokee. I am only one who wants to help.
Pila Maya, Donna

A woman from a reservation in British Columbia wrote asking for help:

Where is the protection of the Canadian Constitution and the Charter of Human Rights and Freedoms for those children, women, and men of native descent or mixed blood descent that do not want to be initiated into a cultural or religious practice that they may or may not want to be a part of?...To volunteer to be grabbed and initiated as a dancer allows for the individual's human and legal rights to be recognized and respected. But to be grabbed and confined for over a 4 to 6 month period of time against one's will is a violation of an individuals basic human and legal rights. ..Not all Indian people want to be initiated into the Bighouse Religion yet many see no way out of the situation for themselves because while native and non native politicians and bureaucrats negotiate over resources and " political self determination " the Indian people's " self determination" and human and legal rights continue to be ignored.. .Everyone has the inherent right to. ..what ever religion or cultural practice that they choose to believe in regardless of their race or ethnic origin.... Cultural identity is not a defense to violating anyone's basic human and legal rights."

An Aide to Senator Gorton called at the beginning of April: Would Roland testify at the Oversight hearings before the Senate Committee on Indian Affairs next Tuesday in Seattle? The hearings were about Senator Gorton's S. 1691, 'The American Equal Justice

Act.' They wanted him to address tribal government abuses of the civil rights of tribal members.

Roland agreed. We found baby-sitters for most of the kids and planned to leave Monday morning and spend the night. However, on Saturday Roland announced that neither of our vehicles could make it. He also wasn't sure if we could afford the trip. Hearing this, Will offered us the use of his car. Another friend paid for our night in the motel, and three other families sent money to help cover the costs.

We got rid of the jitters by reading 18 Psalms during the ride between our hotel and the hearing. We got lost on the way and arrived late. The place was packed. We had to park quite a ways away. Pickets were all over the place - on one side, white people carrying signs in support of Gorton's bill, on the other side, close to the entrance of the hotel, tribal members drumming and holding signs opposed to Gorton's bill.

Scattered in among the tribal members were some white people, wearing khakis and handing out "Free Leonard Peltier" literature to passers by. But we saw no tribal members who, like Roland, allied with the majority of whites in support of Gorton's bill.

Getting to Roland's seat was difficult. We tried to make it through the standing crowd, but that was impossible. We were told to go around through the kitchen, but there was a guy there with a small listening device in his ear blocking the door. We told him Roland was a witness, and he opened the door and let us pass. All kinds of tall men with things in their ears were back there. We made our way in, about ten feet from the senators, when another guy stopped us and tried to herd us back behind a velvet rope. I told him Roland was a witness, and he notified a staff member.

Roland was then seated with the other witnesses. I stood for the next three hours. But that was okay. I wanted to move around anyway. They let me stay where I was now, and even go in and out through the kitchen as I pleased.

I made a foray out to the picket line while I was waiting for Roland to speak and tried to talk to some of the "property rights" picketers outside. I was a little taken aback by some of them. While sharing some information, some of the picketers tried to reciprocate – handing me their bumper stickers encouraging people to 'shoot a buck."

I tried to hide my initial reaction and remained calm. I told them stuff like that makes me fear for my husband, who buys his state hunting license and hunts off the reservation.

"What if he met someone in the woods that really felt that way? And I have several wonderful boys at home that I would hate to see shot, too," I added, "and if the media sees those signs, they will focus on them rather than any truth that is trying to be told.'

I got various reactions from those I spoke to. Two of the men were like bricks. They wouldn't hear a word I was saying.

One of them said, "Signs like these get the point across," and then with a laugh added, "if the moccasin fits, wear it."

One man, I could see in his eyes, did hear me. Just a flicker. He turned his sign around in his hand and looked at it again. Then seeing the eyes of friends watching him, quickly returned the sign to its original position.

But one man down the sidewalk a ways said, "I was trying to tell them that myself."

We spoke for a few minutes about the real problems and where they originate.

"My husband isn't in there testifying because he's afraid someone wants to shoot a buck, he's in there because he loves his family," I told him.

The guy said he understood. He took our information and said he had stuff he would send me.

Another man stood leaning on a car, listening. He never said a word, but as I was leaving, he smiled and gave me a wink of encouragement. I handed out literature to people inside the building also. One group of people in particular was very receptive and kind.

You know, some people make it hard for you to be on their side. Sometimes Roland and I went home thinking we aren't on anyone's side. We have to go at this whole thing, knowing what we know and determined to stand up for it, no matter what anyone else on either side says or intends.

There were two sections of witness panels. The first was about property rights, primarily dealing with current non-member property right issues within the State of Washington. The second was about civil rights, primarily tribal government abuse of such.

Roland was the second to last witness. He was still somewhat nervous and got a little bit tongue tied with having to stand up as a citizen between two governments. He testified in part;

"...I am Indian. When I step foot onto a reservation, State and Federal constitutional rights can be denied me...basic human rights other Americans take for granted, that allow people to live in dignity with their neighbors, are not guaranteed on Indian reservations...

"...It cannot be denied that current federal policy is such that tribal governments financially benefit from the general membership's poverty level staying just as it is...Thus, tribal government needs to keep control of its members, even to the extent of demanding from this Congress that the "tribe shall retain exclusive jurisdiction over any ...Indian child...," as is written in the Indian Child Welfare Act...

"The Indian Civil Rights Act mandates that no Indian tribe in exercising powers of self-government shall violate various basic civil rights. However, when there is no separation of powers within tribal governments and tribal sovereign immunity protects tribal government...

"But many tribal members say nothing publicly. Cronyism, nepotism and ballot box rigging are all part of political reality on many reservations...tribal government controls tribal jobs, HUD housing, tribal loans and land leases...

"...I have seen tribal governments pressure members to rally to their cause and political goals through misinformation, bullying, and even bribes. At a political rally two years ago, in order to portray a good show of force for the media, a tribal government gave its employees the day off and told the employees they were expected to attend the rally. In order to ensure the attendance, the tribal government offered transportation to the rally, free food, and distribution of the employees' paychecks. In another case, the tribal council denied a person running for office in a recent tribal election the right to advertise in the local tribal paper.

"It can be no wonder that Indian people are tired and depressed...

"With the current epidemic of corruption on Indian Reservations, how could tribal members be better protected? ...We can't continue to sit back and watch relatives despair. Let us work together as brothers and sisters to correct the problem..."

People came up to Roland afterwards and congratulated him for his bravery. Three others, a tribal elder, an attorney who has been dealing with tribal civil rights abuses, and Bill Lawrence, the publisher of the "Ojibwe News,' were also seated with Roland and gave very powerful testimony.

A tribal member approached Roland and Bill after the hearing and said she was glad to see them. Having suffered abuse on her Washington State reservation, she and her husband had come on their own in support of Senator Gorton's bill. She'd even made signs to hold up. To stand alone, amidst and in opposition to your very own reservation members was very gutsy. This is exactly the point of Roland's testimony and the reason for his support of Senator Gorton's' bill. It's hard for members to stand up to tribal government when the Tribal Council holds all the strings - controlling your housing and jobs - but can't be held accountable. It amazed us to see this couple do it. Roland and I had to go, but Bill stayed to talk to them.

However, the following day the newspapers only wrote about the property rights issues between members and non-members. They didn't mention the civil rights issues at all. While it is true that much of the media had left before the last panel was seated, they had been given complete witness statements of all the official witnesses, and so had the civil rights testimony in hand.

Realizing papers have limited space, we decided it was understandable that they probably had to concentrate on issues of most concern to the people of its state, meaning the property rights issues that had been news for quite some time. So we hoped that papers from other areas would give better coverage to the civil rights issues. But for the most part, they didn't.

May, 1998 – From Roland
Dear Diane,

Thanks for the tape! I was so moved by it, every time I listen to the tape I really cry. I have a lot of tears because I see my own reflection on what he has to say. And I believe I've drank with him in the city parks. What God can do is a miracle when so many are lost because they don't know where to turn or who to turn to. As I go to Mpls & Cass Lake, even before I get to the city limits I can feel the great oppression and feel so sad and broken hearted. Because what I say don't seem to reach ears. And all I can say is that I'll keep praying for them. And hope they will hear the Word of God and wake up.

Sorry for not answering sooner as I've been very busy trying to get my funds together to go to Wash. DC to help try to push for equal rights and so forth.

I was in Seattle, Wash. last mo to testify on a bill that Slade Gorton is trying to get passed.

I was called a couple of days before the hearing so had to get ready to go. Started praying if I should go. All of a sudden my good car broke down, so I said we'll take my van that wouldn't run either. My wife was talking to a prayer warrior in a different reservation and all of a sudden the line went dead. Evil spirits were attacking us trying to keep me from speaking out about the tribal governments.

Sunday nite I told my wife looks like the lord didn't want us to go. Sunday nite a good Christian friend of ours who is the District 73 Legislator in Helena, the Capitol, called and asked when we were leaving for Seattle. When we told him what happened, he jumped rite in and said you can use my car. Praise the Lord.

So things are really happening around the country for the good of everything.

All I can do is trust in the Lord that he will guide us in everything that we do.

Thanks again for the tape and hope you will be honored if I can make copies of this tape to pass around. And do you know how I could get a hold of Mr. Sky so I can write and thank him personally for the great encouragement that he has given me? And that God does work miracles and if we can trust in him all the time, how can we fail.
And as a song I heard says, "I can walk with Jesus holding my hand." And that has to be every day,

Our prayers
A Brother in Christ
Will be heard
Roland
And answered

By the next Fall, Cheri, the little girl who dreamed of being an architect, was homeless, sleeping in a car. Her fifteen-year-old daughter, Carrie, had been kicked out of her grandma Darlene's home because of her drug and alcohol use, and was living with Misty. Yvonne's youngest boy, Bradley, only sixteen, was serving hard time for robbery and attempted murder, and Joy was on the verge of losing her children, too. We were asked to take in Misty's sixth baby, born very sick from crack. We needed time to think, and social services said they needed time to finish paperwork.

Dear Misty;
I have been doing some writing and reflecting over the last few months. In the last week I realized, as I read what I wrote, that I wasn't fair to you as you were growing up. In fact, I was hateful.
I was angry with a lot of the things you were doing, but my anger went beyond that. I was taking my anger at other people out on you, too.
You were a child. It wasn't fair to you that all the adults around you were acting crazy. While you are responsible for the choices you made when doing the wrong things

you did, it is not your fault that not one of the many adults around you paid enough attention to you to try to understand.

At one time you were just a very hurt and lonely ten-year-old girl, who wanted to have both her parents back together and her family whole again. And not one of us paid attention.

I apologize for taking my anger out on you when you were 13 to 17 years old. I apologize to the little girl you were then, and to the beautiful woman you are now.

I don't want to give you false expectations. Roland's rules still stand as far as visitation is concerned. The nine children have to be given a different chance. But I needed to go back and apologize to you. I was part of the problem of how you got to the situation you are in today.

...You are a wonderful woman, Misty. There is a reason for living. Please don't die.

The kids had all been in bed about an hour when 6-year-old Timothy, rubbing his eyes, came out of his bedroom.

"Mom, I've decided I'm going to grow up and be a genius. I'm going to make big robots"

"Okay, Timothy"

"Goodnight"

"Goodnight"

Beth Ward

NIGHT WINDS

a segment of time
slashes down like
monsoon rain and
one by one the
lights go dark

alleys sleep like
coiled snakes in
the long winter

and lamp posts
walk their
restless dreams
through silent
streets

while night winds
whisper around
the stillness of
buildings gone
dumb

© By **PHONACELLE SHAPEL**

Chapter twenty-two: September, 1999

Praise God that Barb chose that moment to come and deliver two of our children home to us. If she hadn't come right then, Roland would have remained outside working on the van by himself. In fact, shortly before the stroke began, he was test driving the van!

But Barb came, and Roland joined us in the house. The next blessing was that Barb wanted to see the upstairs bedrooms we were working on. So I brought her up the stairs, and Roland followed. This is a blessing because Roland's 'motor' control - or lack thereof – quickly became apparent. He stumbled, then struggled, then started climbing the stairs again, and then stumbled again. Once to the top of the stairs, he began dropping his tape measure. He was also slurring words as he tried to explain what he and his friend Jim had been working on the other day. At this point we knew something was very wrong, so, not wanting him to fall down the stairs, we encouraged him down slowly, ready to grab if we had to. Once at the bottom, Roland turned to face us and we could see the classic stroke 'droop' in his mouth and he was leaning on the wall.

I called our son, Andrew, who then supported Roland and guided him to the van. Roland didn't understand and didn't want to go. Once at the van, he tried to monkey with the engine cover where he had been working earlier, arguing with us in unintelligible language.

Finally getting him into the van, Andrew stayed with Barb and the kids and prayed while Haley came with me. We drove quickly to the hospital, only three blocks away. But when we arrived and

Roland opened the car door, he fell right out onto the pavement. He had lost all function on one side during the trip.

The nurses came quickly with a wheelchair and got him into the emergency room. He had no movement at all on his right side. The doctor arrived and ordered a helicopter right away. He needed to be taken to a hospital with a CAT scan. But while we waited, Andrew must have called half of Ronan.

First Pastor Kirk and Celeste came in and prayed for Roland. Then another Pastor came. When he had finished praying, two other families arrived and prayed for Roland, too. Andrew tells us he practically covered the country calling people to ask for prayer.

So before Roland even left in the helicopter, he was surrounded in prayer. After he was taken, Haley and I went home to get some things and follow in the car. When we arrived at home, we found most of our kids were already gone. Friends had come and taken them. Wow.

By the time we got to the second hospital, the doctors had already identified the type of stroke Roland was having and had begun a new, experimental medication called TPA. Roland said they had started it while he was still in X-ray. We waited about a half-hour for the medication to finish. Then Roland asked me to lift his right hand, and as we did this, his right fingers began wiggling, then his right hand began moving on its own. Elated, he started kicking his right foot.

The doctor came in and explained the drug has been given at this hospital for only about a year. Only about 20 people have received it, and only two people had shown results. And one of those people had only slight improvement. The doctor used the word "miracle" in describing the amount of function Roland was showing. "This just does not usually happen" he said. Even the helicopter pilots had to come in and see!

The Doctor said that although there were some determining factors in Roland's ability to take TPA, the main reason many stroke patients don't get this medication is because it can only be given within three hours of the onset of symptoms. Most patients don't make it in that window of time because they tend to feel tired from lack of oxygen and lay down to go to sleep.

God is so good. The doctors told us that we are very fortunate. The stroke was a bad one but Roland was nearly as good as he was before it happened. The miracle is that we were able to get him to the hospital within that very short window of time.

God is so good. Nothing will make us doubt God's providence.

To the editor; 10/2/1999

A national human rights conference is scheduled for October in Missoula. The newspaper reports "This conference has become the premier conference in the country on this subject,' according to the director of the Northwest Coalition Against Malicious Harassment... its purpose is to inspire people to fight against bigotry, racism, and anti-democratic movements."

Workshops will include issues surrounding treaty rights. One of the workshops, "Margins to the Mainstream," appears to discredit at least one local elected official. Apparently, Human Rights Networks don't feel that everyone in America has a right to respect, or they wouldn't constantly distort the views of our chosen representatives.

What this meeting promotes is exactly what they say they are opposed to, racism, bigotry and anti-democratic movements.

I know we should go listen. Maybe even say something; tell these people the truth about our position. I mean...human rights... they should be interested in what we're really trying to say, right?

But ever since that Conrad Burns event in Billings last year, I haven't wanted to step anywhere near these kinds of people again. The cruel ridicule by our opponents was terrifying. Those of us supporting Senator Burns' proposal were, indeed, maliciously harassed. And that wasn't the first time it has happened. Anytime we've tried to hold public meetings, the same crowd has harassed us. And I've never, ever gone to their meetings and harassed them.

Isn't that funny? I'm afraid the Human rights crowd is going to hurt us.

No... that's NOT funny, is it?

I was told recently that, at one time, there was talk of shooting at our windows. We have nine children in the house, and someone wanted to shut us up by shooting at us. Jesus protect us.

The conference brochure also states that the US Forest Service is a 'supporter'. The US Forest Service-Northern Region is paying for the costs of the keynote speaker.

Please, contact Sen. Burns' office and members of Congress and express displeasure at the inappropriateness of this. Also, please write to Dept. of Agriculture Secretary Glickman.

Beth Ward

We arrived in Bemidji about 2:30 PM Wednesday, and went straight to the hospital. In the ICU, we found Dorothy's room. Her sons Troy and Mickey were there, sitting in chairs next to the wall. There was an old guy half-asleep on a chair too.

Roland went to Dorothy's bed, where she lay unconscious with tubes running out of her body, and I saw him take out his prayer oil. I went over to the other side of the bed. He laid his hand on her forehead to pray and I laid my hand on his. As Roland started to pray, his voice faltered, then broke. He stopped to gather himself, then tried again. As we prayed that God's will be done, I felt a lifting. When we finished, I looked up. Troy and Mickey had their heads bowed. The man on the chair was gone.

We spoke a few minutes with Troy and Mickey. Mickey... You know, eleven years ago (eleven years!) when Mickey took off from Moiese with his girlfriend, Shawna, I didn't know if I would hug him or slug him next time I saw him. Oh, but I hugged him. Boy, did I hug that guy's neck. I still love him so much. And he had a little girl with him! A sweet little baby about a year and a half old, named Kari. Mickey told us he lives in Georgia now and manages a restaurant.

Roland then took us to a motel. Timothy had been sick on the trip, so we didn't want him to stay around Dorothy and Mickey's baby. After settling the kids, Roland, Andrew and I returned to the hospital. This time, there were a lot of people there. The doctor was expected soon, and they were going to make a decision about turning off the life support.

I was surprised by my emotion. There were so many I was so glad to see, so many I was glad to touch. Isn't it funny, I had no idea how strongly I felt. It seems like a whole different life, so long ago. But it all came back. Roland's sisters, Elaine, Yvonne and Annie were all there, and Dale! But Dale, he looked so sick. And who was this young woman hugging me and asking how I am? It was Yvonne's daughter, Sonya. Little Sonya. Dorothy's youngest son, Paul, also was there. He had just gotten out of jail that day.

And the old man that had been sleeping on the chair? It was Yvonne's son, Roger! But Roger is seven years younger than me, how could he look so old? He was baby faced, a happy, bright, kid those few weeks he lived with me. Now he looked as old as Roland. He'd aged so much. And he didn't smile. When I spoke to him, he didn't once look me in the eye. We went for a walk together down the hall and he told me about his lifestyle, not holding anything back. He was ill, physically, emotionally and spiritually.

Others were there, too, including James and Gloria, the parents of that little girl in the cemetery so long ago. There must have been at least 40 people sifting in and out of Dorothy's room or standing in the hallway.

The doctor came and the family trailed him into a meeting room. It was wall to wall people. The doctor said it was over. She has only a 5% chance at survival and it's time to turn everything off. The pastor, a tribal member, said he'd like to wait another day and have everyone pray and fast. He said he wanted to give Jesus a chance to show his power and Glory. He began to pray and I heard Roland, standing near the pastor, praying in agreement. The Holy Spirit seemed to fill the room. Everyone was silent.

Then, his voice breaking, Troy said, "We want to quit. She's suffered too long. It's time to turn everything off." Mickey and Paul stood silently beside him.

Roland was quiet. I wanted to tell everyone about Roland's miraculous recovery. Weren't we in ICU ourselves only a month ago? But it was Roland's place to say it. I watched him. He brought his folded hands up to his mouth and cleared his throat, just like he does before he says something important, but he didn't say anything.

Some people who wanted to leave the machines on got up and left the room. I waited. Another woman agreed with Troy. The room was silent again. Well, you know me. I can't ever keep quiet, even when I know I should.

"I know I'm not part of this family, and the decision is yours, Troy, but I'd just like to say that we were in ICU a month ago..." and I told our story.

The room was quiet again. Then Troy gently said, "I see your point, but as I said, My mom's been suffering (in drugs and alcohol, unhappiness) for a long time. I want her to rest."

The Holy Spirit was there. Life support or not, if God wanted her to live, she would. On the other hand, if He wanted her released, he would release her. Roland then spoke up. He respected any decision Troy and his brothers made. Another woman said the same thing. Others left the room.

Everyone trailed the doctor back to Dorothy's room, where a nurse helped disconnect the tubing. The family packed in to see what happened next. Some drank coffee while they waited. Little children ran up and down the hall. I helped care for them while Roland stood by Dorothy's side, holding her hand and praying.

Later, Mickey told me that when he first arrived, he had brought his baby girl over to his mother's bed. They were meeting for the first time. When he bent to allow his baby to kiss her Grandma, he saw a tear coming from his mother's eye. Soon after, he, Troy and Paul went for a drive alone together. Troy had wanted to have some time with his brothers to talk. He asked them, "What do you think we ought to do?" Mickey and Paul, respecting Troy as the head of their family, responded, "Whatever you think, Troy." Together, they made their decision. They told Roland and a few others, then waited for the doctor to come to tell everyone else.

As Dorothy hung on, people got tired of waiting and drifted away. Many went home.

Dale, shaking from withdrawal, came over to where I stood. He and Dorothy had been drinking buddies these last few years. He was the one that had found her on the floor of her home. He started to cry. The pastor and I went with him to an empty room and prayed with him for about an hour. He asked me over and over again to drop him off in Cass Lake, so he could find a drink and then go in the woods and shoot himself.

I doubted he was going to shoot himself, but didn't want to take him someplace to drink more. I still didn't know how to say, "no." Here I was, again, ten years later, in the same boat I always found myself in. What should I do? I wanted Roland's help, but he was with Dorothy.

Then a niece came and asked Dale to take her and treat her to something to eat. Apparently, he had some cash on him. Well, I knew they weren't going after something to eat. Dale now had his ride to the liquor store and the niece had someone to buy for her.

Later, sitting in the hall talking to three of Roland's nephews, I watched Roland walk by. He was irritated with me. I didn't know why, but I thought maybe I shouldn't be talking to his nephews. So I stood up, went to him, and suggested 16-year-old Andrew drive me back to the motel. I needed to see to our kids. He agreed and gave Andrew the keys.

As I was getting ready to go, Mickey was struggling with his tired baby.

"Do you want me to take her back to the motel?"

"Sure, if she'll go wit you."

He carefully gathered her things together, repacked her baby bag, then had Kari kiss her Grandma, Dorothy, goodbye. He gave Kari a hug and kiss, and told me to call if I had any trouble.

She cried when we left him, but back at the motel, Haley played mom and Kari loved it. The baby was adorable. It was obvious from his attention, her behavior, and even her meticulously kept overnight bag that Mickey was a very good father.

Dale showed up back at the hospital later that night, drunk. He stood at the end of her bed and yelled at Dorothy to get up. The nurses called Security and Dale was escorted from the hospital.

Roland's sister, Dorothy, died at 1:30 am.

The next morning, Roland took us to the cemetery. Alone, we stood in the drizzling rain while Roland showed our children the graves of his parents and other family members. Some mounds were very small...those of children. A few others had gifts of cigarettes, money, and unopened cans of beer. Some had headstones that appeared to be recently placed, but some graves had no headstones or were marked with hand-made crosses bearing no name. A couple crosses had human hair adorning them. We looked, but couldn't find Lila's. She was one of the unmarked ones.

He showed us where he would like to be buried, then took us in the car to an even older cemetery. Here, the mounds were covered with small wooden houses. Rosie, not knowing what it was when we drove up, announced this must be the "dog house cemetery." Roland scowled.

The houses each had just one small opening at one end. Roland said it was believed this was where the spirit went in and out. Some of these graves were as recent as the 1980s. Others were very old, their moss covered boards falling apart.

Roland spent some time wandering the area looking at names. It had started to rain harder, so most of the kids waited in the car. Afterward, we drove to Elaine's house. Several people were already gathered when we arrived. Elaine and Yvonne were at the kitchen table arranging the funeral. When Annie arrived, they and Roland decided to run back up to the cemetery and pick out where to bury Dorothy.

The kids and I stayed at Elaine's and waited. Many young women milled around. They laughed as I tried to figure out who they all were. All these young women, still small last time I'd seen them, now had one, two or three small children of their own.

A couple of them were trying to work on some math for their GED's. They asked Andrew for help. He helped for a few minutes, then wandered away. The girls decided they'd worked enough for one morning. One, who was once a baby girl crying in my basement apartment, looked at the other, who was once a small girl dancing for a blue ribbon at a powwow, and smiled.

"Should we go for a ride in the car?" she asked her.

The other smiled big and said, "Sure!"

Leaving the math books, they each grabbed their small children and some jackets.

"Be right back," they said.

A half hour later they returned, and, smiling, their eyes glazed, sat back down with their math books.

"I just can't get this math," said one, "it makes no sense."

'Well, "I answered, "if you'd stop going for "rides in the car" you could understand your math better."

The girls looked up at me, then at each other, then covered their mouths, laughing in embarrassment.

The funeral was scheduled for Monday. In the meantime, Roland drove us down to the city to see my family, then went back to Cass Lake for the wake.

The night before the funeral, Roland came back to get us. The wake was difficult, he said. He was left alone to watch the casket all night. Someone finally came to relieve him about two in the afternoon. Dale had been signed into a detox but was back out again now. Roland also said that there might be some arguing up there that night. It had been decided the service would be Christian, but a niece had gone on her own and arranged for a drum group. Some are upset about that and Roland said he was glad he wouldn't be there for the arguing.

The next morning, before going up for the funeral, we stopped to pick up Misty's newest baby, Joshua, from the foster home. Social Services gave Roland permission to keep him for 24 hours.

Beth Ward

MOURNING

Mourning is a private sorrow,
tears that fall alone tomorrow.

Mourning is the futile cry,
the always empty why.

Mourning is a frozen smile,
stalling grief for a little while.

Mourning is the love that's left,
that can't be killed by sudden death.

Mourning is the sympathy,
that cannot fill a vacancy.

© By PHONACELLE SHAPEL

Chapter twenty-three:
October, 1999

It was just after lunch when we pulled the blue-gray minivan into the small town of Cass Lake. The autumn air was brisk. Roland was driving. Andrew was in the front seat next to him, and Haley, Heidi, Timothy, Rosie and I were in the back. Roland drove through the streets of the tribal tract housing and pulled into the dirt driveway of a new Veterans Memorial building, built next to the new casino, hotel and Pow wow grounds.

We were a half-hour late coming from the city. Children were outside the building playing when we arrived. Inside, there was a lot of talking and commotion. It was hard to hear the Episcopal minister speak. I didn't see a drum group. Many people turned to greet us. A young woman I didn't recognize came up to give me a warm hug.

In order to hear better, I and a couple of my children sat down with Roland's nieces, (Yvonne's daughters) Sonya and Marci, and their kids. Roland stood in the back with Andrew and Haley. After a while, I got up and went back to him. From out of the crowd, a woman reached out to me. It was Dale's wife, Tammy. After hugging us, she re-introduced me to all her kids – now teenagers.

After the service ended, nephews Verlin and Dale were pallbearers. Both were shaking from withdrawal, although Dale looked much better than he had the day before.

The tiny cemetery was in the heavily forested area near the lake. We followed other cars down the long, narrow, muddy road to get there. Circling through the cemetery, the small area was packed with cars and people. But this time we were near the head of the pack, and parked easily.

Roland, a respected elder in the family, stood at the edge of the grave for the brief service. After the Minister had finished, the pallbearers grouped together, took hold of the straps, and lowered the casket into a wooden crypt. Once it was in place, Verlin jumped in on top and nailed the wooden lid on. Then, family members each grabbed some dirt and threw it on top. A backhoe started up, moved into the group, and filled the rest of the hole. Finally, when the backhoe moved away, Roland, Verlin, and others finished with shovels.

Later, Roland said they had asked that the backhoe not be used at all. He and some of the others had wanted to do it themselves. But there was a miscommunication.

While they worked, Yvonne held and played with Joshua, and I wandered around, looking for the gravesite of a precious sleeping child, a small, dark haired girl in a pretty little dress, no more than two-years-old. I found it; it was unmarked except for a small bouquet of plastic flowers.

Turning away from the small grave, I looked across the grounds and saw Mickey, with Kari on his shoulders, laughing. In his pressed pants, tie, and brown leather jacket, he looked so self-assured. Dorothy would feel proud of him.

Then I saw my Andrew carrying the tiny Joshua. The one born last May, sick, needing a mom.

Roland nudged and, stepping over yesterday's puddles, we began walking back to the car.

The feast was back at the new community center. Many people milled about talking to each other in the main room. Wanda, in her wheelchair, was talking to Annie's daughter, Savannah, over by the window. Roland's niece, Pam, was with her sisters near the door. His brother, Glenn, was sitting at a table. For a very short moment, I wondered how I should act. But then, I knew. While here, I needed to sit with my children, and to look at them and not stare around. I knew to keep my hands occupied with my own business, and not to worry about what others may be doing or thinking. And I knew

I shouldn't worry if Roland wandered off to whatever he had to do. He'd be back in just a short time.

Feeling I could handle all that, I went about the business of making my children's plates. After we sat down to eat, nephew Matthew, Dale's wife, Tammy, and their respective children joined us. Matthew, who's wife, Shanda, died of cancer the year before, was staying sober and trying his best to make it as a single father. Tammy, as usual, made jokes about everything. I told her to get Dale and her kids and come out to stay with us. Tammy laughed and said I hadn't changed a bit. Heidi rocked Joshua, and when someone held up a camera for a picture, others came over. Soon, about half the room surrounded us. It was amazing. After being called a racist for five years in Montana, I didn't expect to come here and be accepted. Nevertheless, for whatever reason, the family still loved us, and I didn't feel alone and out of place anymore.

Verlin, never saying a word, came up from behind, put his arms around me, and kissed my cheek. Never saying a word, he left.

Beth Ward

LEGACY

lie thee deep
and lie thee still
and lie thee there
upon that hill

did thee know
and do thou know
the lamps thee
lit shall always glow

one by one their
lights increase and
warm our dreams
with their heat

lie thee deep
and lie thee still
and lie thee there
upon dreams will.

© By PHONACELLE SHAPEL

Epilogue
June 14, 2004

It was late afternoon when we pulled the red Dodge Caravan into the small town of Cass Lake. Behind us was a small car carrying Yvonne, Dale, Annie and two of Annie's granddaughters. In front of us was a grey Chevy extended cab pickup. It had a short bed, but that was okay because the casket it carried was homemade and shorter than most.

The day was warm and sunny. Andrew was driving the van and Haley was sitting in the seat next to him. I had been sleeping in the middle seat next to my good friend, Ann, and my children, Heidi, Timothy and Rosie were in the back seat.

Our pastor of four years, along with Ron, an elder from his church, had driven Ron's pickup the long miles. Ross and Brooke rode with them the whole way. Caleb and Dewey had been given the choice to come along, but had chosen to wait at home with Will Stanley. We had driven straight through. Haley had fun with the walkie-talkie system between the vehicles, joking with pastor as the night grew long that he should give us a sermon so we could all go to sleep. We stopped at daylight for some breakfast at a McDonalds, where the cashier made the mistake of asking us if we were on a class field trip. The long night had left us rummy, so we answered her truthfully, and emotionlessly pointed to the pickup, then took our food trays and turned away, leaving her wondering if we were pulling her leg.

Andrew now drove through the treeless streets of the tribal tract housing and pulled into the dirt driveway of the Veterans Memorial

Building at the Pow wow Grounds. If we had arrived much later we would have missed the start of the wake.

As Ron backed the pickup up to the doorway, out from the building several nephews emerged and waited on the cement deck to help. They greeted us and explained to Pastor how the wake was going to be held. Our children patiently waited.

Lifting the casket from the truck bed, several helped bring it in. Ron pulled the truck back out from the deck and parked it.

Neither Roland nor I knew how people would feel about our politics. It had been easy to ride in the van, with Pastor taking care of all the thinking and rarely requiring me to make any decisions. My friend Ann was there for comfort, and Roland's sister Annie had arranged most of the Cass Lake details. I don't know what we would have done without her. But now we were here. I was now far away from home and Roland wasn't there to hold my hand. Numbly, I climbed out of the car. I had never been a widow before. What does one do?

As we entered the dark building I stayed close to Pastor, Ann, Annie and my children. A quick glance around the room showed me who all was there. Many people milled about talking to each other in the main room. Shirley was there, as well as Junior and Misty. But the judge hadn't allowed Cheri to leave prison, and Joy had opted not to come. Feeling out of place, I avoided looking at anyone and said little. Annie moved through the crowd to the kitchen. Hands sweating, I stiffly followed. The women in the kitchen were busy preparing food for the feed that would follow the service. I greeted Roland's sister and introduced Pastor.

"Elaine, this is our Pastor."

Elaine looked up from her work and said hello. She and I spoke for a moment, Pastor motioned to me, and I tensely shadowed him back into the main room.

He led me through the crowd toward the beautifully crafted wood casket placed alone by the wall. I actually felt some relief as I trailed him. Standing at the casket would be easier than standing apart in the crowd. Pastor took a moment at the casket and then stepped aside for me to see. Looking down I saw my precious sleeping husband, a frail, grey haired man in his brown ribbon shirt, no more than fifty-eight years old. Although his face was swollen from the cancer medication, he seemed to be laying peacefully.

One of Roland's biggest worries was what would happen to the four grandchildren in our home once he had passed. We had hired an attorney early on in his illness to try to add me to the custody papers. But for one reason and then another, the issue dragged on and on, unresolved. We went for months without hearing anything from him. We attempted to hire another attorney, but she said ICWA cases were very complicated and she would need an extra attorney and a $5,000 retainer. We didn't have $5000.

Just two months earlier, I had tried to write my own papers for custody and had sent them to an attorney friend to proof read. I hadn't heard back from him.

A month ago, against Doctor's advice, Roland flew with Haley and Heidi to Washington DC to speak to Congressmen one more time about federal Indian policy. In addition to speaking to staff at various Congressional offices, he and Haley both spoke about the Indian Child Welfare Act at the National Press Club on Wednesday, May 12, 2004. In a subsequent article on Friday, May 14th, Washington Times intern Jennifer Lehner wrote,

"The ICWA protects the interests of others over [Mr. Ward's] grandchildren," and "[Mr. Ward] said that once children are relocated to the reservations, they are subject to the corrupt law of the tribal government. Instead of preserving culture, he said, the tribal leadership uses the ICWA to acquire funds provided through the legislation. He wants the power over his grandchildren's future to be taken away from the tribal governments and the family to have a say in the placement of the children."

Ms. Lehner quoted Roland as saying that the law is "supposed to help children, but instead it helps tribal governments."

The trip was hard on him, but Haley and Heidi helped by making sure he got everything his needed - including naps - and pushed him in a wheelchair to and from his meetings. Within a few days after he came back, he began to struggle with shortness of breath and was put on oxygen. The very next day, he was hospitalized. I stayed with him most of the time he was there, going home only one night. Haley stayed with him that night in my place. After ten days in the hospital, he was discharged home and a home health nurse was scheduled to visit.

Now, with Roland's illness quickly getting worse, we were no longer able to do anything about child custody. We had no choice but to leave it in the Lord's hands.

That same week, some of Roland's relatives decided to come out to see him. Despite the fact that they had never traveled to Montana as a group before, didn't have a vehicle, didn't have the funds for the trip, and didn't know that this was to be his last week on earth, several showed up.

Roland had a chance to visit with three of his sisters, one brother, a niece, a nephew, three other relatives, and even Joy's two sons, whom he had rarely seen since they moved back to Minnesota. It was a wonderful blessing and comfort. Planning on visiting only a week or so, Yvonne suggested we have an early birthday party for Roland. She had been with us three years earlier on his birthday when we had invited friends over for dinner and sang worship songs. She wanted to do this again. So our Pastor's family, as well as our "grandparents," Della and Marvin, were invited to come for supper on Wednesday, June 9th.

The morning of the 9th, we got a call from our attorney friend that the tribe had decided it wouldn't seek custody of the four grandchildren and was sending papers to that effect. An affidavit was being emailed for Roland to sign, stating that he wanted me to take care of all the kids. Because he was bed ridden at this point, a notary from the bank came over during her lunch hour to witness him sign it.

Now we had reason to celebrate.

After the affidavit was taken care of, Roland read through the final draft of a letter to his four oldest children. It was the way he wanted it, but after reading it through, he was too tired to sign it.

"When should I bring it back?" I asked him.

"Between 8 and 9 pm," he said, "When it's quiet and we're alone."

That didn't seem like a time that would be quiet. There was a lot of people in the house and they would all still be awake. But he was tired and closing his eyes. The letter would wait.

That afternoon, Roland called Elaine and me to his bedside He didn't want there to be any disagreement over his funeral, so he wanted us both to know his wishes. He said that he wanted to have a funeral at the church we had joined four years ago here in Montana, but he also wanted to be buried in his home cemetery at Leech Lake. Further, he wanted both funerals to be an unmistakable witness to the power and reality of Jesus Christ. He made it clear that he wanted the Cass Lake funeral to be in the church and that there should be no traditional religion used. He wanted his family to know that there is only one way, truth and life. Jesus Christ.

Later, while I was cooking dinner for the party, he again called me over to his bed and asked me to stay there. Although unsure of why he had asked me to stay close, I sat down on the edge of his bed and one of his sisters took over the cooking. At one point, while I was sitting on his bed, holding his hand, he asked me who was behind me. Thinking it was a child; I turned around to look. "No one is there," I told him. Roland nodded and again fell asleep.

When he began to feel more uncomfortable, the home-health nurse was called and we began to pray with him, doing whatever we could to bring him comfort. His labor worsened, and I struggled to think of a song off the top of my head that I could sing to him. The first and only song that came to my mind was the song "Surrender." However, because none of my girls were close by to sing the echo, I didn't think I could sing that one. But Roland became more distressed, so I started to sing it anyway just to be singing something. To my surprise, when it came time for the echo, Roland, with all the energy he had, sang it, raising his arm into the air for the Lord.

His final struggle began just after 8 pm. Looking frightened, he grabbed my arm and told me that I was his one, true love. As he struggled to breathe, the nurse gave him some more morphine, then called me out of the room for a moment to tell me he might be passing. Pastor sat next to him and held his hand. In the final moments, Roland looked Pastor straight in the eyes and pointed his other hand up to heaven. When Roland passed on to greater life at 8:10 pm, his good friend Marvin was softly playing Gospel songs for him on his accordion.

After the nurse confirmed he was gone, Roland's brother, Glenn, stepped out into the backyard. He told us later that while out there, he asked for something he had never asked of God before: to see Roland one more time. He told us that the Lord, in his graciousness, gave him a last vision of Roland, with unknown beings around him, standing in light with radiance on his face. Glenn said that Roland looked healthy, young and joyous.

So here we were; the man who did, indeed put his pants on two legs at a time, was now blessed with two funerals. No – we were the ones who were blessed. There had been so much love at the first funeral, and God's Spirit was so fully present that I had wished we had taped it. Further, Roland's pall bearers included not only Andrew and two close friends, but our state legislator, Will Stanley, and a law professor at the university, Rob Natelson. But as the Montana funeral ended, I also felt incredibly blessed by the fact that I didn't have to say good-bye yet. I still had another two days before I had to do that.

Now we are here. He didn't want to have anything traditional, but a sister had insisted that we at least do the all-night wake. How does one sit, what does one look at, what does one do with their hands when at one's husband's all night wake? Turning from the casket, I moved toward a slim young man. Matthew greeted me, along with Troy, Mickey, Paul, Sonya and Marci. Tammy hugged me. Dan Hunter looked straight at me and smiled. Dale and Tammy's youngest daughter was there with her newborn baby. I gave Roland's brother David his boots.

But most didn't stay all night. In the end, it was only Roland's brother, Glenn, my friend Ann, and I that stayed for the entire wake - my children having gone to spend the night at a hotel with my siblings. Some nieces later came back with some beautiful, thick, soft blankets and laid down together and slept. Glenn told Ann that it meant a lot to him to be able to stay awake there all night. His faithfulness was a precious gift Roland would have appreciated.

Dying in Indian Country

Still, Roland's sister later apologized for having insisted we have a wake. Very few people, at least on this reservation, stay for it anymore, she said ruefully.

In the morning, people returned to the building for the service and many were surprised that we were moving Roland to the Christian Missionary Alliance Church for the funeral. There was quite a bit of concern that people might show up at the pow wow grounds and not know where we had gone, so we left a note on the door.

This time, the pall bearers included Junior, Andrew, Roland's brother Glenn, and four proud nephews.

We depended on one of Roland's nephews to direct Ron to the church building, but somehow, he got lost in this very small town and couldn't find it. We ended up going around in circles, crossing through our own procession a couple times. Roland would have gotten a huge kick out of it, but Pastor was pretty concerned that no one in the family seemed to know where the church was in this tiny town. He figured that meant there wasn't much outreach from the church.

Finally arriving, we found three of Roland's political friends waiting, two of whom had been in Washington DC with him just a month earlier. The third man, Frank, a County Commissioner from Mille Lacs, was also a good friend.

The funeral was beautiful. I didn't think anything could be better than the first one, but this one was. Andrew, tasked with reading Roland's biography, instead stood at the altar and asked all of Roland's children, grandchildren, nieces and nephews to stand. When they did, he proceeded to tell them Roland's heart – that he loved them all and wanted them to be saved – not only from the destructive lifestyle, but through Jesus Christ. Andrew's words were so unexpected and so moving, he had several of us crying. After he was finished, two people stood up to testify – one of whom, a relative, had never spoken much publically about his faith. Andrew had opened a door, and the Holy Spirit was flowing through it.

When the funeral ended, it was too soon. Now, without question, was the final time we would see Roland's face. When they closed the casket that last time, Haley, Brooke, Heidi, Rosie and I held onto each other and wept.

The tiny cemetery was in a heavily forested area near a lake. We followed other cars down a long, narrow, muddy road to get there. The road no longer allowed for cars to circle through the cemetery; but because we were at the head of the line we had no trouble finding a place to park. The small area was quickly packed with cars and people.

Standing at the front of the crowd, we watched the ceremony. The graveside service was brief. Too brief for Junior, who had run to find ropes to lower the casket with. Pastor, not knowing he had left, had begun the service, slinging and lowering Roland with very appropriate car battery jumper cables. (Another part of the event that Roland would have loved). Junior returned too late and was very upset - hurt - that the funeral had gone on without him. When I was told about it, I felt hurt for him as well because he had been so kind and good to hurry away to look for ropes – trying to serve the family and Roland in the best way he could. I wished I had known he had left.

As the funeral ended and the first shovel of dirt was thrown into the deep hole, various men moved to grab shovels, our good friend Darrel was among them.

Andrew stepped toward the grave and respectfully stopped some men from putting tobacco in. He explained to them, "Dad said he didn't want tobacco." According to Ann, who witnessed it, that 'in Roland's name' explanation was authority enough for them and they stopped what they were doing. Ann thought Andrew showed great courage and loyalty to his dad and God in what he did.

Although some people began drifting toward their cars, I wanted to wait until the shoveling was done. I asked one of Roland's cousins to sing gospel songs in Ojibwe, and as the sweet sound of his voice filled the air, singing words I couldn't understand but using tunes and a heart that I understood perfectly, I wept imagining the time when I would, by and by, meet Roland by the edge of that beautiful shore.

Pastor nudged and told me that I needed to return to the building; no one could begin eating until I was there. Reluctantly, I began walking back to the car. As I stepped over yesterday's puddles, I glanced back at the almost empty cemetery.

I know what happened to that baby girl, Roland.

Beaten to death twenty-four years earlier; her short life ended with tragic violence. But she is not alone. There is so much pain, hopelessness, desperation, and dysfunction in Indian Country that it is overwhelming. People are dying; some quickly from violence, accidents and drug overdoses, but many others are simply committing slow suicide, spiritually, emotionally, and finally physically. It is a deep reality that few are acknowledging, let alone addressing, but federal Indian policy - the reservation system itself - hurts people. A system created by federal government, it divides people by race, encourages dependency on federal government, and nurtures a "victim" self-concept that hurts tribal members emotionally and spiritually. It has created a two-tiered society that makes no sense. On the one hand, members of tribal communities are afforded special rights that their neighbors aren't given. On the other hand, it has placed tribal members in a "second-class" citizenship when it comes to the Bill of Rights or a Republican form of government. Both of these situations are ultimately destructive.

Why is the reservation system under the wardship of Congress? Why are tribal assets not treated in a more mature fashion, with all the assets held equally by the complete membership in the form of a corporation or co-op? Instead, a political system has been created where US citizens are denied the protections of the Bill of Rights and are under the jurisdiction of rogue leaders.

While praying, we have felt that God's purpose in our work isn't about the bison range, ICWA or senate bills in themselves. It is about injustice, self-destructive behavior, and the systems that nurture it. It's about people dying and others profiting from it.

But mostly, it is about a world-view encouraged by federal Indian policy and those in leadership that is destroying people, discouraging us from trusting God, accepting His guidance in our lives, and understanding His love for us.

I will continue what you started, Roland – working and praying for change.

Appendix: 1

The sweet song by his graveside: • ^" Sweet Bye-and~Bye."^

NUHOUHMOOWIN 27.

1 Ah yah muh gud suh dun uh ke win,

Wah sah dush ke doon zah bun dah naun ^
An duh zhe he e nnng ko so naun,
Wah wa zhe tood ga duh nuh ke yung.

Cho.-^Tuh min wan.. dah gvvut suh..
Nuh quash ko dah de yung ish pe ming
B. Tuh min wan dah gwut, suh tuh min Wan dah gwut, suh, pah mah pee —
Tuh min wan .. dah gwut suh ..
Nuh quash do dah de yung ish pe ming,
B. Tuh min wah dah gwut, suh pah mah Pah mah pee. [pec

2 Ke guh nuh guh mo min ish pe ming,
Ma no tah gwuk in nuh guh mo nun,
Kah we kah ke p;nh mah we se min,
Uh yah wod zha wan dah goo ze jig.

3 Kah shah wa ne me nung koo see non,
Ke guh ke che twah wa ne mah non.
Pa slie gan duh gwuk, ke me ne nung,
Wan je shah wan dah goo ze yung dush.

4 Tuh min wan dah gwud suh pah mah pe

Nuh qua shko dah de yung, ish pe ming
C.'he wah huh mung wah a nwa be jig,
Ewli pa she gan dah gwuk ish pe ming.

1. There's a land that is fairer than day,
And by faith we can see it afar;
For the Father waits over the way
To prepare us a dwelling place there.

Refrain: - In the sweet by and by,
We shall meet on that beautiful shore;
In the sweet by and by,
We shall meet on that beautiful shore.

2. We shall sing on that beautiful shore
The melodious songs of the blessed;
And our spirits shall sorrow no more,
Not a sigh for the blessing of rest.

3. To our bountiful Father above,
We will offer our tribute of praise
For the glorious gift of His love
And the blessings that hallow our days.

4. We shall meet, we shall sing, we shall reign,
In the land where the saved never die;
We shall rest free from sorrow or pain
Safe at home in the sweet by-and-by.

Appendix: 2

SURRENDER

 D
Holy Father,
  C   G
As we stand before your throne,
  C   G
As we look into your face,
  C   A
We confess your matchless grace.

      D
Lord and Savior,
       C   G
We have nothing without you,
      C   G
There is nothing we can do,
 C   A7
But to serve and follow you…

      D
And Surrender (echo)
    G
And Surrender (echo)
    D
To Surrender (echo)
    G

All our dreams (echo)
  Em
All we are (echo)
  C   G
And all that we are to become
D
All our love

Appendix: 3

The Rub Tree; By Don Burgess

From "The Bugle," a publication of the Rocky Mountain Elk Foundation, Jan/Feb 2005 edition.

    Cancer had clamped onto Roland like a wolf on an elk's rear end, and was finally taking him down. Saying our goodbyes up in the hospital room, we recalled some of our hunts. It was a bittersweet time, but far from depressing because Roland was a most peaceful man. He had no fear of dying or anything else that I know of.
    A full-blood Chippewa, born and raised in Minnesota's wild rice country, Roland knew some traditional "medicine" - and a lot of Twin Cities trouble. In his late 30s he'd moved to Montana and started a new family and a new life as a Christian. He viewed the spirit as a person's most vital organ and had figured out how to keep his cancer-free in the face of all manner of difficulties. Looking out the window, oxygen tubes taped in his nostrils, he whispered, "Remember that time we got lost?"
    I could see him standing on a snow-covered Montana ridge in his black stocking cap and faded orange vest, waiting for me to figure out how to get us back to his rig. But I'd taken a wrong turn late that afternoon and wound up with a blowdown-strewn chasm between us and where we needed to be. We dropped into the canyon, clawed our way up the far side in snow above our knees and didn't get back to his rig until well after dark.

Earlier that day we'd cut fresh elk tracks leading down off a ridge into a little basin. Roland looped downhill, staying well to the right of the tracks, while I sidehilled left around the top of the basin. On the far side the breeze said "elk" loud and clear, and I followed the scent-stream downslope toward a copse of Doug fir. Figuring there had to be elk in there and they'd come out when Roland went by on the other side, I sat down and got ready. No elk showed, and when Roland reappeared I angled down to him, wondering how my nose could have been so wrong.

When he said he'd heard some loud purring coming from that thicket, I knew my nose hadn't lied. We'd seen cat tracks earlier, and it didn't take too much ciphering to conclude that there was an elk in there, and Roland had been within a few yards of the happy lion that killed it.

The lion had to have heard and scented him, and I liked the idea of it purring away as he sauntered by. Roland was apparently as unperturbed as the lion, and I wondered where all the equanimity was coming from. I'd have been purring too if I had an elk down, but I tended to thrive on the intensity, danger, extreme-sports brand of hunting, and I wasn't inclined to be so relaxed around my fellow predators. I had never hunted with anyone who wasn't keyed up about such things, and Roland's easy ways mystified me.

On another hunt, Roland's bullet broke the back of a young mule deer buck. He walked slowly up to the struggling animal and circled it once, then stood there looking at it. Watching from a few yards behind him, I grew agitated, wishing he would get it over with, and I thought about doing it myself but held off. The deer soon grew calm and Roland killed it. Later, I asked him why he took so long, and he said he'd been thanking the deer and wishing it well. He wasn't talking out loud, so I guess it was a spirit-to-spirit thing.

My sense of the meaning of coup de grace wavered and shifted after that; quick is good when it comes to delivering death, but I began to think maybe it's also good to wait for - or establish - a moment of tranquility. Clearly, though, you'd have to have it before you could pass it on.

Up in the hospital, remembering that elk hunt years ago, we got to the part where we finally got back to Roland's van. As we headed down the road Roland pulled a couple of ice-cold Cokes from his cooler. I drank mine down and declared it was the best Coke I'd ever had. Roland agreed. Still thirsty, we each opened a second can. Roland said, "This is the second-best Coke I've ever had." Maybe we were just giddy tired, but we laughed long and hard.

Up in the hospital room, the "second-best Coke" line made Roland laugh again. Then the pain cut it off, and as he bent forward with his right hand pressed against his chest, there was the old tattoo spelling out H-A-T-E across the back of his fingers, the part of his fist that would smack somebody if he punched them - a faded memento of difficult days on the far side of another chasm, years before that elk hunt.

When he got a little breath back, we prayed and hugged and said goodbye. Alone in the elevator I shed a couple of tears, but felt peaceful when the door opened on the ground floor…so peaceful it made me wonder if Roland was messing with me, spirit-to-spirit.

____end___

Appendix: 4

Roland, November 2003: Written for Christmas Newsletter

As I reflect on the end of the year, it's really hard to believe that I withstood another year of pain and agony. But <u>Praise the Lord</u> for giving me this much needed time to be with my family again, not knowing how much time I really do have left. Only the Lord knows.

As time goes on, the Lord has put on my heart to believe and trust in Him so that I don't have to suffer so much.

The things He has done for me this past year have been awesome.

1) He has given me one great year.
2) A chance to do a mission trip to Mexico to help the lost and needy.
3) A great gift from the Lord: a RV to travel and do His work.
4) Ability to improve my life with Him (the Lord)
5) Prepare to live one day at a time.
6) Ability to read and study His Word more.
7) Go to Washington DC to help my brothers and sisters fight for freedom.
8) Chance to work at the work I love best (upholstery)
9) Watch my children grow, not only in life but also in the Word.

10) The Lord has been just great, not only to me, but to my whole family (to be closer, travel together, do missions work together, and He will show us what He has in mind for the future for us again.)

If I didn't have Jesus in my heart, I wouldn't have anything in my heart. He is the only way to Salvation and to a new life that can be shared with others.

It is a miracle that I have beaten the Dr.'s on life. It is only by the Grace of God that I am what I am today.

Miracles only happen through the Lord and I am a <u>miracle</u>. Praise the Lord and God Bless you all, and for the ones that are praying for me. Thank you so much for your generosity and I pray to the Lord for more time and for better time.

But how can you ask for more time when He has given me a great year already.

Thank you Jesus.

Appendix: 5

Sampling of emails for Roland, May/June 2004

From: Edith
Sent: May 29, 2004 11:15 PM

Hi [Beth],
 We just want you to know that we are praying for Roland and your family.
 Vicki tried to phone Heidi today, but no one was home in the evening, and only Andrew in the morning.
 Your email is very good. Roland truly has encouraged many people, as he has been able to do so much for so long, even with his condition. Even the last trip to D.C. was a testimony to God's faithfulness.
 …May the Lord continue to strengthen you and the kids through this time, and may you feel His presence with you all in a very real way.
 God Bless. Edith & Rob

From: Howard
Sent: May 31, 2004 4:34 PM

Hi [Beth]... I can honestly say that I have never met another individual that has shown me so much about living and fighting for what you believe in than Roland. Thank him for me and thank him for being my friend and tell him we all love him very much.

From: Frank
Sent: May 31, 2004 6:25 PM

Simply know, [Beth], we love you. More important, He does too... indeed, there is great reason for hope. Please tell Roland I feel very blessed to know him and be able to call him friend. My heart and prayers go out to you.
    Frank

From: Eleanor
Sent: June 2, 2004 9:31 PM

Praise God that Roland knows Him. We all must go to meet our maker someday, and it's good to know Him beforehand. You are in my prayers as I know what a difficult time this is for all.
    Love in Christ, Eleanor

From: Bill
Sent: June 2, 2004 9:37 PM

Roland, [Beth] and kids:
Karen & I have prayed for you and are still praying,
Please keep us on your list of support. What can we do to help?
Bill

From: Andy
Sent: June 2, 2004 11:34 PM

[Beth]
I have been praying for you and Roland, please tell him…

From: Darrel
Sent: June 3, 2004 4:19 PM

[Beth]
I'm sure life is full of many challenges for you right now. Roland has amazed all of us with his tenacity. I pray that he can rally again and that you and your children will also be able to rally spiritually, emotionally, and physically for the challenges you face.

…I have always felt and appreciated Roland's absolute honesty. If he says something, I always know that it is because he believes that what he says is the way it is – no games. I also appreciate his perspective. Without his perspective (and a few others) we would miss a central piece of understanding about federal Indian policy. Roland also serves as a point of reference for me when I think, talk and write about FIP. In other words, Roland serves as part of my "audience." Without knowing him I wouldn't have had that perspective or "audience." I don't know how many times going through that "filter" has changed and improved what I have been doing. Roland, just by being who he is, has had a very valuable and important influence on our group. ...Our thoughts and prayers are with your family.

From: Shelley
Sent: June 9, 2004 8:08 PM

[Beth],
I just wanted you to know that I have been crying with you, celebrating with you, and praying with you... I am so sad for you and your family but so happy for Roland. WOW, face to face with Jesus at last....
I have been passing your updates on Roland and the grandkids onto our prayer chain and they have all been praying for your family.
We love you and your are never far from our thoughts.
Love,
Shelley, Pete and Kids

From: Jim
Sent: June 10, 2004 9:08 AM

[Beth] and Family:
I am so sorry to hear the news; but in another way, we must rejoice that he is in glory! My family and the local prayer group were holding you up in prayer at about that exact time last night, and

we will continue to do so. Be of good courage, be steadfast, hold on the good, lean on Jesus' everlasting arms. May his peace be with all of you. Love Jim Kim family

---

From: Jon
Sent: June 10, 2004 10:17 AM

[Beth], children, and family: Please accept my deepest sympathy for you on Roland's passing. Please also know that in life he earned my deepest respect, and along with [Beth]'s steadfast help and love has made what I think are heroic and very honorable attempts to improve the lot of native Americans in this country. Jon Metropoulos

---

From: Phonacelle
Sent: June 10, 2004 1:35 PM

Oh, [Beth]
    David and I can't begin to express how much we will miss Roland and his strength of character, his dignity, his intelligence and his faith. We know that Roland was at peace, but we also know the loss of his physical presence in your lives will be deeply felt.
    …We are so happy that the matter with the four children has been resolved and just before Roland passed away, it is like a last minute miracle…. All our love goes to you and the children.
Phonacelle and David

From: Edith
Sent: June 10, 2004 8:25 PM

Hi [Beth],
    I am sure you are probably getting flooded with emails now, but we do want to thank you for keeping us informed and giving testimony to the faithfulness of God in all this. Truly He is very involved and concerned about all the details in our lives. We do all send our sympathy and prayers. God has taken Roland to his real home, and I am sure you all do miss him deeply, I just read today that death can be likened to a candle being blown out when morning arrives…
God Bless, Edith & Rob & family

From: Russ
Sent: June 11, 2004 2:20 PM

    Dear [Beth], Though I have not met Roland, through your e-mails, I feel I knew him. Thank you for keeping us posted. You can be assured of our prayer and remember that no trial has overtaken you (including this one) but that it is a trial common to man and God is faithful in that He will not allow you to be tried beyond what you can endure, but will with that trial provide a way of escape in order that you may be able to endure it. 1 Corinthians 10:13.
    God loves you [Beth], proven over and over by His faithfulness, particularly with the joint custody, May He continue to show Himself strong to you as your now new husband of the widows – as scripture promises…
Russ

From: Toni
Sent: June 11, 2004 6:39 PM

Dear [Beth],
    Thank you for your email – how amazing you could write such an email with great clarity, no confusion and with such a sweet, sweet spirit. Last nite I was at Living Faith – Bro, Franz was here and it was announced that Roland had died and we prayed for you and the children. If there was some way someone would drive with me, I would go and support you at this time, I am praying for you and children – what a shock when it was announced, even though I knew it was coming – and it gives me an idea of how to pray for you, because even tho you knew it was coming, still it is a shock. I think because it is our enemy, death. However, the WORD said 'o death, where is they victory, o grave where is thy sting?' So, even tho you feel the shock, the Word is greater and says the sting is gone – may God have mercy on you and children and take away the sting and let His Peace rule in your heart. The victory belongs to Jesus ultimately – He came and overcame sin, satan and death. Praise God.
    I am so glad that God arranged that last evening to include the people who were with you – He loves you so – and at the last minute, all those other issues re the children and guardianship falling into place!!! Who can understand it? But then God's ways are above our ways and His thoughts are greater than ours –
    So, God bless you my dear sister – greet your children for me – those who know me and know that I will be praying and God you courage – "Be strong and of good courage and the Lord will strengthen your heart"…
Love Toni

From: Scott
Sent: June 11, 2004 7:01 PM

[Beth],
   Betty and I send our condolences to you and the kids.

   There is little I can add the kind and thoughtful words and prayers sent to you by your wide circle of friends and admirers.

   I just viewed the video of the DC news conference and I was so impressed by your daughter's maturity and the truthfulness of her words. While Roland may be gone, I can see his good heart and spirit lives on in her....

From: Arlene
Sent: June 12, 2004 3:59 PM

[Beth]
   My sincerest condolences on your loss. Although I did not meet you and Roland in person, I feel I know you. I am saddened by the passing of Roland. He was a magnificent warrior who put himself on the line for the good of all.... I can think of no-one at this time in this dark period of Indian history who is able to speak as Roland has.
   I have been a widow for 11 yrs now. My husband died many times and was revived many times. The first time he died and came back, he couldn't stop talking about the experience of being enveloped in the most indescribably beautiful feeling of being wrapped in a total sensation of his whole being held in safety and love. I now have every assurance that Roland is in the gentle arms of our creator.
   My grandchildren have been my joy and comfort. I wish the same for you.
Arlene

From: Wally
Sent: June 12, 2004 7:37 PM

Dear [Beth] and family, My wife and I wish to express our heartfelt and deepest sympathy upon the untimely passing of Roland. He was one of the great tribesmen as well as a fellow believer and political advocate. He was a personal friend to so many of us who worked with him and believed in the same causes. The many years he devoted to community services and in the helping of mistreated children will be greatly missed in all of the communities that you and he became involved in, May GOD BLESS AND KEEP YOU DURING THESE DIFFICULT TIMES AND MAY YOUR MEMORIES BE A SOURCE OF COMFORT TO YOU AND YOUR FAMILY, NOW AND IN THE FUTURE. Sincerely, Wally and Dolly.

A note sent to us in the mail:

I was very moved by John [Ward] Sr.'s accomplishments as described in his obituary in a Nov. issue of the Minneapolis Star Tribune – Keep up his good work! MC

Appendix: 6

Sample of Letters re: Roland's DVD

March 25, 2006

Dear Beth
    Thank you so much for the DVD. I just cried by myself when I seen Roland in Washington, sick as he was. And his healthy life. I watch it whenever I can. I took it to Cass Lake and most everyone wanted a copy. But I said I don't know where to get one unless they got ahold of you or [Stephanie]. She done such a good job. But I didn't [Haley] when she went thru the woods and the bugs (ha). I just got home here on Wednesday. I was in Cass Lake for a week and in Mille Lacs for a couple days. But am glad to be home. Write again.

Love [Yvonne] and family

P.S. [Troy] is going to make a copy for themselves. They have a beautiful baby girl…. She's only 7 weeks now.

MONTANA HOUSE OF REPRESENTATIVES

Representative Ralph Heinert
House District 1
June 25, 2006

Dear Beth:
    Thank you for sending me the video that was prepared honoring your husband Roland and his beliefs regarding Reservations and the impacts the system has on (it's/their) peoples. I have felt this way myself for many years and your's & Roland's story truly supports that premise.
    I don't know for sure what I can do to help in that cause if I am re-elected to the state House of Representatives. However, I do believe that the education bill requiring Indian Education for all that was passed during the last session just helps perpetuate the things that are wrong with the reservations system. I do believe that Native American culture is worth preserving by the Native American families, but in the same way the immigrants to this country have done. Otherwise we continue to treat American Indians as a separate class.
    I truly admire Roland for the message he was trying to have heard. Again, I do believe the Reservation system has been instrumental in increasing the problems that exist for our Native American brothers & sisters. I am sorry for your family's loss of Roland and wish you all the very best. Hopefully, I will have the opportunity to meet you sometime in the future. I wish I could have known Roland.
                                Thank you
                                  Ralph Heinert

Appendix: 7

Re: Montana Human Rights Network

Factual errors written down for our attorney concerning the MHRN "Confidential Comment Draft" and subsequent 45-page report entitled "Drumming Up Resentment: the Anti-Indian Movement in Montana," which was published in January, 2000.

This is the first publication of the factual errors in their report:

1. Joining ACE:
    a. Prior to ACE, we were active not with them, but outside of them. We only got to know them after we were already working on our own.
    b. Because we were successful in the small organizing we had been doing, ACE asked us to join them.

2. The statement; "She writes…articles for ACE" is written in the present tense. In fact, I haven't written anything for Ace in over two years, having resigned from the group in August of 1997.

3. The statement we "failed to (bolster?) images or to gain new supporters" doesn't apply. Whatever ACE's track record, Roland and I came away from the Bison Range controversy with hundreds of supporters.
    a. In fact, in the next paragraph, MHRN admits, "these controversies…can be used to provide energy and support …" and "helped build membership and infrastructures…"

4. There is no irony in our support of the federal government in the Bison Range controversy, as we are not anti-government.

5. ACE DID NOT organize the Bison Range protest, rallies or petition. I DID THAT prior to meeting them, and only met ACE people through that period of time.

6. The small "organizations" we were involved in prior to ACE were not part of ACE, but were non-professional efforts by some of us residents to do something about the frustration felt by so many.

7. Although we may not have been accused openly of racism at some meetings, the accusation was ever present as this draft document proves.

8. I don't remember organizing a meeting in which Ethel Harding or Bob Keenan were speakers, although I would have welcomed them both.

9. Elderly Angie Read never stated Indians were lazy, and was in fact alluding to the fact that tribal government frequently over-staffs, (see the number of tribal lawyers and tribal police compared to the number of their county counterparts.) Her concern was the amount of taxpayer money that would be spent when tribal government began staffing the Bison Range. Her statement needed to be taken into context with what she was saying prior to it.

10. The AP's failure to report a disruption is no proof it didn't happen.

11. Roland was not drawing on "Indian stereotypes" when he said he'd like to shoot a buffalo with a bow and arrow, but stating a preference. My brother, who is white, also prefers bow-hunting. Many people do.

12. Mock the large ad if you wish, but its presence is proof we had supporters and donors…

13. Yes, this unfortunately, is true. It was sad the rest of the "signatories" wouldn't stand up to identify themselves at that meeting. They were there in the audience. But as they were choosing to remain silent, I didn't feel it was my place to announce them. However, as you know, I never again put myself in the position of being their "fall" person, either.

14. We did raise a respectable amount of money for Roland's campaign.
    a. Around here, many local candidates fund their own campaigns almost entirely.
    b. State legislator campaigns generally cost about $2000.
    c. We easily raised over $2000 and spent very little of our own money.
    d. Our opponent, if I remember correctly, spent less than we did.

15. "Put to rest any doubt about [Ward]' political stance"? Who had doubts? He was always quite clear. Did MHRN have doubts because, as an Indian, Roland wasn't supposed to be conservative? Just who are the racists here?

16. ACE had been non-existent in major controversies for years, long before we became part with them. Why choose March 1999 to point it out? In fact, their mailing list doubled when we came in.

17. The paragraph describing the number of opponents to Senator Burns' bill clarifying jurisdictional disputes fails to mention that the Montana tribal governments sent busloads of high school and college students to the hearings. After arriving by bus, they were given free feasts and entertained with powwows, after which a series of speakers enflamed the crowd. Waving signs proclaimed the bill "genocide". Friends told us that those boarding the busses were asked if they were going to testify against Burns' bill, and those that were not were told not to board the bus. So yes, the majority at the hearings were violently opposed to Burns' bill, and loudly heckled anyone that disagreed.

18. Roland DID NOT identify himself as a representative of ACE at the Gorton Hearings in Seattle. If he was identified as such, it was by others. I know this because I typed his testimony and we pointedly decided to identify only CERA. We felt we were representing CERA, not ACE. ACE was not invited to testify; Roland, as a representative of CERA, was. He did not hand in ACE testimony. There was an ACE member in the crowd that may have.

The person doing ACE's newsletter from the time I'd quit as secretary has, indeed, done a neglectful job of reporting. Roland and I, ourselves, have made that comment, as have others.

20. Our reasons for later lack of involvement in ACE.
    a. ACE was not interested in updating its goals and mission statement. They did not accept the leadership Roland wanted to give.
    b. We decided federal Indian policy could only be changed from the national, not local, level.
    c. Roland and I became more involved with CERA, agreed more with CERA's Mission statement, and knew that's where we had to put our limited energy.

21. The Native American Press began circulating in the Mission Valley in July of 1998.

22. Few would view "We Support Equal Opportunity for All People" an anti-Indian perspective.

23. The tribal government on the Flathead reservation only became incensed with NAP when I started using my by-line (in the fall of 1998) Up till that point, the paper was selling steadily.

24. He inferred there were only two Rocky Mountain articles in the October 30, 1998 edition of the Native American Press, both written by me. In fact, there were four Montana articles, only three of which were written by me.
    a. My commentary about the movie "Pleasantville" was in that edition. As I look through it, I see that I did

also talk about the MHRN. However, contrary to MHRN's inference, the article was not about MHRN.

    b. MHRN mentions the other commentary I wrote, about Rick Jore and the Missoulian. However, not mentioned is the article I had written, titled: "Campaign contributions of the Native Kind." It included information about CS&K Chairman Pablo.

    c. That edition also included an Associated Press article from Great Falls; "Remaining charges in Blackfeet housing fraud case dismissed."

25. Also in that edition were articles from Tucson, Neahbay WA, Los Angeles, Baraboo Wisc, Sante Fe, Sioux Falls, Ledyard Conn. and Washington. Most of the articles of that edition were not Minnesota oriented.

26. Bill Lawrence, publisher of the Native American Press, told the MHRN interviewer this month about the newspaper's mission of pursuing accountability in tribal government, civil rights protections on reservations, and the fact that the paper was instrumental in putting eight tribal officials in prison for federal charges of corruption. Why didn't this get into the report?

27. I'm not working toward getting NAP started out here again. I'd be more interested in helping it get circulated through Barnes and Noble and other national outlets.

28. There is little mention of Roland's involvement with CERA. He is not identified as Vice-chair, nor is his visits to Wash DC mentioned, nor his successful visit with Bruce Babbit's Aide at the Interior building.

29. No mention of [Andrew's] court case.

MHRN, Toole Ignorantly Charge "Racism."
By Attorney Jon Metropoulos
March 25, 2002

This column serves as a partial rebuttal to a charge of racism leveled by the Montana Human Rights Network and its Director, state Senator Ken Toole, D-Helena, against Roland and [Beth Ward]. MHRN was required to post it on MHRN's website and to notify MHRN members of this posting as part of the settlement reached in September 2001 of a defamation and infliction of emotional distress suit brought by Roland and [Beth Ward] against Toole and the MHRN.

The Facts

A member of the Chippewa Tribe of Minnesota, Roland [Ward] is a full-blooded Native American. With his wife [Beth], he has five children, all of whom are members of the Chippewa Tribe. With [Beth], he has received custody of four of his grandchildren, all of whom are members of the Chippewa Tribe. [Beth] and Roland took custody of their grandchildren to protect them from the unending cycle of violence, drugs, alcohol, neglect, abuse and crime they personally witnessed and suffered in the reservation setting. In this process, they have struggled with some of the harsh aspects of the Indian Child Welfare Act ("ICWA"), which protects Tribes even at the expense of individual Indians.

Roland and [Beth] and their children live in northwest Montana in the town of Ronan, within the boundaries of the Flathead reservation. They are not members of the Flathead Tribes, but they live and work and own land and property there. They are not unusual. About 84% of the population of the Flathead Reservation consists of people who are not members of the Flathead Tribes. Because of federal Indian policy, fully 50% of the land mass of the Flathead reservation is not tribal land. Instead, the 84% nonmember individuals, cities and towns, the State of Montana, and the federal government own 50 percent of the land within the exterior boundaries of the reservation. As residents of Montana living in a town within the boundaries of the Flathead reservation, they have firsthand experience with overreaching by the tribal government. Indeed, the Flathead Tribes claim the right to try and punish Roland and his children for alleged violations of the Tribes' criminal code, just because they are Indians, but they do not allow them or any non-tribal member to vote in their elections, run for office, sit on a jury or act as a tribal judge. The Flathead Tribes exclude all nonmembers from these rights simply because of their race or ethnicity, i.e. they are not Flathead tribal members.

The Charge

In January 2000, the Montana Human Rights Network published a 45-page report entitled "Drumming Up Resentment: the Anti-Indian Movement in Montana." As its principle author, Toole labeled Roland and [Beth Ward] racists against Indians primarily because of their opposition to the exercise of tribal governmental powers, termed "sovereignty" or "jurisdiction," over people who are not members of the tribe attempting to exercise such power.

The "Research"

The Report was more than 5 years in the making and, according to Toole in deposition testimony, it took approximately 6 to 8 weeks of his full time labor to draft. His research, however, according to his testimony under oath, consisted of little more than reading newspaper clippings kept by a tribal activist and speaking with a half-dozen or so individuals, almost all of whom were members of the Flathead Tribes or employees or former employees of those tribes. None of the people he spoke with represented any view contrary to the one he held.

While he skimmed one elementary textbook on federal Indian law, and perhaps read a clause or two of a treaty, he did not read a single U.S. Supreme Court decision on Indian law, which is the source of such law, and he did not read a single law review article on the issues.

This refusal to educate himself on the law of tribal jurisdiction over nonmembers - or even to do basic research on the subject - led Toole and MHRN to make uninformed yet serious and harmful charges against Roland and [Beth].

The "Analysis"
According to Toole, the "anti-Indian" movement is "racist at its core" because it "opposes the concept of tribal sovereignty." This movement, he says, consists of three parts, one of which is "lack of knowledge about history and law" relating to tribal sovereignty. Consequently, Toole says people who "oppose tribal sovereignty" are racist, even if they are "well-meaning." Thus, he says, while "there are well-intentioned people who are active in the anti-Indian movement who do not perceive themselves or their cause to be racist. . . [l]ooking at the total picture, we come to a different conclusion."

Note the word "conclusion." After years of simmering the work and months of drafting, Toole betrayed no uncertainty. No equivocal "opinions" for him. Not one sentence in the Report states or even hints that it is relaying mere opinions of the MHRN and Toole. No, after so much scholarly research, analysis, and deep pondering only hard conclusions, judgments really, will do. Uncertainty, equivocation, mere opinion, are too weak for this clear-eyed Torquemada. Only a "judgment" will do.

The "Judgment"
And this was it: Roland, a struggling upholsterer and full blood Indian, and [Beth], a mother to nine Indian children, are "anti-Indian" and "racists," primarily because they oppose the exercise of tribal governmental power over nonmembers, including themselves and their children. But the U.S. Supreme Court agrees with Roland and [Beth] that Tribes rarely, if ever, should have such power. Why? Because of the serious deprivation of civil liberties implicit in allowing a tribal government to control people - non-tribal members - whom

it excludes from equal rights of participation in the political process because of their race. So why does Toole say this is "racist"?

The Explanation

Toole's defense hinges, as one might expect, on his personal definition of "racism," as well as other equally slippery and impossibly fine distinctions. (For example, Toole claimed in his answer to the Complaint that a charge of "racism" is not always defamatory but might have an innocent connotation. Similarly, he maintained, for a while, that actually he only labeled Roland and [Beth] "anti-Indians" and, in another place, said that "anti-Indians" are racists. So, he says, he did not call Roland and [Beth] racists. In his deposition he admitted, under oath, that the "inference is clear.")

Any dictionary, any direct, honest person, sees racism for what it is: "Discrimination or prejudice against someone based on their race." This clear, real definition did not suit Toole's purposes, however, which was to label people who disagree with his notion of tribal sovereignty "racists." So he defined it himself.

Racism, he teaches us, "is a systematic effort to deny legally established rights to a group of people who are identified on the basis of their shared culture, history, religion and tradition."

Thus, Toole claimed alleged "anti-Indians" disagree with the "core concept of (tribal) sovereignty." This, he says, is the "effort to deny legally established rights" that makes such opponents of tribal sovereignty "racist by definition."

But the charge of racism against Roland and [Beth] does not stick even using Toole's personal definition. To determine whether he was justified in labeling Roland and [Beth] "racists" even using his own personal definition requires an answer to the question whether their opposition to tribal jurisdiction over them sought to deny tribes their "legally-established rights" to exercise sovereignty over nonmembers. The answer is unequivocally "no."

The Law of Tribal Sovereignty

First, Toole simply does not know the law of tribal sovereignty as it does or does not extend to nonmembers. As noted above, he failed to read a single U.S. Supreme Court case on the issue, even though in the last 12 years, the Supreme Court handed down six or seven key decisions, each of which comports with earlier rulings and severely limits tribal sovereignty over nonmembers. He failed to read any pertinent law review articles. And he limited the people with whom he spoke about these issues to advocates of expansive tribal power. Toole plainly is in no position to judge.

But Toole, undaunted by his ignorance, remains self-righteously assured. Unfortunately for Toole and MHRN, the law of tribal sovereignty reveals his position as completely uninformed.

In May and June of this year the Court handed down two cases that are the culmination of almost 25 years of consistent decisions by the Supreme Court clarifying that Tribes have few, if any, powers over nonmembers. These last cases, Atkinson Trading Co. v. Shirley and Nevada v. Hicks, hold that tribes almost never have governmental authority over nonmembers. These aren't even close questions - all nine justices concurred in both decisions; i.e. there was not one dissenter. Atkinson held that tribes cannot tax nonmembers within a reservation who are doing business on non-tribal land. Hicks held a tribe and its court didn't have jurisdiction over a nonmember even for his conduct on tribal land. The opinion of the court emphasized that the Court has never found that a tribe had jurisdiction over a nonmember. Justice Souter, whose concurring opinion argues for an even more categorical rule against tribal jurisdiction over nonmembers, emphasized that "the Bill of Rights and the Fourteenth Amendment do not of their own force apply to Indian tribes." He added that a presumption against tribal authority over nonmembers would protect them from "intrusions on their personal liberty" by tribes. The exclusion of nonmembers both from equal rights in tribal processes and from understanding their particular "customs, traditions and practices" could have grave "practical consequences" for the rights of nonmembers.

Thus, even accepting Toole's personal word bending, by his own definition opposing a tribe's assertion of jurisdiction over a nonmember is not racist. According to the Supreme Court anyway, tribes almost never have such power; i.e they do not have "legally established rights" to control nonmembers in almost any case. Roland and [Beth]'s opposition to overreaching by tribes to exert such power is not racism, therefore, even using Toole's definition.

The Importance

Of course, Toole may argue the U.S. Supreme Court itself is a racist institution. One of your Board members, in fact, said so when I presented this rebuttal to them last October. Perhaps the Supreme Court too is "well-intentioned" and does not perceive itself as racist. The Justices must cower at the prospect of Toole's learned judgment condemning them.

But they have good reason to consistently find against tribal jurisdiction over nonmembers.

The foundation of the Court's decisions, and of Roland and [Beth]'s opposition to tribal jurisdiction over nonmembers, is the factual deprivation of basic rights that nonmembers suffer when they are subject to a tribe's governmental power. First you should know that opponents of such power, at least those I defend, do not deny there is a proper role for tribal governmental power, and it is precisely to exercise self-government.

But when such power extends to nonmembers, violations of civil rights occur automatically that we would not tolerate anywhere in the country. People are excluded from participating in government simply because they are not members of the tribe, i.e., they are excluded based on their race, ancestry or ethnicity. Nonmembers are denied the right to vote, hold office, sit on juries. If subject to a tribe's criminal authority, a nonmember Indian could be imprisoned in a tribal jail for years, depending on how the charges were stacked. Yet, he or she has no right even to a fair jury. Simply put, because they are not Indians or are not Indians who qualify to be members of a tribe, nonmembers cannot give the "consent of the governed."

Ponder that lack. When dealing with any other type of government in this country we correctly demand all the rights such consent gets us in exchange. Indeed we celebrate these rights, in particular the right to participate in the government. In the tribal context nonmembers have none of these rights. That is a significant and dangerous deprivation.

The Damage
The charge of racism against Roland and [Beth Ward] by the MHRN and Toole, of course, is absurd. It is defamation arising from willful ignorance or malice. It matters not which.

Notwithstanding Toole's absurd claim to the contrary, racism is never benign. It is never innocent and the charge is always negative, always gives rise in decent people to revulsion and disgust at someone who would act in such a discriminatory manner.

The Remedy
That is why the charge of racism must be correct when it is leveled. You must know what you are talking about, and you must not allow your own biases to blind you. Do your research. You have harmed real people. Playing cute with definitions will not do. Playing fast and loose with the charge, only to admit, as Toole did under cross examination, that it may never have been accurate and that he cannot really know is simply unacceptable in civilized discourse. More, it is cynical, divisive, and dismissive of the accused as a person.

Jon Metropoulos
Attorney

No Response to this Letter was ever received:

Evelyn Staus   November 3, 2007
President
League of Minnesota Human Rights Commissions
4100 Lakeview Ave.
Robbinsdale, MN 55422

Dear Ms. Staus,

I would like to introduce myself. I grew up in the 1960's and 70's in Fridley, Minnesota. My family was middle class and politically active in the DFL. I remember meeting and campaigning for the likes of Hubert Humphrey, Rudy Perpich, Walter Mondale, and Don Fraser. When I was 18, I met a man from Cass Lake, Minnesota, whom I later married.

Let me introduce my husband. A member of the Minnesota Chippewa Tribe, he was born in 1945 in Walker, Minnesota. We were raised worlds apart. But despite the poverty and roughness in which he was raised, he remembered the 1950's and 60's very fondly. He said people seemed a lot closer back then. "Ricing season was almost like Christmas, because people you hadn't seen for a long time would get together while camping by the lake and simply had fun."

Loving and loved by our mutual family members very much, we have taken numerous needy nephews and nieces into our home over the years. One 30 some year-old nephew from my husband's side still calls once a month or so and tells me I'm his "Mom."

- In other words, my husband and I aren't bad people. I was a licensed foster care parent in Minneapolis, a licensed Day Care provider, a staff person at the Minneapolis Crisis Nursery, a Nursing Treatment Assistant at what used to be known as Bridgeway, University Health Care Center, and a Registered Nurse at Cedar Pines Nursing Home in Minneapolis. My husband I have been described as intelligent, loving, patient, kind, and helpful. We have also been described as determined and tenacious, and been known for working with a passion, whether it is my husband's perfectionism in his upholstery craft, or our political concerns.

So it was with great pain that I learned that my husband and I, Roland and [Beth Ward], had been vilified again by the Montana Human Rights Network - this time at the League of Minnesota

Human Rights Commissions 36th Annual Conference in Mille Lacs, Minnesota, on Sept. 29, 2007.

From what I was told, parts of the main conference addressed some very real concerns. It was unfortunate that important time, which could have been put to better use, was wasted by MHRN discussing us. At the time I was told about the conference, I commented to a friend that if the worst that MHRN can come up with as an "anti-Indian" villain to pillory is a tribal member that had passed away three years ago, then Montana must not have much of an "anti-Indian" problem. Roland was not a villain, neither was he a victim of so-called "anti-Indian" forces.

However, as much as I tried to laugh it off, the truth is that, again, MHRN actions have hurt my family very deeply. How do you suppose it feels to the children to hear that MHRN is again dragging their father, a man they miss very much, through the mud? How do you suppose it felt to be a family member present at the conference, seeing someone you loved, someone you knew to be sincere and who couldn't defend himself anymore, be treated this way? That family member, quite upset, left as soon as the MHRN portion ended. McAdam can travel the country trying to distort Roland's message, but Roland's extensive family and friends know, and will not forget, what Roland really believed and stood for. Roland was not anti-Indian, nor a dupe.

I wanted to write to you immediately, and I do apologize for the length of time it took me to respond. I am a single mother now struggling to make a living with several children to care for, as well as continuing the work that our family is interested in, so I don't have lots of time to spend on the antics of the MHRN. I never have had lots of time to spend on their antics, but have been forced to take the time off and on through the years.

That said; I would like you to be aware of a few things.

#1) **My husband's political beliefs were based on the love that he had for his family and friends, the pain he felt watching**

family and friends suffering with drug and alcohol abuse and dying violent deaths, and what he knew in his heart to be true. He wanted change.

#2) The Montana Human Rights Network was told in a letter dated November 29, 1999, <u>prior to</u> the publication of their 2000 report, that "<u>There are numerous factual errors within the MHRN Confidential Comment Draft sent to us by Ken Toole. I would suggest you publish it only after you correct those errors and the equally incorrect assumptions and conclusions. It is your responsibility to ensure the accuracy of your reports.</u>" Again, Roland and I had nine children in the home at the time the draft report was sent to us. Eight of the children were under the age of 11. I did not have any time - or desire to take the time - to sit down and do MHRN's homework for them. But they ignored this warning and published anyway.

#3) Although Mr. McAdam claimed in his September presentation that the settlement of the lawsuit we brought against them confirmed that we were wrong in the suit, <u>that wasn't quite true</u>. In the 2001 Settlement Agreement, the director of MHRN was forced to apologize to us as well as agree to allow our attorney to post a rebuttal on their website and schedule time to talk to their board.

#4) **The apology**, signed by then Director of the MHRN, Ken Toole, stated, *"I accept your earnest assertion that your personal views opposing tribal sovereignty over nonmembers are **not** anti-Indian or racist, and that **you should not personally be labeled** as either anti-Indian or racist. I understand your deep concerns about our publication of matter which you view as defamatory. Please accept my apology for causing you such concern and for any emotional distress this concern may have caused you."*

Having received this apology, can you understand the distress my children and I felt upon hearing that Roland's image was splashed up on the wall in the MHRN power point discussing racism in Minnesota?

#5) **The only reason we settled:** My husband was very sick with cancer at the time and extremely tired. After a certain point, he just wanted it all to be done with. He couldn't fight anymore. I wanted to keep going with the suit because not only had they maligned us so badly, but I had seen so many good, kind people disparaged by the MHRN over the years that I wanted to do something that would help everyone. I hurt for them as much as I hurt for us. Nonetheless, knowing my husband was very tired, and sensing that our attorney was as well, I reluctantly signed. HOWEVER, I wrote next to my signature, (MHRN has a copy), *"Not having been deposed, (and) having much to say, I would rather go to trial, but understand the needs of others at this time, and am signing for the sake of others."* This explains my only reason for signing that settlement.

#6) I was also told that Mr. McAdam took much time in Mille Lacs going over my husband's deposition and essentially mocking it, While some of the deposition quotes I was told Mr. McAdam chose to belittle don't seem that big a deal, (I can understand what my husband was trying to say), I would also like you to know that my husband was hospitalized in Billings a few days before the deposition, on July 4th, 2001, with a sudden, severe pneumonia. (He was okay when we left Minneapolis, having just left the U of M cancer clinic. The pneumonia came on while we were driving home and by the time we got to Billings, I had to drive straight to the hospital). I believe he was discharged on the 7th, and we traveled back to Ronan, where he, still feeling terrible, rested and then reported to Missoula for the deposition on the 10th.

This is important to know, because I sat across from him during the deposition and painfully watched his struggle. Mr. McAdam wasn't there, and even if he had been, he had never met Roland prior and so wouldn't realize the huge difference between a healthy Roland and an ill one. However, the fact that Roland personally testified in numerous State hearings as well as in front of the Senate Committee on Indian Affairs is undeniable, and yet, even the most summary read of this deposition shows that the Roland, on this particular day, was having trouble answering questions as simple as the ages of our children, how many years he went to college, and where we were living at any certain time. On page 17, the questioner said he couldn't understand what Roland was saying, and Roland told the questioner that he didn't understand what the questioner was saying, and it is very clear in the surrounding pages that Roland <u>was</u> totally confused. On page 25, he told the questioner that he was never active on issues related to Indian sovereignty! Yet, further inquiry had him admitting that he had testified in the State Legislature on Indian sovereignty issues. But he couldn't remember what the bills he was testifying about were even for. He also couldn't remember the name of the Interior Department, couldn't remember names of US Congressmen he met with, couldn't remember the platform he ran on for State House in 96, and couldn't even remember the reason for the lawsuit. It wasn't that Roland was trying to lie or hide anything. He was that confused. On page 11 the court reporter quoted me trying to calm Roland when he was stuttering by telling him, "It's okay."

Still, a full read of the deposition doesn't support McAdam's apparent thesis concerning my husband, who, while struggling with most questions, remained adamant that he supported CERA's purposes. Mr. McAdam has read the deposition and should have been able to see that Roland was in distress, but appears to have picked and chosen sentences in attempt to create his own interpretation of Roland's views. Some of us find it pathetic that Mr. McAdam appears to be making a living mocking my husband's responses from that day.
Roland felt he had to be there for the deposition and he did the best he could, and that's that.

Questions: What was the point of Mr. McAdam's presentation? How did picking apart the deposition of an ill man from six years ago further valuable dialogue? How did it help edify and clarify the purposes of the Conference, not to mention the truth and real motivations behind those that are questioning federal Indian policy? Did my husband's deposition prove whatever point Mr. McAdam was trying to make?

Further - we were a team. Why is it that Roland's image was on the power point, instead of mine, a living person that is still politically active – but able to defend herself? Or - why was Roland's image used, and not one of the many white people currently working on issues within federal Indian policy? I honestly don't understand. If anti-Indian racism is indeed a huge problem in America, was there really no one worse than Roland that could have been used as an object lesson?

Or – is MHRN unable to use someone else because, in truth, no one in the so-called "anti-Indian" organizations mentioned is actually doing anything wrong? They are simply average people with simple lives and no fangs. There really is nothing more involved than groups of people with political differences, and thus, no one to single out and specifically accuse, other than a dead man.

Does McAdam need a purpose for his job, and if so, was my husband simply easy pickings?

Needless to say, I wish so badly that I never signed that settlement agreement. It was NOT a good thing to sign. Whether the words I wrote around my signature can help us at all will have to be found out. Ken Toole brought our names up while he was speaking at a conference last year in Missoula; and now this in Minnesota. Who knows where else they are continuing to dredge us up; it appears as if they have absolutely nothing more relevant to talk about.

I am sure you can understand that I owe it to my children to write to you about this. There is no reason for this type of rhetoric to continue. This is America, where everyone, no matter their heritage, is supposed to have freedom of speech and freedom of press. It really is supposed to be okay for a tribal member – or a tribal member's wife - to disagree with the tribal government, isn't it? If it isn't normally okay, is it okay to stand up and begin to disagree if your tribal government has been convicted in federal court of embezzlement and fraud, and if corruption continues to be an issue on your reservation? Please tell us, as I have several children wanting to know: "When <u>does</u> it become okay to have a different opinion?"

All Roland [Ward] Sr. ever did was publish and speak on his thoughts. Very honest and legitimate thoughts, from a man who was in fact very humble in the way he presented himself.

McAdam ended his speech with this phrase, *"It's not always easy, and it's not always fun, but if it's something you believe in – you have to do it."* McAdam was talking about his own agenda, but it could have been Roland's epithet. Roland had a right to stand up for what he believed in.

And we, his family, continue to stand up for him. I am including a video of my husband's life. It includes interviews with family members in Cass Lake and explains his heart better than I can. To those I've carbon copied, if you would like to see Roland's video, please let me know.

I would also love to share with you, at your request, what we had written in relation to the rebuttal posted on the MHRN website (If I remember right, something our attorney had written ended up being posted). I can provide anything we have ever written on request. I can also provide the apology letter from Ken Toole and the Settlement Agreement. Of course, the MHRN already has all of this. They were also sent a fuller length version of the video about two years ago, and yet continue to use Roland for their own purposes. It's interesting that nothing from that video was included in the Mille Lacs presentation.

I can also provide the factual errors written in the MHRN report, which were many. (Yes, at one point in the last seven years I did find time to sit down and type them out.)

- I would also ask, <u>please</u>, for the family's sake, ie his children, grandchildren, and extended Leech Lake family, that an apology be made for what happened to Roland's name and memory in Mille Lacs six weeks ago.

Thank you for your time,

Bless you,
[Beth Ward]
PO Box 93
Ronan, MT 59864

cc. Mary Sam, Chair, MLAHRC
Reverend David Gallus, Co-Chair, MLAHRC, Pastor, Holy Cross Parish
Boyd Morson, Vice-President, LMHRC
Marion Helland, Secretary, LMHRC
Jackie Fraedrich, Board Member, LMHRC
Keith Ellison, U.S. Representative, Minnesota
Arvonne Fraser, Hubert H. Humphrey Institute of Public Affairs
Wayne Simoneau, former MN State Rep.
Minnesota Governor Tim Pawlenty
Velma Korbel, Minn. Human Rights Commissioner
Minnesota State Senator Patricia Torres Ray
Minnesota State Senator Betsy Wergin
Minnesota State Senator Julianne Ortman
Minnesota State Representative Sondra Erickson
Minnesota State Representative Mindy Greiling
Minnesota State Representative Joyce Peppin
Minnesota State Representative Kim Norton
Minnesota State Representative Carolyn Laine
Minnesota State Representative Mike Jaros
Minnesota State Representative Morrie Lanning
Minnesota State Representative Steve Simon
Mille Lacs County Commissioner Frank Courteau
Mille Lacs County Commissioner Jack Edmonds
Mille Lacs County Commissioner Roger Tellinghuisen
Mille Lacs County Commissioner Dave Tellinghuisen
Mille Lacs County Commissioner Phil Peterson
Brett Larson, Editor of Mille Lacs Messenger
Bill Lawrence, Editor, Native American Press
Larry Oakes, Correspondent, Mpls. Star &Tribune

Tom Dennis, Editor, Grand Forks Herald
UPS Store of Golden Valley – conference supporter
Morris Dees, Southern Poverty Law Center
Travis McAdam, Montana Human Rights Network

Delivered to Evelyn Staus -

Label/Receipt Number: **0307 1790 0000 9596 6581**
Status: **Delivered**
Your item was delivered at 9:55 AM on November 8, 2007 in MINNEAPOLIS, MN 55422.

- No Apology was ever given -

_____

Appendix: 8

Family, 2000-2011

<u>Yvonne</u>: *Died of a drug overdose two years after Roland had passed.*

<u>Wanda</u>: *Wanda later became a Christian in the Word of Life Church and believed that by faith her legs, which were amputated after several years due to circulation problems, would grow back. This didn't happen. Discouraged, feeling alone and unloved, she died of an over-dose a few months after Roland, almost 25 years after her accident. Some have thought it was a suicide.*

<u>Roger</u>: *Found dead on the street in late 2001.*

<u>Shanda</u>: *Died of Cancer 2002*

<u>Bradley</u>: *Imprisoned in his late teens for murder*

<u>Savannah</u>: *Died from a drug overdose in Loring Park, 2004*

<u>Wanda</u>: *Died from a drug overdose in her home, 2004*

<u>Elmer Dovetail</u>: *Continued preaching and loving the Lord until his passing, 6 months after Roland.*

<u>Yvonne</u>: *Died in 2009 from an overdose*

<u>Misty</u>: *Died of Liver disease due to alcoholism in 2011*

<u>Bill Lawrence</u>: *Died of Cancer 2010*

<u>Troy</u>: *Happily married, Purchasing clerk for a tribe.*

<u>Mickey</u>: *Happily married, Owner of a flooring company in Georgia.*

<u>Paul</u>: *Happily married, Manages a restaurant near the Twin Cities.*

<u>Ross</u>: *Became one of the best drummers on the college campus we lived on from 2000-2007. Voluntarily reunited with birth parents in 2009.*

<u>Brooke</u>: *Experimenting with chords on her own volition became a wonderful piano player and composed some beautiful music. Voluntarily reunited with birth parents in 2008.*

<u>Caleb</u>: *Amazing athlete; Excellent at every sport he put effort into. Was told by his figure skating teacher in 2004 that he had potential to be in 2010 winter Olympics. Attended Dakota Boys Ranch 2009 – 2010 with good success. Looking forward to attending college in fall 2012.*

<u>Dewey</u>: *Still with us and doing very well. Is on the high school football team, wrestling team, and has been employed at the same facility since he was a freshman in 2010.*

There are many others – all equally loved.

Appendix: 9

Daily Prayer

Praying Scripture for Me
By Carol Ratzlaff

Father, thank You for this brand new day, and for all Your many blessings!!

I pray today that I would seek first the kingdom of God, and his righteousness; and all these things shall be added to me. (Matt 6:33)

I pray that I would give thanks always for all things unto God and the Father in the name of our Lord Jesus Christ;

I pray that I would rejoice in the Lord always: and again I say, Rejoice!!

I choose to trust in the LORD with all my heart; and to lean not to my own understanding.

Father, please help me to redeem the time, because the days are evil. May I not waste time today!

A merry heart does good like a medicine: but a broken spirit dries the bones. I choose to fill our home with joy and laughter – please fill me with Your joy!

Let no corrupt communication proceed out of my mouth, but that which is good to the use of edifying, that it may minister grace to the hearers. And let me not grieve not the holy Spirit of God, whereby I am sealed to the day of redemption. Let all bitterness, and wrath, and anger, and clamor, and evil speaking, be put away from me, with all malice: And may I be kind one to another, tenderhearted, forgiving one another, even as God for Christ's sake has forgiven me.

Hear, O Israel: The LORD our God is one LORD: And I shall love the LORD my God with all my heart, and with all my soul, and with all my might. And these words, which are commanded me this day, shall be in my heart: And I shall teach them diligently to my children, and shall talk of them when I sit in my house, and when I walk by the way, and when I lie down, and when I rise up. And I shall bind them for a sign on my hand, and they shall be as frontlets between my eyes. And I shall write them on the posts of our house, and on our gates.

Father, please enable me to be quick to listen, slow to speak, and slow to get angry.

I pray that I would always submit to my husband as to the Lord.

Please fill me full and overflowing with Your Holy Spirit. May I always hear and obey Your voice. May I be the best helpmeet for my husband, and help me to rest and enjoy our children today. May I see others and myself, through Your eyes.

I love You Lord! Please work in me both to will and to do Your good pleasure. I'm Yours!!

Appendix: 10

Roland

Roland [Ward] Sr.
July 1, 1945 – June 9, 2004

Roland [Ward], Sr., 58, ascended to heaven on Wednesday, June 9th after a four year fight with cancer. Roland, a member of the Minnesota Chippewa Tribe, was born July 1, 1945, in Cass Lake, MN. Ojibwe was his first language, and he grew up fishing, hunting, and gathering wild rice with family and friends. He also played intramural basketball, worked hard in the woods, spent time in a foster home and various jails, drank, smoked, and played guitar with friends at various bars.

Roland went to college in Kansas and was a draftsman for a short time before becoming an upholsterer. While he struggled with many difficulties in his early years, he was a perfectionist with upholstery and throughout his life performed his craft well.

After a life changing spiritual experience with Jesus in 1988, Roland moved his second family to Ronan, Montana to be near his cousin and Christian evangelist, Frank (Scotty) Butterfly. There, in 1992, Roland and his wife created Montana's first patient transportation service, Mission Valley Medicab. They also helped instigate the Montana Passenger Carriers Association and the charitable organization, Valley Missions, Inc., all without tribal assistance.

Roland taught his children about wild ricing, hunting, fishing, and a little of the Ojibwe language. But the biggest, strongest desire of his heart was that his children, grandchildren, and entire extended family come to the saving knowledge and acceptance of Jesus Christ. Having watched many friends and relatives die physically, spiritually, and emotionally from alcoholism, violence, and suicide, Roland could no longer stand aside and do nothing. He was concerned for the children and felt distress at the attitudes of many adults within his community. He wanted the self-destruction to stop.

Roland's relationship with Jesus coupled with his conviction that much of the reservation system was harmful led him to some amazing life experiences. Actively opposing much of federal Indian policy, Roland served as President of the Western Montana organization *All Citizens Equal*, was a board member and Vice-Chairman of the national organization; *Citizens Equal Rights Alliance*, was the Secretary of *Citizens Equal Rights Foundation*.

He also ran as a Republican candidate for the Montana House of Representatives in the 1996 and testified before the US Senate Committee on Indian Affairs in April,1998, the Minnesota Attorney General in 2000, and numerous Mont. State committees. With his family, he also had a private meeting with a member of the President's Domestic Policy Council May, 2002 in Washington DC.

As time progressed, Roland became more convinced of the importance of Jesus in his life. So in 2000 he attended a year of training at the Living Faith Bible College, Canada. Over the last three years, he and/or his family went on mission trips in Canada and Mexico. During a 2003 trip to a children's home in Juarez, Mexico, he fixed most of their dining hall chairs, taught 6 boys how to upholster, donated materials, and preached a Sunday street service.

Through the years, he has appeared in numerous newspaper articles across the country. The last article he appeared in was on Friday, May 14th, in the Washington Times. Reporter Jennifer Lehner wrote, *"the ICWA [Indian Child Welfare Act] protects the interests of others over [Mr. Ward's] grandchildren,"* and *"Mr. [Ward] said that once children* *are relocated to the reservations, they are subject to the corrupt law of the tribal government. Instead of preserving culture, he said, the tribal leadership uses the ICWA to acquire funds provided through the legislation."* Ms. Lehner quoted Roland as saying that the law is *"supposed to help children, but instead it helps tribal governments."*

Finally, in February, 2004, he and his wife founded the *Christian Alliance for Indian Child Welfare.* The purpose of this was to encourage preaching, teaching and fostering of the growth of the Christian Faith in all places, encourage accountability of governments to families with Indian heritage, and educate the public about Indian rights, laws, and issues.

Roland praised God to the very end. When his final struggle began, several of his friends and family were praying with him. When those present sang old-time hymns, he raised his hand in the air for as long as he could. When "Surrender" was sung, he sang the echo. While Pastor sat next to Roland, holding his hand, Roland looked him straight in the eyes and pointed his other hand up to heaven. When he passed on to greater life, his good friend Marvin was softly playing Gospel songs for him on his accordion.

Roland is survived by his wife, nine children, twelve grandchildren and a great grandson.

Roland's loving friend, Jim Ball, crafted a beautiful casket for him as a gift. Funeral services were at the CMA Church in Ronan, MT, on Sunday, June 13, 2004 and the CMA Church in Cass Lake, MN, Tuesday, June 15. He is strongly remembered for his strength, character, and love for the Lord Jesus.

Roland, our husband, father, grandfather, brother, uncle, cousin, and friend; We Love you and Miss you so very much. You are with God now.

Gi gi wah ba min me na wah.

Appendix: 11

Scott Kayla Morrison

Scott Kayla Morrison, (1951 – 2000)

Scott Kayla Morrison, Attorney and Author, grew up on her grandmother's allotment in the old Choctaw Nation, OK, where her family has been living since the Trail of Tears in the 1830s.

In early August, 2000, Scott purchased a rifle. On August 8th her body was found by local authorities.

A month earlier, Morrison was in New York explaining to an audience that there is no guarantee of freedom of press, speech, or assembly on reservations…but that there is retribution against the families of those that speak out against tribal governments. She said she feared for her life and the Choctaw knew she was here "telling on them." 30 days later back in Oklahoma she was found shot dead. The local sheriff ruled the death a suicide with a rifle.

Morrison, a member of the Oklahoma Choctaw tribe, was the recipient of numerous awards, including the 1990 Phillip Hubbard Human Rights Award.

Morrison graduated from the University of Oklahoma in 1987 with a Bachelor's degree in English and a minor in writing. Morrison then attended the University of Iowa Law School where she was

President of the American Indian Law Student Association. While at UI, she was a research assistant to Professor Robert Clinton, a leading Indian law scholar, and did a large portion of the research for the Oklahoma Indian law section of Clinton's textbook: American Indians and the Law.

After graduating from the University of Iowa College of Law in May 1990, Morrison became President of Choctaws for Democracy. In 1991, she was staff attorney and litigation Manager for the Yogesh Nanji, East Mississippi Legal Services on the Mississippi Choctaw Reservation. From 1992 to 1995, she worked as director of the Native American Office of Jobs in the Environment on a campaign organizing Indian communities on environmental issues. In 1995-96, Morrison was a member of The Waste and Facility Sitting Subcommittee National Environmental Justice Advisory Council.

In the May/June issue of 1993, Oklahoma Today named her in its "Who's Who in Indian Country" in recognition of her environmental work. She was also named one of 15 "Women Who Make A Difference" in Minorities and Women in Business Magazine, January-April 1994 issue. In that issue, she was the only woman from Oklahoma and the only Native American profiled in the magazine.

She has also spoke at conferences and published several articles, including a collaboration with LeAnn Howe on the investigative article "Sewage of Foreigners: The Choctaw Survivors" " (Federal Bar Journal & Notes, July, 1992), a detailed exposé that focused on contract negotiations by the Mississippi Band of Choctaw Indians to allow for toxic waste dumps on Choctaw lands in Mississippi. Her short stories and essays appeared in publications including The Four Directions: American Indian Literary Quarterly and Turtle Quarterly (Native American Center for the Living Arts, Niagara Falls, New York), and in the anthology The Colour of Resistance (1994)."

She began her second book on Indian civil rights, called "Nazis and the Indian Mafia," which addressed government policies, reservation scams and scandals and the corruption legacy of the U.S. Department of Interior's Bureau of Indian Affairs, but it is unclear if this book was ever finished.

In the fall of 1994, Morrison, was elected as a member-at-large to the national American Civil Liberties Union board of directors. She was the third member-at-large director elected from Oklahoma in ACLU history, and served a one-year term. She was voted on by all ACLU members from across the country.

"I was thrilled when I was nominated for the national board, and then elected," said Ms. Morrison. "ACLU, with its history in protecting civil rights, has often left out the first Americans. Hopefully, now I can work to begin the shift to help Indians in their civil rights struggles."

In 1995, Morrison began work with attorney Douglas Dry researching Bureau of Indian Affairs Administrative Regulations and drafting civil pleadings and appellate briefs. She assisted in the case Douglas Dry v. Choctaw, which challenged the jurisdiction of the Court of Indian Offenses. In 1997 Morrison practiced in Choctaw tribal court as well as became the President of the Citizens Equal Rights Foundation. Civil Rights and the Indian Child Welfare Act were two areas of particular concern.

She was a member of the Oklahoma and Mississippi Bar Associations, the U.S. District Court for Eastern Oklahoma, U.S. Court of Appeals 5th and 10th Circuits, and the Oklahoma Choctaw CFR Court.

Morrison testified before the Senate Committee on Indian Affairs in 1998, and in June of 1999 opened an office in Clayton, Oklahoma where she had a general practice and consulted on Indian law. Scott Kayla died tragically the following year.

Appendix: 12

Bill Lawrence

Minnesota journalist who was tribal watchdog dies after cancer fight

Park Rapids Enterprise Published March 05 2010 http://www.thedeadballera.com/Obits/MinorLeaguers/Obits_L/Lawrence.William.Obit003.html

Bill Lawrence, a journalist who was a watchdog of Minnesota's tribal governments for more than two decades, has died after a fight with prostate cancer. He was 70.
By: Chuck Haga, Grand Forks Herald
Bill Lawrence, a Red Lake Ojibwe and crusading journalist who hounded tribal officials in northern Minnesota for more than 20 years — and helped send some to prison — died Tuesday in Idaho, where he was being treated for prostate cancer at a Veterans Affairs medical center.
Lawrence, 70, was founder and editor of the Native American Press/Ojibwe News, which he started in 1988 and published in Bemidji. Because of his declining health, his last edition was published last fall.
"I am no longer physically able to do the tasks — computer searches, investigating, seeking ads — that are necessary to put out an edition," he wrote in a final editorial.
Apparently borrowing a line from Chief Dan George in the 1970 film "Little Big Man," he titled the editorial "A good day to die."

In addition to his campaigns against corruption, Lawrence fought for requirements that audits of Indian casinos be made public — he received an award for that in 2003 from the Society of Professional Journalists — and published a series detailing the causes and consequences of fetal alcohol syndrome among Minnesota's Indians.

He was an enrolled member of the Red Lake Band of Ojibwe but grew up in nearby Bemidji, where he was a star high school and college athlete, earning all-state honors in three sports at Bemidji High School. He had a tryout with the Detroit Tigers baseball team and pitched in the Tiger farm system, served with the Marines in Vietnam and worked in tribal government in California and Arizona.

He attended law school at UND but left to work as a miner in northern Minnesota and later a development officer at Red Lake.

'Digging up dirt'

In a March 2005 story on Salon.com, shortly after the shootings at Red Lake High School, Lawrence said tribal press constraints on the closed reservation made it difficult to sort out what happened at the school and hid "systemic problems" on the reservation.

Lawrence had "devoted most of his adult life to digging up dirt on corrupt tribal politicians and shedding light on news neglected by both the tribal and the mainstream press," Salon.com reported.

Lawrence made liberal use of anonymous sources and had what Salon called a "laissez-faire attitude toward journalistic decorum," which drew criticism from some other Native American journalists. His severest critics, though, were tribal leaders who resented and resisted his calls for more transparency in tribal government, including the legendary Red Lake Tribal Chairman Roger Jourdain — who was Lawrence's godfather.

"I should have dropped him in that baptismal font," an unsmiling Jourdain told another reporter in 1990.

When Jourdain died in 2002, Lawrence tempered his assessment of the man. "We had our differences," he said. "But I realized that he was a consummate politician. He brought home a lot of programs. He also established a strong tribal government and worked tirelessly toward self-determination."

He kept railing

Despite Lawrence's efforts to shine light on what he considered systemic problems in the tribal system of self-government, "the reservations of north-central Minnesota remain isolated places, unfamiliar to the society around them," Salon.com noted in the 2005 article.

Months later, in a Star Tribune interview, Lawrence continued to rail against the tribal government's reliance on sovereignty, "which maintains a status quo of unemployment, poverty, civil rights abuses and social dysfunction," he said. "The tribal government is inept. They ... hide behind sovereignty. The social problems — drugs, alcohol, fetal alcohol syndrome, shootings, the kids not going to school — people don't know what to do about them."

David Lillehaug, a former U.S. attorney for Minnesota, oversaw prosecutions which led to prison sentences for former tribal leaders at the White Earth and Leech Lake reservations and a state senator from Leech Lake, all of whom had been targets of Lawrence's reporting.

"Bill Lawrence and the Native American press performed a valuable service in identifying corruption in tribal government," Lillehaug told the Star Tribune at the time of the editor's retirement. "Some of his stories provided leads for federal law enforcement, others were dry holes. But when he was right, he was really right."

Lawrence ran for tribal office in 1970 and 1978, losing what he insisted were rigged elections.

A memorial service is scheduled for 2 p.m. March 13 at Bemidji State University's Memorial Hall.

Appendix: 13

Salvation Assured

With thanks to Dr. William B. Allen for writing this down:

Romans 3
23For all have sinned, and come short of the glory of God;

Romans 6
23For the wages of sin is death; but the gift of God is eternal life through Jesus Christ our Lord.

John 3
3Jesus answered and said unto him, Verily, verily, I say unto thee, Except a man be born again, he cannot see the kingdom of God.

John 14
6Jesus saith unto him, I am the way, the truth, and the life: no man cometh unto the Father, but by me.

Romans 10
9That if thou shalt confess with thy mouth the Lord Jesus, and shalt believe in thine heart that God hath raised him from the dead, thou shalt be saved.
10For with the heart man believeth unto righteousness; and with the mouth confession is made unto salvation.
11For the scripture saith, Whosoever believeth on him shall not

be ashamed.

2 Corinthians 5
15And that he died for all, that they which live should not henceforth live unto themselves, but unto him which died for them, and rose again.

Revelation 3
20Behold, I stand at the door, and knock: if any man hear my voice, and open the door, I will come in to him, and will sup with him, and he with me.

Appendix: 14

Facts and Statistics

#1) The SAMSHA[5] survey and Indian Heath Service reports have found American Indians exhibit higher prevalence of heavy cigarette, alcohol, illicit drug use and need for treatment than the general population.

#3) Millions of dollars in federal funds are spent by tribal officials on lawyers, lobbyists and campaign contributions for the purpose of obtaining and retaining power and more money, rather than invested in reservation growth and economy.[6]

#4) Some tribal governments have become corrupt with unchecked power and money.[7] Unfortunately, the U.S. Supreme

---

5 SAMSHA – Substance Abuse and Mental Health Service
6 In 1996, Tribal entities gave over $1,200,000 to National Party Committees. The Mashantucket Pequot Nation gave over $400,000 in soft money alone. During the 1997 calendar year, lobbyist spending topped $5.5 million, with Mississippi Band of Choctaw Indians topping the list with over $1 million. The National Unity Caucus, a tribal Political Action Committee, reported over $200,000 in contributions from various tribal entities in the year 1996. This money was distributed directly to candidates across the country. *Native American Press, 10/98.*
7 In the summer of 1996, Reservation officials from both the Leech Lake and White Earth Reservations of Minnesota were convicted of millions of dollars worth of fraud and Ballot-box stuffing. During the trials, one witness stated, "That's the reason my parents left the reservation; there is too much corruption and I guess it's still going on." See Native American Press, June and July 1996.

Court ruled in 1978 that there is not federal cause of action to enforce the Indian Civil Rights act (a federal act of limited liberty guarantees) and tribal members must go to tribal courts or councils for redress. That means that tribal members must seek redress from those abusing civil rights to begin with.

#5) Because of the corruption and unwillingness to let go of power and money, tribal government, itself, may be keeping susceptible people in poverty,[8] oppression,[9] and subjugation. The Indian Child Welfare Act[10] is an example.

#6) As long as government is taking care of a man's family through welfare, food stamps, commodities, fuel assistance, Medicaid, and HUD housing, a man does not feel useful. As a result, many tribal members walk through life with no sense of purpose. Many families have come to believe the entitlements are necessary.

#7) As individuals become increasingly dependent, they buy into the idea of being a victim. Believing that others have brought on their problems, they believe they are personally not responsible.

#8) Due to lack of awareness, the general public supports laws that superficially seem to help troubled tribal members but in fact worsen the situation.

---

8 The Minnesota tribal gambling industry placed large newspaper ads using pictures of poor, disheveled elderly and children in the fall of 1997 when the State was considering a tax on tribal gaming revenue.

9 Native American Press publisher Bill Lawrence, while watching a group of homeless men, stated, "these are the ones tribal government likes. The ones who won't fight back."

10 USC 25, 21 § 1911. (a) "An Indian tribe shall retain exclusive jurisdiction over any child custody proceeding that involves an Indian child..." Mississippi Band of Choctaw Indians v. Holyfield: "An Indian tribe and an Indian child have an interest in maintaining ties independent of the birth parents." and "...because of concerns going beyond the wishes of individual parents."

#9) Non-members on the reservations, some of whom whose family have owned land within reservation boundaries from before federal government established the reservation, are becoming increasingly distressed and frustrated, resulting in resentment and animosity. Pro-tribal government groups then falsely label this anger as "racism" and effectively shut off any chance at communication.

Appendix: 15

Senator Conrad Burns

To the Editor: May 2006

Mark Baker, former legislative director for Senator Conrad Burns and recent Burn's campaign chairman, was paid $60,000 to be chief lobbyist for the Confederated Salish and Kootenai Tribes in 2003-2004. Working through his Helena firm, Baker also made $120,000 lobbying for CSKT's S&K Technologies during those years and another $40,000 working for CSKT through the Giacmetto Group. Leo Giacometto was Burns' chief of staff from 1995-1999.

2003-2004 were the same years in which CSKT was negotiating with feds for management of the National Bison Range. Many who signed petitions and wrote letters asking Burns to oppose the transfer were confused as to why Burns had switched sides on the issue since 1997. Denver FWS officials said Burns had the power to stop the transfer, and with his former statements and the need for Western MT federal jobs to remain open to all, many thought he would.

Whether or not one agrees with the transfer, few want Montana issues to be decided on the basis of who can afford the most influence. In 1997, Burns not only stood against the transfer, but introduced a draft opposing tribal jurisdiction AND supported bill S. 1691, opposing Tribal Sovereign Immunity. Burns said tribal sovereign immunity interfered with Fifth Amendment rights. Now, Burns' staff has told Montana citizens that Burns won't support any legislation concerning tribal government unless all 500+ tribes agree to it.

According to a 2006 PoliticalMoneyLine.com report published in Roll Call, Senator Burns pocketed $192,090 from tribal entities over the last few years.

Chain of events:

In June of 1997, my husband had a very good meeting with Senator Conrad Burns. Roland, a member of the Minnesota Chippewa Tribe, was in Washington DC to talk to Senator Burns, other Congressmen, and advisor to Secretary of Interior Babbit, James Pipkin, about Federal Indian Policy and the National Bison Range (NBR). Roland was well received by Senator Burns and they spent about an hour discussing the problems with Tribal sovereignty, including the Indian Child Welfare Act (ICWA), which removes power from parents and gives it to tribal government. But overall, Roland's main concern was that family and friends were living very unhappy and dangerous lives on the reservation. Having watched many relatives die tragically, he believed the reservation system was hurting tribal members and non-members alike. Roland was pleased to find the Senator in agreement.

Later that winter, Senator Burns demonstrated his position by working on legislation intended to "remove certain fee lands located within each Indian reservation in Montana from jurisdiction of the governing body of the Indian tribe..." In a newspaper article from that time period, he is quoted as saying, "The concept of tribal members enacting legislation that will affect all residents of a reservation without allowing all living on the reservation an equal voice goes against the very words which our founding fathers wrote to establish this great country."

About that same time, Senator Burns supported Senator Slade Gorton's bill S. 1691 regarding Tribal Sovereign Immunity, and signed a statement with Senator Gorton urging Congress and the public to defend the Fifth Amendment to the constitution, which declares that no person should be deprived of life, liberty or property without due process of law.

On April 7, 1998, Roland was asked by Senator Gorton to testify in support of S.1691 in Seattle, Washington, and he did so. Both Senator Gorton's bill and Senator Burn's draft were met with heavy opposition by tribal governments, which rallied the membership with angry talk of genocide. Both pieces of legislation were soon dropped. However, with Senator Burns' prominent help, we were able to win the Bison Range issue. Due to the Senator's resistance, the Confederated Salish and Kootenai tribe (CSKT) was not given management of the NBR, and all United States citizens would retain the opportunity to work there.

Roland continued to go yearly to Washington DC to talk to various Congressmen about the negative effects of FIP. At this point, many people were writing or calling us with various issues and problems. ICWA and the NBR were the two issues we received the most correspondence about. Roland visited Senator Burns' office for the last time in May of 2003, when, accompanied by two other men from the Mission Valley, he delivered a Bison Range petition. A year later, he was in DC again. After suffering with cancer for four years, going to DC this last time was his final effort, and he died just three weeks later. My husband stuck to the principles he believed in to the very end. We're not sure of Senator Burns, however.

The realization that his principles had changed came slowly. On November 27, 2000, Senator Burns was still our advocate and wrote an email to me which stated, "I have discussed your request that I write a recommendation for your book "Dying in Indian Country" with the Senate Ethics Committee and I have been told that I may write a forward to the book. I would be happy to do this for you." He then instructed me to speed up communication with him by corresponding directly with his personal assistant, Angela Schulze, and stated that he hoped to work on it in early January. He finished by writing, "I hope Roland is doing well. I look forward to hearing from you soon." A forward for my manuscript was more than I had asked for. We were excited.

I kept in touch with Angela. She told me that she had read the manuscript and thought it was great. She was friendly and encouraging. I tried to always be polite and not push. However, as January passed and time went on, I became more and more concerned. Not wanting to be a pest, I tried to call only every three or four weeks.

In May, 2001, I joined Roland for the first time lobbying in DC and we hoped that we would come home with the forward. We had a meeting scheduled with Sen. Burns, but Senator Burns wasn't able to meet with us. Instead, we discussed federal Indian policy with his chief aide for an hour and a half in the Senator's office. I remember watching the clock now and then, because the aide had assured us that Mr. Burns knew we were there and was going to make every effort to see us. I was hoping he would. But the aide was also blunt in saying that there was nothing Sen. Burns could do to help. If Burns were to introduce anything concerning Federal Indian Policy, he would have 500 tribes down his throat. "Senator Burns can't support any FIP legislation unless all 500 + tribes agree to it."

I also met Angela at that time. She was nice, and apologized for the forward not being ready yet. So when we returned home, I tried to be patient and contact her as little as possible. She wrote to me on August 8, 2001, "[Beth], I talked with Conrad today and he said he would have it done in 2 weeks. He gets back to Billings on Sunday and it's already started on his computer at the house in Billings. I'll get it to you as soon as he passes it on to me."

I think I let two or even three months go by without contacting her. Once, I asked if maybe Senator Burns had changed his mind about the forward. I hoped that if he had, they would just say so. That would be easier then waiting in uncertainty. However, Angela said that wasn't the case. She said he was still interested.

But after a point, Angela no longer answered my email or phone calls. Every now and then I made another polite inquiry, either by phone message or email. But Angela never responded.

In February of 2002, I wrote to Burn's office asking to schedule a meeting in May. I received no response. In April, I called Angela to see if a meeting could be scheduled. I told the secretary my name was "[Beth]." She responded, "[Beth Ward]?" I said, "Yes, how did you know my last name?" She answered, "Oh, it's on a card here on the desk." Angela didn't call back.

Another staffer, who was arranging for our family to have tickets to the Capitol Building, assured me that she had given Angela a message to call me about scheduling a meeting in May. I never heard from Angela.

In early May, I wrote an apology to Burns, just in case there was something I had said or done inadvertently that offended. The only thing I could think of was that I might have called Angela about the forward more than I should have. I was especially apologetic if anything I have done or said was preventing Roland from meeting with Sen. Burns. I received no response.

We were scheduled for other meetings with more receptive Congressmen, though Roland wasn't feeling well, so I went to most of the meetings on my own. I also had a meeting scheduled with BIA Deputy Wayne Smith. Unfortunately, he was fired that same day, and we never met. In his place, I was given a Mr. Fiely, who seemed much in a hurry. After listening briefly, he told me that any changes to Federal Indian Policy would have to happen legislatively. When I told him that Senator Burns' chief staff had told me the year before that changes would have to happen through the BIA, Mr. Fiely laughed.

I wasn't intending to visit Burns' that week in May. However, a colleague urged me that as a Montana constituent, I should enter the office anyway and speak to someone. She told me not to back down. So on the last day of our visit to DC, I walked into Senator Burn's office and asked to see the assistant responsible for tribal issues.

I managed to catch one aide who reluctantly told me she could give me "five minutes". We sat in the entrance room by the hallway door, and I went through our issues concerning ICWA, the NBR, and a Limited Appearance attachment to tribal court summonses. Senator Burns' aide again said that any changes would have to be done through the BIA. I related to her what Mr. Fiely had said to me earlier in the day, and this time it was her turn to laugh. She disagreed with Mr. Fiely and said that Congress has no power to change federal Indian policy. She also told me that Senator Burns has no intention of supporting any legislation that changes Indian law unless all 500 or so tribal governments agree to it.

The idea that I, as a parent of enrolled children, would need 500 tribal governments, who all benefit from ICWA, to agree that ICWA robs me of my parental rights before anything could be done about it felt totally unjust. My husband was dying. I could be the last stand keeping our children from being raised in the same unhealthy situation so many of the people he loved were living in. My voice started to crack, my throat welled up and fought some tears. The Senator's aide (who didn't give me a card, but might have been named Sara) put her hand to her lips and appeared to smile. I responded that Congress has power and I also said something more about ICWA. We didn't talk much longer than that. Embarrassed that I had started to cry, I said thank you and left quickly out the door. She got up and walked away from me just as quickly.

In 2003, the Bison Range issue came back with a vengeance. The tribes were again requesting management of this National Wildlife Refuge. Burns spokesman, J.P. Donovan, stated, "He (Burns) wants this to be vetted in the public process - no behind-the-scenes, closed-door meetings." He went on, "He feels this is a local decision. He really wants to hear from constituents."

Roland arrived to his office in May with thousands of signatures opposing transfer of the NBR in hand, and two other valley residents by his side. Unfortunately, this last effort with Senator Burns bore no fruit, and on March 15 of 2005, the National Bison Range Agreement went into effect.

On March 14, the day before it went into effect, CSKT Chairman, Fred Matt, wrote in a guest column, "Sen. Burns has been a positive and aggressive advocate for Indian Country..." and "Burns fully understands and appreciates consultation with Indian country, our sovereignty, and our right to self-determination." According to the Missoulian, Burns opposed the NBR agreement in the mid-1990s, but seemed to waffle on this round of negotiations.

In 2004, a FWS official from Denver took me aside and told me that it is necessary for us to get Senator Burns' ear on the bison range matter, just as we had in the late 1990's. He said that Senator Burns was the key - the one that could make the decision one way or the other concerning the negotiations. He told me, "Senator Burns can stop this." But I didn't know what to do about it, because it didn't feel to me that Senator Burns was open to us at all anymore.

Interestingly, Mark Baker, a former **legislative director for Burns and recent Burns'** campaign chairman, is partner in the Anderson & Baker law firm in Helena, which was **paid $60,000 to be the chief lobby firm for CSKT in 2003 and 2004.**

The total amount Mark Baker has donated since 2001 to both Senator Burns and his Friends of the Big Sky Leadership PAC, is $9000. But Mr. Baker is also affiliated with the D.C. lobbying firm Denny Miller Associates Inc., whose individuals have donated at least $27,784 to both Senator Burns and his Friends of the Big Sky Leadership PAC since 2001.

Mark also worked through his firm, Anderson and Baker, for S&K Technologies, (a CSKT company) and made $120,000 there in 2003 and 2004, (and made $40,000 working for S&K earlier than that as well, for a total of $160,000).

He also worked for CSKT through another firm he is associated with, the Giacometto Group. Leo Giacometto was Burns' chief of staff from 1995 to 1999. Working for Giacometto, Mark Baker made $40,000 lobbying for the Salish and Kootenai College in 2004.

For the last few years, my husband and I had wondered about the unexplainable change in the Senator's behavior toward us and toward Federal Indian policy. When the Abramoff scandal broke open, I could only wonder if this had anything to do with it. According to a 2006 report by PoliticalMoneyLine.com and published in Roll Call, Sen. Conrad Burns pocketed $192,090 from tribal entities over these last few years. A quick look at the Open Secrets website shows how tribal campaign contributions to Senator Burn's campaign chest have grown since the year 2000, as he has gradually moved to the top of the list of congressmen accepting money from tribal entities.

We have no proof that Senator Burns has sold out our Bison Range in return for donations from tribal entities, (many out-of-state tribes are pleased with the precedent this management transfer has set and would have supported it) nor can we say that he and other Congressmen have sold out our parental rights, as well as the civil rights of non-members living within or near Reservation boundaries. But I think that these are very important things to find out.

National Bison Range

In the 1990s, Burns opposed the transfer of management of the National Bison Range (NBR) in Moiese, Montana, to the Confederated Salish and Kootenai Tribes (CSKT), introduced a draft bill opposing tribal jurisdiction, and supported Senator Slade Gorton's S. 1691, which called Tribal Sovereign Immunity into question. At the time, Burns said that tribal sovereign immunity interfered with citizens' Fifth Amendment rights.

In 2001 and 2002, Senator Burns' policies changed, and his DC staff told citizens of western Montana that he would not support any legislation concerning tribal government unless all 500+ tribes agree to it.

In 2003, the CSKT renewed negotiations over the NBR. Fish and Wildlife officials in Denver stated at the time that Burns had the authority to stop the management transfer. On March 14, 2005 the day before a new NBR agreement went into effect with the tribes, CSKT Chairman Fred Matt wrote in a *Missoulian* guest column, "Sen. Burns has been a positive and aggressive advocate for Indian Country..." and "Burns fully understands and appreciates consultation with Indian country, our sovereignty, and our right to self-determination."

Involvement of staffers and aides

Less than two months after a key earmark by Burns in October 2003, Burns' chief of staff, Will Brooke, went to work for Abramoff at the lobbying firm Greenberg Traurig. [11]

In June 2005, former Burns staffer Shawn Vasell was called as a

---

11   http://www.npr.org/templates/story/story.php?storyId=5299944

witness at the Oversight Hearing Before the Senate Committee on Indian Affairs on the In Re Tribal Lobbying Matters, Et Al. Vasell "was registered as a lobbyist for the Choctaw and Coushatta tribes in 2001, joined Burns' staff in 2002, then rejoined Abramoff's team as a lobbyist for the tribes in 2003." [12], but refused to testify citing his Fifth Amendment right against self-incrimination. [13]

Mark Baker, a former legislative director for Burns, and currently Burn's 2006 campaign chairman, was paid $60,000 to be the chief lobbyist for the Confederated Salish and Kootenai Tribes in 2003 and 2004. Working through his Helena firm, Anderson and Baker, Baker also made $120,000 lobbying for CSKT business venture S&K Technologies during those same years, and another $40,000 working for the CSKT through the Giacmetto Group. Leo Giacometto was Burns' chief of staff from 1995 to 1999. [14][15]

Returning of "tainted" campaign contributions

Burns returned the entirety of Abramoff's personal donations to charity. When possible, Burns has returned contributions to the tribes where they originated.

His attempt to make a $111,000 donation to the Montana-Wyoming Tribal Leaders Council was rejected; the council said the money was tainted because it originally came from Abramoff and his clients. Julia Doney, president of the Fort Belknap Indian Community Council and a member of the tribal leaders' council, said that the tribes are "tired of being used" and didn't want to help Burns with his political troubles. [16]

The Blackfeet Community College also refused to accept money from Burns because it came from Jack Abramoff. James St. Goddard, a Blackfeet council member, told *Great Falls Tribune* that taking the

---

12   http://www.washingtonpost.com/wp-dyn/articles/A61436-2005Feb28_2.html
13   http://www.washingtonpost.com/wp-dyn/content/article/2005/06/22/AR2005062200921.html
14   http://www.publicintegrity.org/lobby/profile.aspx?act=clients&year=2003&cl=L007700
15   http://www.missoulian.com/articles/2005/10/10/news/local/news03.txt
16   http://www.mercurynews.com/mld/mercurynews/news/13660751.htm

money "would have made it look like the money is clean. We do not want Mr. Burns to use the tribes any more for his political gain." [17]

Conrad Burns (R-Mont)

Burns voted yes on the Dodd vote in 2002
$1,500 (2000) $7,000 **(2002)** $38,022 *(2004)* ***$23,985 (2006)***

Keep in mind that 2006 has just begun

Burns' rank as receiver of tribal funds:

2006 - 11th of all tribal gaming recipients, 3rd of all Senators
2004 - 19th of all tribal gaming recipients, 5th of Senators
2002 -- 12th of Senators
2000 -- 17th of Senators

at best, 95% disclosure. At worst, and most recent, 78% full disclosure

1999-
Full Disclosure
$932,487
(85.5%)

Incomplete
$6,250
(0.6%)

No Disclosure
$152,174
(13.9%)

2001-2006 burns

---

17   http://www.greatfallstribune.com/apps/pbcs.dll/article?AID=/20060119/NEWS01

Full Disclosure
$1,702,553
(78.3%)

Incomplete
$9,700
(0.4%)

No Disclosure
$460,928
(21.2%)

Spring 2005 - National Indian Gaming $4985

Appendix: 16

Senator Max Baucus

This letter, describing an opportunity to speak to Senator Baucus while he was campaigning in Ronan, was never answered. In addition to a question about his opposition to 'adversaries' of tribal governments having an opportunity to have their voices heard at Senate Hearings, I had questions concerning tribal government contributions to his campaigns that I never had an opportunity to ask.

I should have gone ahead and asked these questions in front of his constituents and press, but was too polite at that time.

Honorable Senator Max Baucus;

On October 28, 2002, I had the opportunity to speak to you briefly in Ronan, Montana. We walked down the main street sidewalk and discussed a letter I had recently received from you (shown below)
You had seemed confused by the content of the letter and hadn't remembered writing it. My impressions were that you are a very nice man. I would have liked to be able to sit down and talk with you more. I had another question for you, but at that moment, you were very busy.

Your manager suggested that I go ahead and ask you anyway, but he didn't know what my question was. My question was on campaign contributions. I wasn't sure that I should ask that in front of other people. I didn't seem fair to throw it out like that. So I didn't. Your manager asked me to run and get the letter you wrote (below) so you could see it, so I did. My house was just two doors away. While home, I also grabbed all my campaign contribution information. When I returned, you were busy signing autographs and talking to the press. I wondered what to do, and then turned to your manager in private to give him the letter. I also asked him about the contributions. He took the defensive very quickly, and said there is no way Max votes in response to money. I had to calm him down by reminding him that he had told me to ask you the question, but I didn't. I waited and had asked him privately instead. So he calmed down and said, "thank you"

I said, "It doesn't seem to me that Max wrote this letter. When I spoke to him a few minutes ago, he didn't seem to know what I'm talking about. An aide might have wrote the letter. So what my husband, Roland [Ward], and I would really like is an opportunity to speak directly and honestly to Max about the destruction we see Federal Indian Policy doing."

He asked what I meant by that and so I described my husband's family a little. My husband is a tribal member, and we have witnessed a tremendous amount of pain and suffering in his family.

The manager suggested I talk to the Senator's' aide, Sarah Dudley. I told him I already did that in May in DC. Roland has also approached the office staff before. I said, "We'd really like to meet with Senator Baucus. We aren't anybody important. But we have this point of view and we'd really like an opportunity to share it directly with

Senator Baucus". The manager said "You don't need to be "anybody" with Max."

He promised he'd have the scheduler contact us about Senator Baucus meeting with us after the election. I told him "thank you, we'd look forward to that."

So I was wondering if the scheduler would please contact us so we could talk to you. It really feels to me, from my brief contact with you, that if you could hear what we have to say, you would understand.

My sister…is also interested. She has a separate issue, but wondered if she might also be able to speak to you at the same time.

God Bless you and thanks for your time and patience.

[Beth Ward]

His letter to me – emphasis mine ...

----- Original Message -----
From: <max@baucus.senate.gov>
To: <…@ronan.net>
Sent: Monday, October 21, 2002 8:41 AM
Subject: Responding to your message

October 21, 2002

Dear [Beth]:

Thank you for contacting me regarding my vote on the Dodd-Lieberman Amendment. I understand your concerns, and I appreciate hearing from you on this important issue.

As you may or may not know, on the day of this vote on the Senate floor, I was in Montana participating in a debate with the other candidates for the upcoming election. Although I am disappointed that I was not able to participate in the vote, I did submit the following statement for the record:

With regards to the amendment proposed by my colleagues from Connecticut, Senators Dodd and Lieberman, I am forced to disagree with the basis of their amendment. My colleagues from Connecticut have represented their amendment as only codifying existing procedures. But, from what I understand based on the hearing held in the Indian Affairs Committee on September 18, **this amendment in fact requires the implementation of new procedures, including adversarial hearings at the request of any interested party,** raises the burden of proof that a petitioning group must satisfy in meeting the seven mandatory criteria, and requires the Department to provide notice to officials of every state and local government and municipality where a tribal group may have ever been historically located or any geographic area a tribal group may have ever occupied.

In my home state of Montana, the Little Shell Band of the Chippewa Indians have been battling for over a decade for their federal recognition. They have had to jump through many hoops as it is, and they have yet to receive their official recognition.

My Colleague's amendment would not only prolong the Little Shell's recognition, but would only add to the burden they have already carried for over a decade. Based on the outcome of the Indian Affairs hearing and the impact on my tribe at home, I respectfully disagree with my colleagues on this matter and believe it is in the best interest of the recognition process that their amendment was rejected.

Again, I apologize that I was not present to vote on this amendment. I hope this text clearly reflects my opinion. If you should have any further questions or comments, please do not hesitate to let me know.
Thanks again for contacting me.

With best personal regards, I am
Senator Max Baucus

http://baucus.senate.gov

Burns Raked in Campaign Cash From Embattled Lobbyist Jack Abramoff: Ranked #1 Out of 535 Members of Congress
May 24, 2005
By: Phil Singer, DSCC
You Scratch My Back…

Burns Took The Most Money from Controversial Lobbyist Jack Abramoff. Between the years 2001 and 2004, Conrad Burns received more campaign contributions than any other member of Congress from controversial lobbyist Jack Abramoff, his partner, and his tribal clients. During the four year span, Burns received $136,500 from Abramoff and his associates. [Billings Gazette, 5/24/05; Bloomberg News, 5/19/05]

Abramoff Paid for Burns Staffers to Attend Super Bowl. In 2001, Jack Abramoff paid for two Burns staffers to attend the 2001 Super Bowl in Florida. Will Brooke, Former Chief of Staff for Conrad Burns, admitted that "he and one of the senator's appropriations aides received a free trip to the 2001 Super Bowl in Florida." Brooke said they flew on a jet leased by Abramoff and his associates and received a free hotel room and meals. The trip was "underwritten by SunCruz, a Florida-based casino cruise ship company" which is partially owned by Abramoff. He also represented SunCruz as a lobbyist. [Billings Gazette, 4/15/05; Roll Call, 4/11/05]

And I'll Scratch Yours…

Provisions Benefiting Abramoff Client Put Into Appropriations Bill Under Burns's Watch; Admitted It Was Improper. On April 2005, Conrad Burns admitted that provisions "benefiting an Indian tribe were placed in a fiscal 2004 Interior spending bill..." The provision in question was a $3 million school appropriation for the Saginaw Chippewa Tribe in Michigan that had previously been rejected by the U.S. Department of Interior for not meeting requirements for federal funding. While Burns denied knowing the provision was included in the bill, he did admit that "he was not as vigilant as he should have been when his staff was drafting the bill." Burns offered no explanation as to why he didn't monitor the legislation more closely. [Roll Call, 4/11/05; Billings Gazette, 4/17/05]

Headline: "Burns Linked To School Funding for Wealthy Indian Tribe" [Billings Gazette, 4/15/05]

MONTANA DEMOCRATIC PARTY SOUGHT ANSWERS FROM BURNS... MT Democratic Party Called for Senate Investigation. In March 2004, the Montana Democratic Party called for a Senate investigation into whether Burns "violated ethics by supporting a $3 million federal grant to a wealthy Michigan Indian tribe that was a client of Jack Abramoff." [Great Falls Tribune, 4/24/05]

MT Democratic Party Demanded Burns Return Campaign Contributions. In March 2005, the Montana Democratic Party called for Conrad Burns to return all campaign contributions he received from embattled lobbyist Jack Abramoff. Montana Democratic Party Executive Director Brad Martin said, "It's time to come clean Senator Burns, instead of hiring a high-powered lawyer you should start by giving back the $137,000 that Jack Abramoff pushed to your campaign." [Press Release, Montana Democratic Party, 3/28/05]

BILLINGS GAZETTE CONDEMNED BURNS'S ACTIONS... "Burns Must Uphold Higher Ethical Standards". In April 2005, the Billings Gazette published a scathing editorial condemning Burns's for his unethical behavior. In the editorial the Gazette issued the following remark. "A three-term U.S. senator can't avoid responsibility by saying 'I didn't know.' Congressional staff shouldn't be taking vacations paid for by lobbyists or other interest groups. Let the staff pay for their own vacations - like Montanans do." [Billings Gazette, 4/17/05]

ABRAMOFF IS UNDER CRIMINAL INVESTIGATION... Criminal Taskforce of Investigators From FBI, IRS, Department of the Interior, Senate and Justice Department Investigating Abramoff. According to the Washington Post, "A criminal task force of investigators from the FBI, Internal Revenue Service, the Justice Department's public integrity section, the National Indian Gaming Commission and the Interior Department inspector general's office is looking into payments Abramoff and [Abramoff's partner] Scanlon received from an array of clients, including 11 wealthy Indian tribes that operate gambling casinos, according to officials familiar with the investigation." [Washington Post, 7/16/04]

Ø Abramoff Hand Picked Tribal Candidates, Got Them Elected, Then Lobbied for Million Dollar Contracts. Emails uncovered during a Senate investigation show that Abramoff and fellow lobbyist Michael Scanlon hand picked candidates for tribal councils, backed the candidates with money for campaigning, and then cashed in on lucrative contracts after the individuals were elected. "Lawmakers said the e-mails and other documents show that the two men spent tens of thousands of dollars on mailings and other materials for candidates in tribal elections." [Washington Post, 9/30/04]

Ø Abramoff Boasted That One Scheme Would Make "Millions." During the Saginaw Chippewas' tribal election, Abramoff sent Scanlon an email boasting that millions would be made once their candidates took control of the tribal council. "I had dinner tonight with Chris Petras (legislative director) of Sag Chip (Saginaw Chippewas). He was salivating at the $4-5 million program I described to him. He is going to come in after the primary with the guy who will be chief if they win (a big fan of ours already) and we are going to help him win. If he wins, they take over in January, and we have millions." [Washington Post, 9/30/04]

Ø Abramoff and Scanlon Took $66 Million From Tribes. Contrary to a Washington Post report that noted Abramoff and Scanlon receiving about $10 million in compensation from tribes, Sen. Nighthorse Campbell (R-Colo), a leading Senator on the Senate Indian Affairs Committee, said, "The truth is it's much worse."

Campbell unveiled figures that showed Scanlon's PR firms took in $66 million from six tribes. [Roll Call, 3/23/04]

Ø **The Senate Indian Affairs Committee uncovered the following embarrassing and questionable details:**

At least one tribe, the Agua Caliente of California, paid $300,000 into a pool of money Abramoff used to rent box suites at FedEx Field, the MCI Center and Camden Yards." "A Jan. 16, 2002, e-mail from Abramoff to Scanlon talked about needing 'moolah' and set a goal of making '$50M this year (our cut!).'" "In one nine-month period in 2002, Scanlon's Capitol Campaign Strategies sent more than $12 million to Abramoff's Kay Gold Inc." [Roll Call, 3/23/04]

Appendix: 17

The Montana Delegation circa 1990's -

Burns wasn't the only one: Baucus and Rehburg play, too

In Feb. 2004 I wrote
"In Montana, Senator Max Baucus has accepted at least $48,000 from tribal entities: Tribal governments, Tribal PACs, tribally hired lobbyists, and/or their employees. Senator Conrad Burns has begun to accept funds from some of the same sources, and his staff has stated that Senator Burns will not support any tribally related legislation unless all the tribal governments agree to it. Representative Denny Rehberg has also begun to receive campaign funds from tribal entities."

Now this -

Tribes' Donations Since 1999 Top $25M
January 30, 2006, *By John Bresnahan, Roll Call Staff*

American Indian tribes have donated nearly $26 million to the national parties and individual lawmakers since 1999, outpacing the defense industry ($21.9 million) and manufacturers ($18.9 million).

The data on tribal contributions was assembled by PoliticalMoneyLine.com, which tracked donations from more than 200 tribes.

Tribal donations have been recorded under a variety of names, making them difficult to track. For example, one tribe had 78 variations of its name under which donations were recorded. The tribes, which are recorded as individual donors unburdened by the aggregate limits faced by normal contributors, also are not required to report their donations to the Federal Election Commission as do political action committees.

As the scandal surrounding former GOP lobbyist Jack Abramoff has grown, so has the interest in the political activities of tribal leaders. Abramoff, who pleaded guilty on Jan. 3 to fraud, tax evasion and conspiracy to bribe public officials, admitted to defrauding tribes for which he lobbied, to the tune of millions of dollars.

Abramoff used political contributions from tribes to enhance his influence. He was able to steer hundreds of thousands of dollars in contributions from the tribes to certain Senators and House Members, a valuable asset for any lobbyist. Dozens of lawmakers from both parties have now disgorged these donations since Abramoff's guilty plea.

The biggest recipient among lawmakers of tribal donations over the period that PoliticalMoneyLine.com analyzed was Rep. Patrick Kennedy (D-R.I.), with $510,400. Other leading recipients included: Rep. J.D. Hayworth (R-Ariz.), $501,140; Rep. Richard Pombo (R-Calif.), $338,100; then-Sen. Tom Daschle (D-S.D.), $274,650; Speaker Dennis Hastert (R-Ill.), $273,000; Sen. Maria Cantwell (D-Wash.), $266,800; Sen. Patty Murray (D-Wash.), $237,030; Rep. Frank Pallone (D-N.J.), $202,046; **Sen. Conrad Burns (R-Mont.), $192,090**; and Rep. Dale Kildee (D-Mich.), $169,550.

These totals include hard and soft money given to re-election campaigns and leadership PACs. "[18]

See John Bresnahan's article for the the biggest tribal donors ...

---

18   From **Tribes' Donations Since 1999 Top $25M,** January 30, 2006, *By John Bresnahan, Roll Call Staff*

2005-2006

Rehberg
Lawyer groups
16 Denny Miller & Assoc $3,000
16 Giacometto Group $3,000
lobby PACS
2006
Holland & Knight $1,500
Preston, Gates et al $1,000
2004
Greenberg, Traurig et al $1,000
Holland & Knight $1,000
Preston, Gates et al $500
National Indian Gaming Assn $2,000
2002
Dorsey & Whitney $2,000
Greenberg, Traurig et al $1,000
Holland & Hart $500
Preston, Gates et al $1,000
National Indian Gaming Assn $1,000
National Unity Caucus $1,000

Local lobbyist speaks about Burns, Abramoff

By mailto:wwilliams@dailychronicle.comWALT WILLIAMS, Chronicle Staff Writer

As the relationship between Sen. Conrad Burns, R-Mont., and convicted lobbyist Jack Abramoff comes under greater scrutiny, growing attention is being paid to a Bozeman lobbyist and former Burns' staff member.

Will Brooke was Burns' chief of staff from 2000 to 2003, during the time the senator raised much of the money from Abramoff and his clients, perhaps in return for legislative favors. Brooke also was one of two staffers who accepted a Super Bowl trip in 2001 paid for by Abramoff's clients.

Brooke left Burns' office to work for Greenberg Traurig, the lobbying firm that employed Abramoff, and has been interviewed by federal investigators regarding the Abramoff case, although Brooke sought them out himself.

He was the lobbyist who helped developer Dick Clotfelter secure $4 million in federal funding for a downtown parking garage in Bozeman. And he is a lobbyist for the Belgrade biotechnology firm Bacterin Inc., a business relationship that was examined in a recent newspaper report.

...His lobbying efforts for the parking garage and Bacterin have nothing to do with the Abramoff investigation, but the potential scandal has cast a shadow of suspicion over everyone and everything that can somehow be traced back to it.

Brooke said in an interview Friday both the parking garage and Bacterin were worthy projects for the Bozeman community.

"I'm proud of the projects I worked on and the clients I assisted," he said.

ABRAMOFF LINK?

Abramoff pleaded guilty Tuesday to conspiracy, fraud and tax evasion in a deal with federal prosecutors for his cooperation in an investigation into possible Congressional corruption.

Burns received more $150,000 in campaign contributions from Abramoff and his clients -- more than any other member of Congress -- most of it during Brooke's watch as chief of staff, a position that usually oversees fund raising. The senator recently returned the money.

No favors were exchanged for the contributions, Brooke said.

But Brooke may be linked to a controversial $3 million grant Burns acquired for one of Abramoff's wealthy tribal clients.

An e-mail from Abramoff appears to name Brooke in an attempt to get Burns to pull some weight in getting the money -- the message refers only to "Will" -- but Brooke hasn't said whether he was that person, according to news reports.

Brooke talked to federal investigators working on the case last year after contacting the U.S. Department of Justice himself. He stressed he is one of many people investigators have spoken with.

"I talked to the investigators and told them everything I knew, and was forthcoming about everything they asked me about," he said.

The lobbyist said he only worked at Greenberg Traurig for three or four weeks before Abramoff resigned from the firm. He didn't report to Abramoff.

Brooke felt his sole mistake was accepting the Super Bowl trip before thoroughly checking out its legality. The senator only learned about the trip after the fact, he said.

Brooke now regrets accepting the trip because of the perception it created.

Democrats, who are turning up the pressure on the senator as Election Day looms, say Brooke and Burns still have much to explain about their dealings with Abramoff.

"The sooner that Will Brooke and Sen. Burns come clean with the people of Montana about their relationship with Jack Abramoff, the sooner we can put this all behind us," Montana Democratic Party spokesman Matt McKenna said....

....Such grants are hardly unusual for Burns, who has pumped millions of federal dollars into Montana State University research programs and local businesses over the years. MSU even named it one of its buildings after the senator in recognition of that fact.

The money is blasted by critics as "pork" that drives up government spending, but it is used by lawmakers to win voter support back home.

The money for the parking garage didn't originate with Burns but with Rep. Denny Rehberg, R-Mont., in a transportation bill passed by Congress last year. Sen. Max Baucus, D-Mont., made sure the money stayed in the bill when it was in the Senate.

Abramoff-linked probe focuses on 5 lawmakers

By Jerry Seper and Audrey Hudson
THE WASHINGTON TIMES
Published January 11, 2006

A Justice Department investigation into influence-peddling on Capitol Hill is focusing on a "first tier" of lawmakers and staffers, both Republicans and Democrats, say sources close to the probe that has netted guilty pleas from lobbyist Jack Abramoff.

Law-enforcement authorities and others said the investigation's opening phase is scrutinizing **Sens. Conrad Burns, Montana Republican;** Byron L. Dorgan, North Dakota Democrat; and Minority Leader Harry Reid, Nevada Democrat, along with Reps. J.D. Hayworth, Arizona Republican, and Bob Ney, Ohio Republican.

A source working with the Justice Department on the investigation told The Washington Times that Abramoff was questioned during several interviews about the lawmakers and their purported ties to the lobbyist and his former clients.

Mr. Burns, who chairs a subcommittee with influence over funding for American Indian programs, has returned or given to charity $150,000 he received from Abramoff, his partners or his tribal clients. He sent a letter to Attorney General Alberto R. Gonzales on Nov. 28 asking for an investigation in the matter to clear his name, his spokesman, Matt Mackowiak, said.

"Mr. Burns has a long record of supporting Indian tribe education programs, and it goes way back before Abramoff was a lobbyist," Mr. Mackowiak said. "Senator Burns took the lead and was one of the first members to return all contributions, and as a result, more than 100 members will give back money that is linked to Abramoff.

"He believes he will be cleared of any wrongdoing," he said, adding that Mr. Burns told the Justice Department that he would cooperate fully and has directed his staff to do the same.

The Tigua Indian Tribe in El Paso, Texas, said it donated $22,000 to Mr. Burns in 2002 at Abramoff's request, thinking the Montana Republican was part of "Abramoff's group." The tribe hired Abramoff to lobby on its behalf to reopen a casino. FBI agents have interviewed tribal leaders about the donations, the sources said.

Mr. Burns has said the money had no bearing on any of his congressional actions.

Bush, lawmakers returning Abramoff donations
Move follows lobbyist's guilty plea in corruption investigation
The Associated Press
Updated: 7:07 p.m. ET Jan. 5, 2006

December 2005:
Sen. Max Baucus, D-Mont., $18,892 to seven tribal colleges. ... **Sen. Conrad Burns, R-Mont., about $150,000** donated to Native American charities and refunded. Sen. Kent Conrad, D-N.D., $3,750 to North Dakota's tribal colleges. Sen. Byron Dorgan, D-N.D., $67,000 refunded.... **Rep. Denny Rehberg, R-Mont., $19,900 refunded and given to charity.**
URL: http://www.msnbc.msn.com/id/10723902/from/RL.3/

What I wrote...

Tribal governments are taking funds purportedly meant for the good of their membership, and using those funds for the purpose of expanding their power.

Lobbyist Jack Abramoff and Senator Conrad Burns aren't the only ones playing the tribal money game. The amount of tribal gaming money poured into state and federal elections has increased tremendously in the last decade.

Of the top 20 House members receiving donations from the Indian Gaming industry in 2003, 18 were members of the Congressional Native American Caucus, including the two co-chairs, Representatives Dale Kildee and JD Hayworth. Vice-Chair Patrick

Kennedy was at the very top of the list with a whopping $93,550 from tribal government donors and gaming funds.

In addition, at least $225,414 of Indian Gaming funds that year had gone to members of the Senate Committee on Indian Affairs. One tribe alone, the Mashantucket Pequot was a top contributor to Senator Daniel Inouye's war chest with $25,000. The Mashantucket Pequot tribe was also among the top fifteen contributors to Senator John McCain, another member of the Senate Committee, having contributed $38,850 to his campaign.

In fact, the Center for Responsive Politics reported in 2003 that Indian Gaming had contributed over $15,301,273 to federal candidates in individual donations, PAC funds, and soft money since 1990, with $6,590,824 in the 2002 election cycle alone.

What does this buy? A Congress that panders to the demands of tribal governments, allowing them control over their members in a way that no other Americans would tolerate. Despite mounting evidence that large numbers of people on the reservations are suffering from violence, crime, depression, and alcohol and drug addiction, this money buys Congressional acquiescence as tribal leaders push for legislation that benefits their positions of power over the welfare of the membership.

Basic civil rights, including freedom of press, freedom of assembly, fair judicial systems, and even parental rights are not guaranteed within reservation boundaries. Throughout Indian Country, tribal families are being denied their rights in the name of tribal sovereignty.

The family unit used to be of precious importance in the Native communities. Federal Government has contributed greatly to its demise. Federal Indian Policy views Native Americans as helpless wards. As long as government is taking care of a man's family through welfare, food stamps, fuel assistance, Medicaid, and HUD housing, a man loses that feeling of being needed and important to his family.

Parents are not even allowed to choose guardians for their children who live off the reservation or aren't tribal members unless tribal leadership agrees to it. After all, if too many children leave the reservation, tribal leaders will no longer have a kingdom.

All this despite claims from tribal government and the tribal Gaming industry that tribal member interests are best cared for under their direction.

Jack Abramoff Lobbying and Political Contributions, 1999 - 2006
Center for Responsive Politics: http://www.capitaleye.org/abramoff.asp February 17, 2006

Abramoff, who used his connections to influence legislation by enticing lawmakers with golf trips, sporting events or fancy meals at his Washington restaurant. Former House Majority Leader Tom DeLay, who once described Abramoff as a friend, now denies having been tied to him.

Burns PAC - Friends of the Big Sky Leadership PAC of Conrad Burns

Agua Caliente	4,500	2004	5,000	2002		
Abramoff	5,000	2002				
Chitmacha	6,090	2004b				
Coushatta	5,000	2002	1,000	2002b		
Mississippi choctaw	2,000	2004b	5,000	2002	1,000	2000b

	1,000	2002b				
Saginaw	6,000	2004	2,000	2002b		
	4,000	2004b				
SunCruz	5,000	2002				
Tigua	3,000	2002b				

Open secrets:
1990, no records of tribal gaming donations to Senators, and only two reps for a total of $1,750. The donations grew with the tribal gaming industry. In 1992, open secrets records only 4 senators receiving donations, for a total of $4000. Ten Reps received a total of $16,500. So far in this 2006 cycle, the top 20 Senators received $161,335. Top 20 Representatives $527,199. *Total Senators - $170,335, Total Reps - $759,151, primarily to Democrats.\incumbents 2004 - total sen - $716,262*
Reps - $1,574,608

Max Baucus (D-Mont)

Baucus (D-MT) No vote on Dodd
$28,250 **(2002)**

2002 - Max is 12 out of all tribal gaming recipients $28,250, 3rd out of Senators
1998 - 19th of Senators
1996 - 8th of Senators
1994 - 2nd of Senators

Denny Rehberg (R-Mont)

Rep. Rehberg

$14,500 **(2002)** $14,250 *(2004)*   *$8,600 (2006)*

2006 top 17

_____

_____

Appendix: 18

Federal Funding for Tribal Governments based on Census

- *According to the "Tribal Complete Count Committee Handbook", published by United States Census 2000, D-3289 (4-99), (http://www.census.gov/prod/cen2000/d-3289.pdf)*

"**The programs serving tribal residents** (whether operated by the tribal, local, or state government) which **use Federal funding based on population statistics**—for example:
Johnson O'Malley, Headstart, Home Energy Assistance, Housing and Urban Development programs, etc. Develop separate flyers on the benefits those programs provide to tribal residents. Explain how funding allocations are based, in part, on census information." ..."The Federal government uses census data to allocate funds to tribal, state, and local governments for a wide range of programs."

- *According to Jack C. Jackson, Jr., Director of Governmental Affairs, National Congress of American Indians, Statement on the importance of an accurate census to American Indians and Alaska Natives, before the U.S. Commission on Civil Rights, Washington, D.C., February 12, 1999.*
(http://www.ncai.org/ncai/resource/documents/governance/ cvrightcensus.htm)

"....American Indians and Alaska Natives have a significant stake in the outcome of the 2000 census….. **A range of programs now exists** to help Tribes address and overcome barriers to economic advancement and self-sufficiency. **A significant portion of this federal aid is based on the information collected in the census.** Federal programs that distribute aid to American Indians and Alaska Natives based in whole or in part on census data include the *Job Training Partnership Act, Grants to Local Education Agencies for Indian Education, Special Programs for the Aging, and Family Violence Prevention and Services.*"

-According to ACF Administration For Children and Families, U.S. Department of Health and Human Services, May 9, 2007, Child Care Bureau, Office of Family Assistance

"**Tribal Child Counts**
For funds that become available in FY 2008, **ACF will calculate grant awards based on the number of children under age 13**. A Tribe must submit a self-certified Child Count Declaration for children under age 13 (not age 13 and under), in order to receive FY 2008 CCDF funds."

2000 Census –

- There are 4,119,301 people claiming to have American Indians and Alaska Native ancestry in the United States and 562 federally funded Tribes. This population includes individuals who may not be members or eligible for membership in a tribe, as well as individuals who are members of state recognized tribes.

- Approximately **75%** live outside the reservation, with about 55% living in metropolitan areas. Only about **25%** live on the reservations.
- **As much as 45% of reservation residents are non-Indian.**
- On 30% of the reservations, the number of non-members is equal to or greater than the number of tribal members.

The Montana Supreme Court, in Skillen v. Menz, wrote, **"interracial marriages are a fact of life, and, as with other marriages, so are interracial divorces and custody disputes over the children of those marriages."**

According to the 2003 DOI-BIA Indian Population and Labor Force Report, mandated by order of Public law 102-477, "The Indian Employment, Training, and Related Services Demonstration Act o 1992:

- Total number of enrolled tribal members and members from other tribes who live on or near the reservation and are eligible to use the tribe's Bureau of Indian Affairs funded services – **Total 2003 Tribal enrollment - 1,923,650**. 5.9% increase from 2001 labor force report, 34.7% from 1995. The 2003 increase is attributed to updated tribal rolls, improved record keeping procedures, and revisions to tribal enrollment criteria.
- **Total 2003 Service population 1,587,519**. 4.2% increase from 2001 labor force report. 26.0% from 1995. It is also a 216% increase over the Total Service Population reported in 1982. The 2003 Service Population increase is attributed to increased record keeping and improved data collection methods, as well as eligible Indian individuals and families who came to reside in the tribe's service area to benefit from opportunities and services unavailable to them in off-reservation communities.

- 562 Federally recognized tribes
- Several corporate and "at-large" Alaska tribal entities formed by the 1971 ANCS Act.

- *From Indianz.com, "House panel boosts funds for Indian Programs", Monday, <u>June 11, 2007</u>. accessed Aug. 30, 2007 –*

- Indian Education, urban health clinics, law enforcement, and language preservation will see boosts in funding under bills advanced by the House Appropriations committee last week.
- At a markup on Thursday, the committee approved 5.7 billion for Indian programs at the Interior Department and related agencies, including the Indian Health Service….
- The bill "honors our obligations to Native American communities, making investments into better education and healthcare," the committee said of the overall <u>*$27.6 billion*</u> package, an increase of 4.3 percent over current levels."

Appendix: 19

Important Points Concerning ICWA:

1. *Children of tribal heritage should be guaranteed protection equal to that of any other child in the United States.*

2. *Fit parents, no matter their heritage, have the right to choose healthy guardians or adoptive parents for their children without concern for heritage.*

3. *The "Existing Indian Family Doctrine" must be available to families and children that choose not to live within the reservation system.* See <u>In re Santos Y</u>, <u>In Bridget R.</u>, and <u>In re Alexandria Y</u>.

4. *United States citizens, no matter their heritage, have a right to fair trials.*

    (a) *When summoned to a tribal court, parents and legal guardians, whether enrolled or not, have to be told their rights, including* 25 USC Chapter 21 § 1911. (b) "Transfer of proceedings [to tribal jurisdiction] ...<u>in the</u>

absence of good cause to the contrary, [and] objection by either parent..."

(b) ***Under the principles of comity***: All Tribes and States shall accord full faith and credit to a child custody order issued by the Tribe or State of initial jurisdiction consistent within the UCCJA – which enforces a child custody determination by a court of another State – unless the order has been vacated, stayed, or modified by a court having jurisdiction to do so under Article 2 of the UCCJA.

5. ***Adoptive Parents need well defined protections.***

6. ***A "Qualified expert witness" should be someone who is able to advocate for the well being of the child, first and foremost.***

7. ***Finally, if tribal membership is a political rather than racial designation, (as argued) than is it constitutional for the definition of an Indian child to include "eligible" children, rather than "enrolled" children?***

Appendix: 20

For More Information:

Articles:

Allen, William B. "Are Indians Protected by the Constitution? Reflections on the Choctaw Decision." *Okanogan County Chronicle.* Omak, WA. August 2, 1988.

Armstrong, Jeff. "Leech Lake members, residents played key role in White Earth vote conspiracy." *Native American Press/Ojibwe News,* June 7 1996.

Burgess, Don. "The Rub Tree." *Bugle,* Jan/Feb 2005: 118.

Blair, Greg. "Defense overwhelmed by vote fraud evidence in week 4 of Chippygate." *Native American Press/Ojibwe News,* June 7 1996.

Doyle, Pat. "Money is at the core of court queries." *Native American Press/Ojibwe News,* June 7 1996.

Shortridge, Julie. "Sovereignty and Civil Rights." *The Resource.* 1998.

Randall, James. Minn. Court of Appeals. *Indian Country Today.* February 29 1996.

1905-1907 annual report of the American Bison Society

April 27, 1972 issue of *Flathead Courier* re: Payment to CSKT for all land including Bison Range

March 16 & 23, 1972 issues of *Ronan Pioneer* re: Payment to CSKT for all land including Bison Range

Books:

Barsness, Larry. "Hides, Heads, and Horns." *Reed Business Information, Inc.* 1986 edition.

Eguiguren, A. R. "Legalized Racism." *Sun on Earth Books,* Heathsville, VA. 2000.

Fahey, John. "The Flathead Indians." *University of Oklahoma Press.* 1974

Mathie, Peyton. "Shades of Grey." *iUniverse, Inc.* 2004.

Nee, Watchman. "The Normal Christian Life." *Tyndale House.* 1977

Packwood Scoffield, Ruth. "Behind the Buckskin Curtain." *Carlton Pr.* June 1992.

"The Holy Bible"

Court Cases Concerning Tribal Jurisdiction:

Oliphant v. Suquamish Indian Tribe 435 US 191 (1978)
Montana v. U.S. No. 79-1128. Argued December 3, 1980. Decided March 24 (1981)
Brendale v. Yakima Tribes, 492 u.s. 408 (1989)

Duro v. Reina No. 88-6546. Argued Nov. 29, 1989. Decided May 29, 1990. 495 U.S. 676

Hagen v. Utah, #92-6281 (February 23, 1994)

STRATE, BERTHOLD INDIAN RESERVATION V. A-1 CONTRACTOR (April 28, 1997)

ALASKA VS. NATIVE VILLAGE OF VENETIE TRIBAL GOVERNMENT 96-1577, (Feb 25, 1998)

SOUTH DAKOTA VS. YANKTON SIOUX TRIBE, 96-1581, (January 1998)

Arizona Public Service Co. v. EPA, 211 F.3d 1280, 1300, D.C. (2000)

BUGENIG v HOOPA VALLEY TRIBE # 9915654, (October 3, 2000)

Nevada v. Hicks, 99-1994, 196 F.3d1020, 9th Cir. 1999, US Supreme Court (June 25, 2001)

Atkinson Trading Co. v. Shirley, 532 U. S (2001) (slip op. at 13)

Morris v. Tanner, 160 Fed.Appx. 600, 2005 WL 3525598, C.A.9 (Mont.), December 22, 2005 (No. 03-35922.)

Court Cases Tribal Jurisdiction over Children of Heritage:

1. **U.S. SUPREME COURT** – Meyer v. State of Nebraska,325, Decided June 4, 1923."...the right of the individual to ... establish a home and bring up children, to worship God according to the dictates of his own conscience,... long recognized ... as essential to the orderly pursuit of happiness by free men""...and it hardly will be affirmed that any Legislature could impose such restrictions upon the people of a state without doing violence to both letter and spirit of the Constitution." "... the individual has certain fundamental rights which must be respected. The protection of the Constitution extends to all..."
2. **U.S. SUPREME COURT** - Pierce v. Society of the Sisters, Decided June 1, 1925."The child is not the mere creature of the state; those who nurture him and direct his destiny have the right, coupled with the high duty, to recognize and prepare him for additional obligations,"

"...the liberty of parents and guardians to direct the upbringing and education of children."
3. **U.S. SUPREME COURT** – Brown v. Board of Education, Decided May 17, 1954."Segregation is a denial of the equal protection of the laws,"
4. **U.S. SUPREME COURT** – Mississippi Choctaw Indian Band v. Holyfield, et al., April 3, 1989, Definition of "domicile" under the Indian Child Welfare Act / Parental Rights diminished. First case in which the federal high court has construed ICWA.
5. **ALASKA** – In the Matter of F.P., W.M. and A.M, December 18, 1992, Tribal Jurisdiction questioned
6. **CALIFORNIA** – In re Bridget R. (1996) 41 Cal.App.4th 1483 (Bridget R.)., James R. and Colette R. v. Cindy R.et al., January 19, 1996,"The Pomo Twins", IMPORTANT The "**Existing Indian Family**" Doctrine, **Constitutional Limitations upon the Scope of ICWA, Due Process, Equal Protection, and The Indian Commerce Clause and The Tenth Amendment.**
7. **CALIFORNIA** - In re Alexandria Y. (1996), Decided May 31, 1996, IMPORTANT The "**Existing Indian Family**" Doctrine, "neither Alexandria nor Renea had any significant social, cultural or political relationship with Indian life; thus, there was no existing Indian family to preserve."
8. **MONTANA** – In the Matter of the Adoption of Riffle, Decided July 30, 1996, Child's "Constitutional Rights", "Best Interests", and "Good Cause".
9. **NINTH CIRCUIT COURT** - Native Village of Venetie Ira Council v. Alaska, September 17, 1998, "**Full Faith and Credit" given to adoption decrees issued by Tribal Courts**
10. **MONTANA** - In re Marriage of Skillen March 3, 1998, "Indian jurisdiction" law in relationship to UCCJA and PKPA

11. **MONTANA** – In Matter of A.P., Youth in Need of Care , July 16, 1998, Successful "Good Cause", Adoption of Riffle cited, 25 U.S.C. § 1911(b) discussed
12. **MONTANA** – In the Matter of the Adoption of H.M.O. July 16, 1998, "Qualified Expert Witnesses"
13. **MONTANA** – In the Matter of K. H. & K. L. E., Youths in Need of Care , June 3, 1999 (briefs only)
14. **MONTANA** – In re T.A.G., Youth in Need of Care , June 15, 1999, Successful "Good Cause"
15. **MONTANA** – M.P.M. and A.R.M., Youths in Need of Care., April 20, 1999, "Qualified Expert Witnesses"
16. **MONTANA** – In the Matter of C.H., Youth in Need of Care, March 16, 2000, Unsuccessful "Good Cause"
17. **MINNESOTA** – In the Matter of the Welfare of: S.N.R. , September 1, 2000, Determination that a Child is a Tribal Member
18. **CALIFORNIA**-In re SANTOS Y., a Person Coming Under the Juvenile Court Law2001,IMPORTANT RULING re the "**Existing Indian Family**" Doctrine, Constitutional Limitations upon the Scope of ICWA, Due Process, Equal Protection, and The Indian Commerce Clause and The Tenth Amendment. Link to Thomas Sowell article concerning this case.
19. **OKLAHOMA** – In the Matter of Child, B.R.W. September 19, 2003, The "Existing Indian Family" Doctrine
20. **ALASKA** – In the Matter of the Adoption of Keith M.W. October 31, 2003, Voluntary Relinquishment of Parental Rights, Good Cause
21. **CONNECTICUT** - In the Interest of MAKAILA A., a person under the age of eighteen years. December 19, 2003, "Termination of Parental Rights"
22. **MINNESOTA** - Roy E. GERBER v. Phyllis EASTMAN January 20, 2004, "Child Custody Proceeding, " defined, **IMPORTANT – FOUR PRONGS OF ICWA** discussed and agreed upon.
23. **NINTH CIRCUIT COURT** – Mary Doe v. Arthur Mann July 19, 2005, **IMPORTANT** 9th CIRCUIT

RULING – Good news for **Public law 280"** States: Alaska, California, Minnesota, Oregon, Nebraska and Wisconsin, as well as possibly Washington and Idaho; giving those States jurisdiction over children NOT living on the reservation.

24. **MINNESOTA Supreme Court** - In the Matter of the Welfare of the Child of R.S. and L.S., Parents, A101390 October 26, 2011, - **VERY IMPORTANT** - "…transfer of preadoptive and adoption placement proceedings is not authorized under ICWA. We conclude that with respect to an Indian child not residing or domiciled on the child's tribe's reservation, Rule 48 of the Minnesota Rules of Juvenile Protection Procedure, providing for transfer of "the juvenile protection matter" to an Indian child's tribe, is limited to foster care placement and termination of parental rights proceedings."

Government Reports:

Minnesota State Planning Agency. "Report on Indian Needs." *Human Resources Division* Feb 1981.

1990 U.S. Bureau of Census, Department of Commerce.

2000 U.S. Bureau of Census, Department of Commerce.

Records of the Indian Claims Commission (Record Group 279) 1946-83 http://www.archives.gov/research_room/federal_records_guide/indian_claims_commission_rg279.html

Federal Election Commission

Law:

Indian Child Welfare Act – PUBLIC LAW 95-608, 25 USC Chapter 21

The Indian Self-Determination and Education Assistance Act (ISDEAA) Section 403(k)

Online Resources:

Center for Responsive Politics – opensecrets.org

Christian Alliance for Indian Child Welfare (CAICW) - www.caicw.org
CAICW You Tube - https://www.youtube.com/user/CAICW
CAICW Facebook - http://facebook.com/fbCAICW.org
CAICW Twitter - http://twitter.com/CAICW

Native American Law

Handbook of Federal Indian Law by Felix S. Cohen
Indian Child Welfare Act (ICWA) Case Law (CAICW)
Indian Child Welfare Act (Legal Information Institute – Cornell)
Indian Law (Legal Information Institute – Cornell)
National Indian Law Library (NARF)
Native American Constitution and Law Digitization Project (U of Oklahoma & NARF)
Native American Law (New England School of Law)
Native American Law Review (U of Oklahoma – index only on line)
Tribal Court Clearinghouse

Testimony:

Senate Testimony of Scott Kayla Morrison, Choctaw Attorney; Wilburton, Oklahoma; March 11, 1998, Accessed online August 23, 2007, http://www.senate.gov/~scia/1998hrgs/0311_sm.htm

Senate Testimony of Roland Morris, Sr. Oversight Hearing Concerning S. 1691 April 7, 1998 Seattle, Washington - Library of Congress

Senate Testimony of William J. Lawrence, J.D., Oversight Hearing Concerning S. 1691 April 7, 1998 Seattle, Washington - Library of Congress

Legislative History of the Indian Child Welfare Act - Library of Congress

Andrew, January 1983

Dorothy, Andrew, and Walter, June 1983

Oregon coast, 1986; Mickey, Junior, Roland and Andrew

Elmer Dovetail preaching an evening service, 1988

Mickey, Oct 1988, Montana

Roland attaching trailer home to side of old house, 1989

Haley, January 1990

Roland fishing with Andrew, 1990

Timothy

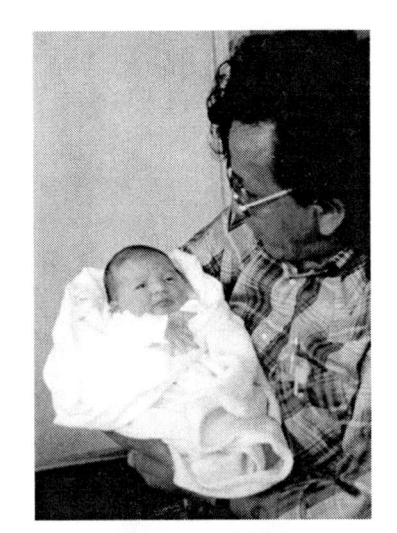

Summer, 1990

Heidi & kitty, 3 years old

Summer 1994

Mission Valley Medicab Van, 1996

Roland and James Pipkin, 1997

Roland and Senator Conrad Burns, 1997

Example of Roland's Work

Roland and Timothy, October 1999

Roland and Don hunting

Traditional cemetery

Roland speaking to MN Attorney General Mike Hatch, 2000

Roland at meeting with BIA staff at Dept of Interior, 2001

Roland and Senator Conrad Burns, May 2003

Roland, preaching Sunday service in Juarez, Mexico, June 2003

Speaking at the National Press Club, May 2004

Beth & daughter, Washington DC, January 2011

Save Veronica Petition, 2012

Roland's Father's house, March 2012, a few weeks after cover picture for book was taken

Family Cemetery